Semantic Atomism

MW01146206

Other Books by Ashish Dalela:

Semantic Reasoning
The Journey of Perfection
Material and Spiritual Natures
Conceiving the Inconceivable
The Science of God
Time and Consciousness
The Balanced Organization
The Yellow Pill
Cosmic Theogony
Emotion
Mystic Universe
Moral Materialism
Signs of Life
Uncommon Wisdom
Gödel's Mistake
Quantum Meaning
Sāñkhya and Science
Is the Apple Really Red?
Six Causes

Semantic Atomism

A Scientific Commentary on
Vaiśesika Sūtras

Original Text Composed by
Sage Kanāda

Ashish Dalela

SHABDA PRESS

Semantic Atomism—A Scientific Commentary on Vaiśeṣika Sūtras
by Ashish Dalela

by Ashish Dalela
www.shabda.co

Copyright © 2021 by Ashish Dalela
All Rights Reserved
Interior Design: Ciprian Begu

All rights reserved. No part of this book may be reproduced in any form without the express permission of the author. This includes reprints, excerpts, photocopying, recording, or any future means of reproducing. If you would like to do any of the above, please seek permission first by contacting the author on www.shabda.co.

Published by Shabda Press

press.shabda.co
ISBN 978-93-85384-41-7

SHABDA
PRESS

CONTENTS

Series Preface

At present, the Vedic philosophical system suffers from many misconceptions—(a) the Vedic texts comprise many disparate or conflicting doctrines that don't form a coherent system, (b) these texts advocate the worship of different deities so the Vedic system must be polytheistic, (c) due to the differences between the various Vedic texts, they must have been authored by different people so they cannot be of divine origin, and (d) the texts produced by various human minds must have originated at different ages and times in history.

Those who want to correct these misconceptions are also making many mistakes. First, they defend the history as being a few thousand years older than modern estimates (when the Vedic tradition is sanātana or eternal). Second, they accept impersonalism as a solution to the supposed polytheism of the Vedas (even though it is solemnly rejected by the Vedic texts). Third, they apologize for the diversity of texts as the intellectual virtue of plural viewpoints (when plurality is different perspectives on a single understanding of reality). Fourth, they visualize Vedic knowledge through the mundane lens of geographical contiguity and genetic resemblances, confusing the correction of mistakes with pedestrian ideals of nationalism, political unity, cultural pride, etc., and the true spiritual foundations under which all material identities of body, gender, society, and nation are rejected as a waste of time, are ignored.

This series of books differs from the above-mentioned goals and aspirations. This may potentially reduce the reader list to a smaller number of people who are truly interested in the truth, not a race, nationality, language, etc. But that risk must be taken in the interest of truth, and broader objectives of Vedic knowledge. The sacrifice of immediate interests is hence a necessary evil.

The primary goal of this series of books is to establish that the Vedas constitute a coherent description of reality, which has to be understood from multiple perspectives to grasp its true nature. This understanding can be broadly classified into the following categories—(a) the study of matter as concepts and qualities, (b) the understanding of the soul and its relation to God, (c) the practices by which this nature of the soul and God are practically realized and experienced, and (d) the system of reasoning and logic that is used to explain it to anyone who might be interested. The study of the nature of the soul and God is theology. The practice by which this nature is realized is religion. The description of matter as categories and qualities is philosophy. And the system of reasoning and logic used to explain it to those who are interested is science.

Each perspective can be, in principle, described and understood without the others. For example, we can practice religious mysticism without perfectly knowing theology. We can know the philosophy of reality without religion or theology. And we can understand the science without practicing mysticism.

Nevertheless, the Vedic texts do not put these into separate boxes. Every text discusses all the subjects—science, philosophy, religion, and theology—but with different relative emphases. Some texts are more focused on science, others more on theology and religion, while others more on philosophy. This unifying tendency in the Vedic system is the antithesis of the modern tendency to compartmentalize, separate one issue from another, focus on narrow problems, and create the illusion of progress by going round and round in circles.

The Vedic system looks at all inquiries holistically, and their answers to one question cannot contradict the answers to any other potential question. If you progress in philosophy, then you also progress in religion, theology, and science. Scientific progress is not contrary to ethics and morality; spiritual development is not contrary to the necessities of life. The Vedic system is not divided into physics, chemistry, mathematics, sociology, economics, psychology, cosmology, theology, and so on, as its purpose is to create wise people—who know everything—rather than professional academics whose solutions are conceived within the narrow ambits of their primary expertise. A wise person is one who acquires broad knowledge needed to consider all aspects of a problem.

The understanding of the knowledge and its application to various areas of human knowledge should be the primary goal, because by achieving that goal, the other goals can be achieved automatically. If the knowledge is useful and true, then each path meant to attain it can be useful for people with different abilities and interests. If the Vedic texts describe reality correctly, then the timelessness of the knowledge would be more important than the age of the text. If the philosophy is consistent and complete, then even plural authorship of the texts would indicate a multitude of mutually coherent viewpoints. If the personalistic and aspected nature of reality is understood correctly, then the myriad personalities would not be contradictory to a single person of God. And the universal applicability and the non-sectarian nature of knowledge would make any national, social, cultural, and political pride completely redundant.

Even as the Vedas are divine knowledge, and many times described as the word of God and transmitted through the creator of the universe—Brahmā—nobody has to accept their divinity a priori. Vedas recommend faith in the teachers because no student approaches a teacher without some faith. But blind faith—as the antithesis of reason and experience—is rejected. The philosophy of the Vedas is meant to be studied, debated, and discussed by all qualified people (the restriction of the Vedas to a certain class is the restriction of qualification). And the knowledge of the Vedas is beyond race, nation, and society. In all these ways, the Vedas constitute a "secular science"—not atheistic, but secular—as they are amenable to reason and experience, open to sincere inquiry and discussion, and not to be conflated with narrow political objectives.

The primary aim of this series of books is to help the readers understand the knowledge. If the truth of the Vedic texts is known, then we can talk about their history. If the unity of Vedic philosophy is known, then we can talk about whether they had different authors. If by learning this philosophy, we can master every subject, then we can talk about its divine and eternal nature. And if all these are achieved, then we can speak of the intellectual, cultural, and social superiority of the people who have preserved, advanced, and propagated this knowledge selflessly. In fact, by establishing the truth, all other questions about history, authorship, and divinity will become moot—we will accept them without an argument, based on their superiority. Without proving the consistency, completeness, pervasive usefulness, and the empirical truth of this knowledge, there is no point in talking about history, authorship, divinity, geographical heritage, and socio-cultural identities. Without understanding the nature of reality, pride in ancient history makes no difference to the present. And without putting that knowledge into practice, all claims remain the subject of endless subjective opinions and pointless debates. If instead, we focus on the truth in the Vedas, then even the temporaneous goals can also be achieved naturally.

The Vedas in fact describe the history of their appearance, but because people don't believe in the Vedic truth, therefore, they don't accept the history. Because the academics have become accustomed to numerous mythological texts in the West, which were repeatedly modified and curated by religious institutions to suit their political objectives, they think that the Vedas too must be myths. But where is the evidence for the doctoring of the Vedas? We can find that evidence in the case of the Bible and the Koran for instance, where books have been revised many times, and the ideas of the doctors were inserted into the books. But the Vedic tradition gives us no such evidence. Instead, there is clear evidence of the separation of the texts from the commentaries on the texts. The texts are always separate from the commentaries by various authors. Therefore, if we rely on the Vedic texts, we can also understand their own history.

To understand the Six Systems of Philosophy, we need to take note of their historical appearance. The Vedas state that their knowledge has existed since time immemorial, and originated in the four Vedas compiled by Brahmā—the creator of the universe—after being inspired in the heart by Lord Viṣṇu. Brahmā imparted this knowledge to his sons—the seven sages, Manu, the four Kumāras, and others. These disciples and their successors then produced a broader oral tradition, which was called the "Vedic system"—because it was based on the original four Vedas narrated by Brahmā to others. This oral tradition was significantly larger than what we know as the Vedic texts today.

Vedic cosmology divides time into cycles of yugas, which are further divided into four sub-ages called Satya-yuga, Tretā-yuga, Dvāpara-yuga, and Kali-yuga. The Kali-yuga is the smallest age and is 432,000 years. Dvāpara is twice that of Kali-yuga, Tretā is three times of Kali-yuga, and Satya is four times Kali-yuga. The present age is Kali-yuga. In the bygone ages—Satya, Tretā, and Dvāpara—which amounts to 3,888,000 solar years, the Vedas existed as an oral tradition, because the people following the system had a great memory.

At the beginning of Kali-yuga, these texts were scribed by Vyāsa, who is also sometimes called Bādarāyaṇa. This is when the oral tradition became a written one. Vyāsa performed a selection from the oral tradition, and the texts he produced by scribing the oral tradition were a subset of the oral tradition.

Vyāsa also divided the oral tradition into many parts, which are today known as Saṁhitā, Upaniṣad, Tantra, Purāṇa, Itihāsa, etc. Each of these classes is further divided into many sub-classes and texts. For instance, there are 108 Upaniṣad and 18 Purāṇa. He then also *composed* the Vedānta Sūtra after *compiling* the other Vedic texts. There is a subtle difference between compiling and composing. A compilation is the selective scribing of the oral tradition. But the composition is solely attributable to Bādarāyaṇa (although he often quotes other sages even in this text). Quite simply, Vedānta Sūtra is Bādarāyaṇa's summary of the oral tradition, after the selective scribing of the oral tradition.

While dividing, scribing, and compiling the Vedic texts, Vyāsa referred to the philosophies of some of the Six Systems such as Sāṅkhya and Yoga and included them into the Vedic texts. He left out some of the philosophies such as Nyāya, Vaiśeṣika, and Mīmāṁsā as they were, and still are, considered supplementary. We might wonder why. And the answer is that Nyāya is a system of logic, Mīmāṁsā is the use of reason for semantic analysis, and Vaiśeṣika is the application of semantic analysis to the study of the material nature. These are, strictly speaking, the applications of Vedic philosophy, which are of great interest to the experts, but not of primary interest to the general population. This exclusion of some philosophies from the primary Vedic texts means that logic, semantic analysis, and its applications to the study of nature, were considered to be not of interest to the people primarily interested in the conclusions.

The selective inclusions and exclusions of some philosophies do not mean that they weren't part of the Vedic tradition. For example, practically everyone undergoing scientific education at present uses logic and mathematics, but the foundations of logic and mathematics are studied only by experts. Similarly, practically everyone masters some language, but the foundations of linguistics are outside the scope for everyone except the experts. The doctors who treat patients learn medicine, but they don't study biochemistry because that is too much unnecessary detail that is not of primary interest to their needs.

Therefore, the inclusion of philosophies of Sāṅkhya and Yoga should be viewed as based on the fact that these were considered general information for everyone's use, while the exclusion of philosophies like Nyāya,

Vaiśeṣika, and Mīmāṁsā should be viewed as something that was needed only for experts.

Quite separately, complete systems of philosophy existed as the Sūtra texts that this series is about. They were authored by other sages (Sāṅkhya by Kapila, Yoga by Patañjali, Nyāya by Gautama, Vaiśeṣika by Kaṇāda, and Mīmāṁsā by Jaimini). These other systems of philosophy are also based on the oral Vedic tradition, which preceded Bādarāyaṇa's selected scribing of the tradition, although Nyāya, Vaiśeṣika, and Mīmāṁsā were not included in the scribing. They too existed as an oral tradition and were scribed by their tradition followers, but their names are not known at present because (a) the texts are relatively small compared to the texts that Vyāsa scribed, and (b) there was no selection performed in the scribing of these texts; they were presented as they were. In that light, we can view Vyāsa as an editor of the Vedic tradition, while the other systems of philosophy had scribes that did not try to edit the Sūtra texts.

The result of this difference between Bādarāyaṇa's selected scribing, and the texts of the other five systems, is that we can sometimes find it hard to cite the claims in the philosophies of Sāṅkhya, Yoga, Nyāya, Vaiśeṣika, and Mīmāṁsā from the Saṁhitā, Upaniṣad, Tantra, Purāṇa, and Itihāsa. This inability to find direct references for one system in another one should not be taken to mean that they are at variance, or that they are not Vedic, or that they were created after the scribing of Vedic texts by other philosophers who did not agree with Bādarāyaṇa's view. We must rather understand that all the Six Systems are based on the oral tradition. Specifically, Sāṅkhya, Yoga, Vaiśeṣika, Nyāya, and Mīmāṁsā had their oral tradition before Bādarāyaṇa scribing a select portion of the oral tradition, followed by composing the Vedānta Sūtra. As far as the historical dates of composing are concerned, Vedānta Sūtra is later. It is for this reason that it is sometimes called Uttara Mīmāṁsā (later analysis).

When we study the Six Systems of philosophy, in one sense, we are studying the much older oral tradition—as it was understood by six different sages. And when we study the Saṁhitā, Upaniṣad, Tantra, Purāṇa, and Itihāsa, we are studying the Vedic system as it was selectively scribed by Bādarāyaṇa. The differences in these systems do not indicate a contradiction, but the fact that the oral tradition was bigger than the combinations of all the texts at present.

The point is this: The Six Systems are Vedic because they are all based on the oral tradition. They are also Vedic because Bādarāyaṇa's texts directly reference Sāṅkhya and Yoga, which are also referenced by Nyāya, Vaiśeṣika, and Mīmāṁsā. Then, several doctrines about the nature of the soul and God are common across the Six Systems and can be found in Bādarāyaṇa's texts. Therefore, the Six Systems are not divergent philosophies, but different streams within the oral tradition that emphasized different aspects, and were thereby encoded as the Sūtra texts, that came to be studied by different students, and that inherited method of teacher-disciple succession created many schools.

And yet, there is widespread perception at present that the Six Systems of Philosophy are divergent, or even contradictory. This perception of divergence is not entirely fictional; it is indeed based on fact. But its appearance is relatively recent. Such deviations appear in the age of Kali-yuga, where people tend to replace understanding with argument, and incommensurate ideas that deviate from the Vedic philosophy appear. To support their contentions, they also reject many essential aspects of the cohesive system of philosophy.

To understand this divergence, we need to consider the last few thousand years of history, in which three philosophies—materialism, voidism, and impersonalism—have dominated. Each of the Six Systems of Philosophy rejects these doctrines. The world, in Vedic philosophy, reflects the properties of God like a mirror reflects a person's image. The mirror is real, and hence, matter is real. The form in the mirror is objective—the image in the mirror is real. Similarly, the reflection in the mirror is not a creation of the mirror, or an illusion, because there is a person outside the mirror. Since there is a transcendent person, therefore, the mirror and the reflection in it are not the only reality; there is also a transcendent reality. By acknowledging a transcendent reality, materialism is rejected. By acknowledging that this transcendent reality is a person, impersonalism is rejected. And by recognizing that the person exists even if not reflected in the mirror—i.e., if the world doesn't exist—voidism is rejected.

The Six Systems texts delve into the details of why materialism, voidism, and impersonalism are false. They describe why God desires to see His reflection—namely, that it is a process of self-awareness and self-cognition. They describe how God is reflected in the mirror—the mirror is also a person, not an impersonal thing; the reflection in the mirror is the mirror "knowing" God; the mirror is then identified as God's energy or Śakti, and two realities—one masculine and the other feminine—are seen as the basis of the world. The immense variety in the reflection is attributed to the myriad aspects of God, which are integrated in God but separated in the Śakti. Thus, the created world is called *duality* whereas God is described as *non-duality*. The separation of the integrated reality is then understood as a mechanism by which God knows Himself—quite like a person looking into a mirror to see his varied features.

Each of the Six Systems of Vedic philosophy goes over these themes in different orders, emphasizing different aspects of this ideology, dwelling more on some things and less on others. Each philosophy refutes impersonalism, voidism, and materialism as these doctrines contrary to the Vedic system.

In the modern context, the criticism of materialism can be equated to the rejection of modern science, and the ideas that underpin it. The Six Systems texts provide alternative descriptions of matter too, which is unparalleled by any other system in the past or present in its breadth and cohesiveness. The methods of realizing the truth of this description—i.e., the methods for practical and empirical confirmations—are also presented. The alternative to materialism is hence also rational and empirical, and without changing the definition of science—i.e., empirical, and rational truth—the reality is presented differently. It is rather the change of the doctrine of matter, with far wider empiricism, that covers the experiences of the senses, mind, intellect, ego, and the moral sense. The criticism of materialism therefore also constitutes an alternative science.

Similarly, in the modern context, the criticism of voidism can be equated to the rejection of Buddhism and allied traditions, which reject the reality of the soul and God. This rejection, similar to the rejection of materialism, is relatively easier, and the Six Systems of Philosophy don't dwell upon it as much.

The greatest focus in these systems—apart from the description of their position on the nature of reality—is to distinguish it from impersonalism, because impersonalism uses more Vedic terminology than voidism. All over the Six Systems texts, we can find the rejection of all the contentions of impersonalism, namely, that—(a) nature is a deluding agency, (b) nature is inert, (c) Oneness is the ultimate reality instead of diversity, (d) this Oneness is formless, and (e) the desire and individuality of the soul are temporary.

All the followers of the Vedic tradition easily accept the rejections of materialism and voidism, but the rejection of impersonalism has become contentious because impersonalism used to be a non-Vedic system until Śaṅkarācārya authored a commentary on the Vedānta Sūtra, to establish that impersonalism was Vedic. This commentary replaced the void of the Buddhists with two realities—called Brahman and māyā—with Brahman being an undivided consciousness, and māyā being inert matter (sort of like the Cartesian mind-body dualism). Since Brahman is undivided, therefore, the analogy of a person reflected in a mirror is modified to say that the mirror—i.e., māyā—creates an illusory picture of the formless. Since māyā is originally formless, and Brahman is always formless, this doctrine runs into difficulties in explaining the origin of forms. Calling something an illusion doesn't make it go away. The doctrine might also sometimes say that even māyā is a conscious entity, which deliberately tries to mislead Brahman into an illusion. This is also problematic, because if māyā is a deluding agency, then everything in the world—including the Vedic scriptures—must be illusory, as they are byproducts of māyā. The evil nature of māyā would entail that Brahman can never be liberated out of māyā because even the supposed sources of enlightenment are merely delusions.

The fact is that Vedānta does not support such an interpretation, because there are explicit statements about devotion to the Lord, the difference between soul and God, and the divine relationship between God and His Śakti. Hence, Śaṅkarācārya's commentary was an ill-conceived misrepresentation. His position was, in fact, subsequently criticized by other Vedānta views, and owing to these successive interpretations, the Vedānta system is popular today.

The Vedic practitioners of that time could have protested Śaṅkarācārya's commentary, but they welcomed it on pragmatic grounds—they saw Indian society afflicted by Buddhism and considered that to be a bigger and more urgent problem. In voidism, every book is a delusion, because the whole world is unreal. Therefore, even the Vedas must be a delusion. Śaṅkarācārya argued against that idea, and his key contribution was to explain why the Vedic texts are not delusions. But he married an un-Vedic doctrine of impersonalism to the acceptance of the Vedic texts as divine knowledge and divine authority.

To support his impersonal doctrine, Śaṅkarācārya also created a schism between the Six Systems, rejecting the other five systems in his Vedānta commentary. Śaṅkarācārya could not comment on Vedānta alone, if the integrity of the other five systems of philosophy—namely, Sāṅkhya, Mīmāṁsā, Nyāya, Vaiśeṣika, and Yoga—wasn't challenged. Historically, these six systems had always supported each other and used each other's doctrines. The schism between the Six Systems of philosophy owes to the criticism of the other five systems by Śaṅkarācārya. Since that time, people began to consider the Six Systems as divergent and inconsistent philosophies, and their teachers began to grow apart, instead of being considered a part of a single coherent system.

Even as later Ācāryas tried to correct this problem by commenting again on Vedānta Sūtra, the results were less than desirable. Three specific problems arose quickly out of these successive commentaries. First, the commentaries of Rāmānujācārya, Mādhavācārya, and others, emphasized the worship of Lord Viṣṇu, instead of Lord Śiva, thus creating a schism between Vaiṣṇavism and Śaivism. Second, they restricted themselves to the discussion of soul and God, neglecting His Śakti. Third, the study of material nature and Śakti was embraced by the Tantra system, and the Vedic system split again into the third sect of Śaktism, which seemed different from Śaivism and Vaiṣṇavism.

The specific outcome of Śaṅkarācārya's commentary was the schism between the Six Systems, and the specific outcome of the later commentaries was the schism between Vaiṣṇavism, Śaivism, and Śaktism. Once these two types of schisms were created, the unity in the Vedic system was effectively lost. The Vaiṣṇavas and Śaivas focused on Vedānta, and the Śaktas took a greater interest in the other five systems of philosophy. Over time, each of these three systems was further split into many subsects, each based on different Vedic texts, but each of them neglecting the principles presented in the other texts. To the outsider, this reinforced the belief that the Vedic system is not just diverse but also disparate; that it is a collection of many contradictory ideologies.

These schisms continue to play havoc on the understanding of the Vedic system even today. For instance, Sāṅkhya is included in all Purāṇas, but practically everyone who reads these Purāṇas glosses over Sāṅkhya and proceeds into the stories because the teachers of the Purāṇas are mostly Vaiṣṇavas and they deemphasize everything other than select aspects of Vedānta. Similarly, the discussion of Yoga forms a core aspect of all the Upanishads, but the teachers of these Upanishads, who are mostly Śaivas, gloss over Yoga philosophy because they are focused on Vedānta.

When outsiders look at these discrepancies, they find it justifiable to create even more discrepancies. For instance, the Yoga Sūtra doesn't speak about the Kuṇḍalinī, although Tantra does. There is no discussion about Chakras in the Yoga Sūtra, although it is present in the Tantras. The Yoga Sūtra speaks of only one Asana or meditative posture, while Tantras speak of 8,400,000 such postures. While Tantra practitioners indulge in sexual practices, the Yoga Sūtra speaks of celibacy. While Yoga Sūtra rejects the pursuit of mystical powers, the Tantra system advocates it. The modern practitioners of Yoga have therefore effectively transformed it into Tantra. This means that even more people who are interested in the transcendental nature of the Six Systems of Philosophy, are repelled from it, as it is now Tantric.

The schisms between the various systems are also exacerbated because the Vedānta school emphasizes the urgency of liberation from the material world, while other systems discuss the nature of the material world. If you think of the material world as a raging firestorm, then Vedānta says that you must quickly get out of it. Sāṅkhya explains how the fire started. Yoga explains how to get out of the firestorm. Nyāya explains how that fire is a logical outcome of the incompatibility between soul and matter. Vaiśeṣika explains how the fire burns. And Mīmāṁsā discusses the protections while trying to get out of the firestorm. Now, it is up to the reader to decide—Do you want to treat the methods of protecting yourself against the fire as a recommendation for permanently living in the fire, or a method to defend yourself while you are trying to escape? Do you want to consider the description of fire and how it burns just an intellectual curiosity or urgent information that matches the urge to escape the fire?

The divergences in the Six Systems are exacerbated when their position in the larger scheme of things is not understood. Then, a method for protection against the burning fire is treated as a recommendation to stay in the fire. Or, information about the fire's burning is used just for intellectual curiosity. This recommendation then is seen as a contrast against the exhortation to escape the fire, and, lo and behold, a contradiction between the texts is produced.

To avoid such misinterpretations, one must study all the Six Systems, because that gives one the conviction that there is a fire (in case you don't believe it), there is a reason why it was started (in case you are looking for a rational justification), there is a method to escape it, and there are methods to avoid its harmful effects while you are trying to run out of the firestorm.

Wearing a mask is not contradictory to running out; understanding that the fire will not die on its own is not contradictory to deciding that one must run out of the fire. In this way, the Six Systems of philosophy are consistent and coherent, despite their diverging emphases. By studying them, we obtain a view into the larger oral tradition, how this tradition was adapted for different purposes, and why all the systems of philosophy are important for different aspects of the problem. These books are the manuals for life—useful for different kinds of issues.

Finally, a few words must be said about the prevalent commentaries, and how the present commentaries differ. The prevalent commentaries today fall into two broad categories. First, experts in one system, trained by their tradition, comment on only one system of philosophy. Second, academics not trained in any system by the tradition, but having some expertise in the Sanskrit language, comment on multiple systems; they produce false interpretations of things that they don't understand because the context in which the text is written completely escapes them. Both these classes seem interesting to historians, but they mean little to most people because their ideas are not compared to modern thinking. The experts are restricted to one system; the non-experts are misleading; and neither experts nor non-experts demonstrate the relevance of an ancient system in a modern world—when so much around has changed.

These commentaries aim to (a) carry out an unthinkable marriage between the text and the broader Vedic context, (b) demonstrate how this knowledge is relevant today, and (c) make it assimilable to people who know little about Vedic philosophy (or even about Western philosophy and modern science).

This series of books is subtitled "Scientific Commentaries", by which I mean reason and experience—something that can be rationally explained, put into practice, and confirmed by experience. I also mean a contrast or similarity to modern science, Western philosophy, and other prevalent systems of thinking. The former is meant to demonstrate that this is not based on "faith"—although enough faith is needed to read the books, put some of it in practice, and realize the truth. The latter is meant to assist with understanding by the modern mind which is accustomed to almost everything other than Vedic doctrines.

We progress from what we know to what we don't. If what we know is true, then it must be confirmed. If what we know is false, then it must be rejected by reason and evidence. The books are meant to provide adequate background to help people understand. This is a different approach to commentaries than those that have been done in the past. The past commentators relied exclusively on referencing other Vedic texts, and that was acceptable in a society where the Vedic texts were popular and their tenets were accepted. It is not useful for a global audience, or those who are educated in modern science but know very little about Vedic texts. They need an alternative, and these books can help.

From an academic viewpoint, the purpose of writing scientific commentaries is also to transform the discussion of Vedic texts from one of history, linguistics, and religious studies to one about science, philosophy, and empirical merit. Unless Vedic texts are seen as technical information, rather than poetry and literature, their content cannot be truly evaluated and appreciated.

Any ambitious project is hard, and anything hard is likely to have flaws. But it is said that thoroughly honest people enjoy and appreciate reading about the truth even if imperfectly composed. I sincerely hope that you will too.

Book Preface

The Vaiśeṣika system of philosophy discusses the following topics:

- It draws a distinction between six categories called object, activity, quality, universal, individual, and inherence. These six categories are variations of the three modes of nature used in Sāñkhya; the object is in sattva-guna, activity in rajo-guna, and quality in tamo-guna. Likewise, the universal is sattva-guna, the individual is tamo-guna, and inherence is rajo-guna. All these categories are called padārtha comprising two terms—pada (word) and artha (meaning). A detailed discussion of how these categories combine to produce ordinary objects that have qualities by which they are perceived, and activities by which they cause changes, follows.
- The discussion now turns toward the nature of the four elements called Air, Fire, Water, and Earth, which are also part of Sāñkhya. Commensurate with Sāñkhya, Vaiśeṣika attributes these elements the properties of touch, sight, taste, and smell, respectively, with each element possessing the qualities of the previous elements. However, in addition, Vaiśeṣika also discusses additional properties such as the fluidity of Water, and the movement of Air, which are not discussed in Sāñkhya. We can distinguish between these as the effects of a single 'atom' of the element vs. the effects of a collection of atoms. The collection has additional properties, and these effects are therefore 'structural properties' of a collection.
- Vaiśeṣika attributes many properties of the mind to the material elements. Two such properties are 'knowledge' and 'absence'. By the property of 'knowledge' each material element acquires a representation of the external reality within itself. And by the property of 'absence' each material element develops a purpose. We can explain this idea by the example of bodily immunity where the body recognizes the alien entities like bacteria and viruses. The original

interaction with the world—which then leads to a representation—is due to an 'absence'. Similarly, the comprehension of an alien entity as a problem, which then necessitates a solution, is an 'absence'. Thus, by knowing the external world, recognizing it as a problem, having the purpose to solve the problem, and then producing a solution, matter appears to act 'automatically'—i.e., even without our conscious intervention. And yet, this material activity—while not conscious in the sense of having a self-awareness—is still cognitive and conative in the sense of having the attributes of the mind.

- The material objects are described as potentials, which are then manifest due to an 'absence'. The doctrine of 'absence' is taken from Nyāya philosophy, where it represents a doubt, question, or problem. The absence is temporary, but the presence of the potential is eternal. Therefore, the potential manifests into a reality when the 'absence' appears—i.e., when it is recognized as a doubt, question, or problem. Vaiśeṣika doesn't explain the origin of 'absence', but from the other descriptions about the nature of consciousness we can discern that it appears due to consciousness. In short, matter acquires a purpose due to the presence of consciousness. The purpose is objectively present within matter, and yet, it is produced only if consciousness is present. Thus, for instance, a living body has a natural survival instinct, but the dead body does not. In these and other ways, the properties of consciousness are delegated into matter such that material objects act just like a conscious person without a conscious intervention, quite like a servant acquires the intentions of the master and does things on the master's behalf without constant attention and supervision from the master.
- Vaiśeṣika presents a description of the various objects, qualities, and activities as modifications of the original object, qualities, and activities such that some aspects of the original are hidden in each thing. Thus, even if something appears to be impure, it has purity hidden within it. Even when there is ignorance, there is knowledge hidden in it. Ultimately, impurity and ignorance have no fundamental basis; the basis is purity and knowledge; however, due to the category called 'absence' this purity and knowledge is gradually hidden. By this hiding, immense variety of imperfect and impure things are produced, but such impurity and imperfection have no reality other than its basis in purity and perfection.

Vaiśeṣika extensively uses the doctrine of Satkāryavāda and the ideas about the five elements from Sāñkhya. It also relies heavily on the ideas of 'absence' drawn from Nyāya. The doctrines about the soul and God are extensively reused from Vedānta, and the doctrines of union and separation, whole and part, are common across all systems. They are called by various names such as abheda (non-separated), advaya (non-dualism), avyatireka (non-exclusive), etc.

Vaiśeṣika is generally considered the description of the material elements, which it is, although it is also much more. The principles of these elements are semantic, because they recognize the existence of universals and inherence, apart from the existence of individuals. Similarly, a distinction between objects, qualities, and activities, the inherence of qualities and activities in the objects, and their manifestation due to the appearance of 'absence' are all descriptions of an atomic reality quite different from how it is conceived presently.

CHAPTER 1

Section 1

Sūtra 1.1.1

अथातो धर्मं व्याख्यास्यामः

athāto dharmaṃ vyākhyāsyāmaḥ

athāto—now, therefore; dharmaṃ—the nature of duty; vyākhyāsyāmaḥ—we shall explain.

TRANSLATION

Now we shall explain the nature of duty.

COMMENTARY

The understanding of duty rests upon the understanding of a person's role. So, to say that we will try to understand duty means that we have to try to understand how something is not just a material object, but also how that object exists in a role, in relation to other objects, which are also existing in a role.

Roles are created through structural relationships between things. For example, people in an organization enter into relations with each other, which gives them a role. That role then prescribes them a duty. Therefore, the study of duty is not merely based on ethical principles, or what is absolutely right and wrong, but also how that principle must be understood in the context of a person's role. The role, in turn, exists upon the understanding of relationships, which must then recognize an objective category that is not merely objects.

Sūtra 1.1.2

यतो ऽभ्युदयनिश्रेयससिद्धिः स धर्मः

yato 'bhyudayaniḥśreyasasiddhiḥ sa dharmaḥ

yatah—by which; abhyudaya—the birth or rising; niḥśreyasa—the most auspicious; siddhiḥ—the achievement; sa—that; dharmaḥ—is duty.

TRANSLATION

By which there is the birth or rising of the most auspicious, the achievement of that is duty.

COMMENTARY

The materialist believes that by understanding the nature of matter, he can build powerful technology by which all problems of life can be solved. By solving those problems, one will obtain happiness. The Vedic system rejects this idea. It says that to become happy, one must perform their duties. Of course, we need to understand matter to perform our duties, but that understanding doesn't guarantee that we will perform our duties. You might as well use that understanding to abuse our freedom, misuse the knowledge, and exploit the opportunities. However, if we do so, then despite our power and knowledge, we will not produce happiness. We will instead produce distress—primarily for ourselves. Therefore, if we want to ensure our happiness, then the understanding of matter is important, but even more important is the understanding of duty. Duty is the means to happiness, and material knowledge is the means to perform our duty. Therefore, we must begin by defining duty, and then we can also focus on the understanding of how to perform the duty correctly.

Sūtra 1.1.3

तद्वचनादाम्नायस्य प्रामाण्यम्

tadvacanādāmnāyasya prāmāṇyam

tadvacanāt—from the statements about that (duty); āmnāyasya—the Vedic knowledge; prāmāṇyam—becomes authoritative.

TRANSLATION

From the statements about that duty, the Vedic knowledge becomes authoritative.

COMMENTARY

The materialist derives his authority from the correctness of the laws of nature. He says: Look, I have discovered these laws, and by those laws I can create the technology, which, as you can see, works. Since the technology works, therefore, my laws are true. The Vedic system instead says: We are telling you about your duty. If you perform these duties, then we guarantee that you will obtain happiness. So, those who follow the injunctions of these duties obtain happiness, and then the truth of the Veda is confirmed. In this way, both systems rely on different kinds of empirical confirmation—the materialist by showing that technology works, and the Vedic system by proving that one becomes happy by their duties. The difference is that even the technology that works may not produce happiness; for example, you may not get access to the technology, or, even if it works, it may still not solve the problem that you were originally trying to solve. This is sometimes paraphrased as "the operation was successful, but the patient died". Thus, the materialist guarantee of technological success is not a guarantee of happiness. But the Vedic guarantee about the performance of duties is a guarantee about happiness. Whether or not you become happy via technology is not very important. The key thing is that you will be happy.

Sūtra 1.1.4

धर्मवशिेष प्रसूतात् द्रव्यगुणकर्मसामान्य वशिेषसमवायानां
पदार्थानां साधर्म्यवैधर्म्याभ्यां तत्त्वज्ञानान्नश्रिेयसम्

dharmaviśeṣa prasūtāt dravyaguṇakarmasāmānya viśeṣasam-avāyānāṃ
padārthānāṃ sādharmyavaidharmyābhyāṃ
tattvajñānānniḥśreyasam

dharmaviśeṣa—specific duties; prasūtāt—from the birth; dravya—object; guṇa—quality; karma—activity sāmānya—universal; viśeṣa—the individual; samavāyānāṃ—inherences; padārthānāṃ—symbols of meaning; sādharmya—that nature; vaidharmyābhyāṃ—and the opposed nature; tattvajñāt—from the true knowing; niḥśreyasam—unsurpassed auspiciousness.

TRANSLATION

From specific duties are born object, quality, activity, universals, individuals, and the inherences of the symbols of meaning; from the true knowledge of that nature and opposed nature there is unsurpassed auspiciousness.

COMMENTARY

Duties are what *ought* to be done, and matter is what *is*. David Hume, a British philosopher, argued that given what the world *is*, we cannot know what we *ought* to do. There is hence a difference between the descriptive statements about what the world is, and the prescriptive or normative statements about what we should do. This sūtra usurps that is-ought distinction and states that the material reality is produced by the execution of our duties. Therefore, if we don't perform our duties, then we don't even get access to the material reality using which we could build technology, by which we want to solve problems, by which we desire to produce happiness. Those who have neglected their duties will remain impoverished and lack access to the said technology.

To understand this doctrine further, we need to grasp the six categories being described here—object, quality, activity, universals, individuals, and inherences. These are variations of the Sāñkhya doctrine of the three modes of nature called sattva, rajas, and tamas. The sattva-guna denotes the object; the rajo-guna denotes the activity; and tamo-guna denotes the quality. Similarly, sattva-guna represents the universal; tamo-guna represents the individual; and rajo-guna represents the inherence. Let's declutter these by using some examples.

What is a universal? It is a general concept or a class. But these classes have three further varieties—objects, activities, and qualities. For example, a 'car' is a general concept or class, in the object-mode. 'Color' is a general class in the quality or property mode. And 'running' is a general concept or class, in the activity mode. Pursuant to these general classes, there can be individual cars, individual instances of color, and individual acts of running. These individual instances of the universals are also called padārtha or symbols of meaning. The term padārtha comprises two parts—pada and artha; the former means word and the latter indicates meaning. These padārthas are produced by the combination of a universal and an individual. So, if 'car' is the universal, and we instantiate that concept into an individual car, then that instance of the concept is the symbol of the idea 'car'. Similarly, if 'wheel' is the universal, and we instantiate that concept into an individual wheel, then the instance of that concept is a symbol of the idea 'wheel'. Finally, a wheel is a part of a car, and that whole-part relationship is called 'inherence'—the wheel exists within the car.

Of course, someone might argue: We can reduce the car to its parts, such as wheels, transmission, steering, seats, engine, etc., so the car is nothing but these parts. The problem is that a random aggregation of the parts would not produce a car. These parts have to be assembled in a specific manner—the 'design' of the car—which is a structure that establishes relationships between the parts, and those relationships are the 'inherence'. To create such relationships, or 'design', the whole must exist prior to the parts. In short, we must begin with the purpose of designing a car, so the definition of a car must exist prior to the parts. Hence, the whole car cannot be reduced to the parts of the car, because the whole existed before the parts. This whole then expands into a structure or design of the car, and functional roles in that structure are populated by components of a car. From a materialistic perspective, the parts can be observed, but the design has no independent existence. Since the design has no independent reality, therefore, the idea of a car that led to the design also has not reality. However, without the idea of a car, and its design, the components of car cannot be assembled. Thus, if the design and the idea are ignored, then science loses predictiveness; as this idea is extended, we fail to see the mental components—i.e., ideas and designs—and focus only upon the parts that are sense perceived. And that sense perceivable reality cannot explain the car's appearance.

This pattern of symbols inhering within symbols can be repeated indefinitely. For example, we can say that the car's wheel can be divided into subparts, such that these subparts have a certain relation to the whole, and that relationship constitutes the design of the wheel. When you come to sufficiently small parts, then, you will have to employ a different kind of inherence in which there is an 'object' which combines 'properties' in a specific manner, and that specific combination of properties (in which the properties are structured in hierarchy, such that some properties are more important relative to the others), is another kind of inherence. Similarly, when we think of the working of the whole car, which can be divided into the working of the car's parts—e.g., the engine, transmission, wheels, etc.—then again an inherence must be invoked: The working of the whole car is the symbol of activity of the working of the whole car, and the parts working within the car are also symbols of (different) activities, and the whole activity (of the car) is a combination of the partial activities (of the parts of the car); that combination of actions is another inherence.

In this way, the concept 'car' can be thought of in three ways—an object, a property, and an activity; then there are instances of these objects, properties, and activities, which create an individual car. And then there are relations between the wholes and parts, such that objects are parts of objects; properties are parts of properties, and activities are part of activities. But we could also use this inherence method to say that activities are part of objects (e.g., the piston of the engine moves); properties are part of objects (e.g., that the car has some weight), apart from saying that objects are part of objects (e.g., that wheels, steering, and engine are part of the whole object—the car). We could also say that objects are part of properties (e.g., the total weight of the car is due to the parts of the car, which themselves have a weight), and activities are part of properties (e.g., the engine's movement is a part of car speed, and it contributes to the car's speed). Finally, we can say that properties and objects are part of activities (e.g., that the movement of the car requires a road apart from the car, and the car is able to gain speed only because it has the property of weight).

The sophistication in this doctrine comes from the use of the three modes of nature, which imply that the same thing can be described either as an object, a property, or an activity. Then each of these could be described as universal, individual, or a relation. The Sāñkhya system summarizes these ideas as the doctrine of three modes, while other systems sometimes elaborate it in new ways. The Vaiśeṣika doctrine above can be understood as that elaboration.

Now we can discuss the claim that this complex system of six categories (which are variations of the three modes of nature) is produced as the consequence of duty performance. To understand this claim, we have to note that prakṛti or material nature is described as a potentiality that exists eternally, but it is not manifest eternally. To convert this unmanifest potentiality into visible reality, an agency is required. The Vedic system describes a system of three agencies called guna, karma, and chitta, which manifest this potentiality.

To illustrate by an example, let's say you are preparing some bread. You need some flour, milk, water, fire, etc. Then you need to know a recipe on how to prepare the bread. Finally, you must want to prepare a certain type of bread. The chitta is your knowledge of recipes; if you don't know certain recipes, then you cannot prepare that kind of bread. The karma is what kind of flour you have, how much milk and water are available, what implements for cooking (e.g., ovens, microwaves, or earthen pots) are available, etc. And guna is your desire for preparing a certain kind of bread. Thus, the availability of ingredients, your knowledge of recipes, and your desire to make a certain type of bread all play a role in determining what type of bread is ultimately produced.

The Sāñkhya system states that all kinds of breads are eternal potentials, but you manifest one potential out of this pool of potentialities by the combination of chitta, guna, and karma. But this sūtra narrows the focus even further and says that the consequences of previous actions determine what kinds of ingredients you will get. How you combine them using your knowledge, with the intention of preparing what kind of outcome, is up to you. Ideally, how you use your knowledge and the goals you try to fulfill are decided by your duties: You should not misuse your knowledge and not aim for goals forbidden by duties. But if you do, then the consequence is that you lose some of the ingredients the next time you try to use your knowledge to achieve some goals.

So, the fact that you have some flour, milk, water, and an oven to prepare a chosen type of bread using the recipe that you know of, is not an accident. You have access to these things due to your karma, and that is in turn produced by the duties you have performed in the past. If you have been dutiful, then you will get access to flour, milk, water, and an oven, and you can prepare the chosen type of bread using the knowledge you have, and then you can satisfy your hunger and feel happiness. But if you haven't been dutiful, then you can desire to prepare bread, and you may have the knowledge to make bread, but you will not get access to the ingredients. Therefore, execute your duties, because by those duties you get access to ingredients, and then you can make bread.

Thus, the is-ought dichotomy that Hume introduced is rejected by saying that what *is* (i.e., the flour, oven, milk, and water) is produced by what *ought* to be done (i.e., the performance of duties). The materialist can describe how to make bread, but he cannot guarantee that you will have access to ingredients. Therefore, knowing the recipe of how to make bread doesn't guarantee satisfaction. The satisfaction is guaranteed only by the performance of duties.

Sūtra 1.1.5

पृथिव्यापस्तेजो वायुराकाशं कालो दिगात्मा मन इति द्रव्याणि

pṛthivyāpastejo vāyurākāśaṃ kālo digātmā mana iti dravyāṇi

pṛthivi—Earth; āpas—Water; tejo—Fire; vāyuh—Air; ākāśaṃ—Ether;

kālo—time; dik—space; ātmā—the soul; mana—the mind; iti—thus; dravyāṇi—are the objects.

TRANSLATION

Earth, Water, Fire, Air, Ether, time, space, soul, and the mind; thus, there are the objects.

COMMENTARY

This doctrine of nature is almost similar to that of Sāñkhya, with two main differences. First, in Sāñkhya, a more elaborate description of the "mind" is provided by dividing it into four parts— (1) the mind that thinks, feels, and wills, and (2) three other instruments called intelligence, ego, and the moral sense, which judge. The intellect judges if the thinking is true; the ego judges whether the feeling is good; and the moral sense judges if the willing is right. In various systems of Vedic philosophy, these distinctions are sometimes elaborated and sometimes summarized. In this case, these are summarized into a "mind".

The second main difference is that the ideas of 'space' and 'time' are added into the material ontology, so we have to discuss what we really mean by them. The term "space" simply means the domain of all the possibilities, and "time" means the agency that controls their manifestation into an experience. Therefore, the five elements of Earth, Water, Fire, Air, and Ether, along with the mind, are potentials that form a "space". There isn't one thing called the "mind". It is rather a category of objects, with many varieties. For example, each species of life has a unique type of mind; even within humans, there are many types of minds. But they are all generically called "mind" just like we might use the term 'car' to describe a variety of vehicles. Likewise, the Earth object is a general class of entities that have the property of smell, taste, sight, touch, and sound. But there are many such types of Earth objects which combine these properties in different ways. Therefore, "Earth" is also a class of objects, but a singular name is used to denote these objects in the interest of summarizing the ontology.

Therefore, there are 5 kinds of objects, that collectively comprise a "space" of possibilities. The origin of all these potentials is also an object, which constitutes the origin of the entire universe. Since these potentials existed in the origin prior to their manifestation, therefore, at one time, the universe was just one thing. Thereby, we can also speak of the space as an individual object. Finally, time is the agency that manifests the possibilities from the origin, and it is, therefore, the ultimate cause of what we perceive in the world. The perceived time begins when the universe springs forth and ends when the universe is annihilated. However, there is a time beyond this perception, which causes the manifestation of the potentials, which is referred to as an 'object' in this sūtra. The perceived time is relative to each observer: It exists only when the observer is perceiving. However, the time beyond the perception exists even if the obervers or their perception doesn't exist; that time causes the potential manifestation. The subjective time is an effect, and the time beyond the subjective experiences is objective. This sūtra refers to the time beyond perception as an object.

If we go deeper into Vedic cosmology, we find that the space of a universe is embedded inside a larger space that comprises infinite universes. Similarly, the time (duration) for which a universe exists is embedded in an infinite time (duration). These latter space and time, which are called 'objects' here, are also understood as persons—Prakṛti and Puruśa—and what we call space and time are the cognitions of these persons. The cognitive capacity of the Prakṛti is the space of all possibilities. And the cognitive capacity of Puruśa is the successive manifestation of these potentials into individual universes and events. Thus, the spaces and times of the universe are "inside" the Prakṛti and Puruśa. The persons whose cognitions these are, are sometimes referred to as 'objects'.

The difference is that these 'objects' are not contained in some 'space', because that will beg the question about the origin of the space and time. This is not a trivial issue, because in science we use nouns like 'space' and 'time' to speak of the universe as a thing, without truly delving into how such nouns could be used. So, the Vedic system changes the paradigm and says that these are objects, but they exist inside the cognitive capacity of a person. That cognitive capacity is the "space" and the person is the "object". The difference is simply that yet another "space" that embeds this "object" is not needed.

The person—which we also call the 'object'—is the *origin* of the space, from which space emanates. The origin is the singularity from which space and time spring, and their combination (i.e., the combination of potentiality and time) produces the perceived reality. Therefore, there is a state in which space and time are unmanifested or unobservable, and then a state in which they are combined and manifest as perceivable reality. If potentiality is separated from time, then the universe disappears, although it exists in a potential form. And if potentiality combines with time, then the perceivable universe is manifest.

Sūtra 1.1.6

रुपरसगन्धस्पर्शाःसंख्याःपरमिाणानि पृथक्त्वं संयोगविभागौ परत्वापरत्वे बुद्धयःसुखदुखे इच्छाद्वेषौ प्रयत्नाश्च गुणाः

ruparasagandhasparśāḥ saṃkhyāḥ parimāṇāni pṛthaktvaṃ saṃyogavibhāgau paratvāparatve buddhayaḥ sukhaduḥkhe icchādveṣau prayatnāśca guṇāḥ

rupa—forms; rasa—taste; gandha—smell; sparśāḥ—touch; saṃkhyāḥ—numbers; parimāṇāni—quantities; pṛthaktvaṃ—separateness; saṃyoga—union; vibhāgau—classification; paratvāparatve—in prior and posterior; buddhayaḥ—cognitions; sukhaduḥkhe—in happiness and distress; icchādveṣau—desire and aversion; prayatna—effort; ca—also; guṇāḥ—the qualities.

TRANSLATION

Forms (vision), taste, smell, touch; numbers, quantities, separateness, union, and classification in prior and posterior; the cognitions, happiness and distress, desire and aversion; and effort; these are also the qualities.

COMMENTARY

The modes of nature are three, therefore, to understand this sūtra, we have to look for triads, but also understand how these triads create diversities.

Let's begin by understanding the nature of counting. It requires three key steps—(a) identification, (b) classification, and (c) ordering. Identification requires two other things that are noted here—namely, separation and union. For example, if you are looking at the sky, then you might see star constellations comprised of individual stars. You put some stars together and call that a "constellation" and you separate some other stars into another constellation. This act of dividing and combining to create groups of things is the first essential step in counting, as it identifies individual things. Then, in the next step, we start classifying these things using some concepts. For example, we might say that this constellation looks like a crab, that one looks like a lion, and another one looks like a girl, etc. This process is called 'classification' in this sūtra. Then, once we have classified things, then we can to also sequence them, which is called priority and posteriority in this sūtra. This sequences everything into an order. Now, we can label these sequenced things as first, second, third, etc. This is called numbering or saṃkhyā in this sūtra. Then if you can count something till the Nth number, you also determine that there are N things. This is called parimāṇa or quantity in this sūtra. We can summarize these as follows. Put all together, these constitute seven different types of processes in counting.

- Identification: pṛthaktvaṃ (separateness) and saṃyoga (union)
- Classification: vibhāgau (classification)
- Sequencing: paratva (priority) and aparatva (posteriority)
- Labeling: first, second, third, etc. — saṃkhyāḥ (numbers)
- Quantifying: one, two, three, etc. — parimāṇāni (quantities)

Now, there are three more steps in counting, which pertain to choices. The first step is that this method of ordering may be true or false. There may be M things, but we might count N things. Then, there may be M things but we might sequence them incorrectly. The job of the intellect, or buddhi, is to determine: Are we identifying, classifying, and ordering them correctly or incorrectly? Next, we might desire to identify, classify, and order them in a particular way. For example, we might want to see the sky in terms of crabs, lions, girls, and rams, when such things may not truly exist (I'm not saying that this classification is false, just highlighting that they may be determined by our desires). So, our desires—which are called desire and aversion (icchādveṣau) in this sūtra—play an important role in identifying, classifying, and ordering. Finally, we might have wanted to see elephants and trees in the sky, but we might not find them, or we might have wanted to see girls and lions in the sky and we might find them. Therefore, once the classification is completed, we also obtain a result—happiness, and distress—which is called sukhaduḥkhe in this sūtra.

This process of counting requires some effort, which is called prayatna, and it operates on some objective reality, which is called forms, taste, smell, and touch. The effort is applied in seven ways to produce a numbered description of reality; this effort is mediated by our desires, the capacity to cognize correctly or incorrectly, and the opportunity to perceive the world in a certain way. Therefore, we can also look at it as the following five-step process below:

- Reality: taste, touch, smell, and form
- Observer: desires, intellect, and relation to reality
- Effort: the seven-fold process that creates number and quantity

- Result: good and bad, true and false, right and wrong
- Consequence: the future potential for an encounter with reality

Now, this sūtra states that this entire system of reality, the observer's capacities, judgments, and preferences, the efforts that are applied to the instruments of cognition, judgment, and preference, and their results and consequences, are simply the three modes of nature. This is a bold and encompassing statement that concludes that the Sāñkhya system of philosophy (which describes the nature of the three modes) is accepted, but also extended. The acceptance pertains to the understanding of reality and the observer. But the extension pertains to additional categories of effort, result, and consequence.

As we saw earlier, this text began with the desire to study the nature of duty. What is duty? It is the study of how to apply our effort, to obtain the results that are mandated by duty, so that we can reap auspicious consequences later. In this sūtra, the Vaiśeṣika system accepts all that the Sāñkhya system provides, and then moves forward: Using that system, let us study the nature of duty, how effort, if dutiful, leads to good results, and, if undutiful, leads to bad results. The differences of focus between these systems are not indications of contrary viewpoints; they are rather supportive and progressive claims.

The Sāñkhya system says that they don't advocate the Vaiśeṣika categories like object, quality, and activity, or space, time, and actors. The Sāñkhya system also states that by delving into the detailed manifestations of the three modes, we do not get detached from the modes. Hence, there is an important distinction between Sāñkhya and Vaiśeṣika: The former imparts knowledge of the material modes to ensure that the soul is detached from the material world by this knowledge, while the latter imparts knowledge of the material modes to ensure that the soul can understand reality enough to perform his duties. These two are called nivṛtti and pravṛtti methods in Vedic philosophy; the former advises detachment and the latter recommends engagement—as methods for liberation. Their goals are identical (liberation); their understanding of reality is identical (based on the three modes). And yet, the philosophy of detachment for liberation gives the overview without the details, and the philosophy of engagement for liberation provides the details, to help a person do their duties.

Sūtra 1.1.7

उत्क्षेपणमवक्षेपणं आकुञ्चनं प्रसारणं गमनमिति कर्माणि

utkṣepaṇamavakṣepaṇaṃ ākuñcanaṃ prasāraṇaṃ gamanamiti karmāṇi

utkṣepaṇam—rising up; avakṣepaṇaṃ—falling down; ākuñcanaṃ—contraction; prasāraṇaṃ—expansion; gamanam—movement; iti—in this way; karmāṇi—the actions.

TRANSLATION

Rising up, falling down, contraction, expansion, and movement; in this way, are the actions.

COMMENTARY

Modern science describes everything in terms of motion, which is called 'movement' here, and this motion occurs in a flat box-like space comprised of points. Space, in the Vedic system, is hierarchical as an inverted tree, and movement is therefore not just the change of the position of an object vis-à-vis the point position in a flat space but also the evolution of the space itself. To understand this new kind of dynamic, we can think of a person moving from one organization to another. The organization structure is a hierarchical 'space' in which people have 'positions'—that are higher and lower. So, what we call 'motion' or 'movement' is a person moving from one organization to another. Then, within that organization, a person can move up or down. Finally, the organization itself can expand or contract. We have to recall that space was earlier described as an *object*. So, the dynamics of the organization—namely, expanding and contracting—is also an object's dynamic. Likewise, since something can move inside that space—e.g., rising up and down—therefore, that movement is also a type of object motion. Then, since something can move from one organization to another, therefore, that is also a type of motion. Thus, if we think of space as a flat or linear structure, then there is only one kind of motion—the motion of a particle from one point to another. But if we think of space as an inverted-tree-like structure, then objects can move up or down, and the space itself can expand or contract. The upward and downward movement can also be applied to space—it is like one branch of a tree changing its point of attachment on the tree. Likewise, expansion and contraction just mean that the hierarchy is increasing or decreasing. In this way, there are five motions.

We can illustrate these ideas with more examples. For instance, if you join an organization, then you have a certain 'position' in it, which is the relative importance assigned to you in an organization. But then the organization grows and there are many more people in the organization. Then, your 'position' is automatically reduced. You might say: I hold the same title, do the same job, I am paid the same salary. So, how can my position reduce? The answer is that when the organization grows, it steepens in its hierarchy. So, if there were some levels above your level previously, then the number of levels increases after the growth. Now, your position is farther relative to the top-level position, and therefore, your position is now 'lower'. Likewise, if an organization shrinks, the then number of people reduce, and the hierarchy flattens. Now, your position is closer to the top-level position, so relative to that, you are now 'higher'.

Similarly, if you jump from one organization to another, and get a promotion, then you have a 'lateral' move which is called 'movement' here, and then you have an upward 'jump' which is called 'rising up' here. So, one change is comprised of two components—lateral movement and an upward movement. Then, if you get laid off from your job, and accept a lower-paying position in another company, then you have movement (from one company to another), and 'falling down' change from a higher position to another. If you subsequently rise up due to your work, that is again an upward movement. And if you are working to expand the organization, hoping to get promoted (and that promotion arrives), then there is a combination of two distinct changes—the organization expands, and then you move up in the new organization.

In this way, the modern scientific ideas of what we mean by 'motion' undergo a radical transformation when we change our notions of space. Instead of monolithic 'motion', we get five distinct broad classes of position changes. This sūtra refers to this five-fold movement as 'activity' or 'actions'. There is a subtle difference between the two; the activity is the change occurring, and the action is the cause that makes that change. Therefore, we can use the five-fold classification for both the appearance of changes and the cause of changes.

In one sense, the 'space' in which change occurs is three-dimensional. But since each branch or twig in a tree is a dimension, therefore, the space is infinite-dimensional. And yet, since we describe changes to this space and the object in it, in terms of five distinct components of change, therefore, the space is also five-dimensional. There is no contradiction between these descriptions, but they are alternately employed depending on the context and the problem.

Sūtra 1.1.8

सदनित्यं द्रव्यवत् कार्यं कारणं सामान्यविशेषवदिति द्रव्यगुणकर्मणामविशेषः

sadanityaṃ dravyavat kāryaṃ kāraṇaṃ sāmānyaviśeṣavaditi dravyaguṇakarmaṇāmaviśeṣaḥ

sat—eternal; anityaṃ—temporary; dravyavat—like objects; kāryaṃ—effects; kāraṇaṃ—causes; sāmānyaviśeṣavat—like general and particular; iti—thus; dravya—object; guṇa—quality; karmaṇām—activities; aviśeṣaḥ—universals.

TRANSLATION

The eternal and temporary, like objects, effects, and causes are both generals and particulars. Thus, object, quality, and activities are universals.

COMMENTARY

In an earlier sūtra, two triads were described. The first triad was universals, individuals, and inherence. The second triad was objects, qualities, and activities. We can see how each of these is both universals (if we treat them as concepts), and also individuals (if they are instantiated into individuals). For example, a cow is an object, whiteness is a quality, and running is an activity. These are universals. Then, the instance of cow is an individual instance of the concept cow; the whiteness of the cow is the instance of the quality of whiteness; and the running of the cow is the instance of the universal activity of running. Thus, the concepts of objects, qualities, and activities are eternal, but the individual instantiation of these concepts is temporary. These individuals are produced by the combination of universality and individuality. Thus, the things of the second triad (objects, qualities, and activities) could sometimes be treated as universals, and then at other times as individuals. This doesn't mean that they are identical. It just means that based on the context, we must know which "mode"—universal or individual—is being employed while using them.

This is a pervasive fact about all words. For example, the word 'president' can indicate a universal— "the head of a state". And then, 'president' can also mean a specific person, who is the head of the state. So, if someone says: "you should become the president", they are referring to the universal idea. And if they say: "you should meet the president", then they mean an individual.

Sūtra 1.1.9

द्रव्यगुणयोःसजातीयारम्भकत्वं साधर्म्यम्

dravyaguṇayoḥ sajātīyārambhakatvaṃ sādharmyam

dravya—object; guṇayoḥ—and qualities; sajātīya—of the same class; ārambhakatvaṃ—the originators; sādharmyam—of similar nature.

TRANSLATION

The objects and qualities of the same class are originators of similar nature.

COMMENTARY

Each of the universals can further be divided into other universals (not merely instantiated into individuals). For example, a mammal—which is a universal—can be divided into other universals like cows, horses, dogs, cats, etc. Likewise, the universal 'dog' can be further divided into species like Alsatian, Poodle, Bernese, etc. These concepts are also the *instances* of the previous higher-level concept, although they are not individuals. For example, all Alsatians are also dogs, which are also mammals, which are also animals, etc. Thus, a conceptual hierarchy—which looks like an inverted tree—is constructed in which the abstract concept (e.g., a mammal) expands into subsidiary concepts like dogs, which then expands into further subsidiary concepts like Alsatian. The same claim can also be applied to qualities. For instance, the concept 'color' is instantiated into the concepts of red, blue, and green. Then, 'red' itself can be instantiated into Maroon, Crimson, Carmine, etc. thus creating an inverted tree. As we climb up this tree, we get more abstract ideas; as we descend down this tree, we get more detailed ideas. At every level, we can draw a 'class'—with some level of abstraction—that is the 'originator' of similar things of its own nature. This sūtra refers to such an expansion of concepts into concepts.

Sūtra 1.1.10

द्रव्याणि द्रव्यान्तरमारभन्ते गुणाश्च गुणान्तरम्

dravyāṇi dravyāntaramārabhante guṇāśca guṇāntaram

dravyāṇi—objects; dravyāntaram—differences of objects; ārabhante—originate; guṇāśca—also the qualities; guṇāntaram—the differences of qualities.

TRANSLATION

The objects and differences of objects (i.e., numerous objects) also originate the qualities and the differences of qualities.

COMMENTARY

The hierarchy of concepts has several levels, and in these levels, the *type* of the concept changes. This sūtra notes one such *type of* change, by saying that as the conceptual tree expands, at some point, the type changes from *objects* to *qualities*. For example, we can say that a "dog *has a* weight" or a "dog *has a* color", whereas, previously we said that a "dog *is a* mammal". So, the object is thought to be the whole, and the properties are the aspects or parts of the dog. These properties can further expand. For example, we can say that a "dog *has a* color which *is* black". Subtle nuances between these expansions exist in various languages. For example, in English, we use the connective *is-a* to expand mammal into a dog (a dog is a mammal), the connective *has-a* to expand the dog into properties (a dog has a color), and the connective *is* to expand one property into another (the color has a color, which is black). Much confusion is created in languages when these connectives are contracted. For example, we could say "the dog is black", where the property of color is contracted along with the *has-a* connective (we have removed the part which says "the dog has color"). Similarly, we can say that "the animal is black", thus contracting multiple stages of the conceptual hierarchy (i.e., a mammal is an animal, a dog is a mammal, a dog has color). We should set aside these contractions for the time being, and consider the complete hierarchy that involves an animal expanding into a mammal and a mammal expanding into a dog, both of which are expansions in the object-mode. Then, the expansion of the dog into color, and the expansion of the color into black are expansions in the quality-mode. This sūtra simply notes that objects also expand into qualities, but the picture is quite complicated when we try to understand the different classes of expansions.

A similar type of expansion is that of activity. For instance, we can say that "a man has the power of holding, and he is holding a pen". But when this sentence is contracted, we simply say "a man is holding a pen", although due to our innate capacities to distinguish between nouns, verbs, and adjectives we don't feel confused when the *is* connective is employed both for saying that "a man is tall" and "a man is holding a pen", when in other cases we use other connectives such as has-a (a man has a weight), or is-a (a man is a mammal).

The point is this: There are different kinds of expansions— (1) the expansion of an abstract object into a contingent object, (2) the expansion of an abstract quality into a contingent quality, (3) the expansion of an abstract activity into a contingent activity, and (4) the expansion of objects into qualities and activities. We can set aside the nuances of which of these expansions are clearly demarcated by the use of different connectives (is-a, has-a) and which ones are not so demarcated (is), although we know that there is indeed a difference. In a properly constructed formal language, such things could be properly distinguished by employing different terms, or different kinds of connectives.

This idea of properties and activities expanding from the object is noted even in Sāñkhya, although in a different way when it is said that the senses of knowledge (taste, touch, smell, sound, and sight) and the senses of action (speech, procreation, excretion, holding, and movement) are expanded from the mind. The mind grasps objects—e.g., a cow. The senses of knowledge grasp a quality—e.g., a color. And the senses of action grasp the activity—e.g., running. As a result, the three modes of nature—object, quality, and activity—are now connected by saying that qualities and activities are expansions of the object. The senses of knowledge are the instruments that capture qualities, and the senses of activity are the instruments that capture activities. Once these things are captured, the mind combines them to construct a picture of the object. Similarly, while creating an object, we first conceptualize an abstract form, then we create a design of how a thing looks, and then we create a mechanism of working. Depending on the context, you could say that the activity is an expansion of the quality, or the quality is the expansion of the activity. This nuance is not discussed in this sūtra; it just says that qualities are expanded from objects.

Sūtra 1.1.11

करम करमसाध्यं न वदियते

karma karmasādhyaṃ na vidyate

karma—the activities; karmasādhyaṃ—the objects attained by the activity; na—not; vidyate—do not exist.

TRANSLATION

The actions do not exist in the objects attained by the actions.

COMMENTARY

Any object with its qualities can be constructed by many methods. Once the construction is complete, we cannot know the process by which it was constructed. This is the rejection of determinism in which every current state has exactly one possible past state, and the trajectory by which the current and the past states are connected is deterministic. When determinism is rejected, then there is more than one trajectory—a sequence of steps—leading to the same destination. That trajectory represents the activity. If nature were deterministic, then given any current state, we could perfectly trace the past state from it. And that would mean that the action in some sense 'resides' in the objects. Therefore, the rejection of action residing in the object is the rejection of determinism.

Sūtra 1.1.12

न दरव्यं कारयं कारणं च भवति

na dravyaṃ kāryaṃ kāraṇaṃ ca bhavati

na—not; dravyaṃ—the objects; kāryaṃ—the effects; kāraṇaṃ—cause; ca—also; bhavati—becomes.

TRANSLATION

Also, the objects do not become the causes or the effects.

COMMENTARY

The objects are treated as inert entities—neither causes nor effects. The next sūtra attributes this causation to qualities (e.g., taste, touch, smell, sight, etc.).

Sūtra 1.1.13

उभयथा गुणाः

ubhayathā guṇāḥ

ubhayathā—both (causes and effects); guṇāḥ—are qualities.

TRANSLATION

Both causes and effects are qualities.

COMMENTARY

This doctrine is similar to modern science where causation resides in the properties. The difference is simply that modern science views properties physically (e.g., energy, momentum, mass, charge, etc.) while Vaiśeṣika views them as qualities (e.g., taste, smell, touch, sight, etc.). Yet another difference is that in modern science the properties are attached arbitrarily to objects; for example, any particle could have any mass. But in Vaiśeṣika, the qualities are manifest from the objects (as noted in the earlier sūtra). Thus, for instance, a cow could not have an arbitrary mass; the property of the cow's weight is partly decided by something being a cow. Since objects manifest properties, therefore, they can be called the cause of the effects produced by the properties. And yet, when the effect is produced, it is not the object, but the properties that cause it.

A later sūtra will note how the qualities themselves are present in an object due to activities, which cause the qualities to combine and divide into objects. This leads to a question: If the cause of the qualities combining and dividing is activity, and not the qualities, then what kind of causes are qualities? And the answer must be nuanced to say that they are the causes of perception. If an object has no qualities, then it cannot be perceived. But if it has some activity, then it can still produce effects or quality changes, which can then be perceived. Thus, qualities are akin to what is perceived by the senses of knowledge, and activities are akin to what is achieved through the senses of action. By our senses of action, we can transform the groupings of qualities, and that change would be perceived by the senses of knowledge—if there were some qualities. Of course, as we have seen earlier, any kind of distinctness, the ability to prioritize things, or even number or count them, entails the presence of qualities. Finally, desire and aversion, happiness and distress are also qualities.

Thus, a 'pure object' is something that exists as an individual, but it cannot be distinguished, ordered, and counted. It has no attraction or repulsion. We can call it a pure thing-in-itself (this term is employed in Western philosophy to describe the reality that exists in and of itself without being perceived).

Sūtra 1.1.14
कार्यविरोधि कर्म
kāryavirodhi karma

kārya—effect; virodhi—opposes; karma—action.

TRANSLATION

The effect opposes the action.

COMMENTARY

There are some similarities between this idea and the physical notion of 'inertia'. When a force is applied to an object, the object resists it, which is called its 'inertia', and equated to a property called 'mass'. The difference here is that the thing opposing the action is the effect, rather than the property. To understand this idea, we have to think of the effect as the intended state which exists as a potential right now. When an action is performed, the current state is transformed into the intended state. The modern physics description states that it is the present state which offers a resistance to change, while the Vaiśeṣika description says that it is the future state that offers a resistance to change.

We can illustrate this difference by an example. Suppose you are trying to walk from place A to B, and you need to apply some effort to move. According to modern physics, the thing that resists the movement is your own weight. And according to Vaiśeṣika, it is the future state (i.e., where you are intending to go) that offers resistance. Thus, according to modern physics, all heavy people will have the same difficulty in moving, and that difficulty will not change based on their destination. But according to Vaiśeṣika, the difficulties in movement will be determined by the destination that a person is going to. Thus, a heavy person will move easily toward some destinations and not others, while another person will move easily toward a different set of destinations.

Modern physics solves this problem by saying that there can be a 'force' that pulls something toward the destination; whatever is pulled with greater force moves easily, and whatever is not pulled in this way, moves with difficulty. Thus, there are two distinct ideas—inertia and force—that are combined to produce a result: Inertia resists change, and force causes a change.

In the case of Vaiśeṣika, the force is applied by the moving object, and the resistance is offered by the destination state. So, the destination state is not pulling the object toward itself, with the object itself resisting the change. Rather, the object is trying to move toward the destination, and the destination state is resisting it. The roles of inertia and force are thus reversed in the two cases. In modern physics, the moving object is inertia, and the force is external; in Vaiśeṣika, the moving object is the force and the inertia to change is external.

Sūtra 1.1.15

क्रियागुणवत् समवायिकारणमिति द्रव्यलक्षणम्

kriyāguṇavat samavāyikāraṇamiti dravyalakṣaṇam

kriyāguṇavat—the activities and qualities; samavāyikāraṇam—the cause of combination; iti—thus; dravyalakṣaṇam—the symptom of the object.

TRANSLATION

The symptom of the object is thus being the cause of combining qualities and activities.

COMMENTARY

An earlier sūtra stated that an object is inert, and the qualities are both causes and effects. And this sūtra says that the object is the cause of combining the activities and qualities. The qualities and activities are thus two complementary ways of describing an object. For instance, a car can be described by its qualities—e.g., its shape, size, weight, etc. And it can be described by its actions—e.g., that it can move on a road. Something that merely moves on a road is not necessarily a car (trucks can also move on a road). Likewise, something that merely looks like a car but doesn't move, cannot be considered a car. The 'car' is defined by the combination of how it looks and how it works. This combination is called an 'object' and it is different from both qualities and actions.

Sūtra 1.1.16

द्रव्याश्रय्यगुणवान् संयोगविभागेष्वकारणमनपेक्ष इति गुणलक्षणम्

dravyāśrayyaguṇavān saṃyogavibhāgeṣvakāraṇamanapekṣa iti guṇalakṣaṇam

dravyāśrayi—sheltering in the object; aguṇavān—devoid of qualities; saṃyoga—union; vibhāgeṣu—division; akāraṇam—not a cause; anapekṣa—independent; iti—thus; guṇalakṣaṇam—the symptoms of qualities.

TRANSLATION

Sheltering in the object which is devoid of qualities, not an independent cause of union and division (into things), thus are the symptoms of qualities.

COMMENTARY

This sūtra describes how the qualities and the objects are distinct and yet combined. The distinction is that the causation is in the quality, and the combination is that each quality is attached to an object. The union and separation of qualities, however, is not due to the qualities, but due to the objects. This description is nearly identical to that used in modern physics, with some notable exceptions. The properties in modern physics are conserved, but the division of these properties into objects cannot be gleaned from the properties themselves. For example, the total mass is conserved, but the division of this mass into individual particles is not determined by the mass. This determination is made in Vaiśeṣika by the 'objects', which in classical physics would be 'particles'. However, only Vaiśeṣika considers these objects real; they are not real in classical physics.

For instance, if N particles collide, then according to classical physics, the result can be M particles; the total number of particles would not be conserved, which entails that they are not real, but the total value of the properties (e.g., mass) would be conserved. In contrast, in Vaiśeṣika, both qualities and objects would be conserved, although the qualities can be distributed among objects in different ways. Thus, the fact that properties are tied to objects is the similarity between classical physics and Vaiśeṣika. And the difference is that particles are not conserved in physics, whereas they are conserved in Vaiśeṣika. The situation is akin to saying that we are allowed to distribute 10 liters of water into a fixed number of buckets—in Vaiśeṣika. In classical physics, the 10 liters of water is fixed, but the buckets (particles) are not fixed.

Sūtra 1.1.17

एकद्रव्यमगुणं संयोगविभागेष्वनपेक्ष कारणमिति कर्मलक्षणम्

ekadravyamaguṇaṃ saṃyogavibhāgeṣvanapekṣa kāraṇamiti karmalakṣaṇam

eka—one; dravyam—object; aguṇaṃ—without qualities; saṃyoga—union; vibhāgeṣu—division; anapekṣa—independent; kāraṇam—cause; iti—thus; karma—activity; lakṣaṇam—the symptoms.

TRANSLATION

Residing in one object devoid of qualities, the independent cause of union and division (of the qualities), thus are the symptoms of activity.

COMMENTARY

This sūtra notes that something called 'activity' resides in the objects themselves, and it is the cause of the union and division of the qualities. In other words, the number of objects and the total instances of various qualities are fixed. But they are redistributed among the objects due to the 'activity' in them. An earlier sūtra noted that the qualities are both the causes and the effects. And this sūtra states that the presence and absence of the qualities are due to the activities. This leads to two notions of causation. The qualities are the causes and effects of our perception. For example, if you see, taste, touch, smell, etc. then the effects are due to the qualities and the effects that we perceive are also the qualities. But why some object has a particular set of qualities is not explained by these qualities. Rather, it has to be explained by the presence of activities. That activity refers to the action of aggregating qualities into the objects.

Sūtra 1.1.18

द्रव्यगुणकर्मणां द्रव्यं कारणं सामान्यम्

dravyaguṇakarmaṇāṃ dravyaṃ kāraṇaṃ sāmānyam

dravyaguṇakarmaṇāṃ—of the objects, qualities, and activities; dravyaṃ—objects; kāraṇaṃ—the cause; sāmānyam—the general class.

TRANSLATION

Of objects, qualities, and activities, the cause of objects is a general class.

COMMENTARY

Earlier sūtras have discussed two distinct things. First, qualities and activities are produced from the objects. Second, objects, qualities, and activities can be treated both as individuals and universals. Now, this sūtra states that the cause of the (individual) object is the universal idea denoted by that object. These objects, as we have discussed, are symbols of meaning. The meaning is the universal, and the symbolling of that meaning is the instantiation of that meaning. Thus, an individual cow is the instance of the idea of 'cow'. Thus, the process of creation of things is that from the general idea of a cow, an instance of cow is created, but this is merely an object right now, devoid of qualities and activities. Then, from this instance of cow, qualities such as shape, size, color, etc. develop. This development can be attributed both to the manifestation from the object cow and to the activity of transferring these qualities from other things. For instance, when a calf is conceived, there is an innate tendency in the object to manifest the properties of shape, size, color, etc. This tendency to manifest only some qualities means that the calf will not have an arbitrary shape, size, color, etc.; the qualities it will acquire will be decided by the object cow (and not the object horse, for instance). But activities are also important in that they will transfer the qualities from the environment as food, air, water, etc.

Thus, we can say that the object cow determines *what* the qualities will be; the activity determines *how* these qualities will be acquired; and the quality instances outside the cow (e.g., water, air, food) are the causes of the qualities in the cow, and when they are added to the object by the activity, they become the effects. The activity selects a particular instance of the quality so that instance is also a cause (before addition to cow) and an effect (after the addition). In this way, the objects, activities, and qualities are all causes, but in different ways. The object decides what will happen; the activity determines how it happens, and the qualities are the perceived causes and effects of the changes.

Someone who sees this process will likely attribute causality to the qualities, as they cannot see the activities or the objects. Thus, if you see a calf growing, then you will likely attribute the growth to grass, water, and air. What you cannot understand in this mechanism is why the calf doesn't grow into an elephant (even if it is a miniature elephant)—since that is due to the qualities manifesting from the object cow. The universal cow delimits which shape, size, color, etc. are permitted by the object. Even though the object is not those qualities, still, it defines what qualities are consistent with being a cow. Likewise, you cannot understand why this calf only eats grass—rather than dead things—because that is due to the activity manifesting from the object cow. Just like the qualities, the object cow defines what types of activities are possible. The fact that an object cow conforms to the definitions of a universal concept, is therefore explained by asserting that this individual is manifest from a universal.

Sūtra 1.1.19

तथा गुणः

tathā guṇaḥ

tathā—in the same way; guṇaḥ—the qualities.

TRANSLATION

In the same way, (the cause of) qualities (is a general class).

COMMENTARY

An earlier sūtra stated that objects, qualities, and activities can all be treated as universals and individuals. An earlier sūtra also stated that the cause of qualities is the object. The last sūtra stated that the objects are caused by the universal. And this sūtra states that the qualities are also caused by the universals of the qualities. This raises the question: Is the quality caused by the instance of the object? Or is it caused by the universal of quality? And the answer is both. The universals of qualities expand into other universals; for example, the universal 'color' expands into the universal 'red', which then expands into the universal 'maroon'. But the *instance* of the universal 'color' expands from the *instance* of the object 'cow'. And the instance of the 'cow' expands from the universal 'cow'. In this way, we can say that "red is a color" just like we can say that "a cow is a mammal". Then, we can say that "cow has color and color is white". Finally, if this statement is contracted, then we can say that "cow is white". Thus, while looking at these expansions of objects, qualities, and activities, we must consider the differences between universals and individuals.

Sūtra 1.1.20

संयोगविभागवेगानां कर्म समानम्

saṃyogavibhāgavegānāṃ karma samānam

saṃyoga—union; vibhāga—division; vegānāṃ—impetus; karma—activity; samānam—the universal.

TRANSLATION

(The cause of) the forces of union and division are the universals of activity.

COMMENTARY

We have earlier discussed how the activities are also universals, and they are derived from other universals, although there wasn't a sūtra making that claim. This claim is made in this sūtra. For example, we can say that "swimming" is a universal, and "freestyle swimming" and "backstroke swimming" are two derived activity-concepts. In some languages, which do not see the hierarchy of conceptual derivation, one could say that "swimming" is a verb and "freestyle" and "backstroke" are nouns. Likewise, we can add qualities or adjectives to this derivation and say "slow backstroke swimming" or "fast freestyle swimming", and if we don't see the conceptual relationship, one could say that "fast" and "slow" are adjectives, which are attached to nouns such as "backstroke" and "freestyle" which are then attached to the verb "swimming". This is indeed what happens in languages like English, where "slow backstroke swimming" is treated as a verb phrase, which is then divided into a verb, noun, and adjective. A problem arises if we apply our previous claim about an object combining quality and activity to this case, because the object, in this case, is a noun—backstroke or freestyle—and if we tie the quality (fast) and activity (swimming) to that object, then we would arrive at the erroneous conclusion that backstroke and freestyle were derived from an object called 'body'. This is a false conclusion because backstroke and freestyle are attributes of swimming. Therefore, even when seemingly nouns and adjectives are used to describe verbs, we must note that if the top-level concept is an activity-concept, then the derived concepts must also be activity-concepts. In this case, "slow backstroke swimming" and "fast freestyle swimming" are activity-concepts. Only if the instances of these concepts are derived from the instances of the objects, then we can say that they are still activity-concepts, but attached to an individual.

Sūtra 1.1.21

न द्रव्याणां कर्म

na dravyāṇāṃ karma

na—not; dravyāṇāṃ—the objects; karma—activity.

TRANSLATION

The objects are not activities.

COMMENTARY

Modern science employs some object-concepts like a 'wave', which are not truly objects; they are actually activities. When the 'wave' is applied to a 'rope', the distinction between object and activity is maintained. However, in the case of electromagnetic waves, the object-concept is completely dispensed with, as there is nothing that the wave is actually the activity *of*. In an electromagnetic wave, there are two orthogonal components—electricity and magnetism—and each component creates the other component. As a result, when we study classical electricity and magnetism, then there is a particle with a property, which is called an electrical charge (positive or negative) and a magnetic monopole (positive or negative). But in the electromagnetic wave, both the particle and the property are dispensed with. This subsequently creates problems in understanding photons in quantum theory because these are detected as particles, and they have the property of energy, but the quanta itself is just 'action'. The manifest issue is whether the photon is a particle or a wave, but there is also the issue of whether there is an action that causes changes vs. the existence of the property of energy. This latter issue arises because the photon can be absorbed in one of the many possible destinations, which cannot be explained if we say that there is simply energy. Thus, the solution to the quantum problem also requires three distinct concepts—an object (a photonic particle), a property (its energy), and an activity (which decides where the photon is absorbed causing a change). The conclusion is that we cannot reduce objects to properties to activities.

Sūtra 1.1.22

व्यतिरेकात्

vyatirekāt

vyatirekāt—due to the mutual separation.

TRANSLATION

(The objects are not activity) due to the mutual separation.

COMMENTARY

In the last sūtra, we discussed why the reduction of objects to activities to qualities creates conceptual issues in causality. We also noted how some intractable problems in science are produced due to this reduction of one category to another. Such types of reductions have been carried out in mathematics too, where a word is alternately interpreted as a noun and an adjective, and a general class and an individual member of that class, and the results can be contradictory. For example, Mr. Barber is not necessarily a barber; Mr. Carpenter is not necessarily a carpenter; if we reduce the individual to the universal, we will run into such problems. Such problems produced from reduction are avoided if the distinction between object, quality, and activity is maintained. This sūtra states that the object is not activities due to their mutual separation. More generally, the object is in sattva-guna, the activity is in rajo-guna and the quality is in tamo-guna. If we reduce one thing to another, then we also create confusion between the three modes, treating one mode as another. This cannot be permitted.

Sūtra 1.1.23
द्रव्याणां द्रव्यं कार्यं सामान्यम्
dravyāṇāṃ dravyaṃ kāryaṃ sāmānyam

dravyāṇāṃ—the many objects; dravyaṃ—a single object; kāryaṃ—the effect; sāmānyam—a universal.

TRANSLATION
The many objects are the effects of a singular universal object.

COMMENTARY
In earlier sūtras, we have discussed how an individual is instantiated from a universal, but the sūtras themselves did not make that contention. We elaborated that idea to make things clearer by noting the general pattern of instantiation of a universal. Previous sūtras have discussed how a more abstract concept instantiates a less abstract concept (e.g., color instantiates red), which is the expansion of one universal into another. And this sūtra talks about the expansion of the universal into an individual. The sequence of the sūtras makes it tricky to explain all the concepts without creating confusion. Therefore, we have noted these ideas in earlier sūtras, even if they weren't explicitly stated. I hope that the readers will excuse this repetition as it helps the understanding.

Sūtra 1.1.24
गुणवैधर्म्यान्न कर्मणां कर्म
guṇavaidharmyānna karmaṇāṃ karma

guṇa—qualities; vaidharmyāt—from the opposed nature; na—not; karmaṇāṃ—the varied activities; karma—activity.

TRANSLATION
An activity is not the combination of many activities (or even caused) from the opposed natures of (many) qualities.

COMMENTARY

This is the first sūtra that speaks about the atomism or irreducibility of activities, but this irreducibility is tricky when we consider complex actions such as "slow backstroke swimming". To understand the irreducibility properly, we have to separate each of these as separate 'atomic' actions, which are structured hierarchically. Thus, 'swimming' is an atomic activity, which is modified by 'backstroke' which is again modified by 'slow'. We can think of swimming as the trunk branching out of the root 'activity', which then produces a branch 'backstroke', which then produces a leaf 'slow'. The activity of "slow backstroke swimming" is, therefore, the composition of three different activities, such that the backstroke modifies swimming, and slow modifies backstroke. The implication is that even abstract concepts are irreducible atoms or units. This is important to ensure that abstract ideas are not reduced to contingent ideas.

For example, in modern mathematics, the concept 'color' is nothing but the collection of all shades like yellow, green, blue, red, etc. There is no such thing as 'color' itself, apart from the collection. Then, there is also nothing called 'yellow' because it is merely a collection of sub-shades of yellow. When concepts are reduced to their collection in this way, all concepts are eliminated from the language, because *in principle* there is simply no limit to how much we can go on reducing these things. As a result, we cannot say that "yellow is a color" because the claim requires 'color' to exist prior, but it can exist only after all the shades have been collected. Since the collection of shades includes 'yellow', therefore, we cannot define 'yellow' in terms of 'color' because the concept 'color' has become posterior to yellow, instead of being prior to yellow.

The limit to reduction, however, arises *in practice* when we find that we are unable to reduce indefinitely. Atomic theory for instance tells us that there are 'packets' of 'action' called the "quantum of action". A quantum of energy is defined by the equation $E = hv$ where v is the frequency. Since there is no theoretical limit to how small that frequency can be, there is no limit to how small the energy can be. Then the question arises: What do we *mean* by frequency or energy? Shouldn't it be the smallest unit of energy or frequency possible? But there is no answer to this question in quantum theory; as a result, we continue to use everyday *macroscopic* standards, even while studying the quanta.

The fact is that physics uses properties like 'energy' and 'frequency' without truly defining them—as concepts, or even as real entities. These properties are defined in relation to macroscopic measurement instruments, which are in turn comprised of a very large number of atomic particles. The situation is just like saying that color is nothing but the collection of all shades; in this case, the property of 'frequency' or 'energy' is assigned to atomic particles, but it is *measured* by the collection of a very large number of particles. Effectively, 'frequency' and 'energy' are macroscopic, rather than atomic concepts. Ideally, we should never use them in atomic physics, but since we cannot conduct any science without them, hence, they are still used without adequate justification.

In Vaiśeṣika, and in the model of causation used in Vedic philosophy, all concepts are real, and they are produced out of more fundamental, general, or abstract concepts. Therefore, for instance, 'color' is real before 'yellow' is real. Hence, we can say that "yellow is a color" due to this derivation. This, however, requires a hierarchical construction beginning with a root concept to the leaf concepts. Each of these concepts is 'atomic' or irreducible; so, for instance, 'color' is not just the aggregation of all shades. Rather it is truly an indivisible concept.

This sūtra explains this general idea in relation to activities. A complex activity like "slow backstroke swimming" is certainly comprised of parts, but it is not comprised of *contradictory* parts. Why? Because it is a particular chain of atomic concepts. We can trace this chain if we move from the leaf to the root. Of course, an object can have contradictory properties or even contradictory actions. But the actions or properties themselves cannot be contradictory. We will see later how this leads to property, activity, and object atomism. Since it is based on concepts, therefore, we can call this position "Semantic Atomism".

Sūtra 1.1.25

द्वित्वप्रभृतयःसंख्याःपृथक्त्व संयोग वभिागाश्च

dvitvaprabhṛtayaḥ saṃkhyāḥ pṛthaktva saṃyoga vibhāgāśca

dvitva—duality; prabhṛtayaḥ—brought forward; saṃkhyāḥ—the numbers; pṛthaktva—separateness; saṃyoga—union; vibhāga—division; ca—also.

TRANSLATION

The numbers brought forward by duality are also separateness, union, division.

COMMENTARY

To count a certain number of things, we must identify them as distinct things; this requires their 'separateness'. But this separateness doesn't help us order or sequence those things; separate things just remain distinct entities. Therefore, modern mathematics adds an Axiom of Choice to say that there are potentially many methods by which distinct things can be ordered or sequenced, and the choice of one such method produces a specific order or sequence. But what is this choice? If you are given a collection of balls, then you might decide to order them first based on color, then based on size, then based on weight, etc. This is obviously a choice, but is it a random choice? You can say that it is random, and then it just remains an Axiom of Choice. Or, you can say that there is actually some rationality in this randomness because we have *reasons* because of which we will measure color first, measure size next, measure weight after that, etc. What are those reasons? You might say we will prioritize color over size over weight because we find that easier. What is easy? Is it a random choice, or is there some rationality in it? The answer can be that some methods are cheaper, or more accurate, or more popular, require less effort, etc. But which of these criteria comes first? Should we prioritize lower cost over lower effort? Or lower effort over greater accuracy? In this way, the problem of choice keeps getting deeper, and ultimately it comes down to: I like this more than the others because it is relevant to the problems that I'm trying to solve, or I think this is the right thing to do, and I consider this to be the correct method of ordering based on my preconceived notions about the nature of reality.

Sāñkhya philosophy describes the *ideal* hierarchy and method of prioritization. If everyone orders or prioritizes things in that order, then we can obtain perfect knowledge, perfect happiness, and perfect morality. But of course, we are free to order things in other ways, which will not be perfect knowledge, perfect happiness, and perfect morality. Hence, there is a "choice", but we are not "free", in the sense that certain choices result in the perfect truth, right, and good, while other choices create numerous falsities, wrongs, and miseries.

The meaning of 'duality' is that the parts are created by removing something from the whole and, therefore, the parts are incomplete. If we follow the correct hierarchy from bottom to top, then we can obtain completeness. But if we don't, then we get many kinds of incompleteness. However, completeness is attained when the whole truth is understood as the purpose of everything that exists. When the whole truth enters every part—as the purpose of existence of that thing—then everything is inside everything, because the whole truth is inside everything. When everything is united in the purpose of their existence, then the apparent differences are simply diversity, not mutual oppositions. The common purpose becomes the unifying principle among the diversities.

There is still a choice—which thing we want to be, but that choice is like being situated on the branch of a tree; the tree itself is the universal space in which things are counted from top to bottom. If the root of the tree is disregarded, then everyone counts things starting from themselves—e.g. I am the first and the most important thing to be counted—and that creates oppositions between the different methods of counting. Thus, the meaning of 'duality' is that the methods of identifying, distinguishing, and ordering are employed randomly. And the meaning of 'non-duality' is that there is a fixed and universal method of identifying, distinguishing, and ordering, which forms an inverted tree, but each individual has a choice of where they want to be on the tree.

Even the material world can be understood as non-duality if we recognize this universal tree, which is described in Sāñkhya philosophy. But if we don't, then we will produce arbitrary methods of ordering, which then seem opposed to the other methods of counting. Thus, duality *appears* from non-duality due to ignorance, illusion, or deception. The result of this duality is that the knowledge is false, actions are wrong, and feelings are misery. Thus, the Axiom of Choice in counting exists, but it is does not mean equivalence of all methods of ordering, sequencing, or prioritizing. We cannot simply order things in whichever way we like, creating whatever prioritization system we choose. Rather, we have to choose the prioritization based on the time, place, situation, or where we are situated on the tree. If we learn how to use our choice correctly, then despite the changes in position, there will be truth, right, and good.

Sūtra 1.1.26

असमवायात् सामान्यकार्यं कर्म न विद्यते

asamavāyāt sāmānyakāryaṃ karma na vidyate

asamavāyāt—from being disparate; sāmānya—the universal; kāryaṃ—the effect; karma—activities; na—not; vidyate—known or understood.

TRANSLATION

From being disparate, the activities that will produce the effect of universality are not known or understood.

COMMENTARY

We can envision a space like an inverted tree, in which every person is at some or the other trunk, branch, twig, or leaf. The problem is that each person thinks that they are the root or the origin of the coordinate system of this space. In modern science, this is called 'relative space', and it seems that all such spaces are equivalent because space is like a box, rather than a tree. The existence of absolute space is rejected in modern science because no such space could be conceived *if* space were a box. But if space is an inverted tree, then there is a universal space, there are many relative coordinate frames in which each person can falsely consider themselves to be the origin, and this falsity can be corrected if we understand the true origin. This true origin would be understood only if we begin to grasp how diversity emerges from unity. That unity and diversity in turn require us to view reality semantically. The origin of all the problems is therefore physical thinking; it leads us to think that there are many disparate things. Then we cannot understand their unity. Then, we cannot see how the diverse locations are not equivalent locations in space. And then we cannot act in a way that will correct the false perceptions of everything and everyone being equivalent. Thus, materialism leads to the false notion of equivalence, which then leads to oppositions and clashes among the various parts, and those clashes then mutually abolish each other. Materialism is thus self-destructive. It is also ignorance. If we want to be knowledgeable, then we have to change our thinking from materialism to semanticism. Then we can see how all meanings are expanded from an original meaning, how these expansions are not equivalent, how we can choose to be one of these expansions, and despite this choice, and immense diversity, there can be perfect unity and harmony.

Sūtra 1.1.27
संयोगानां द्रव्यम्
saṃyogānāṃ dravyam

saṃyogānāṃ—the unities; dravyam—objects.

TRANSLATION

The unities are objects.

COMMENTARY

In the inverted-tree-like space, each branch can be treated as an 'object' relative to the twigs it emanates—which can be qualities or activities. If we invoke the Sāñkhya understanding, then the object in sattva-guna emanates an activity in rajo-guna, which then emanates a quality in tamo-guna. As we have noted earlier, the mind is an object. This mind then emanates the activities of the indriya or the senses, which then emanates the qualities or tanmātra, which have been earlier described as taste, touch, smell, sight, etc. These qualities then emanate another group of objects, namely Earth, Water, Fire, Air, and Ether (which alongside the mind, have also been called 'objects' previously). Thus, the mind is an object, and the five gross elements are objects. But they are connected by two other things—the indriya or the senses which are activities, and the tanmātra, or the properties like touch, smell, sound, and sight, which are qualities. However, this is just one way of looking at things. We can also treat the mind as an activity, which then produces the qualities of the senses, which then produces the objects called tanmātra, which then produces another activity as the five gross elements called Earth, Water, Fire, Air, and Ether. Finally, we can say that the mind is also qualities, which then emanates objects called the five senses, which then emanates the activities called tanmātra, which then emanates qualities called the five gross elements. As a result, the same thing can alternately be called an 'object', a 'quality', and an 'activity'. We call it an object when we see the higher entity in the inverted tree as a quality and the lower entity as an activity. A good example of this fact is the concept of 'color'. Normally, we will say that it is a quality. But when we think of it in terms of something that creates an effect, then it becomes an object, and the many effects that it creates become the activities. Similarly, if we say that color is the effect of a quality called "visibility", then "visibility" is a quality, and "color" is an object. This process can become difficult to grasp because the same thing is alternately an object, a quality, and an activity. But nothing is simultaneously these things. Therefore, the 'object' vision of something is that which diversifies into many activities, which then create effects, which are then perceived as qualities.

For example, if an object exerts a force on another object, then there are three visions or descriptions. First, we can say that there is an 'object' that existed prior to the effect. Second, we can say that the object emanates a force which is the activity. Third, this activity then produces a quality of 'speed'. This 'speed' can in turn become an object, that acts as a cause, and then produces another quality, which can call 'heat' (e.g., if the object collides with a wall).

The notable thing here is that 'speed' is a quality for those people who see things moving, but it is an 'object' when we describe its effects on other things. If we don't adopt this view and say that 'speed' is a quality of some 'object', then we get a new problem—how can some quality become activity? In some cases, properties that separate from an object can become objects in their own right. The transformation of a property into an activity or even an object then produces category confusions, unless we say that we can treat the same thing either as an object, activity, or quality, so it is all those things, but not simultaneously. Of course, this problem is not directly indicated by this sūtra, but it is important to note this issue so that we can understand how objects, activities, and qualities are just modalities of linguistic description; they are not physical entities that are somehow joined (even though we say that the object joins the qualities and activities) because that joining requires yet another entity.

Sūtra 1.1.28

रूपाणां रूपम्

rūpāṇāṃ rūpam

rūpāṇāṃ—the many forms; rūpam—form.

TRANSLATION

The 'form' is the unity of the many forms.

COMMENTARY

When we study individual subjects like physics, chemistry, biology, etc. then we can say that we are all pursuing 'knowledge'. We make the claim that 'physics is knowledge', 'chemistry is knowledge', and 'biology is knowledge'. But we never say that 'knowledge is physics, chemistry, or biology'. This fact rests on the recognition that there is a primordial 'form' called 'knowledge', which is then modified or expanded into many forms such as physics, chemistry, and biology. Thus, each of these subjects is the diversity, and the unity is that they are all knowledge. This unity is in one sense outside the diversity because knowledge is not physics or chemistry or biology. And yet, the unity is immanent inside the diversity because physics, chemistry, and biology are knowledge. So, something called 'knowledge' unites physics, chemistry, and biology from the 'outside'—i.e., as a transcendent entity. And 'knowledge' also unites physics, chemistry, and biology from within as an immanent form. We cannot understand these claims—e.g., how knowledge is both transcendent and immanent to all the individual subjects—without the semantic approach.

The last sūtra stated that objects are unities and this sūtra says that unity is a form that unites many forms. This can be easily understood if we say that 'knowledge' is an object, and physics, chemistry, and biology are the diverse aspects or qualities. Then, since these qualities can have effects, therefore, they are also activities. Then each of these subjects can also be treated as an object in turn, which has further subdivisions, each of which can be treated as an object, quality, or activity. Thus, instead of using three terms—object, quality, and activity—a simpler language of forms is employed. We can also understand these 'forms' as sound symbols. Just like a word can be treated alternately as a noun, verb, or adjective, similarly, there is an objective reality that doesn't seem to have a meaning unless it is interpreted as a noun, verb, or adjective. So, the physical picture of reality is a byproduct of not thinking about the reality as things, qualities, and activities, but reducing everything to some objective existence. The problem is that we cannot construct a science of this reality without using nouns, adjectives, and verbs. So, not using terms such as an object, quality, and activity will not salvage the situation. It will just make the reality unknowable. To explain how that reality is knowable, we must say that it is the combination of the three modes, such that one mode appears at one time.

Sūtra 1.1.29

गुरुत्वप्रयत्नसंयोगानामुत्क्षेपणम्

gurutvaprayatnasaṃyogānāmutkṣepaṇam

gurutva—heaviness; prayatna—effort; saṃyogānām—combinations; utkṣepaṇam—moving up.

TRANSLATION

The combinations of heaviness and effort result in moving up.

COMMENTARY

When we describe space as an inverted tree, then moving up means moving up the hierarchy in the tree. It can mean a change in the object, property, or activity. For example, if someone moves up in an organization's ladder, then the type of work they were doing previously changes. Likewise, Vedic texts describe that when a soul moves upwards in the universe, then the qualities of its body changes. Finally, by moving up, the mind also changes. The 'heaviness' noted in this sūtra is the resistance to upward movement, but it is not the only type of resistance; given a certain type of body, mind, and position, there can also be resistance to moving downward, and that resistance would also be experienced as inertia or 'heaviness'. This inertia or heaviness arises merely because of an incompatibility between the current and the future states (object, quality, or activity). To overcome this incompatibility, some effort is required. And if that resistance is countered by the effort, then the change occurs.

Some commentators on Vaiśeṣika like to think of 'gurutva' as 'gravitation', and the 'effort' is then described as throwing up a ball in the Earth's gravitation field. This is almost completely wrong because the modern ideas of moving out of earth's 'gravitational field' don't involve a change in the body, mind, qualities, or activities. For example, a person who moves into space into a rocket has the same body, mind, qualities, and activities, and so, this type of movement isn't considered 'moving upward'. It is simply the 'zooming out' of the vision, which occurs when we weaken our interaction with certain things. To understand this idea, we have to note the general process by which we are able to focus and defocus our attention on things. For example, if you are absorbed in reading this book, then you might not be aware of the pressure of the chair, the mild blowing of a breeze, the chirping of birds, or of people talking in the distance. It's not that they don't exist. And yet, they don't have any effect on you. When we focus deeply on reading, we decrease the distance to the book and increase the distance to the other things. In this process, there is a small change to our body, mind, qualities; some change in the activity; and yet, a great change in the awareness of the surrounding. It is as if we have been lifted into a new world where birds, trees, people, and things around us simply don't exist.

What we call 'distance' to things in modern science is therefore not an objective reality in Vedic philosophy; it is a byproduct of our interactions with those things. A good example of this fact is looking into a microscope, by which we can see microbes as if they were the size of our hands. So, peering into the microscope is decreasing our distance to the perceived object, without significantly altering our body, mind, qualities, and activities. Things appear bigger and closer through a stronger interaction, and they become smaller and farther through a weaker interaction. Another easy example is seeing another person through a video conference; they seem close to us because there is a process by which the strength of interaction between two objects has been increased.

The process of going into 'space' using a rocket should be seen in the same vein. It is not a change in the body, mind, qualities, and activities. And yet, we see proximity to things that were far earlier and distance to things that were closer earlier. That change in proximity is the byproduct of changing strengths of interaction, and it gives the impression of movement without a movement. The yogis are also capable of such movement and they move by changing the strengths of interaction with other objects. The Yoga Sūtra describes these 'mystical powers' which arise by our capacity to control the mind and the prāṇa, using which we can, by our will, decrease the proximity to the things in this world, and create proximities to things in another world—without changing our body, mind, qualities, and activities. The 'effort' in this case is the prāṇa changing the interaction strengths with other objects, and that process is similar in nature to focusing on a book, peering into a microscope, or meditating.

The process of meditation is described in Yoga Sūtra to teach the yogi how to control the prāṇa and then the mind to change our focus and hold it there. When control over prāṇa is obtained, then the yogi can focus on one thing for a very long time (yogis can remain in meditation for hundreds of years), and that gives them the ability to control their interaction with other things. By the ability to control the interactions, the yogi can pass through walls because he knows how to create proximity to things 'beyond' the wall, without creating proximity to the wall itself. So, when the yogi passes through the wall, he does so without interacting with the wall. This seems surprising to people who are thinking in terms of physical reality, but it is not surprising to a person who has developed the ability to control their prāṇa and are able to change the interaction strengths. They can become proximate to certain things and distant to other things because what we call distance in modern science is perception, not reality.

Therefore, the term 'gurutva' should not be equated to 'gravity', and moving upward should not be considered the same as going up in a rocket. There is a *real* upward movement due to changes in body, mind, qualities, and activities, and there is an *apparent* upward movement due to changes in the strengths of interactions with the things in the world. Modern gravitational theory is an incorrect description of the latter because it treats the perceptual space itself as the real space, and the space of conceptual qualities, conceptual objects, and conceptual activities is considered unreal. But if the latter type of space becomes real in science, then the former type of space would become a perceptual illusion. Just as two people talking over a video conference are not close—because they have different types of thinking, feeling, willing—similarly, the objects around us are not truly close to us. And yet they seem close because there is an interaction with them. The process of this interaction involves many factors, including guna, karma, chitta, prāṇa, and time, but it can be summarized simply as the 'strength' of interaction which then creates proximity. Such apparent proximity is different from the real proximity to a certain type of reality based on the change in the qualitative or conceptual nature of something.

Sūtra 1.1.30

संयोगविभागाश्च कर्मणाम्

saṃyogavibhāgāśca karmaṇām

saṃyoga—union; vibhāga—division; ca—also; karmaṇām—the actions.

TRANSLATION

Union and division are also the actions.

COMMENTARY

The previous sūtra spoke about how things can change by altering the conceptual nature of objects, qualities, and activities, and this sūtra talks about how this change arises by the union and separation of qualities. For example, if someone is interested in changing their mind, then they can acquire knowledge. When we hear a knowledgeable person speak, then the words are embodiments of meaning, and as these meanings are assimilated into our minds, some other ideas are displaced. The assimilation is 'union' and the displacement is 'division'. The displacement of ideas due to a union occurs due to the incompatibility in their meanings. If two contradictory beliefs are brought within a single system, then a struggle for domination ensues and one of those ideas survives, while the other is eliminated. This process is slow if we are unprepared to give up our old ideas. It becomes rapid if we are prepared for change. Therefore, the willing student can quickly learn very difficult subjects, while the unwilling student struggles to "fit" everything into their understanding without realizing that it doesn't have to be "fitted". It requires the learner to throw away whatever incorrect beliefs they already hold, and whatever struggle they are facing in integrating the new learning is because of holding onto earlier beliefs.

Sūtra 1.1.31

कारणसामान्ये द्रव्यकर्मणां कर्माकारणमुक्तम्

kāraṇasāmānye dravyakarmaṇāṃ karmākāraṇamuktam

kāraṇa—cause; sāmānye—in the universal; dravya—objects; karmaṇāṃ—the activities; karma—the action; akāraṇa—uncaused; muktam—free.

TRANSLATION

In the universal cause, the objects and activities are free as uncaused action.

COMMENTARY

The Six Systems of Vedic philosophy are theistic so they also describe the nature of the origin of everything in God—He is referred to here as the "universal cause". But He is also referred to as a sāmānya or an idea, a general class, or a universal. He is the original conceptual object, of which the other conceptual objects are parts. He is the original conceptual quality, of which the other conceptual qualities are parts. And He is the original conceptual activity, of which the other conceptual activities are parts. These parts are semantic rather than physical, so they manifest from the original cause, and they can go back into the original cause. Just like the idea mammal manifests the idea cow by dividing itself into parts, similarly, all objects, activities, and qualities are manifest from a universal cause. When these aspects are manifest, then God is different from these manifestations, and yet, these manifestations carry the nature of God. And yet, God is different from the manifestations emanating from Him. This is just like saying that a "cow is a mammal" but "a mammal is not a cow". Now, this sūtra says that the manifestation of these objects, qualities, and activities is uncaused in the universal cause—i.e., God. This 'uncaused' is also called 'free' or mukta, which can be understood by contrasting it to 'forced'.

What is forced and what is free? Whatever is caused due to an external agency is 'forced', and whatever is caused by something internal is 'free'. Since we generally think of causes as something external, therefore, the 'free' causation is also sometimes called 'uncaused'. We can say that it is spontaneous. This spontaneity is simply a person's free will, which is the original nature of the 'object'. The original object is a person with a personality of likes and dislikes. The object and the personality are identical such that there is a natural tendency in each object to desire certain things. Even the varied species of life in this world must be defined as various kinds of desires. From this desire spring some qualities such as the different capacities to perceive, think, feel, etc. And along with these potential capacities are activities that convert these potentials into an experience. Thus, the original cause is a personality or desires, and everything appears due to a purpose. These desires are also called guna or 'nature', but it is the nature of a person, from which the nature of a body and the nature of activities are produced. Whatever is caused due to desires is considered free, especially since prior to the manifestation of other things, there is nothing external. Thus, the world is manifest due to the desire in God. It is like the ability to think is converted into an activity, which then appears as a thought, and that activity of thinking (and its result—thought) is produced due to a desire.

Section 2

Sūtra 1.2.1

कारणाभावात् कार्याभावः

kāraṇābhāvāt kāryābhāvaḥ

kāraṇābhāvāt—from the nature of the cause; kāryābhāvaḥ—the nature of the effect.

TRANSLATION

From the nature of the cause comes the nature of the effect.

COMMENTARY

This statement is easily understood when we understand how effects are created from the cause by conceptual expansion. A cow has the properties of a mammal. Backstroke swimming has the property of swimming. Yellow is the property of color. Mathematics has the property of knowledge. In this way, everything that is expanded from a concept inherits its properties as well.

Sūtra 1.2.2

न तु कार्याभावात् कारणाभावः

na tu kāryābhāvāt kāraṇābhāvaḥ

na—not; tu—but; kārya—effect; abhāvāt—from the absence of; kāraṇa—the cause; abhāvaḥ—the absence of.

TRANSLATION

But from the absence of effect, the absence of cause is not concluded.

COMMENTARY

When the cause is an abstract concept, it is possible that it hasn't manifested the contingent concept. These contingent concepts lie within the abstract concept in an unmanifest state. So, when the contingent concept hasn't manifested, we cannot conclude that either the abstract or the contingent concept don't exist. Their existence can be understood as a possibility that has to be converted into an observation. All causes are eternally possible, but they are not eternally manifest. Thus, from the absence of effects, the absence of causes is not inferred. It is understood that everything can be manifest if the conditions are right.

Sūtra 1.2.3

सामान्यविशेष इति बुद्ध्यपेक्षम्

sāmānyaviśeṣa iti buddhyapekṣam

sāmānya—the universal; viśeṣa—the specific; iti—thus; buddhi—knowing; apekṣam—relatively or in comparison.

TRANSLATION

Knowing the universal and the specific thus is relative or in comparison.

COMMENTARY

When we understand the conceptual hierarchy, then we can see how what is specific from one perspective is general from another perspective. For example, seeing is general, and color is specific. Then color is general and red is specific. Then red is general and maroon is specific. In this way, if something is viewed as a general concept, then it is a comparison to the more specific, and if something is viewed as a specific concept, then it is in relation to the more general concept. The conceptual hierarchy is their mutual or relative definition.

Sūtra 1.2.4

भावो ऽनुवृत्तेरेव हेतुत्वात् सामान्यमेव

bhāvo 'nuvṛttereva hetutvāt sāmānyameva

bhāvah—the nature; anuvṛtteh—repeated; eva—certainly; hetutvāt—from the cause; sāmānyam—the universal eva—alone.

TRANSLATION

The repeated nature is certainly from the reason of the universal alone.

COMMENTARY

A materialist believes that the human body has been produced due to millions of years of random mutation and natural selection. But the Vedic philosophy states that the human body is created from a universal or a concept, which exists eternally. This concept diversifies in many ways, thus creating many colors, shapes, and sizes. But despite these variations, there is something common in all humans—namely, that they have developed minds and intellects; they have the capacity to learn and understand languages; and most of all, they can ask questions about their origin and the origin of everything around them. Humans are capable of reasoning and creativity; they produce art and poetry, music and science. Again, these capacities are developed to various degrees in various individual members of species, but they are the definition of what it means to be 'human'. The existence of all these qualities, this sūtra states, is to be exclusively attributed to the preexisting universal concept of humanity.

Sūtra 1.2.5

द्रव्यत्वं गुणत्वं कर्मत्वं च सामान्यानि विशेषाश्च

dravyatvaṃ guṇatvaṃ karmatvaṃ ca sāmānyāni viśeṣāśca

dravyatvaṃ—object-hood; guṇatvaṃ—quality-hood; karmatvaṃ—activity-hood; ca—and; sāmānyāni—the general; viśeṣa—specific; ca—also.

TRANSLATION

Object-hood, quality-hood, and activity-hood, are also both general and specific.

COMMENTARY

An earlier sūtra explained how objects, qualities, and activities can be both universals and individuals. An example is the concept of cow and an individual cow. This sūtra states that each of these three can be general concepts and specific concepts. The term viśeṣa can be used to indicate individuality and specificity. Since the claim about objects, qualities, and activities being sāmānya and viśeṣa is repeated, we must understand that one statement is about universals and individuals, while the other is about general and specific universals.

Sūtra 1.2.6
अन्यत्रान्त्येभ्यो विशेषेभ्यः
anyatrāntyebhyo viśeṣebhyaḥ

anyatra—others; antyebhyo—till the end; viśeṣebhyaḥ—are specifics.

TRANSLATION
The others, till the end, are specifics (of the original general concept).

COMMENTARY
The inverted tree of concepts expands unhindered until we reach the point where we obtain the most complex idea, the most complex quality, and the most complex activity. The original idea is, in contrast, the simplest. For example, 'knowledge' as the original idea is very simple. But as it expands into divisions of knowledge, then individual subjects like mathematics, physics, and chemistry are more complicated ideas. Then, individual theories like quantum mechanics and relativity are even more complicated ideas. In this way, complexity is constructed hierarchically until we reach the point where we cannot understand, create, use, or perceive the complexity. This limit is not a *theoretical* limit to complexity; theoretically, the complexity is infinite. But it is a limit to how much complexity will practically exist. As we have discussed, the complexity manifests from within the simplicity, and we can go on creating this complexity as long as we *want*. But ultimately, everyone gets tired of this complexity because to understand, create, and use complexity, our senses, minds, and intellects must also be capable of this complexity. This means that only a mind and intellect that is supremely complicated can create, understand, and use such complexity. The practical limits of complexity are the practical limits to our senses, minds, and intellects. As this complexity expands, it is always an additional layer of information on top of the previous layers of information. Thus, this sūtra states that other than the original universal, everything else is specific—"till the end"—implying that we can go on limitlessly if we so want.

Sūtra 1.2.7
सदितियतो द्रव्यगुणकर्मसु सा सत्ता
saditi yato dravyaguṇakarmasu sā sattā

sat—eternal truth; iti—in this way; yatah—from which; dravya—object; guṇa—quality; karmasu—and actions; sā—that; sattā—preponderance.

TRANSLATION

In this way, the eternal truth is that from which the object, quality, and actions (emerge). That (eternal truth) is the preponderant (reality).

COMMENTARY

The eternal truth is sat-chit-ānanda. The tripartite distinctions between objects, activities, and qualities are the divisions of the chit or the cognitive capacity. The cause of this expansion is the ānanda or the desire. And the capacity of the truth to divide itself to manifest the variety is sat. Thus, if we understand the hierarchical relation between object, activity, and quality, then we can understand that everything is manifest from a single source. Then we can understand how the manifested reality existed inside the source (chit) in an unmanifest form. And finally, we can understand how the desire in the original truth, which is called ānanda, uses its consciousness, which is called sat, to divide itself by itself. The thing being divided is the chit; the reason it is divided is ānanda, and the mechanism by which it is divided is sat. Thus, the chit is *what* is divided, the ānanda is *why* it is divided, and sat is *how* it is divided.

However, even after the original truth has expanded into parts, It remains the preponderant, complete, and eternal truth. The Iśopaniśad states that "after the complete has been removed from the complete, the balance is still complete". In this way, the texts of Vedic philosophy explain the truth, but to varying levels of detail. The Upaniśads summarize the truth, the Purana expand it more, and the Six Systems of Philosophy expand it in the greatest detail.

Sūtra 1.2.8

दरव्यगुणकर्मभ्योर्ऽथान्तरं सत्ता

dravyaguṇakarmabhyor'thāntaraṃ sattā

dravya—object; guṇa—quality; karmabhyoh—and actions; athāntaraṃ—the differences of meaning; sattā—preponderant reality.

TRANSLATION

The differences of meaning in the preponderant reality are object, quality, and actions.

COMMENTARY

The impersonal philosopher believes that the Absolute Truth is devoid of qualities, and qualities are added *externally* to this truth. This sūtra rejects this contention. The differences between quality, object, and activity are present in the Absolute Truth, and they are not added externally. The impersonalist distinguishes between Brahman and māyā and says that māyā is all the qualities, activities, and objects, and Brahman is the observer, and māyā is external to Brahman. But this doctrine is contrary to all Vedic texts. Maya is a Śakti of the Absolute Truth, and She exists as part of the Absolute Truth. This Absolute Truth then divides into desire and power; the desiring aspect of the Absolute Truth becomes the Supreme masculine person, and the powerful aspect of the same truth becomes the Supreme feminine person. When the capacity for desire and the capacity of power were combined, the desire did not exist and the power was not used. This state of reality is sometimes called Param Brahman, but it is still not impersonal. It is like a person in a sleeping state. Just like a person when asleep doesn't use the power to fulfill the desires, but when he wakes up, power activates the desire, and the desire then utilizes the power. In the same way, there are not two things—Brahman and māyā; there is just one reality which has aspects, and that aspected nature is due to personhood.

Sūtra 1.2.9

गुणकर्मसु च भावान्न कर्म न गुणः

guṇakarmasu ca bhāvānna karma na guṇaḥ

guṇakarmasu—in qualities and activities; ca—also; bhāvāt—from the being; na—not; karma—activities; na—not; guṇaḥ—qualities.

TRANSLATION

Also, the qualities and activities in the being from which everything expands are not qualities and activities.

COMMENTARY

The qualities and activities of the material world have the property of duality—everything that is X is not non-X, which is also called mutual exclusion. This makes everything duality because it is opposed to something else. But this property of exclusion doesn't apply to the Absolute Truth. The Nyāya Sūtra explains this in great detail by describing how every aspect of the whole truth is present in each aspect of that truth. God, for instance, can eat by looking, hold things by His vision, go close to something just by seeing it, and even impregnate material nature by His vision, apart from the regular job of seeing. Thus, God's eyes are not like our eyes—which can only do the job of eyes. Rather, with His eyes, He can do the job of every part of His body. Likewise, His curse and benediction are like the scolding and pampering of a mother; they are both meant to correct the soul. He deludes the arrogant soul and enlightens the humble person. Thus, Nyāya Sūtra describes how God appears to be whatever we are. That is, He reveals an aspect of His nature depending on our nature. And within each of these aspects, the other aspects are immanent. Thus, if we think that God is like a father, then His mother-like, son-like, sister-like, brother-like, friend-like, and teacher-like qualities are all present within the father-like demeanor. Thus, God's qualities and activities are not like the mundane qualities. All the qualities and activities are therefore the full truth, as they contain all the truths, but an aspect becomes manifest and visible due to the nature of the person who is seeing. Our vision is therefore limited, but the reality is not.

Sūtra 1.2.10

सामान्यविशेषाभावेन च

sāmānyaviśeṣābhāvena ca

sāmānya—the universal; viśeṣa—individual; abhāvena—the absence; ca—also.

TRANSLATION

There is also the absence of the distinction between universal and individual.

COMMENTARY

In the Lord, the universal is the chit or the cognitive and conative capacity. His personality of ānanda is the individual. And His consciousness or sat is the relational capacity that divides the whole into parts, and then connects the parts to the whole. The sat-chit-ānanda are not separate, but three modalities of understanding the Absolute Truth. Therefore, if we want, we can know the Absolute Truth as the original idea, and, if we want, we can know the Absolute Truth as a person who embodies that idea. Finally, if we want, then we can know the Absolute Truth as omniscience. The impersonal philosopher says that God is nothing other than omniscience. Scientists like to think of God as the original idea. And religious people would like to know Him as a person. But perfection is knowing Him as the original idea, the omniscience, and the personality.

The distinction between universal and individual is useful while understanding the many expansions because these expansions are either the parts, or the instances, or both of the whole. The concept cow is a part of the concept mammal. An instance of a cow is an individual that instantiates the concept of the cow. The individual cow is distinct from the universal concept of a cow in the sense that if the cow died, the concept would not cease to exist. Likewise, if all cows died, and the concept of the cow itself ceased to exist, the concept mammal would still exist. Then, if horses appeared, the concept cow would be contextually contrasted to the concept horse, and the individual cows will be contrasted to the individual horses. To accommodate all these truths, a distinction between universal, individual, and contextual is made. But universality, individuality, and contextuality are combined in the Absolute Truth. As a result, we can make assertions, but not negations. An assertion can say that God is an individual, but that doesn't mean that He is not the universal idea. Similarly, we can say that God enters various contexts, but that doesn't mean that He is not the original individual or the universal idea. Thus, if we limit ourselves to assertions, then there is no problem. But that is not the nature of ordinary individuals and universals, which involve both assertions and negations. Therefore, this sūtra states that the Absolute Truth is not an ordinary universal or individual. He is rather that entity to which all assertions apply, and no negations do.

Sūtra 1.2.11

अनेकद्रव्यवत्त्वेन द्रव्यत्वमुक्तम्

anekadravyavattvena dravyatvamuktam

aneka—many; dravyavattvena—by these objectivities; dravyatvam—objectivity; uktam—is expressed.

TRANSLATION

By these many objectivities, objectivity is expressed.

COMMENTARY

When the concept cow expands from the concept mammal, then the concept mammal is present in the cow. By being the source of the concept of cow, the mammal is transcendent. And by being within the cow, the concept of mammal is immanent. This sūtra speaks about immanence, as transcendence has already been discussed. The Lord is present in everything and this presence is called the Paramātma or the "Supreme Soul". The mammal is the ātma or the "soul" of a cow. And the animal is the ātma of the mammal. The mammal is immanent within the cow, and the animal is immanent within the mammal. Then, what is the ultimate ātma beyond which there is no more "soul"? That ultimate soul which is inside everything, and was previously transcendent to everything is the Paramātma. The transcendent form of the Lord is also called Bhagavan. For example, if an author writes a book, then the author who wrote it is transcendent. But when that book has been produced, then the author's personality and nature are also present within the book, and by reading that book, the readers can associate with that person. The book is the ukta or expression of the author, and the author is immanent in the book. If an author writes many books, then he is immanent in each of the books, but each book partially expresses his personality. In the same way, the expansion of the visible world is like the paintings of an artist, the musical compositions of a musician, or the books of an author. The artists, musicians, and authors expand their work from within themselves, because of their desire to become many things from one thing. This expansion is an expression by which the author, painter, or musician realizes his complete nature. The Lord's creation is also a work of art, music, or literature. He expands merely to realize His complete personality.

Sūtra 1.2.12

सामान्यविशेषाभावेन च

sāmānyaviśeṣābhāvena ca

sāmānya—the universal; viśeṣa—individual; abhāvena—the absence; ca—also.

TRANSLATION

There is also the absence of the distinction between universal and individual.

COMMENTARY

This sūtra is the exact replica of the statement made in the last but one sūtra. The difference is simply that the last but one sūtra spoke about the transcendent Lord, and this sūtra talks about the immanent form of the same Lord. The meaning is that the form of the Lord that is immanent in everything as the Supreme Soul also doesn't have a distinction between universal and individual. This means that there is a person immanent in everything, and that person is the universal idea. Since a person is immanent in many things, therefore, some people might tend to think that there are many 'copies' of Paramātma, but that is not true. There is only one Paramātma, and yet, He becomes visible in many things. Just like you and I can look at the moon at night from our windows, and we can say: "The moon is inside the window". Since each person sees the moon within the window, therefore, it appears that there are many moons—after all, they are inside so many windows. But there is still a single moon. So, the immanence of the Lord in everything doesn't mean that He is *not* transcendent.

Sūtra 1.2.13
तथा गुणेषु भावाद्गुणत्वमुक्तम्
tathā guṇeṣu bhāvādguṇatvamuktam

tathā—in the same way; guṇeṣu—in the qualities; bhāvāt—from the being; guṇatva—the quality-hood; muktam—free.

TRANSLATION

In the same way, in the qualities manifested from the Being, the Being is free of quality-hood.

COMMENTARY

When the reflection of moonshine is seen in many pots of water, one might say that the moonshine has become contaminated by the water in the pot. But that is our mistaken conception. The moon is not contaminated by the pots of water, but it can still be seen in the pot of water. In the same way, the Paramātma can be seen in everything—if our vision is advanced to understand the complete hierarchy of essences inside everything. But that doesn't mean that the Paramātma is physically contained inside each thing, and therefore, contaminated by that thing. The problem of contamination arises when we think of matter as something physical. If we think of matter semantically, then the mammal is inside the cow, and the animal is inside the mammal. And yet, these are also transcendent. So, the problem of inside and outside is a result of misunderstanding the nature of matter, which is then transformed into a misunderstanding about the nature of God. The impersonalist says that when God advents into this world as an incarnation, then He is covered by material qualities. They even use the term Saguna Brahman to describe such incarnations. But they don't know that God is already inside everything in the world and He is not contaminated by the material qualities. The Paramātma exists within each atom, and yet, He is transcendent to all these atoms. Thus, mundane ideas about the nature of God are based on mundane ideas about the nature of matter.

The fact is that impersonalists should stop speaking about the soul, God, Brahman, etc., and just study material nature. If someday they can understand the nature of tables and chairs, then they will also understand the soul and God. This is not just our prescription; it is stated in all Vedic texts as well. They first describe the nature of the material world and then describe the nature of the soul and God. The impersonalist rejects that material knowledge as an "illusion" and focuses on Brahman. But that "illusion" is also an expansion of God, and God is present inside that illusion, and yet, He is transcendent to that illusion. Just like if a movie script writer authors a movie script, then even if the script is a false story, it is a reflection of the author's ideas and personality, which are embedded in the script. Even if we know that the movie is false, we can still understand that the movie was produced by a person, for the entertainment of people who are interested in illusory stories rather than the nature of truth. Thus, if we properly understand the illusion then we also know the truth.

Sūtra 1.2.14

सामान्यविशेषाभावेन च

sāmānyaviśeṣābhāvena ca

sāmānya—the universal; viśeṣa—individual; abhāvena—the absence; ca—also.

TRANSLATION

There is also the absence of the distinction between universal and individual.

COMMENTARY

This sūtra is the exact replica of the statement that has been made twice in the prior sūtras. The difference is that the previous statements spoke about the transcendent and immanent objects, and this sūtra speaks about their qualities. The next sūtra will speak about the activities, and the sūtra following that will make the exact same statement regarding the activities. The claim of this sūtra is that in the Absolute Truth, there is no distinction between the universals of qualities and the individuals of qualities. For instance, in this world, the property color is different from the property yellow; these two properties combine to create the 'yellow color' property. But 'color' and 'yellow' are separate atoms, with the 'color' atom being logically prior to the 'yellow' atom, such that there can never be 'yellow' if there is no 'color'. But there can be 'color' even if there is no 'yellow', 'green', 'blue', etc. Similarly, there can be instances of 'yellow' that are distinct from the concept 'yellow'. Such distinctions between abstract and contingent qualities, and universal concepts and individual instances do not exist in the Absolute Truth. The Lord is all the qualities but each person sees different qualities based on the qualities within them. Thus, the materialist sees God as the source of fear and oppression and materialistic religions, therefore, create an oppressive, fearful, and angry image of God. The true devotees see God as the source of love and compassion, and truly spiritual religions, therefore, create a beautiful, loving, and happy image of God. Both images are true, but they are based on the nature of the person practicing that religion. So, all these qualities are simultaneously existing in the Lord, but they are not visible to everyone simultaneously. They manifest depending on our own nature.

Sūtra 1.2.15

कर्मसु भावात्कर्मत्वमुक्तम्

karmasu bhāvātkarmatvamuktam

karmasu—in the actions; bhāvāt—from the Being; karmatva—the activity-hood; muktam—freedom.

TRANSLATION

In the actions manifest from the Being, there is freedom from activity-hood.

COMMENTARY

A materialistic person might think that when the Lord punishes, then He is not rewarding. That when He deludes, He is not enlightening. That when He takes us through the cycle of birth and death, He is not giving us liberation. These dualistic visions of the Lord are not factual. His punishment is the reward of education that we should not repeat the mistakes. His delusions are the source of enlightenment that we must give up our arrogance. And this dragging the soul through the cycle of birth and death is to help us recognize our ignorance about the true nature of the soul. If you really think that there is no soul, then you will be repeatedly forced to accept birth and death. If you think you are the most intelligent, then you will be forcibly confused to a point where you cannot understand anything. If you think you are the master, then you will be punished so much that you will forget all about your mastery. So, these apparent actions of unkindness, delusion, and punishment are actually kindness, enlightenment, and rewards in guise. But one must have the vision and understanding of the whole truth to understand the Lord's non-dualistic nature.

Sūtra 1.2.16

सामान्यविशेषाभावेन च

sāmānyaviśeṣābhāvena ca

sāmānya—the universal; viśeṣa—individual; abhāvena—the absence; ca—also.

TRANSLATION

There is also the absence of the distinction between universal and individual.

COMMENTARY

This is the fourth occurrence of the same statement; the previous three occurrences spoke about the transcendent and immanent object and His qualities, and this sūtra speaks about the absence of universal-individual distinction in His activities. An abstract activity is a large-scale action, and a detailed activity is a small-scale action. The head of the nation performs the activity of "governing the nation", while a bureaucrat performs the activity of "typing a report". These distinctions exist in this world, where there is higher and lower, general and specific. But the Lord is "governing the universe" and "moving each specific atom". There is an aspect of His person which performs the high-level task, and then there are aspects of His persona that do the low-level tasks. These personas are not different *persons*. They are varied aspects of the same person.

As a result, in this world, we find that the CEO who is running a company is incapable of doing low-level tasks such as manufacturing, programming, or moving things from one place to another. At the very least, if the CEO did all these low-level tasks, then he would not have the time to run the company. But the Lord is not like that. He is simultaneously doing the high- and the low-level tasks. It is not merely that He has the capacity and ability to do all of them simultaneously, but He is also doing them. Therefore, the mundane distinctions between general task and specific task, or universal definition of a task and the individual instantiation of the task, are not to be found in the Lord. If someone thinks that if the Lord rules the universe, then He would not have the time, energy, patience, or the ability to control each atom, then they are wrong.

Sūtra 1.2.17

सदिति लिङ्गाविशेषात् विशेषलिङ्गाभावाच्चैको भावः

saditi liṅgāviśeṣāt viśeṣaliṅgābhāvāccaiko bhāvaḥ

sat—eternal; iti—in this way; liṅga—forms; aviśeṣāt—from the universal; viśeṣa—the specific; liṅga—forms; abhāvāt—from the absence of; ca—also; eka—one; bhāvaḥ—existence or nature.

TRANSLATION

In this way, the eternal form is the source of the universal and specific forms, which are also (separated) from the absence of one nature.

COMMENTARY

A table doesn't have the properties of a chair, but it has the property of being an 'object'. Color doesn't have the property of taste, but it has the property of being a 'quality'. Swimming is different from writing, but it has the property of being an 'activity'. Thus, in every object, quality, or activity, the concept of objectivity, quality, and activity is immanent, and yet, these concepts are also transcendent because they are not *confined* or *limited* to one object, quality, or activity. Thus, the same truth is understood in three distinct ways, which can be called transcendent, immanent, and variety. The variety is produced from the transcendent source, which is one. And the qualities, activities, and objectivity of the transcendent source are also immanent in each thing. Just like a mammal is transcendent to cows and horses, and the mammal is immanent in cows and horses, similarly, the Absolute Truth is transcendent to variety, it is all the variety, and it is immanent in each variety. And yet the variety itself is not the transcendent source of the immanent truth, because each thing among the varied things is missing the objectivity, qualities, and activities of the other things. This doctrine is called by other names like abheda (non-separated), advaya (non-dualism), avyatireka (non-exclusive), etc. and it pervades all the Vedic systems of philosophy such as Vedānta, Sāñkhya, Yoga, and Nyāya.

The same idea is also presented in Vaiśeṣika. The difference is that we arrive at the same view in different ways. The doctrine of objects, qualities, and activities, universal, individual, and inherence, is rather unique to Vaiśeṣika. But the same doctrine is presented as three modes in Sāñkhya. The conclusion in all these philosophies is identical—the non-separated, non-dualistic, and non-exclusive nature of the variety from the source of the variety. This non-separated, non-dualistic, and non-exclusive nature is not "oneness", nor is it the rejection of personality, individuality, and variety, as some kind of "illusion". It is rather a far more nuanced understanding based on the nature of concepts. When reality is treated physically, then variety is rejected as an illusion of oneness. But when reality is treated conceptually, then the variety is a part of the oneness, manifest from the oneness, and the oneness enters that variety to be the immanent truth that can be known from the variety. Thus, unity is both inside everything and outside everything; the one truth can be known by transcending all individual things, and it can be known by going deeper inside each thing.

Thus, that one truth is beyond all the things, all the things collectively, and inside each of the things. These three visions of the truth are called Bhagavan, Brahman, and Paramātma. Brahman is the collection of all the individual truths in the universalist mode of knowing, such that individuality is not visible. Just like if we see a clump of trees, but we don't distinguish between them individually and just see a single type of thing—treeness. Paramātma is the individualist mode of knowing the same thing where the similarity of these things is disregarded, and they are just viewed as separated things. Finally, Bhagavan is the contextualist mode of knowing in which there is a whole thing comprised of parts that are mutually entangled with each other through their being a part of the whole. In scientific terms, we can say that Brahman is the undifferentiated sea of individual things, Paramātma is the separation of the particles as individual things, and Bhagavan is the separated particles that are not truly separated because they are the parts of a whole. Bhagavan is the source of Brahman or the individual truths. And Paramātma is the immanent truth inside the variety. Impersonalists claim that Brahman is real, and Bhagavan and Paramātma are unreal. But this is not the position of any system of Vedic philosophy. The correct understanding is that all three visions are correct, but how they are simultaneously true needs a non-physical semantic understanding of reality.

CHAPTER 2

Section 1

Sūtra 2.1.1

रूपरसगन्धस्पर्शवती पृथिवी

rūparasagandhasparśavatī pṛthivī

rūpa—form; rasa—taste; gandha—smell; sparśa—touch; vatī—possessed of; pṛthivī—the Earth.

TRANSLATION

The Earth is possessed of form, taste, smell, and touch.

COMMENTARY

The next few sūtras describe the nature of the five elements. These are nearly identical to that in Sāñkhya with one difference, namely, that the property of sound (which is said to be that of space) is omitted. This is also explicitly stated later. This difference between Sāñkhya and Nyāya is explained later.

Sūtra 2.1.2

रूपरसस्पर्शवत्य आपो द्रवाःस्नग्धाः

rūparasasparśavatya āpo dravāḥ snigdhāḥ

rūpa—form; rasa—taste; sparśa—touch; vati—possessed of; āpah—Water; dravāḥ—fluid; snigdhāḥ—sticky or viscous.

TRANSLATION

Water possesses form, taste, and touch, and is fluid and sticky or viscous.

COMMENTARY

The number of properties present in the Water element is lesser than those present in the Earth element; the Water element doesn't have the property of smell. Similarly, even though both Earth and Water possess the properties of touch, there is further subcategorization of these properties. This sūtra notes that Water is sticky or viscous on touch, implying that it has form, but it is not fixed. This subclassification of properties was not noted for the Earth element. We must remember that Earth, Water, Fire, and Air were noted as 'objects' in the last chapter, and taste, touch, smell, and sight were noted as qualities.

In modern science, when we assign fluidity to Water, we are assigning it to a *collection* of water particles. But Vaiśeṣika and Sāñkhya assign them to *each* particle. Therefore, we cannot equate the atomism of modern science to that in Vaiśeṣika. Instead, by attributing properties like viscosity and fluidity to each Water particle, a distinction between modern science and Vaiśeṣika is apparent. Then, ordinary water has the property of fluidity but it is far less viscous than other things like vegetable oils, milk, or mercury. Of course, oil and milk also have a smell, but mercury has no smell. So, why should this element be called 'Water' when it could be equally well called 'mercury'? The answer is that 'Water' doesn't denote any of the things that we normally associated it with. It is not a property of viscous liquidity, and it is not merely odorless liquids.

The rationale for using terms like 'Earth' and 'Water' is not apparent, but we can understand these names as a technical nomenclature that gives some intuition of what we are talking about without indicating those very things. A good analogy in modern science is the use of terms like 'waves' for light, as they produce interference patterns just like water waves. Or, calling planets like Earth and Moon 'particles' when they are not infinitesimal because the mathematical formulation of the theory of motion uses infinitesimal points. Thus, just as 'particle' and 'wave' are theory-laden constructs, similarly, 'Water' and 'Earth' should be understood as technical terms, not ordinary things.

Sūtra 2.1.3
तेजो रूपस्पर्शवत्
tejo rūpasparśavat

tejo—Fire; rūpa—form; sparśavat—just like touch.

TRANSLATION

Fire has the properties of form and touch.

COMMENTARY

As we can see, the number of properties from Earth reduces as we progress into these elements. Thus, Water doesn't have a smell, and Fire doesn't have a taste. The point about technical naming still holds true, because if we wanted to identify things that are odorless and tasteless, then many liquids would fit the bill equally well, and the term 'Fire' would not have to be employed.

Sūtra 2.1.4
स्पर्शवान् वायुः
sparśavān vāyuḥ

sparśavān—possessed of touch; vāyuḥ—the Air element.

TRANSLATION

The Air element is possessed of touch.

COMMENTARY

As we come to the end of this list of elements, one obvious conclusion is that there are some objects which have four properties; other objects which have three properties; and yet other objects which have two; and finally, just one property. These objects are respectively called Earth, Water, Fire, and Air.

Sūtra 2.1.5
त आकाशे न विद्यन्ते
ta ākāśe na vidyante

ta—these; ākāśe—in space or Ether; na—not; vidyante—are present.

TRANSLATION

These do not exist in the Ether or space.

COMMENTARY

The term 'these' can be understood in two ways here. First, we can say the qualities of smell, taste, sight, and touch described previously do not exist in the Ether. That would also be consistent with Sāñkhya. However, the issue is why the quality of space—which is called 'sound' in Sāñkhya—has been omitted from Earth, Water, Fire, and Air. This sūtra can also be seen as a clarification of that difference—by explicitly stating that these, i.e., Earth, Water, Fire, and Air, are not present in Ether. The 'presence within' is conceptual in nature. For example, we can say that dogs are present within mammals, which simply means that the dogs have the quality of mammals. So, by saying that Earth, Water, Fire, and Air are not present in Ether, we can conclude that these don't have the property of sound. This latter interpretation of the sūtra requires a nuanced understanding of what we mean by 'space', to which we turn now.

As we have discussed previously, counting requires individuating, distinguishing, and ordering. Earth, Water, Fire, and Air have been called 'objects' earlier, so they are conceptually distinct types of things, and we can also extend that to say that there are also individual instances of these conceptual types. They can also be distinguished from each other based on the above properties, which are also universals, and we can extend that to say that the properties are also individuated by the particles. The net result of these individuations would be that there are many particles with different properties. But that doesn't tell us which particle is the first, second, third, or fourth particle. That *ordering* of particles requires a 'space', which, as we have discussed, creates a hierarchy. If that hierarchy or structure among the particles is missing, then we can say that there is no space. Thus, the statement that "these are not in space" is equivalent to saying that there is no structure, order, or sequence between them. We can also say that these objects have not been labeled or numbered as the first, second, third, fourth object. Equating the absence of labeling to the absence of space is the rejection of a "substance" notion of space as a container in which things exist. This absence was introduced in modern science by Einstein who argued that there is no such thing as "space" beyond what we call "coordinate systems", which are introduced by "observers". The world of matter itself exists objectively, but an order or sequence is introduced by a coordinate system.

A similar idea was introduced by Immanuel Kant in philosophy when he said that space and time are modalities of perception, and therefore, introduced by observers. Space and time are therefore not "out there"; they are "inside" the observer. Of course, Kant believed each observer carried their own Euclidean coordinate system, which Einstein rejected. But the fundamental idea that space is tied to the observer, rather than to the world of material particles has been prevalent in various forms in Western science and philosophy. Kant's philosophy also required a distinction between 'mind' and 'matter'. The 'mind' for example would supply space and time, while 'matter' would be just particles. This distinction was collapsed in Einstein's theory of relativity where particles themselves were identified with space and time. The trouble is that a particle is dimensionless, so each particle can be said to be at the origin of infinite orientations of three perpendicular axes. Similarly, each particle can be associated with infinite coordinate systems that don't use perpendicular axes (e.g., employing a circular coordinate system). Einstein did not delve into this problem of identifying which coordinate system is being employed; he simply stated that all these coordinate systems are 'equivalent' so any of them could be used. Regardless of which of these coordinates are used, the 'distance' between particles would remain unchanged, even though we would label these points by different numbers. This claim, however, is a flawed view of space and time.

As we have discussed earlier, the proximity to something in space depends on our interaction with that thing. If we interact strongly, then that thing is 'close' and if we interact weakly, then it seems 'far'. When a coordinate system is changed, and these coordinates are viewed semantically, then just by changing the coordinates, the distances between particles would also change. Why? Because a semantic coordinate system is a system of priorities—that puts something nearer and something else farther. By changing these priorities, we change what we perceive and don't perceive, what we consider near or far. Thus, Kant's contention that each person orders or sequences things in the same way is false. But so is Einstein's contention that even if we use different coordinate systems, the distances are identical. As a result, despite introducing a radical idea that space and time are properties introduced by the observer, the truly radical conclusion of this idea was not understood in these theories.

That understanding can be obtained if we say that what we mean by 'space' is an ordering system, and each observer has a choice of a coordinate system or a method of ordering things. By that choice, the distances to different things are changed, thereby creating a perceived structure in which what is 'near' may be considered very far and hence invisible, while what is 'far' for some may be considered very near and hence visible by the others. Now, 'space' is a method of ordering, sequencing, and numbering things, which creates a distance.

We can now understand why in Sāñkhya all these things are "in space" and why in Vaiśeṣika they are not. Our ability to reorder things in space doesn't mean that there isn't an objective order. If this were true, then the external world would be like a bag of balls that we can order in any way we like. The existence of an objective order among the objects is an objective space, and Sāñkhya speaks of it. But this objective space can be disregarded in our perception if we decide to interact with things strongly thereby creating proximity. Since perceived distance is an observer construct, therefore, we can say that there is no objective space. These two claims, while seemingly contradictory, are totally consistent with each other, and hence, there is a space, and yet, there is no space until the observer interacts with matter to create a perception.

The problem comes down to what we mean by 'space'. In Yoga philosophy, four such spaces are identified; they are called vaikharī, madhyamā, paśyanti, and parā. The vaikharī is the space of objects as they exist independent of our observation. The madhyamā is the space of conscious experience, in which we see things as being near or far, higher or lower priority. The paśyanti is the system of priorities, which is also the unconscious biases and preferences we carry. And parā is the choice of one such system of biases and preferences that the soul chooses. Since the choices of one soul are distinct from those of the others, therefore, there is an objective distinction between the souls. Since there is a distinction between one system of biases and preferences, therefore, the space called paśyanti is the space of all such 'coordinate reference frames', which are tied to the observer. Since each person's perceptual experience is different from those of the others, therefore, they are in the same 'space' of perceptions, conceptions, and judgments, but they are also distinct. Finally, since the objects, qualities, and activities can exist independent of our observation, therefore, there is a space of objective reality, which is incorrectly studied in modern science—this world should be described in terms of qualities like smell, taste, sight, and touch, but it is described as physical properties like energy and mass. Even in modern science, there is an objective distribution of mass and energy, which can be called 'space', but it is different from the perceptual space where distances can be longer or shorter, and things can be nearer or farther. Therefore, the issue is: What do we *mean* by space? If we say that space is created in our perceptual experience, and produced by a system of biases and preferences, then the objective world is not in that space. But if we say that there is an objective reality that is prioritized and ordered without an observer's intervention, then these things are in space. Thus, both statements are true, but their truth depends on what we mean by 'space'. When the broader picture of four spaces is considered, then this problem disappears, and both claims become true.

As an aside, we must also remember that there are two kinds of Earth, Water, Fire, Air, and Ether, and their properties such as smell, taste, sight, touch, and sound. The first is the objective reality that exists independent of observation (which modern science incorrectly describes as mass and energy). And the second is the perception, conception, and judgment that exists because of an observer (which modern science generally ignores, and, if they are considered, they cannot be explained based on scientific properties like mass and energy). The fact that we may not accurately measure or perceive the true nature of things doesn't make the perception unreal—in the sense that it doesn't exist. We must rather recognize *two* instances of Earth, Water, Fire, Air, and Ether—one that is the perceived world, and the other that is the objective reality (that exists independent of our observation). The former is called madhyamā, and the latter vaikharī. But since both these spaces can use the same five elements and their properties, therefore, Sāñkhya just speaks about the five elements and their properties. In Yoga philosophy, a distinction between vaikharī and madhyamā is drawn, so, both objective reality and its subjective perception are considered. Then, in other systems, such as Vaiśeṣika, which we are discussing here, the same five elements are just seen as objective reality or vaikharī.

If we try to understand these systems collectively, then we will see why there is no contradiction between them—even if the statements seem contradictory. They are describing different things, but the same names must be used because what we perceive, conceive, and judge can also be potentially true. Even if our perception, conception, and judgment are false, ultimately, they have to be described in terms of the perceived qualities. For instance, even if we say that 'energy' is an objective property of matter, the fact is that we never measure energy. We measure motion, which we call 'kinetic energy', by our eyes. We measure heat, which we call 'thermal energy', by our skin. And when we cannot measure anything, but we must suppose that it exists, we call that 'potential energy', which is a pure concept understood through the mind. Thus, even if believe that physical properties are *real* (i.e., they exist), we must know that they are not *fundamental*. Just as apples are real but not fundamental, similarly, the properties of physics can be real (which is why science works in a limited sense) although these properties are not fundamental. The fundamental properties are those in terms of which we perceive, conceive, and judge.

Sūtra 2.1.6

सर्पिर्जतुमधूच्छिष्टानां अग्निसंयोगाद्द्रवत्वमद्भिःसामान्यम्

sarpirjatumadhūcchiṣṭānāṃ agnisaṃyogāddravatvamadbhiḥ sāmānyam

sarpir—clarified butter; jatu—lac; madhu—honey; ucchiṣṭānāṃ—the waste or leftover; agni—fire; saṃyogāt—from the union with; dravatvam—objectivity; adbhiḥ—etc.; sāmānyam—similarity.

TRANSLATION

The waste leftover from the union of fire with clarified butter, lac, and honey, has similar objectivity, etc. (i.e., they are of the same universal class, which includes the type of object, the type of qualities, and the activities).

Sūtra 2.1.7

त्रपुसीस लोह रजत सुवर्णानामग्निसंयोगाद्द्रवत्वमद्भिःसामान्यम्

trapusīsa loha rajata suvarṇānāmagnisaṃyogāddravatvamadbhiḥ sāmānyam

trapu—tin; sīsa—glass; loha—iron; rajata—silver; suvarṇānām—and gold; agni—fire; saṃyogāt—from the union with; dravatvam—the objectivities; adbhiḥ—etc. (i.e., object, quality, activity); sāmānyam—of the same class.

TRANSLATION

Tin, glass, iron, silver, and gold, from the union with fire, have the objectivities, etc. (i.e., object, quality, and activity), of the same class.

Sūtra 2.1.8

वषिाणी ककुद्मान् परान्तेवालधिःसास्नावान् इतिगोत्वे दृष्टं लङि्गम्

viṣāṇī kakudmān prāntevāladhiḥ sāsnāvān iti gotve dṛṣṭaṃ liṅgam

viṣāṇī—horns; kakudmān—possessing a hump; prānte—in the end; vāladhiḥ—hairy, etc.; sāsnāvān—possessed of a dewlap (folds of skin under the throat); iti—thus; gotve—in cowness; dṛṣṭaṃ—are seen; liṅgam—signs.

TRANSLATION

Horns, possessing a hump, hairy in the end, etc. (speaking of the tail), possessed of a dewlap (folds of skin under the throat), thus are the signs seen in cows.

Sūtra 2.1.9

स्पर्शश्च वायोः

sparśaśca vāyoḥ

sparśa—touch; ca—also; vāyoḥ—of Air.

TRANSLATION

Touch is also the property of Air.

COMMENTARY

The previous sūtras identified multiple properties in each type of object, and this sūtra is an indication that each type of object possesses a unique property due to which it is distinguished from other object types. For example, the object-type Earth is distinct from the object-type Water because Earth has the quality of smell, which Water does not. Similarly, Air has the unique property of touch, which contrasts to Ether, which is devoid of touch, sight, taste, and smell.

Sūtra 2.1.10

न च दृष्टानां स्पर्श इत्यदृष्टलिङ्गो वायुः

na ca dṛṣṭānāṃ sparśa ityadṛṣṭaliṅgo vāyuḥ

na—not; ca—also; dṛṣṭānāṃ—being visible; sparśa—touch; iti—thus; adṛṣṭa—the invisible; liṅgah—symptom; vāyuḥ—Air.

TRANSLATION

(Air) is also not visible (to the eyes); thus, touch is the invisible (to the eyes) symptom of Air.

COMMENTARY

Modern science often supposes that if something exists, then it must also be visible, but in Sāñkhya and Vaiśeṣika, this is not necessary. There can be matter which creates a force, pressure, and movement, but it remains invisible to our eyes. In modern cosmology, this type of reality is called "dark energy" and "dark matter". Why dark? Because we cannot perceive it with our eyes. In simple terms, it emits no light. And yet, it creates effects—pressure, movement, force—which must be attributed to something, so we suppose that there must be some matter. Modern cosmology similarly speaks about "black holes", which are invisible, and yet they exert an enormous force around them. These black holes are supposed to be infinite condensation of visible matter, and cosmology postulates that the gravitational pull of an infinite concentration of matter prevents light from 'escaping' the black hole. In Sāñkhya and Vaiśeṣika, these hypotheses are not needed, because there is a class of matter—the Air—that exerts force, pressure, and creates movement, but it is not visible. We detect its presence by the *effects* it creates on our sense of touch. The conclusion is that even when you see something, that vision is also an effect produced by something. The difference between "visible" and "dark" matter is that the visible matter comprises Fire (and other elements) whereas "dark" matter comprises only Air. The notable point is also that even when Fire exists, Air may not be absent! Therefore, when we attribute forces to gravity due to some visible matter, that is not the only force; there is also force due to Air, which is invisible. Thus, if we truly understand "dark matter" and "dark energy" it will disrupt all cosmological theories based on gravitation because the effects we attribute to visible matter are not completely due to the visible matter—i.e., Fire. There are effects due to Air, which is invisible. Since we are attributing all the effects to Fire, therefore we are overestimating the presence of Fire, and neglecting the presence of Air. All calculations of modern cosmological models such as distance and motion are thus incorrect as matter is both visible and invisible.

Sūtra 2.1.11

अद्रव्यवत्त्वेन द्रव्यम्

adravyavattvena dravyam

adravyavat—as if non-objectivity; ena—in this; dravyam—object.

TRANSLATION

As if non-objectivity in this object.

COMMENTARY

This sūtra acknowledges that most people would like to think of Air as if it were not a real thing—simply because we cannot see it by our eyes. The use of the term "Air" gives us this idea intuitively—most of us cannot see Air. But the air we breathe can still be analyzed spectroscopically and when light is diffracted, reflected, or absorbed, then the changes to light indicate that ordinary air that we breathe also comprises Fire, not just Air. The Air in the air we breathe is that which is invisible to spectroscopic analysis; and yet, it can create force, pressure, and movement. Since modern science is focused on "seeing" things by eyes, therefore, an entire realm of matter is hidden from our perception. We think that everything is molecules that we can see by analyzing the light reflected, refracted, and absorbed, but that is false. Even our bodies comprise Air, but since modern science reduces everything to Fire (i.e., what we can see), hence, it cannot completely understand the working of the living body. In this way, modern science is incapable of not just understanding the nature of the senses, mind, intellect, ego, and the moral sense, not just inadequate to understand the nature of dreams and the unconscious, and not just impoverished to explain consciousness, soul, and God. It is also incapable of understanding "gross matter" in Sāñkhya and Vaiśeṣika because it is focused on what we can "see".

Sūtra 2.1.12

क्रियावत्त्वात् गुणवत्त्वाच्च

kriyāvattvāt guṇavattvācca

kriyāvattvāt—as if from the actions; guṇavattvāt—as if from the qualities; ca—also.

TRANSLATION

Also, as if from the actions, as if from the qualities.

COMMENTARY

The same effect can be explained in two ways—based on qualities or activities. Since the quality explanation works, therefore, we can say that it is "as if" the qualities are causing it. But since the activity explanation also works, therefore, we can say that it is "as if" the activities are causing it. Then, we might ask: If each explanation works, then why do we need two explanations? And the answer is that each explanation underspecifies the object. For example, a knife can be used for cutting or piercing, but so can a nail. The activity of piercing doesn't completely specify the knife. To say that the thing used to pierce is a knife, we must say that it had a certain shape, size, weight, etc. But if something has the same shape, size, and weight, but cannot be used for piercing—e.g., it might be a cardboard knife—then we cannot infer a knife from the properties. Then, even if there is a real knife, but it hasn't been used to pierce, then we cannot attribute the effect to that knife; we might attribute it to the nail. Then, a knife may not always have the same shape, size, weight, etc. There can be knives that have other shapes, sizes, weights. And they may not be used for piercing; they also can be used for cutting wood or vegetables.

Thus, all concepts involve an underdetermination—(1) a knife doesn't have a fixed shape and size, and may not always be used in the same way, so activity and quality underdetermine the knife, (2) all things that look just like a knife may not be knives, and may not work as a knife, and therefore, the qualities underdetermine the activity and the object, and (3) the activities of cutting and piercing may not be performed by knives or even certain fixed shape and size, and therefore, the activities underdetermine the object and their qualities.

This underdetermination requires us to use three ontologies—objects, qualities, and activities—because a single ontology cannot complete the causal description. Since each ontology can explain the effect, therefore, we can say that the effect was "as if" caused by that ontology. But the complete explanation requires the determination of all three ontologies—namely, that there are some qualities, which can be used to perform some activities, and then an object with the capacity for those qualities and activities was indeed used to produce an effect. The ontologies in one sense are equally *sufficient* in causing an effect. And still, all of them collectively are *necessary* for a complete explanation.

Sūtra 2.1.13

अद्रव्यत्वेन नित्यत्वमुक्तम्

adravyatvena nityatvamuktam

adravyatvena—in non-objectivity; nityatvam—permanence; uktam—said or expressed.

TRANSLATION

In this non-objectivity, permanence is expressed.

COMMENTARY

The element Air was called an object in the last chapter. Then in the last but one sūtra, Air was termed 'non-objective object', because it is not visible to the eyes. In the same way, Ether is not visible to the eyes, and not perceivable by touch; the Ether is a method of sequencing or ordering things, and it has an effect, which appears when something becomes nearer or farther as a result of our ordering. But proximity and distance are again not perceived as objectivity because the causality of pressure or force is assigned to the other elements. Thus, relative to our vision, Air is a non-objective, and relative to our touch, Ether is a non-objective. When the term 'non-objectivity' was introduced earlier, it was also with the caveat of "as if", by stating that if there are effects caused by Air, but we cannot perceive the cause, then it is as good as saying that nothing can be held responsible for the effects; the effects are as if just 'magic'.

The problem is that these effects don't go away. They are repeatable, persistent, and lasting. Therefore, if we say that there is nothing called Air, then we would be hard-pressed to explain the repeatable, persistent, and lasting effects. Thus, the last few sūtras should be viewed as acknowledging two key things—(1) you cannot visually see Air, and yet (2) you can perceive the effects. The conclusion is that we must allow the existence of Air to explain these effects. This is a well-acknowledged paradigm even in modern science where to explain the effects, we can postulate the existence of the cause—even if we cannot directly perceive the cause. Science doesn't become less empirical by such postulates because the effects are still empirical, even if the causes are not.

Sūtra 2.1.14

वायोर्वायुसंमूर्छनं नानात्वलिङ्गम्

vāyorvāyusaṃmūrchanaṃ nānātvaliṅgam

vāyoh—of Air; vāyu—Air; saṃmūrchanaṃ—merger through collisions; nānātva—the plurality; liṅgam—symptom.

TRANSLATION

The merger through collisions of Air with Air is the symptom of plurality.

COMMENTARY

Modern science postulates the existence of 'fields'—such as a gravitational field—which we cannot perceive, although the effects can be perceived. The difference is that such fields are not particles—i.e., they do not collide. Rather, even if two objects exert separate fields, the fields merge into a single field. The quantum fields, however, are different as they can be treated both as particles and fields. When the quantum is treated as a field, then it is inseparable from other fields (as a result, there can be a bosonic 'sea of particles'). But when the quantum is treated as a particle, then it is separable from other particles.

This raises a question: is there a quantum 'particle' or is it just a 'field'? The answer is there are some particles that can become indistinguishable from one another as if they have coalesced into a single thing; this is described by the term saṃmūrchanaṃ here—"fainting together". The three modes of nature, namely, universality, individuality, and contextuality, help explain this problem. In the universality mode, there is a "field" devoid of separation, because we are observing the 'type' of thing, rather than individual things. In the individuality mode, there are many particles, because we are looking at the individuality rather than the type of object. And in the contextuality mode, these particles are entangled as if they were neither a field (a single thing) nor a particle (many independent things). This understanding can be applied to all the elements, and this sūtra notes its application regarding the element Air.

The notable thing is that the modes seem contradictory so they cannot be applied simultaneously, but they can be applied alternately. Thus, the 'particle', 'field', and 'entangled' modes are alternately true, not simultaneously true. So, occasionally, the 'field' magically produces individual particles, and then the particles merge into the field, and then the particles seem to be entangled. What is the reality? The answer is that it exists in three modes of understanding. Each mode can lead to the other mode; therefore, it is the proof of itself and the other modes. This sūtra specifically notes that since the Air-objects can collide and merge, therefore, they should be treated as individual particles. This merger by collision isn't the merger of classical physical particles where the particle identity is lost; if that were the case, then the collision would be the evidence that the particle identity is lost, and therefore, the particles are not 'real'. But in the universality mode of knowing, the particles become indistinguishable because distinguishability is a 'mode' of knowing the reality as individual things. But the individuality is not lost even if we don't know the reality in the individual mode. That aspect of reality is hidden, and another aspect is revealed.

Sūtra 2.1.15

वायुसन्नकिर्षे प्रत्यक्षाभावात् दृष्टं लङिगं न वदियते

vāyusannikarṣe pratyakṣābhāvāt dṛṣṭaṃ liṅgaṃ na vidyate

vāyu—Air; sannikarṣe—proximity and attraction; pratyakṣa—direct observation; abhāvāt—from the absence; dṛṣṭaṃ—the vision; liṅgaṃ—symptom; na—not; vidyate—known.

TRANSLATION

From the absence of direct observation of the proximity and attraction of Air, the vision of the symptoms (of proximity and attraction) is not known.

COMMENTARY

As we have discussed earlier, if we cannot see the movement of certain types of objects, or we cannot perceive their interactions, we can still say that such things are real—provided that postulate helps us explain what we can perceive. The mathematical equations of modern science postulate numerous such entities which cannot be directly perceived, but their effects can be perceived. This sūtra notes that we cannot perceive the movement, attraction, and proximity of the Air particles, by our vision. We also cannot perceive these things through touch, because touch is the phenomena being explained. So, this movement has to be grasped through mental perception, and that is also the way in which a scientific theory postulates the changes to reality mathematically.

Sūtra 2.1.16

सामान्यतो दृष्टाच्चाविशेषः

sāmānyato dṛṣṭāccāviśeṣaḥ

sāmānyato—the general; dṛṣṭāt—from the vision; ca—also; aviśeṣaḥ—the universal.

TRANSLATION

From the vision of the general class, also the universal truth (is obtained).

COMMENTARY

All of us have the capacity to perceive concepts in the world of specific things. For example, you may see many cows, and you can say that there is a type of thing called a 'cow' which is present in each individual cow. If we rise up this hierarchy of generalities, then we can say that cows are mammals, mammals are vertebrates, and so on. But what happens when the individual things are themselves not visible? This is when mental intuition must operate independently of sense perception. By this intuition, we can see the conceptual cause of a certain class of phenomena. In the case we are discussing, that general class of phenomena is the 'touch' sensations, and their explanation requires a mental intuition about the conceptual cause of these phenomena. This requires two kinds of classifications—(a) recognizing that the touch sensation is indeed a general class of sensations, and (b) seeing that this class has a common cause. In modern science, touch is not recognized as a general class, but its subclasses are recognized. For instance, in physics, heat—which is a subclass of 'touch'—is recognized as a valid class of phenomena, leading to a theory of the motion of heat, which is called thermodynamics. But other phenomena such as hardness, heaviness, roughness, etc. are not grouped into the same class as heat. Why? Because modern science doesn't recognize the reality of sense perceptions. Hence, it doesn't group heat, hardness, heaviness, and roughness into the same broader category, and doesn't seek a common explanation for them.

Thus, this sūtra uses two terms—sāmānya and aviśeṣa—which can mean to indicate the same thing—i.e., a "general class". But there is a subtle difference: the term sāmānya denotes the general class of phenomena related to touch, and the term aviśeṣa represents the universal object concept Air. The claim is that we can explain all the touch phenomena by the concept Air. Therefore, by Air we mean that object-concept which explains heat, hardness, roughness, heaviness, and possibly other things perceived as touch sensation.

Sūtra 2.1.17

तस्मादागमिकम्

tasmādāgamikam

tasmāt—from that; āgamikam—the access road to approach.

TRANSLATION

From that (recognition of a universal concept that explains a general class of phenomena, we conclude that Air is) there is an access road to approach.

COMMENTARY

The root gama means 'going', and āgama denotes the road by which we can approach something. This āgama emerges out of the destination, like a rivulet coming out of a lake of water. The Vedic scriptures are thus sometimes called āgama, as they are the road to approach the Absolute Truth. The elements such as Air are called āgama here, after noting that we cannot perceive them sensually, and yet, if we recognize the general class of sense perceptions, then we can understand the object-concept that is used to explain them. Thus, the recognition of the general class of sensations, and then mentally intuiting the object that can explain all these sensations, is the "road to approach" Air.

Sūtra 2.1.18

संज्ञाकर्म त्वस्मद्विशिष्टानां लिङ्गम्

saṃjñākarma tvasmadviśiṣṭānāṃ liṅgam

saṃjñākarma—the nouns and verbs; tu—but; asmad—us; viśiṣṭānāṃ—superior in many ways; liṅgam—symbols.

TRANSLATION

The nouns and verbs are but symbols used by those superior to us.

COMMENTARY

This sūtra generalizes the previous discussion in several ways. First, it extends the discussion about the element Air to all 'nouns'—i.e., the object-concepts, which include Fire, Water, and Earth. The implication is that we cannot perceive these objects, but we can perceive their effects. Second, it also states that the 'verbs'—i.e., the activities of these objects are also in the same category, which means that we also cannot perceive their existence by our senses.

Then what can we perceive? The answer is the third category—the adjectives or properties such as taste, touch, smell, sound, and sight. We can illustrate this idea by an example from classical physics, which postulates objects like 'particle', and activities like 'gravitational force', which then produce the quality of heaviness. We can perceive neither the particle nor the gravitational field, but we can perceive heaviness. And yet, to explain the perception of heaviness, we must postulate the existence of a particle and a gravitational field. In that sense, the particle and the gravitational field remain pure theoretical constructs, but they are necessary to explain the observed perception of heaviness. This sūtra also states that some beings, who are "superior to us", can perceive the particle and the gravitational field. Who are these superior beings? They are the people who have the mental intuition to see abstract concepts like particles and gravitational fields, formulate a theory based on this mental intuition, and then present the theory to everyone else, who then take these ideas for granted.

The implication is that the concepts of Air, and the activities of Air, are theories and descriptions of "superior beings" who have the mental intuition to see the world in this way, present a theory for the 'ordinary beings', who can then test their correctness by using and applying them, not by questioning the mental intuition itself. If some 'ordinary being' challenges these ideas on the grounds that we have no 'evidence' for their existence, then we can ask them to present an alternative theory that explains the observations better. If such challengers have the mental intuition to see things, and if their theories work better, then they can be accepted, although the fact is that the problems of non-perceivability of nouns and verbs will arise even in these theories. The challenges of 'ordinary people' are based on the false idea that nouns and verbs are perceived when they are only grasped by mental intuition. And the challenges of "superior beings" are acceptable if they can produce a better theory. Those theories will be equally unperceivable; however, they will explain qualities better.

Sūtra 2.1.19

प्रत्यक्षप्रवृत्तत्वात् संज्ञाकर्मणः

pratyakṣapravṛttatvāt saṃjñākarmaṇaḥ

pratyakṣa—direct perception; pravṛttatvāt—produced or proceeded from; saṃjñākarmaṇaḥ—the nouns and verbs.

TRANSLATION

The nouns and verbs are produced or proceeded from direct perception.

COMMENTARY

This sūtra further explains the idea describe in the last sūtra, namely, that nouns and verbs are not perceived, and yet, they are inferred from that perception. For example, when you say "I see a table", someone can say: "I don't see any table; I just see some shape, size, color, etc.". Likewise, if you say "I see a man running", then someone can say: "I don't see a man running; I just see a succession of shapes, sizes, and colors". In this way, if we are pedantic about nouns and verbs, then we can try to eliminate them from our discourse, and a doctrine of Western philosophy called Positivism made such an attempt by trying to reduce all nouns and verbs to the adjectives of sense perception.

The problem is that if we remove nouns and verbs—which are not directly perceived—then we cannot construct an explanation of the qualities. Yes, we can perceive the qualities, but there will be no theory of why and how we see them. We will just be able to say what we see, without an explanation of why and how. The why explanation requires an object-concept, and the how explanation requires the activities. To conduct science, we need the answer to what, how, and why, and that means that the how and the why must be inferred from sense perception, or what we can perceive. That inference requires a superior being who has the mental intuition to see beyond the sense quality façade.

David Hume had a similar critique of science where he said that causality requires a necessary and sufficient connection between the succession of states, but we cannot perceive that necessity and sufficiency in the sense perception itself. Then how can we say that there is indeed a real cause if such a cause is only a mental intuition rather than sense perception? This critique of science was so devastating that Immanuel Kant revised the empiricist doctrine to say that we—as observers—supply the ideas of objectivity, causality, concepts such as force, and even the ideas of space and time, which are then added onto the sense perception to structure, organize, and explain their occurrence. Thus, the inadequacy of sense perception is widely recognized in both Western and Vedic philosophy, with additional clarity being presented in this sūtra, namely that of the three ontologies of nouns, verbs, and adjectives (objects, activities, and qualities), we cannot perceive the nouns and verbs. We rather infer them from the adjectives, which requires a mental intuition, available to "superior beings".

Sūtra 2.1.20

नष्क्रिमणं प्रवेशनमित्याकाशस्य लिङ्गम्

niṣkramaṇaṃ praveśanamityākāśasya liṅgam

niṣkramaṇaṃ—egressing; praveśanam—ingressing; iti—thus; ākāśasya—of the Ether; liṅgam—the symptoms.

TRANSLATION

The symptoms of the Ether are thus ingressing and egressing (only).

COMMENTARY

This sūtra can be understood easily if we think of space as an inverted tree. The egressing occurs from the root of a tree, whereby the whole expands into parts. And the ingressing occurs in each part as the whole is embedded inside the parts. For example, yellow expands from color, and the color is embedded inside yellow. As a result, we can say that color is both transcendent to yellow and immanent in yellow. Since the whole truth is immanent in everything, therefore, just by knowing one thing completely, we can know everything. Likewise, if we know everything incompletely, then by combining all these things together, we can know the whole truth completely. Hence, complete knowledge can be obtained by studying the entire universe as comprised of partial truths (if the embedded truths in each thing are ignored). And, complete knowledge can also be obtained by studying a single atom if all the embedded realities in that atom are fully understood. The embedding of the part inside the whole is accessible in the physical way of thinking, but the physical thinking actually becomes reductionism due to which the parts remain real, and the whole becomes an epiphenomenon of the parts. The embedding of the whole inside the parts is simply not accessible without a semantic worldview. Therefore, both to avoid the fallacy of reduction, and to understand how the whole exists inside each part, it is essential to treat reality semantically, and in practical terms, this means treating space as an inverted tree. But we must bear in mind that we cannot still view space as a physical tree, because then we cannot understand how the root exists inside each branch, how the branch exists inside each leaf, and so on. Thus, the inverted tree analogy also fails if we are accustomed to physical thinking, although it works perfectly for a conceptual hierarchy.

Sūtra 2.1.21

तदलिङ्गमेकद्रव्यत्वात् कर्मणः

tadaliṅgamekadravyatvāt karmaṇaḥ

tat—that; aliṅgam—non-symptoms; eka—one; dravyatvāt—as if from an object; karmaṇaḥ—the actions.

TRANSLATION

The actions are the non-symptoms as if from that one object (Ether).

COMMENTARY

This sūtra explains the doctrine of the three modes in another way, by saying that the activity mode, which is also called rajo-guna, is manifest from the object-mode, which is sattva-guna. The term "as if" is used to indicate that these are not created, but hidden inside the object mode. Similarly, the qualities, which are tamo-guna, are hidden inside the activity which is rajo-guna. The actions are called 'non-symptoms' here because as we have discussed earlier, they are not perceivable; only the qualities are perceived by the senses. Similarly, Ether or space is not perceivable, which means that the conceptual object, the individual thing, and the embedding of the whole into the part is not sense perceivable. However, all these notions are necessary to explain sense perceptions. For instance, to say that yellow is color, and the color is also red, we need a conceptual hierarchy in which yellow and red are parts of color, and the color is embedded inside both yellow and red. Then, to say that a shade of color has effects, we must say that the quality can also be spoken of as an activity, and the activity is produced from a more abstract activity, which is also embedded inside the more contingent activity. In this way, an inverted tree-like hierarchy is produced from just three modes, but this tree becomes enormously complicated because qualities, activities, and objects produce other qualities, activities, and objects, and are embedded inside the produced qualities, activities, and objects. This complexity is simplified if we adopt a semantic view of nature in which everything is meaning, there are three kinds of meanings, and one meaning produces another meaning (egress) and enters that meaning (ingress).

Sūtra 2.1.22

कारणान्तरानुक्लृप्ति वैधर्म्याच्च

kāraṇāntarānuklṛpti vaidharmyācca

kāraṇa—cause; antara—differences; anuklṛpti—the peculiarities or uniqueness; vaidharmyāt—from another nature; ca—also.

TRANSLATION

Also, the peculiarities or uniqueness from another nature lead to differences in the causes.

COMMENTARY

The meanings of red rose, red cross, and red light, are slightly different. Red rose denotes love and passion. Red cross denotes life and blood. And red light denotes danger and stop. All these meanings—love, passion, life, blood, danger, and stop—are inherently present within redness, but by association with a rose, cross, or light, one particular meaning is selected and manifested. Accordingly, the same redness by association becomes the cause of a different effect. This idea of the changes in the causes, which then lead to different effects, is contrary to the modern physical doctrine in which each property is always a unique cause and effect. In the same way, the activity of 'running' changes its meaning depending on whether we are running away from a tiger, running to complete an assignment, or running for an election. Running away from a tiger indicates escaping danger; running to complete an assignment indicates a shortage of time, and running for an election indicates a goal and purpose. An object such as a knife is an instrument of cutting in relation to fruit, and it is a paperweight in relation to a wind that can blow away a stack of papers.

Thus, when we describe reality semantically, then contexts become very important. The varying associations of the qualities, activities, and objects change the meanings of each of the qualities, activities, and objects. That change of meaning then changes the causes and effects. The world is no longer independent things with possessed properties that act universally the same in all places, times, situations, and for all people. Rather, everything has an effect on everything else, and we must consider the entire hierarchy of relationships between objects, activities, and qualities, to explain the causes and effects.

Sūtra 2.1.23

संयोगादभावःकर्मणः

saṃyogādabhāvaḥ karmaṇaḥ

saṃyogāt—from the union; abhāvaḥ—absence; karmaṇaḥ—activity.

TRANSLATION

From the absence of union, there is (the absence of) activity.

COMMENTARY

Matter lies in a state of potentiality in which it remains inactive unless this potentiality is manifest through a combination with another aspect of matter. In the last sūtra we noted how the varied meanings of redness are manifest from redness, by association with other objects, qualities, and activities. This association is called 'union' in this sūtra. If there is no 'union' then matter lies inactive. Even the three modes of nature are potentials that remain inactive unless they are combined. Thus, the uncombined state of the modes is called 'unmanifest' while the combined state is called 'manifest'. This is because the combination of the modes causes the expansion of new kinds of meanings, which then combine with other meanings, thereby manifesting even more meanings. The manifestation of this meaning from the unmanifest state is 'activity'. Activity is not the production or creation of anything new that did not previously exist in an unmanifest form. But it remains unmanifest unless there is a combination.

Sūtra 2.1.24

कारणगुणपूर्वकःकार्यगुणो दृष्टः

kāraṇaguṇapūrvakaḥ kāryaguṇo dṛṣṭaḥ

kāraṇa—the cause; guṇa—the qualities; pūrvakaḥ—preceded by; kārya—the effect; guṇah—the qualities; dṛṣṭaḥ—the manifestation of.

TRANSLATION

The manifestation of the qualities of the effect is preceded by the qualities of the cause.

COMMENTARY

This sūtra evokes the doctrine of Satkāryavāda from Sāñkhya where the effect prior exists within the cause and is manifest from the cause. The previous two sūtras have described how the combination of things manifests new effects from the cause, and this sūtra states that these qualities already existed in the cause, but were hidden. For example, if a person gets angry upon being insulted, then the insult is the trigger for the manifestation of the anger, which prior existed within him. If someone feels desire or love upon seeing another person, then the person they see is the trigger, and the love or desire preexisted in them. Sometimes you see a block of wood, and you think: "This is a chair". Then, the property of chairness is manifest from within the block of wood. Similarly, a knife has the property of being a weapon, but it is manifest by the combination with a person in an angry mental state. All good inventions of science become sources of problems when they combine with the materialistic mind imbued by greed, lust, jealousy, and pride. Similarly, the Absolute Truth is the potentiality for every possible manifestation, and based on our desire, attitude, and nature, a certain aspect of that complete reality becomes manifest to us.

In one sense, nothing is ever created or destroyed; whatever seems to be created is manifest from within something else, where it previously existed as a potential. Thus, a person who has been purified of all material desires cannot produce anger even if subjected to an insult. It is because there is no pride within them. Consequently, if an insult produces anger, it means that the person is not purified of pride. Thus, if we understand how the manifestation emerges from the unmanifest, then we can say that the qualities we see in the effect were previously present in the cause from which they were produced.

Sūtra 2.1.25

कार्यान्तराप्रादुर्भावाच्च शब्दःस्पर्शवतामगुणः

kāryāntarāprādurbhāvācca śabdaḥ sparśavatāmaguṇaḥ

kāryāntara—the different effects; aprādurbhāvāt—from not produced; ca—also; śabdaḥ—sound; sparśavatām—as if touching; aguṇaḥ—a non-quality.

TRANSLATION

From the different effects not being produced also, the (contact with) sound is as if touching a non-quality.

COMMENTARY

One of the peculiarities of modern physics is that it hypothesizes the existence of forces that change their effects with increasing or decreasing distance. For instance, the gravitational force is said to increase as the distance between two objects decreases. Thus, physics claims that objects near Earth appear heavier than if they were in space. Vaiśeṣika would instead say that the heaviness of the object is an innate property of that object but it is *manifest* due to an interaction with the Earth, and *unmanifest* when the interaction disappears.

As we have discussed earlier, the proximity to Earth is a byproduct of an interaction between the object and the Earth. A stronger interaction reduces the perceived distance, and that can also make the thing seem heavier. A physicist would say that the distance reduced and therefore the force increased. And Vaiśeṣika would say that the interaction strengthened, due to which two things happened—(a) the perceived distance reduced, and (b) the quality of heaviness became more manifest. At this stage, both descriptions seem equivalent from an observational standpoint, and it is hard to distinguish between them.

The distinction arises when our bodies seem to be close to other things, and yet, heaviness is not perceived, such that even on the surface of Earth things can seem weightless. An easily understandable example of this phenomenon is a person standing in a crowded room who escapes into another world of their own thoughts and never hears the noise. From the perspective of a structural relation, the person is standing in a crowded room, and he should therefore hear the noise just like everyone else. However, from the perspective of interaction, the person is actually very far, and hence he doesn't perceive the effects of the crowd. This difference between structural proximity and the proximity created by interaction is used sometimes by yogis to perform miracles such as walking on fire, walking through walls, or walking on water. There is structural proximity but there is no interaction. Hence, despite proximity to the fire, the yogi's body is not burned; despite being surrounded by walls, there is absolutely no hindrance to the yogi's movement; and despite seeming to touch water, the yogi's body is not wetted due to the absence of interaction.

With this background, we can understand this sūtra. What is contact with sound? As the property of Ether, sound represents the number assigned to an object in a coordinate system. In a simple sense, we can call this structural proximity. But this structural proximity is not the cause of evoking or suppressing any properties. The real cause—as we have discussed—is due to an interaction. Of course, when we come into contact with other people, then our consciousness is drawn toward them. But the question is: What do we mean by 'contact'? Is it simply structural proximity? If so, then how can we keep our attention away from them and not be disturbed by their presence? To explain this anomaly, we have to say that 'contact' is not the structural proximity. It is only interaction. We can be very close to something structurally and yet, not feel its effects. And we can be very far from something structurally and still feel its effects. Both these exceptional scenarios require us to completely reject structural proximity as having an effect on the manifestation of properties.

Hence, there is no such thing as long- or short-distance forces. Modern physics believes that gravity is a long-distance force and electromagnetism is a short-distance force. According to Vaiśeṣika, distance has absolutely no role in creating an effect. Hence, regardless of the number we assign to an object, it has no effect on the effects and properties that the object manifests. Those effects must be explained entirely based upon the interaction between two things.

Now, one might say: If I am in a crowded room, then there is a likelihood of hearing the noise. If I'm in a forest, away from a crowd, that possibility is almost nil. The answer to that is also interaction: Our desire to interact with something creates an interaction, which manifests a certain type of property, which then has a strong effect on us. But we can interact even if there is structural distance, and not interact even if there is structural proximity. Hence, the causal explanation has to be based on interaction instead of proximity.

Sūtra 2.1.26

परत्र समवायात् प्रत्यक्षत्वाच्च नात्मगुणो न मनोगुणः

paratra samavāyāt pratyakṣatvācca nātmaguṇo na manoguṇaḥ

paratra—elsewhere; samavāyāt—because of the combination or interaction; pratyakṣatvāt—as if from direct perception; ca—also; na—not; ātma—the self; guṇah—qualities; na—not; manah—the mind; guṇaḥ—qualities.

TRANSLATION

Elsewhere (i.e., not in case of the sound of Ether, new properties are visible) because of the combination or interaction, as if from direct perception; also, these are not the qualities of the self and not the qualities of the mind.

COMMENTARY

We normally think that heat is an unavoidable property of fire; wetness is the unavoidable property of water; heaviness is the unavoidable property of macroscopic things, etc. But we have to think a little deeper about the problem. If you sit on a block of wood, then it becomes a chair; if you keep things on that block of wood, then it becomes a table. Even a criminal may display kindness toward his children, while he displays cruelty toward others. The properties of table and chair are hidden inside the block of wood, and they are manifest due to interaction; the kindness or cruelty of a criminal are hidden inside the criminal and they are manifest due to an interaction. In the same way, the wetness of water, the heat of the fire, and the heaviness of things are properties hidden inside those things and they are manifest due to an interaction. When these things are manifest, we have their direct perception, and we might say: I have seen these things, so they must indeed exist. This is true; what we are seeing is indeed the nature of the things and not merely a hallucination or illusion produced by our mind or the senses (as this sūtra notes). However, everyone may not see the same things. So, there is something in us, which causes the manifestation of these properties, but the properties themselves are not due to us.

For example, if you make a person angry by insulting them, then the anger is their property, which is manifest from within the insulted person. But the insult is caused by you. Therefore, you can attribute the insult to you (as a cause) but you must attribute the anger to the person who has insulted (also a cause). These two kinds of causes are sometimes distinguished as 'efficient' and 'material' causes. The insult is the efficient cause of anger, but the anger manifests because it preexisted in the person, and hence it is a material cause.

This phenomenon is also observed in the quantum slit experiment. As the number of slits is changed from two to three to four, etc., the wavefunction that describes the probabilities of quanta observation changes. The wavefunction is the description of the whole object, and yet, it can be expressed in infinite ways—called the "eigenfunction bases" of the wavefunction. By changing the number of slits, one such basis is selected, which then changes the observations. The slits are not interacting with the radiating body through a "force". Instead, the mere presence of the slits (and their changes) changes the eigenfunction basis. As a result, physicists might sometimes say that the radiating body, the slits, and the detectors form a single system—as far as the observations are concerned. But they are factually not a single system; the slits are the *efficient* cause of the change in eigenfunction basis, while the particles observed are the *material* cause. The change in the efficient cause alters the nature of the material cause, which means that what we observe in an experiment depends on both the material and the efficient causes because the efficient cause evokes a different kind of material property out of the collection of all possible properties.

Sūtra 2.1.27
परशिेषाल्लङ्गिमाकाशस्य
pariśeṣālliṅgamākāśasya

pariśeṣāt—from the exhaustion; lliṅgam—the symptoms; ākāśasya—of the Ether.

TRANSLATION

The symptoms of Ether from the exhaustion (of other symptoms).

COMMENTARY

The last sūtra used the term 'paratra' or 'elsewhere' after speaking about the Ether, indicating that changes to properties are produced by a combination of other elements—i.e., Air, Fire, Water, and Earth—not due to the Ether. This sūtra confirms this understanding by saying that when all the symptoms (i.e., the perceived qualities) are stripped, then we get the nature of space. The meaning of these two sūtras is the same, but they are presented in two distinct ways. As we have discussed, by Ether we mean space, and by space we mean the numbers assigned to the objects, activities, and qualities. There are two kinds of numbers—(a) that represent the objective reality, and (b) that represent our perception of that reality. As a result, there is an objective space, which we can call the 'absolute space' and there is a perceptual space, which we can call the 'relative space'. This 'space' simply comprises of locations, which are assigned numbers. The difference in Sāñkhya and Vaiśeṣika is that this numbering is hierarchical whereas in modern science the number is linear. In a linear ordering system, a change in order doesn't change anything; but in a hierarchical ordering system, a change in order alters the *boundaries* of systems. Such a change produces effects on our perception, but the effects are visible only through the other properties of touch, sight, taste, and smell. In this way, the Ether or the ordering system is objectively real and has effects on our perception, and yet, those effects are visible only when other elements are added into the picture. We can say that all methods of dividing space using system boundaries are equivalent to empty space—i.e., devoid of Air, Fire, Water, and Earth. However, when these other properties are added, this equivalence disappears.

Sūtra 2.1.28

द्रव्यत्वनित्यत्वे वायुना व्याख्याते

dravyatvanityatve vāyunā vyākhyāte

dravyatva—objectivity; nityatve—in the persistence; vāyunā—from Air; vyākhyāte—explained or ascribed.

TRANSLATION

The persistence in objectivity is explained or ascribed from Air.

COMMENTARY

After describing the nature of 'empty space', this sūtra states that the objects (and thereby the qualities and activities) appear beginning with Air. We might recall that when objects, qualities, and activities were described in the last chapter, Ether was left out of this description. This sūtra now explains why that is the case—after describing the nature of empty space—namely, that the Ether doesn't have touch, sight, taste, and smell. It doesn't mean that the Ether doesn't have any properties; as we have discussed, the Ether is a method of ordering things, and since the ordering is hierarchical, therefore, what we mean by Ether is the division of space into boundaries of systems. This system of boundaries is studied non-semantically in modern set theory, and numbers are constructed by creating a hierarchy of sets. For example, the empty set or {} is taken to represent the number zero. Then, the set that contains the empty set or {{}} is taken to represent the number one, and so on. In the hierarchical representation, zero must contain one and must be contained inside one. Zero is that state in which all the variety is unmanifest and we cannot distinguish one thing from another. As variety is manifest, a hierarchy of system boundaries is produced. However, this hierarchy of system boundaries—which is like sets—doesn't yet contain any objects. These sets are just numbers, which have a meaning, and yet, there is no object, activity, or property that makes the meaning perceivable.

We can illustrate this idea by an example. Suppose you are designing a house, and you divide the space inside the house (after drawing the house boundary) into separate spaces like kitchen, bedrooms, living room, bathrooms, garden, library, etc. The numbers in the Ether are these names—bathroom, garden, bedroom, etc. But this division of the space is just nomenclature without a physical realization. You cannot touch, see, taste, or smell these spatial divisions. If the house hasn't been constructed, then you can also redesign the house without any perceivable effects, because there are no objects, activities, and qualities. Thus, what we mean by 'Ether' is this hierarchical division of space into subparts, prior to the design being converted into a perceivable reality by the use of house construction materials. The design is real and objective, and yet we cannot touch, see, taste, or smell it. Hence it is also not an *object*.

To an extent, these distinctions of the object vs. non-object are disputable, and they are disputed in Sāñkhya and Vaiśeṣika. For example, Sāñkhya would say that even space where we have simply constructed imaginary boundaries is objective because we have designated them by names such as kitchen, bedroom, bathroom, etc. And Vaiśeṣika would say that we begin our consideration of objectivity only from the point where we can perceive things, not just talk about them using words or numbers, or think about them using concepts, etc.

The problem comes down to: What do we mean by a house? Is it only that thing which we can be touched, seen, tasted, and smelt? Or even the design of the house produced by an architect can be called a house? The architect would of course say that "I'm working on building a house", and a construction worker would also say that "I'm working on building a house". So, these disputes about what we mean by a "house" are not fundamentally contradictory. They are merely positions in philosophy taken from different viewpoints. The key point to remember is that the house springs out from the house's design. Thus, when something is designated as a kitchen, the details of that kitchen are produced after we have determined that it is a kitchen. For example, one would not create a place for a dishwasher or kitchen sink if it were a bedroom. So, the nomenclature of the place as a 'kitchen' plays a key role in the subsequent manifestation of the details, and hence the house emerges from the design.

Sūtra 2.1.29
तत्त्वम्भावेन
tattvambhāvena

tattvam—the essence; bhāvena—exists in this (Ether).

TRANSLATION
The essence (of Air, Fire, Water, and Earth) exists in this (Ether).

COMMENTARY
After stating that the objectivity begins from Air in the last sūtra, this sūtra states that the essence of that objectivity exists in the Ether. That essence is the division of space into boundaries, designating these boundaries by names such as kitchen, bedroom, bathroom, etc., and ordering these places in different directions (such as east, west, north, and south). In the Vedic system of architecture called Vāstuśhāstra, there are ideal places for each part of the house. If for some reason, the bedroom has to be moved from one part of the house to another, the things inside the bedroom must be rearranged to make it an ideal living place. Some elements of this science of space are also employed in Chinese Feng Shui. The basic idea is that the locations in space are not uniform or identical. Rather, there is an ideal macroscopic design, and if this ideal is not followed, then ideality can still be created partially by moving things inside the new location. The rearrangement of bedrooms, kitchen, bathrooms, etc., therefore, plays a role in the rearrangement of things inside these places. That rearrangement constitutes the full design of the house, and that design is the 'essence' of the house.

Thus, we can see that the dispute between Sāñkhya and Vaiśeṣika regarding Ether is not as deep as we might think. Sāñkhya considers the design of the house as being objective, while Vaiśeṣika considers those things that can be touched, seen, tasted, and smelt as objective. And yet, even Vaiśeṣika agrees that the essence of what is later manifested as a house exists in the Ether.

Sūtra 2.1.30
शब्दालिङ्गाविशेषाद्विशेषलिङ्गाभावाच्च
śabdāliṅgāviśeṣādviśeṣaliṅgābhāvācca

śabda—sound; aliṅga—non-symptoms; aviśeṣāt—from the universal; viśeṣa—the specifics; liṅga—symptoms; abhāvāt—from the absence; ca—also.

TRANSLATION

From the universal (conceptual) non-symptoms called sound, the specific symptoms are also manifest from the absence (of those specifics).

COMMENTARY

This sūtra further closes the gap between Sāñkhya and Vaiśeṣika by stating that the specific symptoms—i.e., Air, Fire, Water, and Earth—are manifest from the non-symptoms called the sound in the Ether. The difference is what we consider "symptoms". Vaiśeṣika will say that Air, Fire, Water, and Earth are symptoms, while sound, numbering, words, or design are non-symptoms. And Sāñkhya will say that since we can speak about the house using words, numbers, ordering, or design, therefore, those things are also the symptoms.

This sūtra also invokes the Nyāya doctrine of absence, by using the term abhāva which means "absence". The idea is that the absence exists in the presence as a question; the presence and absence interact with each other as a premise interacts with a question, thereby generating an answer, which becomes a new presence, although it also has another question—an absence—within it. For example, the concept 'mammal' is a presence, but along with that presence are many questions about the true meaning of mammal. Does a mammal have two legs or four? Does a mammal have horns or not? How big is the mammal? What are the shapes and colors of mammals? Etc. The Nyāya system states that this absence interacts with the presence to produce an expansion. In this example, the concept 'mammal' must interact with the questions about the meaning of mammal to produce varieties of mammals such as cows, horses, dogs, etc. Thus, the idea of 'mammal' diversifies into a lot of variety due to 'absence'.

The same idea is applied here as well in the context of space. For instance, once we have designated something as a 'kitchen', then there is an absence or question about what we truly mean by a kitchen. Does it have storage space? Does it have a dishwasher? How big is the kitchen? Does it have a modernist design or a traditional design? Etc. These questions are then used to produce a more detailed design of the kitchen, and as the details accumulate, they become touch, sight, taste, and smell. Thus, the kitchen that we see is produced from the word 'kitchen' but after it has been subjected to many questions. All the varieties of kitchens are hidden inside the word 'kitchen' and they are manifest from that word depending on various choices. These choices are the different ways of answering the aforementioned questions about the meaning of the kitchen. Thus, there is an objective reality in the existence of the word 'kitchen', which contains all the varieties of kitchens as a potentiality within. When this objective reality is subjected to questions, then it projects different details based on the questions and the choices of the answers. Since the variety was previously hidden, therefore, all that subsequently manifests is also objectively real. And yet, since the manifestation is based on a choice of how the question is answered, therefore, the production of reality is also caused subjectively.

Sūtra 2.1.31

तदनुविधानादेकपृथक्त्वञ्चेति

tadanuvidhānādekapṛthaktvañceti

tat—that; anuvidhānāt—from a proper arrangement (the design of order in space); eka—one; pṛthaktvam—separated; ca—also; iti—in this way.

TRANSLATION

In this way, from that proper arrangement (the design of order in space), the one also becomes separated.

COMMENTARY

This sūtra almost nullifies the distinction between Sāñkhya and Vaiśeṣika by stating that all that we touch, see, taste, or smell springs from space. The variety that we perceive through our senses is "separated" because it was previously unseparated in the "proper arrangement" of the "essences" in space. This springing forth is due to the Nyāya doctrine of 'absence', whereas what we call 'space' is not truly empty: It comprises the arrangement of essences. Now, whether we call this proper arrangement as a quality, activity, and object or not, hardly matters because the proper arrangement can also be described as an object, a set of qualities, and a set of activities. The activity is that it produces variety; the objectivity is that there are separate components of the design; and the quality is that each component has a unique property like being a kitchen, bedroom, bathroom, etc. These systems of philosophy differ in their emphasis upon what they present earlier or later, what they might consider visible vs. invisible, the level of detail they elaborate on, etc. But they are not contrary theories of nature. Once we understand what they are saying, they become identical.

Section 2

Sūtra 2.2.1

पुष्पवस्त्रयोःसति सन्निकर्षे गुणान्तराप्रादुर्भावो वस्त्रे गन्धाभावलिङ्गम्

puṣpavastrayoḥ sati sannikarṣe guṇāntarāprādurbhāvo vastre gandhābhāvaliṅgam

puṣpavastrayoḥ—the garment and flowers; sati—exist; sannikarṣe—in proximity; guṇāntara—different qualities; aprādurbhāvah—not produced; vastre—in the garment; gandha—smell; abhāva—absence; liṅgam—the symptom.

TRANSLATION

The garment and flowers exist in proximity with different qualities; the smell is not produced in the garment; the symptom being its absence.

COMMENTARY

After discussing how qualities are manifest from objects in the presence of other objects, this sūtra states that this is not always the case; the counterexample being the presence of smell in a cloth imparted by a flower. The cloth doesn't draw out the smell from the flower; that smell already exists in the flower. In the same way, if we mix sugar and salt, the property of saltiness is not drawn out of sugar. That property already existed in the salt itself. As a result, we can distinguish between two kinds of mixtures. A classical mixture is one in which the qualities preexisting in one thing are imparted to another thing (e.g., the smell of flowers is imparted to the cloth). A quantum mixture is one in which qualities in one thing are drawn out of that thing due to the presence of other objects. These qualities are preexisting, although invisible, in the object to which they are subsequently attributed. The context makes those qualities visible.

Sūtra 2.2.2
व्यवस्थितिःपृथिव्यां गन्धः
vyavasthitaḥ pṛthivyāṃ gandhaḥ

vyavasthitaḥ—situated within; pṛthivyāṃ—in Earth; gandhaḥ—smell.

TRANSLATION

Smell is situated within the Earth.

COMMENTARY

As we have discussed, activities emerge from objects, and qualities emerge from activities. The activity and the quality may sometimes be hidden. For example, if perfume is placed in a glass bottle, then the quality is unmanifest, even though it exists in the perfume. When the bottle is opened, and our senses interact with the perfume, that property is manifest. Now, there are two ways to describe this manifestation. First, in the classical mechanical sense, we can say that the smell was always manifest in the perfume, but the bottle was preventing the spread of the smell. Second, in the quantum mechanical sense, the perfume in the bottle had a smell hidden when it was in the bottle; it manifested from the perfume when the bottle was opened. Most of us think of the perfume in the classical mechanical sense—i.e., that the smell in the perfume is always manifest, but it is unable to 'escape' the bottle. But the Vaiśeṣika way of thinking would say that the smell is not manifest in the perfume, and hence there is no question of 'escaping'. Rather, our sense of smell cannot penetrate the bottle, and hence, it cannot smell the perfume. In short, if the perfume is in the bottle, then the context which causes the manifestation of the smell is absent. Therefore, the smell is unmanifest due to the absence of the interaction between the perfume and our sense to smell, and then manifest by that interaction.

If we change our way of thinking about matter, then all classical physical ideas about the world are overturned, and the world is understood as meaning. The smell in the perfume is like the meaning in the book. If we keep the book closed, then we cannot understand the meaning. The meaning is in the book, but it is unmanifest unless there is a capable reader. If someone doesn't know the language in which the book is written, or doesn't have the concepts that are essential to understand what the book discusses, then the meaning in the book is unmanifest to such an ignorant reader. The meaning is, however, manifest to the educated and learned reader, so we must acknowledge that the meaning exists in the book. And yet, the ignorant reader cannot find it, since their minds are the precondition to the meaning manifesting from the book. Similarly, opening the bottle is like opening a book, and interacting with the smell that preexists in the perfume, but it remains unmanifest until our senses can interact.

An illustration of this fact is that dogs can smell things inside closed boxes. How? The answer is that the dog's sense of smell can penetrate bottles and boxes, and the properties are hence manifest to their sense of smell alone. The difference in smell between humans and dogs is therefore due to their senses, and not due to the boxes and bottles, or the things inside those containers.

Sūtra 2.2.3
एतेनोष्णता व्याख्याता
etenoṣṇatā vyākhyātā

etena—in this way; uṣṇatā—heat; vyākhyātā—is explained.

TRANSLATION
In this way, heat is explained.

COMMENTARY
People who have become accustomed to living in hot climates don't feel the heat as much as those who come to live in those climates from cold places. Conversely, those who live in cold climates don't feel the cold as much as those who have immigrated to live in those places from warm or hot places. If we took a thermometer and measured the temperature, we will find it objectively hot or cold. But the sense perception of hot and cold is different from the temperature. So, is this sūtra speaking about the objective heat or its sense perception? If we take this sūtra to be talking about objective heat, then by the previous sūtra we can say that the heat objectively rests in the objects. But if we broaden the meaning, then we can say that even though heat objectively rests in the objects, it is not always manifest to sense perception. The reason is that the senses are not blank slates. They have tendencies of their own, and that tendency is defined in three ways. First, it is the desire to perceive certain things,

which is called guna. Second, it is the capacity to perceive certain things, which is called chitta. And third, it is the opportunity to perceive certain things, which is called karma. When the senses are repeatedly subjected to a certain type of sensation, they develop the capacity to perceive it (if they weren't previously able to identify it), and they also get habituated to that perception (if they weren't previously habituated). However, capacity and habituation also reduce the interaction with those objects. As a result, one has the capacity to bear the heat or cold, is habituated to heat and cold, and yet doesn't perceive the heat or cold as much. Thus, if we broaden the discussion from the objective existence of heat to the perception of heat, then we can say that even though heat objectively exists in things, the perception of the heat is based on the interaction of the senses with the objects, thereby resulting in varying notions of hot and cold.

Sūtra 2.2.4
तेजस उष्णता

tejasa uṣṇatā

tejasa—Fire; uṣṇatā—heat.

TRANSLATION

Heat exists in the Fire element.

COMMENTARY

As we have discussed earlier, the successive elements of Air, Fire, Water, and Earth carry successively greater properties such that heat is a property of touch, but it is also a property of things that can be seen. The difference is that if you stand in sunlight, your eyes do not see the heat; the heat is perceived by the skin. And yet, the Fire element carries both heat and light, such that the heat is perceived by the skin, and the light is perceived by the eyes. The complete perception of Fire is therefore not possible with just the sense of seeing. It also requires the sense of touch. Modern science converts both heat and light into 'energy', but Sāñkhya and Vaiśeṣika separate them into heat and light. The reason is simple: You can feel the heat even if there is no light—e.g., in a dark room. Similarly, you can perceive light even if there is no heat. If heat and light were simply 'energy' then more light would mean more heat and vice versa. This is not always the case, and hence, these two properties must be separated.

Sūtra 2.2.5
अप्सु शीतता
apsu śītatā

apsu—Water; śītatā—coldness.

TRANSLATION

The Water element has the property of coldness.

COMMENTARY

One might say that ordinary water can be heated, and then it will also have the property of heat, but Sāñkhya and Vaiśeṣika would say that when ordinary water is heated, then a property of 'heat' is added to water, and since heat is a property of Fire, therefore, we must say that Fire was added to Water. Without this addition, Water has the property of touch, and that touch is coldness.

In this way, even though Air, Fire, and Water all have the property of touch, the *values* of these properties possessed by these elements are different. The notable example here is that the Fire element has the touch which is hot, and the Water element has the touch which is cold. Thus, having the property of touch doesn't mean Water itself becomes hot; rather, heating the element Water requires the addition of the element Fire; the result is the combination of two elements—Fire and Water—just like the combination of a flower and a garment creates a sweet-smelling garment. Since hot and cold are properties of two distinct elements, both properties are simultaneously real—although in different elements. Hot and cold are mutually opposed properties, but reducing the heat in Fire doesn't mean it has become Water. Likewise, reducing the cold in Water doesn't mean it has become Fire. The simultaneous reality of hot and cold properties means that the properties don't cancel each other if these are mixed. Rather, both hot and cold exist as distinct properties. The cancellation of properties occurs in our perception since one property is now dominant. Nevertheless, if our senses are advanced to perceive the individual sensations, then we can perceive both kinds of sensations separately. For example, while drinking hot water, you can also perceive coldness, even though the heat is dominant.

Sūtra 2.2.6

अपरस्मिन्नपरं युगपत् चिरं क्षिप्रमिति कालिङ्गानि

aparasminnaparaṃ yugapat ciraṃ kṣipramiti kālaliṅgāni

aparasmin—that which is inferior; aparaṃ—inferior; yugapat—coinciding with; ciraṃ—long; kṣipram—short; iti—thus; kāla—time; liṅgāni—symptoms.

TRANSLATION

The symptoms of time are short and long, which coincide with the inferior, and the inferior to the inferior.

COMMENTARY

Time, like space, is also described hierarchically in Vedic philosophy. A close analogy of this type of time is its description in terms of years, months, days, hours, seconds, etc. The higher-level time—e.g., a year—is longer. And the lower-level time—e.g., a month—is shorter. Thus, the lower-level time is the 'inferior' time, and the higher-level time is the 'superior' time. However, both long and short are inferior relative to eternal time. Thus, this sūtra uses the terms 'inferior' and 'inferior to the inferior' in the description of observed time; the former for the longer durations and the latter for the shorter durations.

Sūtra 2.2.7

द्रव्यत्व नित्यत्वे वायुना व्याख्याते

dravyatva nityatve vāyunā vyākhyāte

dravyatva—objectivity; nityatve—persistent; vāyunā—of Air; vyākhyāte—explained.

TRANSLATION

The persistent objectivity of Air is explained (based on time).

COMMENTARY

The hierarchy of time has a correspondence with the hierarchy in conceptual space in the sense that the entities higher up in the conceptual space are also longer-lived, while the entities lower down in the conceptual space are shorter-lived. The element Air is considered a subtle element relative to Fire, Water, and Earth, and it is hence higher-up in the conceptual hierarchy. This also means that it is longer-lived. This doesn't mean that the individual objects called Air are eternal; as we have discussed, these objects are combinations of the universal and the individual; the individuality and universality are eternal, but the combination of the two is not. Nevertheless, even as all the element instances are temporary, Air is longer-lived compared to the other elements. These longer and shorter durations of existence are attributed to time hierarchy. In simple terms, the abstract view or the "big picture" changes slowly, while the detailed view or the "details in the picture" evolve faster in comparison.

Sūtra 2.2.8

तत्त्वम्भावेन

tattvambhāvena

tattvam—essential; bhāvena—nature of this.

TRANSLATION

(Time has) an essential nature.

COMMENTARY

Time, like space, is also conceptual which means that different moments in time are not identical; each moment in time has a different *type*. A common example of this typed-nature of time is the division of the day into morning, afternoon, evening, and night, which have a different nature. Similarly, the days of the week have different natures; the months have different natures, etc. Due to this typed nature of time, different material types become dominant or subordinate. This creates cycles of changes in nature where the older type of phenomena are repeated, and this repetition of types creates a cyclical time.

Sūtra 2.2.9

नित्येष्वभावादनित्येषु भावात् कारणे कालाख्येति

nityeṣvabhāvādanityeṣu bhāvāt kāraṇe kālākhyeti

nityeṣu—in the permanent; abhāvāt—from the absence; anityeṣu—in the temporary; bhāvāt—from the presence; kāraṇe—the causalities; kālākhyeti—named as time.

TRANSLATION

From the absence in the permanent, and from the presence in the temporary, are the causalities named as time.

COMMENTARY

The abstract and the contingent are both incomplete—the abstract because the details are absent, and the contingent because the whole truth represented by the abstract is absent. The absence of the whole truth in the contingent defines its nature. For example, a cow is a mammal, but other properties of mammals found in horses, dogs, cats, etc., are absent. The absence of the other qualities of mammals defines the cow (in the contextual mode). Similarly, the absence of details about cows, horses, dogs, and cats, defines the concept 'mammal'. These absences become the question, and the change that ensues is the answer to that question. For instance, the absence of the details in a mammal becomes the question: What is a mammal? The answer to that question is the expansion of the mammal into the concepts of cow, horse, dog, and cat. However, once that question has been answered, then the concept of mammal is immanent in the cow, horse, dog, and mammal. Therefore, if you were studying these contingent concepts, and you delve deeper into the nature of each type, you will find a more abstract concept—the mammal. Then, you can ask: What is a mammal? And that question requires us to return to the concept of mammal where the details of cow, horse, cat, etc. are absent. Thus, the absence of the details in the abstract produces the details, and the absence of the understanding of the abstract in the details reverts these details back to the abstract.

The concept mammal is relatively more permanent than the concept cow, and hence longer-lived. But since the details are absent in this longer-lived concept, therefore, the absence of the details is the causal effect called 'time'. Likewise, the understanding of the abstract is missing in the details, and this absence is the causal effect called 'time'. Thus, the doctrines of logical reasoning in Nyāya and the doctrine of the nature of matter in Vaiśeṣika are connected.

Such a connection between logical reasoning and time is absent in modern science. As a result, why nature evolves as the result of logical inference is missing in science. The inferencing mechanism was created by Newton and Leibniz in calculus, which uses the concept of "rate of change with time" and equates it to some material property. This formulation foregoes the age-old debate about what *causes* changes, and focuses on the "rate of change". These two ideas seem almost synonymous because if the rate of change is zero, then we can take that to mean the absence of change. But it makes a crucial assumption—namely, that time is *passing*. How does time pass? Why does it pass? Is it another kind of motion? If so, that motion also requires yet another time to pass, which then leads to an infinite cascade of times that must pass for the time used by physics to pass, which can then be used to compute the rate of change. The modern doctrine of time and change, therefore, assumes a parallel between logical reasoning—i.e., that premises lead to conclusions, the premises are prior in time and the conclusions are later in time—without explaining how logic is connected to time. That explanation, as we saw, is present in these sūtras.

Sūtra 2.2.10

इत इदमिति यतस्तद्दिश्यं लिङ्गम्

ita idamiti yatastaddiśyaṃ liṅgam

ita—from this; idam—this; iti—in this way; yatah—from which; tat—that; diśyaṃ—directionality or space; liṅgam—symptoms.

TRANSLATION

From this, this, in this way, from which, that, are symptoms of space.

COMMENTARY

Space is a method of identifying, distinguishing, and ordering objects, qualities, and activities. The method then gives us the ability to count and organize them in a hierarchy. That hierarchical construction is like an inverted tree. There is an objective individuality, distinction, and order among the objects, activities, and qualities, which this sūtra speaks about.

But there are also subjective methods of identifying, distinguishing, and ordering, as we have discussed before. As a result, we can sometimes misperceive the distance to things, think that something is background when it is foreground, mistake the cause as one thing when it is another. This reordering of things, however, doesn't have a causal effect unless there is an interaction with those things. When that causal interaction occurs, the perceived distance depends on the strength of the interaction.

Sūtra 2.2.11

द्रव्यत्व नित्यत्वे वायुना व्याख्याते

dravyatva nityatve vāyunā vyākhyāte

dravyatva—objectivity; nityatve—persistent; vāyunā—of Air; vyākhyāte—explained.

TRANSLATION

The persistent objectivity of Air is explained (based on space).

COMMENTARY

This sūtra repeats the statement made in regards to time. As we noted in the case of time, matter is organized hierarchically in which the elements higher up in the hierarchy are also more persistent. Similarly, the elements lower in the hierarchy are shorter-lived. The long and short life pertains to the combination of universality and individuality, which are separately eternal, but the combination is temporary. This temporary combination, however, can be long- or short-lived. The Air element is higher in the hierarchy, and that higher position is due to the spatial organization. This element is longer-lived relative to the other elements such as Fire, Water, and Earth, which are shorter-lived.

Sūtra 2.2.12

तत्त्वम्भावेन

tattvambhāvena

tattvam—essential; bhāvena—nature of this.

TRANSLATION

(Space has) an essential nature.

COMMENTARY

Classical mechanics thought of space as a physical entity, which used to offer 'resistance' to movement. Later in relativity theory, this physical entity was discarded and reality remained the metric distances between locations. Since these distances are just numbers, and science is accustomed to a physical conception of reality, therefore, it is sometimes said that space is unreal. And yet, the metric distances are supposed to have properties like 'curvature', which means that the shortest path between two points is not necessarily a straight line. All these concepts about space are replaced in Vedic philosophy by treating it as a domain of concepts. These concepts constitute universality, individuality, and contextuality. Then, within each of these, there are divisions of objects, activities, and qualities. Thus, three kinds of hierarchies can be constructed—if we keep the universality, individuality, and contextuality separate. But these three hierarchies are also combined because the activity springs out from the object, and the quality springs out from the quality. Likewise, universality springs from individuality, and contextuality from individuality. Thereby, a semantic space of universality, individuality, contextuality, objectivity, activity, and quality is constructed. The distances in this semantic space are based on conceptual differences, and hence space has an "essential" nature.

Sūtra 2.2.13

कार्यविशेषेण नानात्वम्

kāryaviśeṣeṇa nānātvam

kārya—the effects; viśeṣeṇa—from these specifics; nānātvam—numerous.

TRANSLATION

The effects produced from these specifics are numerous.

COMMENTARY

Once the space of diverse meanings has been constructed, numerous kinds of effects can be produced by an interaction between the components of the space. What is an effect? It is the manifestation of something that preexisted within but was previously invisible. Similarly, it can also be the hiding of something that was previously manifest. Thus, by the interactions between the parts of the tree, the tree itself can evolve—it can manifest new trunks, branches, and leaves, or it can hide some manifest trunks, branches, and trees. The effects of causality, which we call 'change' is the evolution of the semantic tree. Vedic texts describe how the entire universe springs out like a tree growing from a seed, and then collapses back into the seed. Even when the tree is manifest, it grows new branches and then collapses them. All the possible trunks, branches, and leaves are conceptually eternal possibilities. Hence, the universe is said to be eternal. And yet, it is not eternally manifest. Thus, change doesn't mean the absence of eternality, and eternality doesn't mean the absence of change.

Sūtra 2.2.14

आदित्यसंयोगात् भूतपूर्वात् भविष्यतो भूताच्च प्राची

ādityasaṃyogāt bhūtapūrvāt bhaviṣyato bhūtācca prācī

āditya—the sun; saṃyogāt—from the union; bhūtapūrvāt—from that which is past; bhaviṣyato—that which is in the future; bhūtācca—also all the beings (that are existing at the present); prācī—directed from east.

TRANSLATION

From the union with the sun, from that which is past to that which is in the future, also the beings (that are existing at the present), are directed from east.

COMMENTARY

In an earlier sūtra, we discussed how time was moving as logical inference due to the nature of presence and absence. In abstract reality, the contingent is not visible, and in contingent reality, the abstract is not visible. Both the abstract and the details are eternally present as possibilities, but their visibility is limited. Which limited reality leads to which another limited reality creates time. In short, when something new becomes visible, something that previously existed becomes invisible. There is a logical connection between the past, the present, and the future because the question follows logically from the premise, and the answer follows logically from the question. And yet, this logical inference is not deterministic. Given a certain premise, many questions can potentially arise from it. Likewise, given a question, many potential answers can be given.

Time selects one of the possible questions from a premise, and one of the possible answers from a question, thus constructing a narration or story of the universe. However, in another sense, this time is also deterministic because the *type* of question and answer at a given time is fixed. For example, if your friend says: "I'm going shopping", then you can potentially ask him many possible questions: "Where are you going shopping?" or "What are you planning to buy?" or "When will you be back?" or "Will you also get something for me?", etc. The *type* of the question is in the words such as where, what, when, will, etc. They select one out of the many possible questions that could be asked. Similarly, there are many types of answers. Since the questions arise from premises, and the answers arise from the questions, there is always contextuality in the progression of time, due to which we do not see determinism. But it is still deterministic in the sense that each moment in time represents a *type*, which produces a different kind of question or answer, which then produces a new reality and hides another reality. The determinism becomes visible over a long period of time when the same patterns are seen to repeat cyclically.

This background helps us understand what we mean by "time"—it is the deterministic succession of types, but since a different question is applied to a different premise, or a different answer is provided to a different question, hence, immense variety is created from a deterministic succession of types.

This succession of types in time is represented in Vedic cosmology by the movement of the sun. As the sun passes through the different zodiac signs, the time changes its nature, which then produces different questions, answers, and premises, whatever seemed like the "choice" of question from a premise, or the choice of an answer based on a question, becomes deterministic. This determinism is however attributable only to the story or narration—which is like the script of the drama. This script limits what the soul can choose, but it doesn't completely determine the soul's choices. Thus, just like a script can be enacted by different actors, similarly, the soul can choose whether or not to participate in a certain role in the script.

Alongside the determinism of time and predictiveness of the future, there is perfect free will in the choice of the drama roles.

This sūtra attributes ordinary changes to the movement of the sun, but this movement must be understood in the context of the previous discussion about presence and absence, the process of logical inference, and the transcendence of the soul from material nature. Once all these things are understood, then we obtain an alternative semantic process of history, time, and evolution, in which we can construct a cyclical sequence of events, making nature perfectly deterministic. That deterministic predictiveness is the foundation of alternative science that is based on meanings rather than physical properties of things. It follows a different kind of logic, has a different understanding of numbers, describes space, time, and matter in a completely different way. And yet, it is capable of explaining not just the evolution of physical particles, but also of minds, bodies, societies, ecologies, planets, and the entire universe itself.

Sūtra 2.2.15

तथा दक्षिणा प्रतीची उदीची च

tathā dakṣiṇā pratīcī udīcī ca

tathā—in the same way; dakṣiṇā—south; pratīcī—west; udīcī—north; ca—also.

TRANSLATION

In the same way, from the south, west, and north, also.

COMMENTARY

Vedic cosmology describes how the sun rises and falls in its orbit as it goes around the Earth. The rise and fall are attributed to the Earth's tilt in its axis in modern astronomy. The difference is that the space in which the sun's rise and fall are described is semantic in nature. Thus, for half the year, the sun moves "northward" and that phase is called Uttarāyaṇa. Then, for the remaining half of the year, the sun moves "southward" and that phase is called Dakśhiṇāyaṇa. Similarly, the cosmology texts describe how the sun moves counterclockwise but its movement is offset by a clockwise movement of the zodiac, just like an ant moving counterclockwise on a potter's wheel that is moving clockwise. The clockwise motion of the zodiac gives the sun an "eastward" movement, while the counterclockwise motion of the sun gives it a "westward" movement. The zodiac moves 365.25 times faster than the sun, such that the sun reverts to its position relative to the zodiac after 365.25 days, which is called a solar year. But during this time, the sun is simultaneously moving northward or southward, eastward and westward. The type changes in the semantic space arise due to these movements. Factually, the sun is not moving; the motion is attributed to a soul, called Sūrya Nārāyaṇa, who moves from one "body" to another. All these "bodies" are the different locations along the zodiac. Therefore, the sun's movement is not the physical movement of an object, but the soul's transmigration from one body to another, thereby acquiring various types of bodies.

These body types are thus 'activated' and 'deactivated' or 'manifest' and 'unmanifest' by the soul's presence. And that activation and deactivation of the type cause their activation and deactivation in other things in the universe. The last sūtra described this succession of types simply as movement from east to west. And this sūtra adds northward, southward, and westward movement to this. In short, the soul called Sūrya Nārāyaṇa moves in a three-dimensional semantic space, and that movement is the cause of all other material changes. The sun's movement is further said to be caused by eternal time, which can be understood as the time which is topmost in the hierarchy of progressions.

Sūtra 2.2.16

एतेन दगिन्तरालानि व्याख्यातानि

etena digantarālāni vyākhyātāni

etena—by this; digantarālāni—the differences in directions and extensions in space; vyākhyātāni—are explained.

TRANSLATION

By this, the differences in directions and extensions in space are explained.

COMMENTARY

The locations and directions in a semantic space are not identical. As we have discussed earlier, the locations in a house are designated as a bedroom, bathroom, kitchen, etc. Similarly, the directions east, west, north, and south are given different meanings. Modern science strips all these meanings from the locations and treats all locations and directions as being equivalent. There is, hence, nothing up or down, east or west, in space itself. No location is higher or lower. This non-semantic space is rejected all over Vedic texts. Space is that which has meanings; the meanings are abstract or detailed; the directions represent objects, activities, and qualities. Thus, all directions and locations are not considered identical. Movement in this space is not simply the change in position, but also a change in meaning. That change in meaning means that the type of object, the type of activity, and the type of quality have changed. Change can also mean that the personality of likes and dislikes, priorities, and preferences have changed. Finally, change can also mean that the roles or characters of the actor have changed. This complicated dynamic of the change in the three types of meanings (and their various subtypes) is described as "motion". Causality is then attributed to the change in these meanings. A red rose and a red light have different meanings than a yellow rose and a yellow light. The effects created by these qualities are also different. Therefore, by the change of meanings, new effects are created, and that change is controlled by the sun's motion.

Sūtra 2.2.17

सामान्यप्रत्यक्षाद्विशेषस्मृतेश्च संशयः

sāmānyapratyakṣādviśeṣasmṛteśca saṃśayaḥ

sāmānya—the general class; pratyakṣāt—from direct perception; viśeṣa—the specific; smṛteśca—also from the recollection; saṃśayaḥ—doubt.

TRANSLATION

Doubt is the result of the (incompatibility between) the general class arising from direct perception and the recollection of the specific from memory.

COMMENTARY

If you have always seen white cows in the past, then your memory carries the notion that cows are always white. So, if you see a black cow and cognize it as a cow—because all the traits except the color of the cow match—then doubt is created: Is this really a cow or not? Contradictions between the universal, the individual, and the contextual are the norm, rather than the exception in this world. No two cows are alike, which makes the understanding of what we truly mean by a cow difficult. Sometimes, the preconceived notion of a cow can be used to reject something perceived as being a cow, because the thing that we are seeing is incompatible with our idea. At other times, the preconceived notion of a cow can be modified by what we are perceiving. In this way, when the preconceived idea dominates, then the specific thing is not classified by that idea. And when the specific thing dominates, then the preconceived idea is modified. Doubt is the prior state that leads to this modification, and it represents an incompatibility between the general class ideas and the specific perceptions. Change thus results from contradictions, incompatibilities, and inconsistencies among the meanings. This is a different mechanism of change than the one noted earlier, which was about the absence of something in the presence of something else. The Nyāya Sūtra discusses both these mechanisms—(a) that arises from incompatibility and is called 'doubt', and (b) that arises from the 'absence'. The third mechanism which involves ejecting a new meaning out of a preexisting reality when the two are brought into contact is not discussed in Nyāya but has been discussed at length in the Vaiśeṣika Sūtras earlier.

Sūtra 2.2.18

दृष्टञ्च दृष्टवत्

dṛṣṭañca dṛṣṭavat

dṛṣṭam—that which was seen; ca—also; dṛṣṭavat—just like what is seen.

TRANSLATION

When a thing seen is just like what was seen earlier (it) is also (cause of doubt).

COMMENTARY

If you have seen a storm and a tornado only once, it is possible that you will classify them both into the same category—e.g., a storm. But if you see repeated instances of storms and tornadoes, then you will realize that they are different, and then you will also classify them into separate categories—i.e., storm and tornado. On the encounter with repeated instances of storms and tornadoes, a doubt arises: Are these really the same thing or a different thing? The comparisons of similarities and differences then lead to two separate classifications.

Our identification thus depends on two methods—(a) perceiving the similarities, and (b) perceiving the differences. If only differences are seen, then everything is an individual thing, and there are no classes, and in this case, there is no doubt, but there is also no conceptual knowledge. Knowledge begins when we start seeing similarities between things, by which we categorize them into different classes. But which thing goes into which class? Should we put storms and tornadoes into the same class because both involve fast winds? Or should we put them into separate classes because in a storm wind blows linearly while in a tornado the wind blows cyclically? Generally, if enough differences are not recognized, then a single class of similarities suffices. Then, when the differences are recognized, different things are categorized into separate classes.

Thus, doubt can arise in two ways. First, we focus on the similarity and if we don't find enough similarity, the result is a doubt—does this thing really belong to the class? This type of doubt was discussed in the last sūtra. Second, we can focus on the differences, and we might not find enough difference, which then leads to doubt—does this thing really deserve another class? This type of doubt is discussed in this sūtra. These two kinds of doubts reach a tipping point when there are enough similarities and enough differences. Then, we are unable to create a separate class due to similarity, and we cannot bundle things together due to the differences. This confusion then leads to the creation of a hierarchy in which a higher class is postulated in which the similarities are emphasized, and the lower classes are postulated wherein the differences are emphasized. Doubt is the mechanism by which (a) contradiction is created, (b) the resolution of the contradiction creates a class hierarchy, and (c) individual things are placed into different classes based on similarity and difference.

Sūtra 2.2.19

यथादृष्टमयथादृष्टत्वाच्च

yathādṛṣṭamayathādṛṣṭatvācca

yathā—just as; dṛṣṭam—has been seen; ayathā—just as not; dṛṣṭatvāt—from the seeing; ca—also.

TRANSLATION

Doubt is also caused by the types of things that were seen or not seen.

COMMENTARY

This sūtra discusses the role of familiarity in the creation of doubt. If you have never seen black cows, then the unfamiliarity will lead to doubt on the vision of a black cow: Is this really a cow or something else? Conversely, if you have seen a number of black and white cows, then such doubt doesn't arise.

Sūtra 2.2.20

वद्यिावद्यिातश्‍च संशयः

vidyāvidyātaśca saṃśayaḥ

vidyāvidyātah—from knowledge and ignorance; ca—also; saṃśayaḥ—doubt.

TRANSLATION

Doubt is also caused by knowledge and ignorance.

COMMENTARY

If we have acquired false ideas about the nature of reality, then we might see radically different things, and yet bundle them into the same category. For instance, a materialist might say that the body and the mind are not truly different; they are just chemicals. Similarly, the soul is not separate from the body; even consciousness is the byproduct of chemicals. This is because the materialist doesn't understand the nature of the mind and its unique properties, which are not found in physical things. But a materialist may still have some doubts: Is the mind or consciousness attributable to a new property in matter that we have thus far never theorized about? Or is the mind a byproduct of the already well-known properties? Similarly, if one acquires an understanding of the three modes of nature, then he can classify people into the modes of sattva, rajas, and tamas, which others—who are ignorant of this method of classification—cannot. Such a person may have a doubt: Is this person dominantly in the mode of rajas or tamas? But such a doubt would never arise in the other people.

Thus, false ideas create their own certainty and doubts, just like true ideas. The general principle of truth is that certainty increases and doubts decline when the true nature of reality is understood. Therefore, if doubts are declining, then we can understand that we are headed toward the truth. But if the doubts keep increasing, or they merely change form from one type to another, then we must know that whatever we think is true, should not be considered true.

Sūtra 2.2.21

श्रोत्रग्रहणो योऽर्थः स शब्दः

śrotragrahaṇo yor'thaḥ sa śabdaḥ

śrotra—the sense of hearing; grahaṇah—perception; yah—that which; arthaḥ—the object; sa—that; śabdaḥ—sound.

TRANSLATION

The object which is perceived by the sense of hearing, that is sound.

COMMENTARY

Language is the method of *naming* objects, qualities, activities, universals, individuals, and relationships. These names create a space of sounds to which the mind assigns meanings—i.e., identifies each name as some object, quality, activity, universal, individual, or relationship. The sound is itself comprised of objects—e.g., words. It has some qualities—e.g., pitch, tone, and form. And there is an activity—e.g., the utterance or non-utterance of words. The sense of hearing produces the identification of different sounds as objects, qualities, and activities. Likewise, the sense of hearing also understands pauses, which are sometimes interpreted as creating structure within a sentence, and then sometimes as different sentences. All these properties, which can be gleaned by the sense of hearing, are collectively called 'sound'. It includes forms such as alphabets, words, and sentences. It also includes tonality and pitch. The sound perception is not merely cognitive; it also includes the perception of emotions based on tones and pitches. Thus, the sense of hearing produces three kinds of meanings—the words, their structure into sentences, and emotions.

Sūtra 2.2.22

तुल्यजातीयेष्वर्थान्तरभूतेषु विशेषस्य उभयथा दृष्टत्वात्

tulyajātīyeṣvarthāntarabhūteṣu viśeṣasya ubhayathā dṛṣṭatvāt

tulya—comparison; jātīyeṣu—in the classes; arthāntara—the difference of meaning; bhūteṣu—in that which exists, or the material elements; viśeṣasya—of the specific; ubhayathā—both; dṛṣṭatvāt—from the perception.

TRANSLATION

From the perception of both the specific things that exist and the difference of meaning in the classes through comparison.

COMMENTARY

As we have discussed earlier, perception involves three activities—identification, distinguishing, and ordering. The ordering in the case of sound is relatively easy in the case of speech as it is expressed as different moments in time. But as we hear someone speak, the sequence of sounds must be bundled into words. This requires identification and distinguishing. For example, we must be able to distinguish when one word ends and the other begins. And then we must also be able to identify each word as representing something meaningful, or, otherwise, the distinction between words would not be considered correct.

This process is also visible in a written text when the words are incorrectly spelled, or spaces between words are absent. By the process of identifying, we break the text down into individual words, even if spaces between them are absent. Then, by the process of distinguishing, we determine if the separation of letters into words is correct. Again, by the process of identifying, we determine if some word has been misspelled. And then by the process of distinguishing we decide if some partial groups of letters should be merged into a longer word. The process of identifying, distinguishing, and sequencing is iterative, and it continues until we find a properly framed sentence or statement. This statement is then presented to the mind, which then decodes the meaning, and again goes through the process of identification, distinguishing, and sequencing. If the meaning is incompatible with what was said earlier, or the context in which it is said, or something is not understood the first time it is read, then the process reverts to reading. This sūtra emphasizes the process of identifying and distinguishing the words as the present context is about the hearing of sound.

Sūtra 2.2.23
एकद्रव्यत्वान्न द्रव्यम्
ekadravyatvānna dravyam

eka—one; dravyatvāt—from the objectivity; na—not; dravyam—object.

TRANSLATION

Individuality is based on objectivity, rather than the objects.

COMMENTARY

Visual illusions are based on the inability to correctly identify a boundary in our perceptual field that clearly demarcates one thing from another. Similarly, correct perception is based on demarcating sensations in our perceptual field by drawing boundaries. Assuming that there is something real corresponding to the sensations, what corresponds to the boundary in space?

A materialist would say that the boundary is just the collection or aggregation of sensations, and there is nothing real corresponding to it. For example, we can draw lines on the land demarcating countries, but that doesn't make each country a different 'object'. Likewise, we can draw imaginary lines in space dividing the stars into 12 zodiac signs, but there is nothing real about that division. What we call a 'country' or a 'zodiac sign' is an arbitrary construct. But the same idea about space cannot be easily extended to our bodies. For example, if we say that people's hands are not truly part of their body, but some imaginary construct about drawing boundaries in space, then I doubt anyone would agree. So, what is the difference between imaginary boundaries on the land that identify countries, and the boundaries that demarcate your body?

The answer is conceptual objectivity. When a region in space, or on land, represents a unique conceptual type, then it is appropriate to identify it as a separate object. For example, national boundaries would become real if people in each country had a unique cultural, philosophical, social, economic, and political outlook. Their ideological differences would identify them as a unique nation, which is quite different from arbitrarily drawing boundaries in space based on administrative control. Similarly, if regions in space represent different meanings, then those regions can be given different names; such is the case with the zodiac signs. Then, if your body represents a different mentality or ideological existence than the table on which your hands are kept, then that hand is part of your body, but the table is not. Similarly, a prosthetic for human body parts attached to your biological system is actually a part of your body, but if you attached artificial wings to your back, they would not be body parts. This is because a human is identified as an idea-like existence that constitutes its objectivity. By the physical way of thinking, either artificial wings attached to your back would also be considered a human body or prosthetics for limbs would not be considered your body. To allow for prosthetics to be your body, and wings to not be your body, we must equate objectivity to the idea.

Sūtra 2.2.24

नापि कर्माचाक्षुषत्वात्

nāpi karmācākṣuṣatvāt

na—not; api—even; karma—activities; acākṣuṣatvāt—from being invisible.

TRANSLATION

Not even activities (can lead to objects) due to being invisible.

COMMENTARY

All activities involve a succession of states, and we call them an activity because something changes thereby creating a trajectory. But we also associate that activity to an object and call that the activity *of* the object. For example, in classical physics, we can associate a trajectory with a particle, and say that the same particle is moving in space. The problem is that we never see the particle itself. So, how can we say that the *same* particle moved to another position in space? This problem is incorrectly solved in classical physics by the concept of continuity of the trajectory, but if atomism is adopted then this continuity is false. Now, you just have a discrete succession of states, and the objectivity that binds these states into the trajectory of a single particle is not visible because there is no continuity. Therefore, we must again employ conceptual unity. For example, we can say that a person is walking, where the 'person' is conceptual objectivity, and 'walking' is conceptual activity. The conceptual activity is based on the *form* of the trajectory, and not merely a succession of states. If a person fell down while walking, we would not include that falling state into the walking state. That is because the form of walking and the form of falling are different. But what is form? It is a pattern in the succession of states, and it is conceptual in nature; many ways of falling would be classified into 'falling' due to the pattern in the states being similar. Thus, again, when we say that a person fell, or a person is walking, then we require concepts to identify the activity.

Sūtra 2.2.25

गुणस्य सतो ऽपवर्गः कर्मभिः साधर्म्यम्

guṇasya sato 'pavargaḥ karmabhiḥ sādharmyam

guṇasya—of the qualities; satah—existence; apavargaḥ—fulfillment; karmabhiḥ—of the activities; sādharmyam—similarity of nature.

TRANSLATION

The existence of qualities, upon the fulfillment of the activities establishes the similarity of nature (between the quality, activity, and the objectivity).

COMMENTARY

As we have discussed earlier, something that looks like a car, but doesn't work as a car, is not truly a car (it could just be the model of a car, for example). Likewise, something that works as a car, but doesn't look like a car, is not a car (it could a truck for example). But if something looks like a car, and works like a car, then it is a car. The objectivity of a 'car' is given by two things—qualities and activities—and hence it is separate from both qualities and activities.

This sūtra, however, gives priority to the activity over the quality. It says that if an activity has been completed, and then if the qualities are also present, then we can identify the similarity between the qualities and activities and arrive at the conceptual object. For instance, if someone was transported over a long distance in a short time, then we can say that the cause can be a car, truck, boat, or an airplane, but it could not be a horse, goat, table, or chair. Thus, when an activity is completed, a number of object-types are eliminated from the possible causes. But there are still many object-types which are equally possible. The quality now acts as a selector among these possible object-types. For instance, you can identify that the cause of transportation was a car by observing its shape, size, color, etc. But the activity selection comes prior to quality selection. In short, before you consider something to be a car by its shape, size, color, etc., you must judge its working condition, fuel efficiency, speed, etc. If those conditions are satisfied, then you can also look at the shape, size, color, etc.

A car that works and looks good is better than a car that works and looks bad. But a car that just looks good but doesn't work is not a car. A bad-looking car is still car, if it works. But a non-working car is not a car, even if it looks good. The activity method for deciding an object is more important than the quality method.

Sūtra 2.2.26

सतो लिङ्गाभावात्

sato liṅgābhāvāt

satah—existence; liṅga—the symptoms; abhāvāt—from the absence.

TRANSLATION

The existence (of objects) can be decided from the absence of symptoms.

COMMENTARY

If someone was transported over a long distance in a short time, then we can say that the cause can be a car, truck, boat, or airplane. Now, qualities of shape, size, color, etc. can be used to decide if the cause was one of these. This sūtra says that we can apply the method of elimination to determine if the cause was a car. For example, if we say that the cause only weighed one ton, then we can eliminate a truck and an airplane from the potential causes. Then if we say that the cause of transportation did not have wheels, then we can eliminate the car from the cause, and conclude that the cause was a boat. In this way, the object can also be decided by the absence of properties, rather than just their presence. That identification, however, is contextual and assumes that we know all the potential causes that could have produced the same kind of effect. If the list of potential causes is not exhaustive, then the method of elimination can lead to a false conclusion. Likewise, if the list of potential causes is exhaustive, but the eliminating factors are insufficient, then we will be uncertain about the cause, although know about it with greater certainty than if the method of elimination was not used. Our perception always operates in both modes; while mentally searching for the perfect idea that matches the qualities and activities, we narrow down the list of potential ideas by the method of elimination, and then we identify the best fit within the narrower list. For example, people who want to buy a car would narrow down the possible list of candidate cars by filtering on price and type of car and then identify the best match in that filtered list.

Therefore, the methods of selection and elimination are complementary approaches used to identify or select something, and this applies to cognition as well. Sometimes, if the method of selection is not working, then the method of elimination can be used to arrive at the final determination of objectivity.

Sūtra 2.2.27
नित्यवैधर्म्यात्
nityavaidharmyāt

nitya—persistent; vaidharmyāt—from the opposing nature.

TRANSLATION
(Objectivity can be decided) from the presence of opposing nature.

COMMENTARY
The last sūtra spoke about the absence of qualities, and the sūtras before that spoke about the presence of qualities, as the method for deciding the objectivity. This sūtra speaks about the presence of *opposing nature*, which is different from the absence of nature and the presence of the intended nature. For example, ideally, you might want to buy a car with zero emissions, which we can call the absence of the quality of emission. Electric cars would work in this case. But you may also not want the burden of having to recharge the electric car frequently so that consideration acts as the presence of an opposing nature—the electric car indeed requires you to charge it frequently. By applying two criteria—(a) low emissions, and (b)

infrequent recharging—you can arrive at a car that is still based on carbon fuel but has low emissions. You may, however, have to pay higher for this car. If instead, your consideration was very low price, then a higher priced carbon fuel car would have the opposing nature.

The same principles can also be applied to perception. If you see a big hump, then objectivity cannot be a horse, as the horse has no hump. But if you see very big ears, then the objectivity cannot be a horse, as the horse has ears, but they are small. In the former case, the absence of a hump decides a horse, which was cited in the last sūtra. And in the latter case, the presence of a small ear decides the horse, and the presence of big ears rules out a horse. Thus, objectivity can be determined by the presence of the desired quality, the absence of some quality, or even the presence of a quality opposite to the desired one.

Sūtra 2.2.28
अनित्यश्चायं कारणतः
anityaścāyaṃ kāraṇataḥ

anitya—temporary; ca—also; ayaṃ—this; kāraṇataḥ—having its cause.

TRANSLATION

This (objectivity) can also be decided from the temporary (incidents or observations) having its cause (in the object).

COMMENTARY

The last sūtra spoke about persistent qualities which are opposed to an object's nature, and this sūtra speaks about temporary manifestations as the means to identify an object. For example, cows regurgitate previously consumed feed and chew on it further. Unlike the cow's tail, hump, or horns, this is a temporary symptom of the cow. And yet, it can be used to identify a cow because other animals don't ruminate. This adds another method to how conceptual objectivity can be identified apart from (a) permanent presence of qualities, (b) permanent absence of qualities, (b) permanent presence of opposing qualities. The temporary presence can further be applied to both desired and undesired qualities. For example, if something even occasionally roars, then it cannot be a cow. And if it even occasionally ruminates then it can be a cow.

All these things might seem trivial to many people because we use them so often intuitively. But these should not be taken trivially as even if our cognition process works so easily, we don't really understand how it works. So, these sūtras should be taken as the description of how cognition works, and the many factors such as (1) activities over qualities, (2) the presence and absence of permanent qualities, (3) the presence and absence of permanent opposing qualities, and (4) the presence and absence of temporary favorable or opposing qualities, that are responsible in the process of identifying the nature of something.

Sūtra 2.2.29
न चासिद्धं विकारात्
na cāsiddhaṃ vikārāt

na—not; ca—also; asiddhaṃ—unachieved; vikārāt—from the modification.

TRANSLATION
Also, (objectivity) is not determined from unachieved modifications.

COMMENTARY
The last sūtra spoke about how temporary manifestations can lead to the determination of an object-type, and this sūtra says that if those temporary manifestations are not seen—after all, they are manifest temporarily—we cannot conclude the absence of objectivity. For instance, a cow can be determined because of rumination. But if the rumination is not observed, it doesn't automatically mean that it is not a cow. After all, the rumination is temporary.

Sūtra 2.2.30
अभिव्यक्तौ दोषात्
abhivyaktau doṣāt

abhivyaktau—the expression or manifestation; doṣāt—from the faults.

TRANSLATION

(The objectivity is not determined) from the manifestation of faults.

COMMENTARY

Ideally, a cow can get pregnant, so pregnancy can be a deciding factor. But if the cow is not getting pregnant, we cannot automatically assume that it is not a cow, because there can be some 'faults' in the cow's reproduction system.

The order among these sūtras is very important, as they indicate the order in which we must apply the principles of conceptual determination. For instance, we must first note that something functions as it is expected to function, then observe its qualities, then observe that opposing qualities are absent, then note that the temporary qualities are present. In this process, we might say that getting pregnant is one of the functions of the cow, but since the cow is not getting pregnant, therefore, it cannot be a cow, and that would stop the process of conceptual determination at the first step itself. This sūtra cautions against that conclusion, by stating that even if something is not working correctly, it may be due to a fault. For instance, a car may have a broken carburetor, and it may not function as a car, but that doesn't mean that it is *not* a car. By the ordinary method of deciding that something is a car if it works as a car, we would have ruled out a faulty car as something that is not a car. But that would result in an erroneous judgment. Therefore, if something doesn't work as a car, we have to dig deeper into the mechanism—which is again qualities, activities, and objectivity—to determine if it is truly not a car or just a dysfunctional car.

This problem makes the conceptual determination an iterative process where just because something works or doesn't work as a car, doesn't mean that it is, or is not a car. For instance, a car may only work occasionally, although when it works, it works perfectly. Likewise, it may occasionally not work perfectly, because it requires maintenance. Thus, we cannot simply determine the conceptual nature by observing the macroscopic phenomena; we must also delve into the deeper mechanisms. Likewise, we cannot conclude anything simply from the microscopic functioning; we must also look at the macroscopic functioning. In this way, knowledge remains incomplete until we understand what a thing is (by observing its permanent qualities and activities), what it is not (by eliminating things that don't have the requisite qualities or have the opposing qualities), by considering the temporary qualities, but not making conclusive decisions based on either the presence or absence of temporary qualities. The problem is that everything is potentially a temporary quality. The color, shape, and size of a car can be changed; its fuel consumption can be altered; we may add truck accessories to the car, and we may remove some things that are typically found in cars, and even car's working can be temporary.

Thus, if we cannot make positive or negative conclusions based on temporary qualities, and everything is potentially temporary, then how do we decide anything? And the answer is that when the nature is temporary, nothing can ever be said with certainty. All conceptual determinations—when the nature is temporary—are therefore potentially false. We might still make a determination based on a majority of factors in favor, and a minority of factors in opposition, but we cannot be certain if that determination is indeed correct. This fact about the material world makes it impossible to know the true nature of things, which is one reason why the material world is considered mostly ignorance in Vedic philosophy. Since things are always changing, whatever ideas you apply today may not work tomorrow. What works in one situation may not work in another. And what seemed to work in one place may not work in another.

Temporariness is the bane of all knowledge, and the last two sūtras drive the nail in the coffin by saying that if something is not always manifest then you cannot conclude a nature because that nature is occasional. Similarly, if it is not manifest then you cannot conclude a nature because there could be faults. You can still try to determine the nature by observing over long periods of time and ruling out the faults. But that requires much more effort. For example, how long must we wait for a temporary nature to appear, before we conclude that the temporary nature is absent? And even if it is found to be absent over a long time of observation, how do we know that its absence should not be attributed to a fault, and not its real nature? The conclusion is that the process can be infinite. Whatever we see can be due to a fault. Whatever we don't see can be due to a fault. And that means that we must rule out the faults to decide anything. But the process of ruling out can also be potentially faulty. And that leads to an infinite regress of ensuring that the faults are eliminated at various levels.

Sūtra 2.2.31
संयोगाद्विभागाच्च शब्दाच्च शब्दनिष्पत्तिः
saṃyogādvibhāgācca śabdācca śabdaniṣpattiḥ

saṃyogāt—from the union; vibhāgāt—from the division; ca—and; śabdāt—from the sound; ca—also; śabda—the sound; niṣpattiḥ—decided.

TRANSLATION

From the union, from the division, and from the sound, also the sound is decided.

COMMENTARY

This sūtra identifies three methods by which names are assigned: identifying, distinguishing, and ordering. For example, if you are looking at a painting, then you group different dots in the picture into groups; this grouping is the act of distinguishing things. Then, we identify each grouping as a different type of object—e.g., mountain, rivers, trees, sun, etc. Finally, we perform an ordering: The sun is far, the mountains are slightly closer, the river is even closer, and the trees are the closest. The śabda or name denotes three things accordingly. First, it identifies a physical collection or boundary, which is then identified as an object. Second, the object is also associated with a type—e.g., mountain or river. And then, the object is also associated with a priority order which we call distance. In modern science, we use the object distinction and the priority order, and these two are equated as a number relative to the observer's coordinate reference. But the painting is objectively real, so the objects are not merely the numbering in the coordinate system; there is also an objective numbering that must distinguish the objects relative to each other. Finally, in ordinary language, we associate these objects with types such as a mountain, river, tree, sun, etc. which are 'names' or 'words', which are similar to numbers, but they have a meaning or type and are not merely quantities, things, or some order.

We can also say that a mountain in the picture is the combination of a type or universal, and an individual which we identify as a boundary in space. And the combinations of these universals and individuals are ordered from the perspective of an observer, which is contextuality. Thus, the same three methods of identifying, distinguishing, and ordering can also be called universality, individuality, and contextuality. The important thing is to understand what these words mean, and then the nomenclature of these meanings becomes clear.

Sūtra 2.2.32
लिङ्गाच्चानित्यःशब्दः
liṅgāccānityaḥ śabdaḥ

liṅgāt—from the symptoms; ca—also; anityaḥ—temporary; śabdaḥ—sound.

TRANSLATION
From the (temporary) symptoms, also the temporary sounds (or names).

COMMENTARY
If the things in the picture we are seeing were temporary, then the methods of identifying, distinguishing, and ordering would also become temporary. Then, the names assigned to these things would also become temporary. So, in an everyday sense, we can denote the changing picture by the changing numbers. But we can also say that underlying the changing picture there is a process of changing identification, discrimination, and ordering. As a result, change can be described either phenomenally as the changing numbers, or as the underlying causality of changing universality, individuality, and contextuality.

Sūtra 2.2.33
द्वयोस्तु प्रवृत्त्योरभावात्
dvayostu pravṛttyorabhāvāt

dvayoh—both; tu—but; pravṛttyoh—produced; abhāvāt—from absence.

TRANSLATION
Both (i.e., the sounds, words, names, or numbers, and the underlying distinguishing, identifying, and ordering) are but produced from absence.

COMMENTARY

This sūtra revives and repeats the Nyāya doctrine of absence as the cause of change. As we have discussed earlier, this absence is the question, problem, or goal, which produces a change and the result is an answer, solution, or achievement. The question, the answer, and the goal reside in the present, but they are not visible as answers, solutions, or achievements. So, they are called 'absence', because the answer, solution, or achievement is missing. When something 'missing' is treated physically, then we get the false impression that absence creates a presence, which means that something must come out of nothing, and the entire doctrine of causality becomes scientifically untenable. But when the absence is treated semantically as a question, problem, or goal, then the same doctrine becomes tenable in a new sense that change occurs only because there is a question to be answered, a problem to be solved, or a goal to be achieved. If there is no question, no problem, or no goal, change will stop.

Sūtra 2.2.34

प्रथमाशब्दात्

prathamāśabdāt

prathamā—the first; śabdāt—from the sound.

TRANSLATION

The first from the sound.

COMMENTARY

This sūtra describes the Vedānta doctrine of śabda-brahman which is the sound representation of Brahman, which means "everything". The first manifestation of the word "everything" is "one thing", but this production of "one thing" is colored by māyā, so it is also *not* something else. But the soul focuses on the "one thing" and it is called pradhāna, which also means "boss" or "master". Sāñkhya describes how subsequent to pradhāna, prakṛti is manifest, which is the desire for different types of mastery. For instance, some people want to be great intellectuals, others want to be very beautiful, and yet others want to be very rich and powerful. Based on these respective desires for mastery, a unique set of ideals or mahattattva are selected. For instance, a great intellectual values novelty and innovation in ideas. But the person who just desires richness and power doesn't care about novelty and innovation; he rather values other qualities like discipline and order. In this way, the prakṛti acts as a selector for what we consider ideals and greatness. Then, based on these ideals, a further identity called ahaṃkāra or "ego" is created, which is the pride, as the soul believes not just that it is a master, that it desires to be a master in a certain way, or that certain qualities of greatness are required for someone to be a master, but also that he already has those qualities, and hence it is already great.

The intellect, mind, senses, and the body are then manifest as proofs or evidences for that pride or ego. In simple terms, if we give up the idea that we are masters, and the idea that possession of certain qualities like hard work, honesty, etc. will make us master, and that we have such qualities already which entitles us to be masters, then we can be free from the material bondage.

The ideas of greatness and mastery seem similar but they must be distinguished. A person with qualities of greatness may not be the boss or master, and a boss or master may not have the qualities of greatness. In the material world, in both these situations, the person remains unhappy. For example, people who have great qualities but are not masters, feel that their greatness is not recognized. But even those who become masters without having great qualities, remain insecure as they know that their position of mastery has no foundation. Thus, the soul tries to combine mastery with greatness with its individuality, to become just like God—i.e., one who is the master because of His greatness.

Together with the soul, therefore, Sāñkhya describes five categories called Brahman (the soul), pradhāna (mastery), prakṛti (choice of a specific type of mastery), mahattattva (the ideals of greatness), and ahaṃkāra (the identity).

The devotees of the Lord are not covered by pradhāna because they don't want to be masters; they just want to serve the Lord. Their prakṛti is that they want to serve the Lord in a certain specific way. Their mahattattva is that they adopt certain ideal standards for performing their service. And their ahaṃkāra is that they are proud of being the Lord's servants. Thus, for the devotee, even if the pradhāna is destroyed, the prakṛti, mahattattva, and ahaṃkāra are not. Rather, they are purified as the desires for the Lord's service, the ideal standards for that service, and the pride in being the Lord's servant. The impersonalist claims that all desires, ideals, and pride are false. But the devotees don't agree. They just replace the pradhāna or the idea of mastery by the idea that we are the Lord's servant, and everything else is naturally transformed. Their intellect, mind, senses, and body are expressions of service to the Lord.

Sūtra 2.2.35

सम्प्रतपित्तभिावाच्च

sampratipattibhāvācca

sampratipatti—complete truth; bhāvāt—from the existence; ca—also.

TRANSLATION

Also, (the sound) is also from the existence of complete truth.

COMMENTARY

As discussed above, the śabda-brahman is a sound representation of Brahman, just like the word "everything" is a representation of everything. The sound representation is the expression and expansion of the complete truth. Just like an artist manifests a painting that previously existed in him as an idea, or a musician produces a composition which earlier existed in him as a form, similarly, the complete truth manifests His own sound representation called śabda-brahman. This śabda-brahman is also sometimes called the mantra OM. Brahman and śabda-brahman have the same meaning—i.e., "everything". But the word "everything" is produced from the source which is everything. In that way, a subtle distinction between Brahman and śabda-brahman is drawn.

Sūtra 2.2.36

सन्दग्धिाःसता बहुत्वे

sandigdhāḥ sati bahutve

sandigdhāḥ—uncertain or doubtful; sati—existing; bahutve—plurality.

TRANSLATION

The uncertainty or doubt in the existence creates plurality.

COMMENTARY

As we have noted, the complete truth is also the abstract truth, and it is uncertain because it is not yet defined in terms of details. This uncertainty in the abstract produces the details, in order to create certainty. Nyāya Sūtra describes a reverse process in which once certain details have been created, there is the absence of the abstract summary. For example, if someone asks you a question, and you provide a simple and short answer, then the listener might say: It is not clear to me; can you elaborate? Then you can explain the same answer with extensive details, and the listener may get tired of these details and say: Can you just summarize it for me? We can also visualize this process by an artist producing a painting. First, the artist draws an outline which is the abstract representation of the picture. Then, he delves deeper into each part of the picture, painting then minuscule details. Finally, when the picture is complete, the artist steps away from the details and looks at the whole painting, and admires it as his own creation. This sūtra just notes the initial process of expansion where the uncertainty in the abstraction causes the production of details.

Sūtra 2.2.37

संख्याभावःसामान्यतः

saṃkhyābhāvaḥ sāmānyataḥ

saṃkhyā—number; bhāvaḥ—nature; sāmānyataḥ—the general concepts.

TRANSLATION

The general concepts have the nature of numbers.

COMMENTARY

As the details manifest one after another from the complete truth, they are also partial truths. And the succession of these concepts can be numbered as one, two, three, etc. The representation of the whole truth (or śabda-brahman) is thus the number one, the first manifestation from that representation is two, the second representation is three, and so on. This sequence of manifestations produces an inverted tree-like structure because at each step there is some uncertainty (as noted in the last sūtra) which is resolved by providing more details. Thus, the larger numbers represent more complex and yet partial ideas, whereas the smaller numbers represent simpler and yet more complete ideas. Just like mammal is more abstract, complete, and yet simpler compared to a cow, which is more complex, detailed, and yet a partial idea, similarly, as the whole truth expands, the successive ideas are also numbers, but the larger number is a complex, incomplete, and detailed idea, while the smaller number is a simpler, more complete, and more abstract idea. This sūtra equates these concepts to numbers, which means that numbers are ideas, rather than quantities.

Of course, once a million such ideas have manifest, then we can count them as first, second, third, etc., and then say that the total number of manifested ideas is a million. But that cardinality of all the ideas, which creates the quantitative view of the numbers, doesn't tell us what the first, second, and third ideas *mean*. In modern mathematics, cardinality is given the greatest importance, the sequencing of first, second, and third is only part of mathematical foundations, and the things being sequenced and how they are manifest from a singular concept are completely disregarded. The fact is that ordering things requires us to identify and distinguish things, which then requires us to treat them as conceptual entities. The order among these things also depends upon the order among the concepts—i.e., which concept is more fundamental than other concepts. Therefore, it is impossible to create correct mathematical foundations unless we delve into the nature of concepts, understand their hierarchical nature, and how they are sequentially produced from prior—more abstract—concepts.

This sūtra simply summarizes this understanding by stating that things are produced from a single source, and successively manifest due to uncertainty, following which we can number things; therefore, these ideas are themselves numbers. This doesn't deny the quantitative view of numbers but states that the quantitative view is based on the more fundamental conceptual view.

CHAPTER 3

Section 1

Sūtra 3.1.1

प्रसिद्धा इन्द्रियार्थाः

prasiddhā indriyārthāḥ

prasiddhā—famous; indriyārthāḥ—the objects of the senses.

TRANSLATION

The objects of the senses are famous (as numbers).

COMMENTARY

The last sūtra spoke about the conceptual nature of numbers, and this sūtra states that numbers are well-known only as ways of identifying sense-objects, or the ordinary things like tables and chairs that we perceive by the senses. This is the acknowledgment of the fact that most people don't understand or view numbers as conceptual entities, or as embodying different kinds of meanings. They simply view them as representing ordinary perceived objects.

Sūtra 3.1.2

इन्द्रियार्थाप्रसिद्धिरिन्द्रियार्थेभ्योऽर्थान्तरस्य हेतुः

indriyārthāprasiddhirindriyārthebhyor'thāntarasya hetuḥ

indriyārtha—the objects of the senses; aprasiddhih—not the common view; indriyārthebhyah—from the objects of the senses; arthāntarasya—of the difference between the meanings; hetuḥ—due to the reason.

TRANSLATION

The objects of the senses are not commonly viewed (different) from other objects of the senses due to the reason of differences between the meanings.

COMMENTARY

This sūtra indicates that the differences between objects are not because of these objects being "things in themselves". The plurality of these objects is rather because they embody meanings, which differ from the meanings in other objects. In very simple terms, no two objects are conceptually identical. All differences in objects arise due to some difference in meaning. We can contrast this idea of difference to that used in modern physics. For instance, in classical mechanics, there is only one *type* of object—the particle—but there are numerous instances of particles. A type of object is defined by the laws that govern it, and all particles are governed by the same laws (e.g., the conservation of momentum and energy). If instead, we say that all objects are distinct from one another because of the differences in meaning, then the implication is that each unique object is also a unique *type* of object. The laws that govern that object are associated with that conceptual type, and hence no two objects in the universe can be governed by the same mathematical laws. To formulate the laws of these objects, we must formulate the laws of meaning, which are in turn comprised of fundamental meanings. Thus, universal laws of objects can be created, but they must be based on how complex meaning is produced from simple meaning and the understanding of the laws governing the simple meanings.

Sūtra 3.1.3

सो ऽनपदेशः

so 'napadeśaḥ

sah—that; anapadeśaḥ—false view.

TRANSLATION

That (which sees objects as not different due to meanings) is a false view.

COMMENTARY

The last sūtra stated that most people don't view the differences between objects as caused due to differences of meaning, and this sūtra explicitly states that such a viewpoint about the objects is a false understanding of the objects.

Sūtra 3.1.4

कारणाज्ञानात्

kāraṇājñānāt

kāraṇa—the cause; ajñānāt—from the ignorance.

TRANSLATION

(The false view arises) from the ignorance of the cause (of differences).

COMMENTARY

All philosophy begins with a difference between appearance and reality. The appearances are that there are separate objects, and the materialistic view converts this appearance into reality by postulating individually distinct things such as particles and waves. This sūtra rejects this view and says that such a viewpoint that treats things as physically distinct entities is ignorant about the cause of differentiation. As we have discussed, all differentiation requires concepts; these include the concepts of qualities (such as taste, touch, smell, sound, and sight), the concepts of objects (e.g., tables and chairs), and the concepts of activities (e.g., running, writing, eating, etc.). When we see different objects, qualities, or activities, that appearance is caused by the application of differentiating concepts. As a result, concepts are not simply mental entities by which we cognize the world; they are also the entities by which the world is distinct. We can term this viewpoint conceptual or semantic realism in which the world is itself comprised of concepts, which then create different appearances.

Sūtra 3.1.5

कार्येषु ज्ञानात्

kāryeṣu jñānāt

kāryeṣu—of the effects; jñānāt—from the knowledge.

TRANSLATION

(The false view arises) from the knowledge of the effects.

COMMENTARY

By the distinction between kāraṇa and kārya or cause and effect, this sūtra along with the previous one explicates the difference between appearance and reality. The "effects" are the appearances, and the "causes" are the reality. The reality is semantic or conceptual, while the appearances seem to be physical.

Sūtra 3.1.6
अज्ञानाच्च
ajñānācca

ajñānāt—from ignorance; ca—also.

TRANSLATION

Also, (the false view arises) from ignorance (even of the effects).

COMMENTARY

The physical model of causality was created by Newton's mechanics and later extended to other areas like heat and light. But this model of causality was ignorant about the true nature of atoms, or the discrete nature of space and time. The study of atoms has shown that they are not independent physical things because changes to the state of one particle alter the states of all the particles in the system. Similarly, the fact that the same reality produces different observations based on the changes in the instruments used for measurement indicates that we are no longer measuring physically independent things. Thus, this sūtra states that the physical view of things is not just ignorance about the causes, but also the ignorance about the true nature of effects. The last sūtra stated that the physical view arises due to the knowledge of effects, which can be seen as the limited ways in which classical mechanics works. Then, this sūtra states that the physical view arises from the ignorance of the effects, which can be seen as the inability to sustain this view even in the case of the observation of atoms.

Sūtra 3.1.7
अन्यदेव हेतुरित्यनपदेशः
anyadeva heturityanapadeśaḥ

anyat—others; eva—certainly; hetuh—the reason; iti—thus; anapadeśaḥ—an invalid argument or false conclusion.

TRANSLATION

Others certainly say that the reason (of the ignorance of the effects as being the basis for the physical view) is an invalid argument or false conclusion.

COMMENTARY

Ever since the birth of atomic theory, there have been numerous attempts to explain away the observed discrepancies between the classical and quantum experiments. Quantum theory describes matter as a state of possibility and these attempts to resurrect determinism in science claim that there must be other material mechanisms that convert this possibility into a reality. All such attempts have failed over the last century, but there is no dearth of people who keep trying to find some new mechanism to preserve the physical view. This is an example of how people resist rejecting the physical view despite the empirical evidence. They want to preserve the prevalent dogmas because acknowledging the necessity of an alternative would mean that everything done so far in modern science over the last 400 years was essentially a mistake. Such an acknowledgment would completely ruin the prestige of modern science.

Sūtra 3.1.8
अर्थान्तरं ह्यर्थान्तरस्यानपदेशः
arthāntaraṁ hyarthāntarasyānapadeśaḥ

arthāntaraṁ—the differences between meanings; hi—because; arthāntarasya—of the difference of meaning; anapadeśaḥ—invalid conclusion.

TRANSLATION

The differences between meanings exist because of the invalid conclusion about the difference of meaning.

COMMENTARY

Everything in this world is something which the other things are *not*. This makes everything an incomplete meaning. Even our bodies and minds are different from the bodies and minds of other living entities because each of the bodies and minds embodies an incomplete meaning. These partial meanings have separated from a whole meaning, and if we look at the reality semantically, then we can see how these realities are like the trunks, branches, twigs, and leaves emanating from a root. That is, underlying this diversity is a unity from which it has sprung, which controls it, and which is the whole truth. But if this unity is not accepted, then only diversity is seen. Each person thinks that they are independent; each body is considered an independent particle or object. This sūtra says that we are in this world of mutually exclusive diversities because we are unable to see how each individual thing is manifest from the unity, has the unity immanent, and is controlled by the unity. By our desire to be independent, we enter a world where things are mutually exclusive.

Everything mutually exclusive is incomplete, and therefore insufficient or inadequate. But since it has chosen independence, the insufficient thing must be responsible for its own existence. Thus, by desiring independence, we become incomplete, insufficient, isolated, and lonely. This is not how reality itself is, but it is how it seems under our desire for independence. Therefore, the "invalid conclusion about the difference of meaning" is that meaning is merely in our minds, or our creation, and has no objective basis. And the existence of the difference of meaning is the mutual exclusion of one thing from another, which makes everything incomplete and isolated, and makes existence miserable. And the root of the problem is our desire to be independent of the whole truth.

Sūtra 3.1.9

संयोगि समवाय्येकार्थसमवायि विरोधि च

saṁyogi samavāyyekārthasamavāyi virodhi ca

saṁyogi—the thing that joins; samavāyi—the inherent; ekārtha—one meaning; samavāyi—the inherent; virodhi—the thing that opposes; ca—also.

TRANSLATION

The thing that joins is the inherent one meaning; the inherent is also the thing that opposes.

COMMENTARY

The mammal is inherent in cows, dogs, cats, and horses, so it is the cause of their unity—they are all mammals. But mammal is also a multifaceted idea, such that different facets of that idea are expressed in cows, dogs, cats, and horses. So, the multifaceted nature of unity is also the cause of diversity.

The Absolute Truth is thus present in every part, but it is immanent and unmanifest. Since it is present in everything, therefore, it is the unity underlying the diversity. However, since that immanent truth is unmanifest, and explicates only one aspect in each thing, therefore, the manifestation of different aspects is the cause of the diversity and differences between individual things. In this way, the Absolute Truth is the cause of diversity and unity. This idea is explained in Vedānta Sūtra as a transcendent truth that produces many parts or aspects, and that truth then becomes embedded in each part as their purpose. Just like the whole divides into parts, and the whole is present in each part as the purpose for the existence of the part, similarly, the Absolute Truth is both the transcendent whole and the immanent purpose in each of the parts. Finally, the parts are nothing other than the aspects of the Absolute Truth. In this way, the Absolute Truth is studied in three ways—(1) the whole truth, (2) the aspects of the whole truth as variety, and (3) the purpose that is immanent in each of the aspects, which then refers to the whole truth. This doctrine can also be understood as a body, which is the whole, its various parts which are the aspects of the body, and the purpose of serving the body which exists in each part.

Sūtra 3.1.10

कार्यं कार्यान्तरस्य

kāryaṁ kāryāntarasya

kāryaṁ—the effects; kāryāntarasya—of the differences of effects.

TRANSLATION

(The differences of meaning are) the effects of the differences of the effects.

COMMENTARY

This sūtra can be easily understood if we visualize an inverted tree in which the root diversifies into trunks, which then diversify into branches, which then diversify into leaves. The trunks are the effects of the root and they represent different aspects of the meaning embodied in the root. Then, as each trunk diversified into branches, the differences of meanings in the trunk become the source of the differences of the meaning in the branches. Therefore, the branches are the effects, and they are the effects of the differences in the trunks. Thus, the Absolute Truth is the kāraṇa, and the manifest world is the kārya.

Sūtra 3.1.11

वरिोध्यभूतं भूतस्य

virodhyabhūtaṁ bhūtasya

virodhi—the thing that opposes (i.e., divides the whole into parts); abhūtaṁ—is the non-existence; bhūtasya—of the existence.

TRANSLATION

The thing that opposes (divides the whole into parts) is the non-existence of existence.

COMMENTARY

The Nyāya doctrine of abhāva is again noted, and this time, 'absence' is called 'non-existence'. This absence or non-existence is the missing details. The absence of details is the question, and the production of details is the answer. The primordial state of the Absolute Truth is that it is some existence and some non-existence, and the non-existence exists within the existence, just like a question exists within the premise, and is manifest from the premise. This question within the premise is also called the desire in the Absolute Truth, and when it arises, then the whole is divided into parts. These parts are also existents but they are now the answers to the question. And the connection between the whole and the part becomes the conditions for truth, right, and good. If the answer satisfies the question, then the answer is true, right, and good. But if the answer becomes connected to something other than the question by which it was produced, then it becomes false, bad, and wrong. An example of this process is the soul, which is manifest from the Lord as the answer to some questions in the Lord. If the soul remains connected to the Lord as the answer to the Lord's desires, then it also remains true, right, and good. But if the soul becomes disconnected from the Lord, and connected to other things that are not truly the questions perfectly suited for the answer, then it becomes false, wrong, and bad. In this way, everything is like a proposition with a question within. The proposition is the existence, and the question is the absence or non-existence.

Sūtra 3.1.12

भूतमभूतस्य

bhūtamabhūtasya

bhūtam—the existent; abhūtasya—for the non-existent.

TRANSLATION

The existent is for the non-existent.

COMMENTARY

When we study the world as material things, then we just speak about which and how many things exist. But if we study them as conscious beings or even things with meaning, then we also ask: Why do they exist? In what way are they useful or important? What is the purpose of their existence? This sūtra makes the contention that the existent is for the non-existent. For example, we are existing because of a purpose. That purpose is not yet fulfilled, and therefore it is non-existent. And yet, we exist to fulfill that purpose. Therefore, the purpose is the real thing, and the existent is a property of that existent. Just like a master employs some servant to fulfill its purpose, similarly, the existent is the servant, and the purpose is the master. The servant is *of* the master, or *for* the master. Modern science focuses only on the 'what' and 'how' questions, but neglects the 'why' question. Why do we exist? Science has no answer, but the materialist would say that the question is itself meaningless. This is because modern science has grown out of the idea that existence is primary and non-existence is secondary. In short, things just exist even if there is no purpose. This sūtra counters this idea and says that the purpose is the primary cause, and whatever exists is the subordinate entity only because of the purpose.

Sūtra 3.1.13

भूतो भूतस्य

bhūto bhūtasya

bhūtah—the existents; bhūtasya—for the existent.

TRANSLATION

The existents for the existent.

COMMENTARY

The last sūtra stated that the existents exist for the non-existent and we might ask: If each thing has a purpose, then what is that purpose? This sūtra answers that question: That purpose is also some existent. For example, in this world, people are chasing property, wealth, knowledge, fame, etc. Within the people who are chasing these things, property, wealth, knowledge, and fame are non-existents, but those things they are chasing are existents. Similarly, when the Absolute Truth divides into parts, the parts are the non-existence in the Absolute Truth, and the whole is the non-existence in the parts. The question in the whole is: What are the parts? And the question in the parts is: What is the whole? Since they are mutually the answers to each other's questions, therefore, they are connected to each other. If they were separated, then the parts would lose the purpose of their existence, as the question would remain unanswered. Likewise, the question in the Absolute Truth would remain unanswered. So, the whole and the parts are both existents, and they are mutually the answers to each other's questions. As a result, this sūtra says that the existent is also for an existent; that is, there is an object which is different from the object, but it constitutes the reason for the existence of the object. This purpose now binds the various objects together, and the manifest reality is not a collection of purposeless fragmentary parts; it is rather a purposeful existence.

Sūtra 3.1.14
प्रसिद्धिपूर्वकत्वादपदेशस्य
prasiddhipūrvakatvādapadeśasya

prasiddhi—the common opinion; pūrvakatvāt—from the previously produced; apadeśasya—the faulty conclusion of this (existent for the existent).

TRANSLATION

The common opinion (that effects are produced) from the previously produced, is the faulty conclusion of this (existent for the existent).

COMMENTARY

Modern science postulates deterministic laws of causation in which an effect is produced from a cause, due to a *rule*, which is called the *law* of nature. But one can ask: Why this rule and not some other rule? What is the reason that the laws of nature could not be different? Modern science has no answer to such questions. It says: These are just rules, and we should not question them. Thus, when the rules are accepted, then the necessity of the rules is ignored.

This sūtra says that this causation by rules is the faulty conclusion of the real fact which is that things are happening due to a purpose. The necessity and sufficiency of logic, or the mathematical laws of nature, are all useless instruments without a purpose because the effect is an answer to the question posed by the cause. If the cause doesn't have a question, why should logic and reason be employed to produce an answer? Conclusions do not follow from the premises without a question. The existence of the question involves a choice, based on a purpose. Thus, all the effects are produced from a cause because there are questions and purposes. The common opinion that things are happening automatically due to some laws of nature, or logic and mathematics, is a false mischaracterization of the real process, which is occurring because of a purpose.

This fact has been proven in modern science as numerous cases of probability and indeterminism arise in every area of science. If we postulate deterministic laws, then we find that their predictions don't match reality. If we reject all laws, then science ceases to exist. So, we postulate some probabilistic laws. Such laws work because, given any premise, there are certain limited questions and answers that make sense—the domain of outcome is not infinite but some limited outcomes. There is also a greater and lesser likelihood of such questions and answers being produced, based on the meanings of the premise, question, and answer because all questions cannot arise from all premises, and all answers cannot be given to all questions. Some questions are more likely for a given premise, and some answers are more likely for those questions; the likelihood is based on meaning, but it is measured as a probability. But the scientific theory cannot capture the underlying mechanism of a premise producing a question and then an answer unless we adopt a semantic view of nature.

Sūtra 3.1.15

अप्रसिद्धो ऽनपदेशो ऽसन् सन्दिग्धश्चानपदेशः

aprasiddho 'napadeśo 'san sandigdhaścānapadeśaḥ

aprasiddhah—uncommon opinion; anapadeśah—faulty conclusion; asat—not existing; sandigdha—suspicious; ca—also; anapadeśaḥ—faulty conclusion.

TRANSLATION

The uncommon opinion about the faulty conclusion is that it doesn't exist, it is suspicious, and also a faulty conclusion.

COMMENTARY

The term 'faulty conclusion' has been used a few times earlier, and this sūtra adds two other conclusions, namely, that the claim of physical reality (which is separated and independent objects) is (a) suspicious, and (b) doesn't exist. The 'faulty conclusion' premise arises from the nature of concepts and how they are used to understand reality. If reality is independent objects, then the properties of concepts—such as abstraction and detail, reference or using one object to talk about another, and representation in which the nature of one object is encoded by another object—become impossible. The impossibility of concepts makes knowledge impossible. This is can be called the *epistemological* route to the conclusion that reality must be conceptual. But there are two other routes—ontological, and moral. In the ontological route, we can bring in empirical evidence to say that collections of objects have different properties than if they were merely a set of independent things. Sometimes additional properties are manifest in the combination, and sometimes the manifest properties are hidden. A collection of things is organized hierarchically rather than linearly. By postulating his hierarchical semantic nature, we can explain empirical differences with a physical collection. This argument against the physical doctrine is called the uncommon view that a physical reality 'doesn't exist' in this sūtra. Then, there is also a moral route to the same conclusion, namely, that if everything was independent objects, then what are the mechanisms for their aggregation that lead to bodies, societies, and other higher constructs? A materialist says that these aggregations are produced randomly, but the problem is that randomness can produce infinite possible collections. So, why this particular collection and not something else? Again, a materialist would say that it is an accident, but a moralist would say that it is not; life has a purpose and nothing happens randomly. The claim that nature is purposeless, that our lives have no meaning, and things are happening due to random aggregations is highly suspect. This moral argument for rejecting the physical view is called 'suspicious' in this sūtra. In this way, we can reject the physical view based on epistemology and philosophy, empirical evidence, ontology, and science, and even based on moral arguments about the existence of purpose and choice in our lives.

Sūtra 3.1.16

यस्मादविषाणी तस्मादश्वः

yasmādviṣāṇī tasmādaśvaḥ

yasmāt—because; viṣāṇī—horns; tasmāt—therefore; aśvaḥ—horse.

TRANSLATION

Because it has horns, therefore, it is a horse.

COMMENTARY

This sūtra compares the 'faulty conclusion' noted in the last few sūtras to the claim that because something has horns, therefore, it must be a horse. As we know, horses don't have horns, so the inference from the symptoms to the reality is false. The 'horns' in this case refer to the common observation that the world comprises of tables, chairs, houses, cars, etc. and since we can break each of these down into smaller parts, therefore, they must have been built up from smaller parts. The common observation doesn't analyze reality as being comprised of the sensations of touch, smell, taste, sound, and sight, which is what the uncommon viewpoint does. There are thus two analysis methods.

For instance, if you were given an apple and asked to explain what it was comprised of, then you can analyze the apple in two ways. First, you can cut the apple into smaller parts, and the limit of that cutting the apple would be considered the most fundamental reality. Second, instead of cutting the apple into smaller parts, you can separate the sensations from one another; for instance, you can say that the apple has both color and shape, but these are different properties, so the apple is produced from their combination. The common view of cutting the apple says that we must break it down into smaller pieces of apple. And the uncommon view says that we must separate the properties and treat those properties as the fundamental ingredients of reality.

Now, it is imperative to note that both methods of cutting are possible, so let us call them 'structural cutting' and 'conceptual cutting'. The structural cutting produces smaller physical parts, but it progresses hierarchically—namely, you first cut the apple into two pieces, then each of the two pieces into further two pieces, and so on. Once you get to the smallest pieces of apple, then you cannot cut the apple without separating the properties such as taste, smell, touch, sound, and sight. This method of cutting is also hierarchical, but it involves a conceptual hierarchy. The physical view neglects this fact. It says: If I have been able to cut the apple into smaller parts using a knife, then I should be able to carry on this process until I find the smallest physical parts. The conceptual view of cutting says that once you reach the smallest objects, then you can still cut them by separating out the properties into "property atoms".

Of course, the fact is that due to the hierarchical nature of both structural and conceptual organization, the reality is not independent things, and this becomes evident due to the failure of classical physical theories. But the materialist wants to claim that if we can imagine that an apple could be comprised of some physical particles, then it would indeed be such a thing. This idea of imputing properties of entanglement, organization, and structure to something that can never in principle have such thing is called a "horse with a horn" in this sūtra. The horse is the materialism, and the horn is the observed properties. Someone who infers the presence of the horns into the existence of a horse makes a false conclusion because they are fundamentally incompatible. But supposing that there could be some horses with horns—even if we have no way of explaining how—is the favorite delusional pastime of the materialist.

Sūtra 3.1.17

यस्मादविषाणी तस्मादगौरितिचानैकान्तिकस्योदाहरणम्

yasmādviṣāṇī tasmādgauriticānaikāntikasyodāharaṇam

yasmāt—because; viṣāṇī—horns; tasmāt—therefore; gau—cow; iti—thus; ca—also; na—not; ekāntik—only one; asya—of this; udāharaṇam—example.

TRANSLATION

Because there are horns, therefore, it must be a cow; thus, also the example of this (interpretation of reality from the observation) is not only one.

COMMENTARY

This sūtra further demystifies the last sūtra by saying that even if "horse with horns" is a fallacious conclusion, the "cow with horns" is not. In other words, there is more than one way of interpreting the observations into an understanding of reality, if we simply understand that hierarchical organization is found in everything, so matter cannot be independent physical particles.

Sūtra 3.1.18

आत्मेन्द्रियार्थसन्निकर्षाद्यन्निष्पद्यते तदन्यत्

ātmendriyārthasannikarṣādyanniṣpadyate tadanyat

ātma—the self; indriyārtha—the sense objects; sannikarṣāt—from the combination by attraction; yat—that which; niṣpadyate—falls out as being produced; tat—that; anyat—is different.

TRANSLATION

That which falls out as being produced by the combination of the soul and the sense objects is different (from the common opinion of people).

COMMENTARY

This sūtra goes to the root of materialism and identifies it as the rejection of the soul, and the misunderstanding about a living and a dead body. The body is the instrument of sensation, cognition, judgment, intention, and valuation. Accordingly, there are many levels of semantic reality that act as the goggles of perception. The observer or the soul interacts with the sense-objects through these goggles and obtains the sense percepts, concepts, judgments of truth, good, and right. Something is considered good if it aligns with our goals, and something is considered right if it matches our system of values. Therefore, the moral sense, ego, intellect, mind, and the senses are considered the 'covering' of the soul, because the same soul can also perceive the world as a different set of values, goals, beliefs, thoughts, and sensations. When the soul is removed from the theory of experience, then gradually, each of the levels of morality, intention, judgment, thought, and sensation is gradually collapsed and one ends up with just the body. Now, this body is described as a physical thing, and even though the theory cannot explain the conscious experience or even the material phenomena, the materialist insists that he will one day find that explanation. In short, the delusion is maintained by postponing the problem. If instead the soul is recognized, then the numerous levels of reality such as valuation, intention, judgment, thinking, and sensation are realized. Then, the body is also described differently—compatible with the existence of the varied levels of meaning. And even ordinary objects like tables and chairs are understood differently. Thus, the recognition of the soul is not merely a religious or spiritual idea; it has a direct impact on the understanding of inanimate objects too.

Sūtra 3.1.19

प्रवृत्तनिवृत्ती च प्रत्यगात्मनि दृष्टे परत्र लिङ्गम्

pravṛttinivṛttī ca pratyagātmani dṛṣṭe paratra liṅgam

pravṛtti—engagement; nivṛttī—detachment; ca—also; pratyak—in the opposite direction; ātmani—in the soul; dṛṣṭe—are seen; paratra—elsewhere; liṅgam—the symptoms.

TRANSLATION

The engagement and detachment are also in the opposite direction to the vision in the soul; they are the symptoms of things that exist elsewhere.

COMMENTARY

When materialism is rejected, and the soul's existence is recognized, then a doctrine—called Idealism—is touted to be the answer to all the problems of materialism. It says: There is no external world; all the so-called reality is merely an impression in our consciousness. Therefore, what we call 'matter' is conscious experience, and what we call the 'observer' is consciousness. However, this 'matter' acts on the consciousness to create the impression of external reality, when there is no such reality. This doctrine of Idealism is also called Advaita; it recognizes two categories—Brahman and māyā; Brahman is the observer, and māyā is the cause of experience, which creates the delusion of reality. This sūtra rejects the conclusion of Idealism and says that the engagement and detachment with the sense objects are in the opposite direction to the vision of the soul; that is, there is a real external reality. Furthermore, our experiences are not merely in our consciousness; they are rather the symptoms of an external reality. This doctrine is sometimes called Realism, but it is different from materialism because the external reality is semantic rather than physical. Thus, the Vedic viewpoint should be seen as opposed to both materialism and idealism; while advocating the reality of the soul, the reality of the world is not rejected. But because both realities exist, the nature of matter must be altered to explain morals, intentions, judgments, thoughts, and sensations, besides the objects. This is possible if matter is itself semantic; each tier of reality is semantic, but it is more abstract than the previous reality. This means that even tables and chairs have a deeper structure of the organization in which we speak of them not just as physical things, but also as object-concepts, embodying a belief system, meant to fulfill some intentions and by-products of a moral system.

Section 2

Sūtra 3.2.1

आत्मेन्द्रयिार्थसन्निकिर्षज्ञानस्य भावो ऽभावश्च मनसो लिङ्गम् ३,२.१ ।

ātmendriyārthasannikarṣajñānasya bhāvo 'bhāvaśca manaso liṅgam

ātma—the soul; indriyārtha—the sense objects; sannikarṣa—union by attraction; jñānasya—knowledge of; bhāvah—the nature; abhāva—the non-nature; ca—also; manasah—the mind; liṅgam—symptoms.

TRANSLATION

The knowledge of nature and non-nature, produced by the soul's union by attraction with the sense objects, is also a symptom of the mind.

COMMENTARY

The senses, mind, intellect, ego, and the moral sense are all different types of goggles through which we perceive the world. The sense goggles give us sensations; the mind goggle tells us about the object concepts; the intellect goggle tells us if the perception is true or false; the ego goggle tells us if this perception is good or bad for us, and the moral sense goggle tells us if the perception is right or wrong. Each of these goggles is ideological. That is, we will perceive the world in terms of the ideas that we have already acquired. If we have come to believe that the world is particles and waves, then wherever we look, we will only find particles and waves. As the saying goes, the world looks like a nail to one who only has a hammer. The purpose of informed education is to give us the correct goggles so that we can see the world in the correct manner.

Thus, this sūtra talks about the influence of the mind on correct perception. If we don't know what a table is, but we are acquainted with chairs, then if a table was presented to us, we will think of it as a large chair with missing hand rest and arm rest. Similarly, if we have acquired false beliefs, then the truth will seem false to us, and the falsity will seem true. If our intentions are bad, then those with good intentions will be considered evil, and those with evil intentions will be considered good. If we have wrong moral ideals, then those with similar moral ideals will seem to be right, and others with the right moral ideals will seem wrong. Thus, what we perceive, understand, judge, intend, and value is a by-product of the mental conditioning of ideas, beliefs, intentions, and values. The mind's conditioning also filters things that don't fit the goggles. Thus, a person accustomed to thinking that things happen randomly, will not see the order in nature; he will think that this order is also randomness.

Thus, if the soul acquires contaminated goggles, then the reality is either filtered or distorted or both, in our perception. Therefore, this sūtra says that nature and non-nature produced by the interaction of the soul with the sense-objects depends on the mind (not just on the senses, as in the last sūtra).

Sūtra 3.2.2

तस्य द्रव्यत्व नित्यत्वे वायुना व्याख्याते

tasya dravyatva nityatve vāyunā vyākhyāte

tasya—its (referring to the mind); dravyatva—objectivity; nityatve—persistence; vāyunā—of Air; vyākhyāte—is explained.

TRANSLATION

The objectivity and persistence of that mind is explained as of Air.

COMMENTARY

The statement "dravyatva nityatve vāyunā vyākhyāte" was made twice earlier—once referring to space and then referring to time. As we noted then, the more abstract reality is longer-lived. Since Air is more abstract relative to Fire, Water, and Earth, therefore, it is also considered to be longer-lived. This sūtra extends the previous statements about the objectivity and persistence of Air to the mind. The mind is even more abstract, hence even more persistent.

Sūtra 3.2.3

प्रयत्नायौगपद्याज्ज्ञानायौगपद्याच्चैकम्

prayatnāyaugapadyājjñānāyaugapadyāccaikam

prayatna—effort; ayaugapadyāt—from the non-simultaneity; jñāna—knowledge; ayaugapadyāt—from non-simultaneity; ca—also; ekam—one.

TRANSLATION

From the non-simultaneity of effort, also from the non-simultaneity of knowledge, (we conclude that there is only) one mind.

COMMENTARY

We have five senses of knowledge and five senses of action. But we can only draw attention to one of these senses at one time. If you are focusing on sight, then the sound is unheard; if you are focusing on hearing, then the sight is invisible. However, because the mind rapidly moves attention from one sense to another, therefore, we don't notice this mutual exclusivity of sensations. The Yoga practices thus teach a person to focus on one thing—the sound of a mantra—in order to concentrate the mind and cease its movement from one sense to another. If the mind can be stopped in this way, then wherever the mind is concentrated, that specific sense or faculty becomes extremely strong and capable. The mind itself becomes very powerful simply by concentration, which anyone can test by practicing. Thus, this sūtra says that the mind is constantly moving between the senses of knowledge and action and the mutual exclusivity of our attention to one of these things means that there is only one mind.

Sūtra 3.2.4

प्राणापाननिमेषोन्मेषजीवनमनोगतीन्द्रयान्तर विकाराः सुखदुखेच्छाद्वेष प्रयत्नाश्चात्मनो लिङ्गानि

prāṇāpānanimeṣonmeṣajīvanamanogatīndriyāntara vikārāḥ sukhaduḥkhecchādveṣa prayatnāścātmano liṅgāni

prāṇa—ascending breath; apāna—descending breath; nimeṣa—closing eyelids; unmeṣa—opening eyelids; jīvana—life; manogati—the movement of the mind; indriyāntara—between senses; vikārāḥ—modification;

sukha—happiness; duḥkha—unhappiness; icchā—desire; dveṣa—aversion; prayatna—effort; ca—also; ātmanah—of the soul; liṅgāni—the symptoms.

TRANSLATION

Ascending and descending breath, the opening and closing of eyelids, the movement of the mind between senses, the mind's modifications of happiness, unhappiness, desire, aversion, and effort, are also the symptoms of the soul.

COMMENTARY

This sūtra clearly identifies the symptoms of a living body that must be attributed to the soul's presence. When the soul leaves the body at death, these symptoms end. This includes purely mechanical processes like the opening and closing of the eyes. The list is well-known to everyone, and yet, the materialist likes to believe that he can explain these things without the soul. When those claims are not successful, the materialist changes the parameters by which the success must be measured—to whatever he has already achieved materially. This sūtra lays down an unchangeable set of parameters to decide whether a body is living or dead (without, of course, the influence of external agents).

Sūtra 3.2.5

तस्य द्रव्यत्वनित्यत्वे वायुना व्याख्याते

tasya dravyatvanityatve vāyunā vyākhyāte

tasya—of that (soul); dravyatvanityatve—objectivity and persistence; vāyunā—of; vyākhyāte—explained.

TRANSLATION

The objectivity and persistence of the soul are explained as Air.

COMMENTARY

The principle of abstraction leading to longevity, which was previously applied to Air, and then applied to the mind, is here applied to the soul. The soul is eternal because it is more abstract than all of the properties in matter. Just like color is abstract because it can be associated with innumerable shades, and yet, it is not any of those shades, similarly, the abstractness of the soul is that it can be associated with innumerable material bodies and minds, and yet it is not any of these bodies and minds. The difference between matter and soul is that matter has the property of representing the knowledge of other things, but it doesn't have the property of self-representation or self-knowledge. The soul, therefore, uses matter to know material things, but it doesn't need matter to know itself. If it uses matter to know itself, then it is a false identification because self-knowledge is not other-knowledge. The knowledge of other things requires some effort but the knowledge of the self is sprung spontaneously from within—provided we stop the identification with false material identities.

Sūtra 3.2.6

यज्ञदत्त इति सन्निकर्षे प्रत्यक्षाभावात् दृष्टं लिङ्गं न विद्यते

yajñadatta iti sannikarṣe pratyakṣābhāvāt dṛṣṭaṁ liṅgaṁ na vidyate

Yajñadatta—name of a person; iti—thus; sannikarṣe—proximity and attraction; pratyakṣa—direct observation; abhāvāt—from the absence; dṛṣṭaṁ—the vision; liṅgaṁ—the symptoms; na—not; vidyate—known.

TRANSLATION

From the absence of direct observation arising due to proximity and attraction, only Yajñadatta is seen as symptoms (of the soul); (the soul) is not known.

COMMENTARY

As we have discussed earlier, sometimes the cause is not empirical, but its effects are empirical. Those empirical effects require us to postulate the existence of a non-empirical cause—if only to explain the empirical effects. If we attribute the empirical effects to some material causes, then the explanation would never be consistent and complete. As we approach greater completeness, we will also find more contradictions in our theories. And if we resolve those contradictions, then the theories will be more incomplete. Thus, the necessity of the non-empirical reality is forced by theoretical conditions of consistency and completeness. In this case, the soul is the non-empirical cause of the empirical effects such as breathing.

Hence if we reject the soul's existence, then we cannot explain the empirical effects of the soul's presence consistently and completely.

Sūtra 3.2.7

सामान्यतो दृष्टाच्चाविशेषः

sāmānyato dṛṣṭāccāviśeṣaḥ

sāmānyatah—general class; dṛṣṭa—seeing; ca—also; aviśeṣaḥ—universal.

TRANSLATION

The universal is also the seer of the general class.

COMMENTARY

To directly observe an entity, the instrument of observation must be at least of the same level of abstraction as the entity being measured. For example, color is more abstract than yellow, and hence, the instrument (e.g., the eyes by which we see) that embodies color can be used to measure yellow. Instruments that encode meanings less abstract than the soul cannot detect the soul's presence.

Thus, the materialist claim that the soul's existence must be confirmed empirically already assumes that all things are of the same type—the soul and the instrument measuring it are of the same type. If instead matter encodes abstract and detailed meanings, then the instruments of detailed variety cannot measure the objects of an abstract variety. This principle also applies to the soul—to measure the soul, the instrument of measurement must be at least as abstract as the soul. Therefore, if the direct perceptual capacities of the soul were developed, then it can perceive the existence of other souls. Until that development, one can only infer the soul's presence from theories that can explain the effects.

Sūtra 3.2.8

तस्मादागमिकः

tasmādāgamikaḥ

tasmāt—therefore (because the previous sūtra said that the soul cannot be perceived by the material body); āgamikaḥ—it is known via scriptures.

TRANSLATION

Therefore (because the previous sūtra said that the soul cannot be perceived by the material body), the soul is known via scriptures.

COMMENTARY

Many modern religions have corrupted the meaning of 'scripture' as a collection of rules and principles to be accepted on faith and obeyed without questioning. Otherwise, in the Vedic system, scripture is a scientific theory established by questions and answers, arguments and justifications, evidence and reason. Therefore, if we say that the soul's existence must be accepted based on scripture, the real meaning is that the scripture presents arguments about why the soul is real, what its real nature is, and how that nature can be realized through the practice of various Yoga forms. Thus, there is preliminary motivation, detailed theoretical explanation, and practical confirmation by practice. However, because the meaning of 'scripture' has been corrupted by other religions, therefore, the statement that the "soul's existence must be accepted based on scripture" is generally taken to mean—(a) no theoretical formulation, (b) no practical method to realize the theory, and (c) no scope for questioning.

This, however, is not the meaning of 'scripture' here. By 'scripture' we don't mean just any book that just claims to be God's revelation. That revelation must be established based on rational discussion, should be consistent and complete, and its truth must be confirmable through the practice of some method. There must also be examples of people who have confirmed it by that method. All these conditions are satisfied in the Vedic scriptures which provide: (1) theory of the soul, (2) its empirical symptoms, (3) the methods of practice, and (4) the examples from the lives of the great personalities who have realized it.

Sūtra 3.2.9

अहमिति शिब्दस्य व्यतिरेकान्नागमकिम्

ahamiti śabdasya vyatirekānnāgamikam

aham—"I-ness"; iti—thus; śabdasya—the sound of this; vyatireka—exclusive; na—not; āgamikam—the teaching of the scriptures.

TRANSLATION

The teaching of the scriptures is not that the sound of the word "I-ness" means exclusiveness (to the other individuals who use the sound I-ness).

COMMENTARY

So many people have been murdered in the name of religion in modern times that we can easily say that the killers thought that they were exclusive from those whom they killed. Any religion that gets mixed up in political or national ideology leads to the idea that "we are exclusive from the others". That exclusion is presented as racial, national, or ideological superiority over others, and the nations and people then kill each other to establish their superiority. All such religions mixed with politics are the mundane ideas of the ignorant. They have nothing to do with the soul's true nature and its connection to God. Vedic texts describe how God is the whole, and the soul is the part. God and soul are not identical, but also not separable. Likewise, the souls are also different and yet not separable. This doctrine is called by various names like Advaya or non-opposed, Avyatireka or non-exclusive, Abheda or non-separable.

Sūtra 3.2.10

यदि दृष्टमन्वक्षमहं देवदत्तो ऽहं यज्ञदत्त इति

yadi dṛṣṭamanvakṣamahaṁ devadatto 'haṁ yajñadatta iti

yadi—if; dṛṣṭam—observation; anvakṣam—afterward; ahaṁ—"I ness"; devadattah—the person's name, Devadutta; ahaṁ—"I-ness"; yajñadatta—another name, Yajñadatta; iti—thus.

TRANSLATION

If a person right after saying "I" is observed to say "Devadutta", or "I am Yajñadatta", thus (we can know that he is not following the scriptures).

COMMENTARY

A common cultural difference between West and East is that people in the West introduce themselves as "I am John", whereas a person from the East will generally say "My name is John". The fact is that "John" is the name tied to the body, not to the soul. Therefore, if someone says "I am

John" it is obvious that he thinks that he is the body called John. But if they say that "My name is John", then it is obvious that "John" is how they can be called, but they are not John. The distinction between the body and the soul means that the name doesn't refer to the true nature of the soul, its qualities, or even its eternal identity. A person who legally changes their name doesn't cease to be the person that he was.

This sūtra refers to "I am Devadutta" and "I am Yajñadatta" phenomenon as the root of the idea that Devadutta and Yajñadatta are mutually exclusive.

Sūtra 3.2.11

दृष्ट्यात्मनि लिङ्गे एक एव दृढत्वात् प्रत्यक्षवत् प्रत्ययः

dṛṣṭyātmani liṅge eka eva dṛḍhatvāt pratyakṣavat pratyayaḥ

dṛṣṭyātmani—seeing the self; liṅge—in the symptoms; eka—one; eva—certainly; dṛḍhatvāt—from the conviction; pratyakṣavat—as if directly perceived; pratyayaḥ—the attributes.

TRANSLATION

Certainly, from the conviction in the soul, the self is seen in the symptoms, as if directly perceived in the attributes.

COMMENTARY

The deeper levels of material reality may not be directly perceived by the senses, but their effects can always be directly perceived. For example, when a person is angry or happy, we cannot perceive anger or happiness, but we can perceive its symptoms in the body. The beliefs and moral values of a person may not be perceived by the senses, but their effects can be perceived in what the person says and does. The intentions of a person are also not seen by the senses, but their effects on the body are seen in the person's activities. Similarly, the choices of the soul have effects on the body which can be perceived, although the soul cannot be perceived. Thus, a person who has developed the conviction in the soul's existence is able to see all the deeper levels of reality including the soul, in the bodily parts which are called pratyaya in this sūtra. One who has advanced perception can understand a person's mentality, beliefs, intentions, morals, and choices, just by the observation of the body.

Sūtra 3.2.12

देवदत्तो गच्छतियज्ञदत्तो गच्छतीत्युपचाराच्छरीरे प्रत्ययः

devadatto gacchati yajñadatto gacchatītyupacāraccharīre pratyayaḥ

devadattah—the person called Devadatta; gacchati—goes; yajñadattah—the person called Yajñadatta; gacchati—goes; iti—thus; upacārāt—from the secondary movements; śarīre—in the body; pratyayaḥ—parts.

TRANSLATION

Devadatta goes, Yajñadatta goes, thus from the secondary movements in the bodily parts.

COMMENTARY

The material body, senses, mind, intellect, ego, moral sense, etc. are just potentials. They cannot act on their own. They become active in the presence of the soul. The materialist believes that matter moves automatically because he doesn't understand that matter moves only under the presence of the soul. Thus, if a person is walking, there is a will or choice that triggers that movement. Just like a fan rotates when the switch is turned on, the switch is turned on by our hands which act under the mind's influence, the mind acts under the control of the intellect, the intellect under the control of the ego, the ego under the control of the moral sense, and the moral sense under the control of the soul. There is indeed machinery in which a number of steps are automated. But there is still something that is not automatic—it is the choice of moral values, which creates goals, which accepts some beliefs that satisfy the goals, which generates some thoughts compatible with the beliefs, which translate into sense activity, which alters the state of the body, which pushes on the fan switch, which then causes the fan turn. The materialists remain unaware of this hierarchical and complex process by which the soul's will is translated into the fan's movement, and he thinks that if the body is the cause of the fan's movement, and the body is material, therefore, the soul's choices must also be material. Bur this sūtra rejects such conclusions. The bodily activities are imputed to the soul because there is a choice that converts the body's potentiality into an observable reality.

Sūtra 3.2.13
सन्दग्धिास्तूपचाराः
sandigdhāstūpacārāḥ

sandigdha—doubtful; tu—but; upacārāḥ—the secondary actions.

TRANSLATION
The secondary actions are but doubtful.

COMMENTARY
The bodily actions underdetermine the thoughts, but the thoughts determine the bodily actions. Similarly, the thoughts underdetermine the beliefs, but the beliefs determine the thoughts. The beliefs underdetermine the intentions, but the intentions determine the beliefs. And intentions underdetermine the moral values, but the moral values determine the intentions. In this way, if we simply observe bodily activity, then we can neither predict nor explain its occurrence until we also understand the deeper levels of reality. If the deeper level reality is known, then the shallower level reality is predicted and explained. Thus, this sūtra states that the secondary actions are "doubtful". What is this doubt? It is the indeterminism in predicting and explaining bodily activity. When something is indeterministic, the results cannot arise randomly. Indeed, since matter exists in a state of potentiality, therefore, it will remain a potential until sufficient reason is present. Thus, deeper levels of reality become necessary in science to solve the problem of predictive indeterminism. The soul is a deeper level of reality that addresses some forms of indeterminism in matter (God is similarly necessary in science to address other forms of indeterminism).

Sūtra 3.2.14
अहमिति प्रत्यगात्मनि भावात् परत्राभावादर्थान्तर प्रत्यक्षः
ahamiti pratyagātmani bhāvāt paratrābhāvādarthāntara pratyakṣaḥ

aham—"I-ness"; iti—thus; pratyagātmani—recovered in the soul; bhāvāt—from the existence; paratra—in the place beyond; abhāvāt—from the absence; arthāntara—the differences of meaning; pratyakṣaḥ—direct observations.

TRANSLATION

The "I-ness" is thus recovered in the soul; from the existence in the place beyond (the material existence), and from the absence (the feeling of incompleteness in the soul) the differences of meaning become directly observable.

COMMENTARY

The soul is transcendental to the material nature, but when it is outside the relationship to the Lord, then it feels incomplete. This incompleteness is called māyā, and it is termed abhāva or absence in this sūtra. Everyone in this world is insecure and fearful because they feel incomplete and they try to overcome that incompleteness by acquiring material things. Some people thus find security in wealth, some in knowledge, some in fame, some in beauty, and so on. From the insecurity in the soul arises the need to become the master and boss. From the need to be the master, arises the principles of greatness by which one can be a legitimate master. From that greatness arises the false ego that one is capable of becoming great because one has some quality of greatness. From that goal of becoming great in a specific manner arise some beliefs about how one can become great. Those beliefs then lead to thoughts, which then produce sensual activity, which then translate into bodily actions, which then manipulate the material objects—all with the goal to become great and overcome the innate sense of insecurity and incompleteness. However, no matter how much fame, power, wealth, knowledge, beauty, or other forms of greatness are acquired, the sense of insecurity is never overcome unless the soul is situated again in the relationship to the Lord. This process can begin only when one realizes that the soul is different from the body, senses, mind, intellect, ego, the moral sense, and the sense of incompleteness. If the soul is not accepted, then the further steps of realizing the spiritual identity do not occur, and one iterates from one body to another, simply trying to overcome the incompleteness in various ways.

Sūtra 3.2.15

देवदत्तो गच्छतीत्युपचारादभिमानात्तावच्छरीरप्रत्यक्षो ऽहङ्कारः

devadatto gacchatītyupacārādabhimānāttāvaccharīrapratyakṣo 'haṅkāraḥ

devadattah—Devadatta; gacchati—goes; iti—thus; upacārāt—from the secondary activities; abhimānāt—from the pride; tāvat—in that way; ca—also; śarīra—body; pratyakṣah—direct observation; ahaṅkāraḥ—the false ego.

TRANSLATION

"Devadatta goes" is thus from the secondary effects (of the body) and from the pride also; in that way, we can directly observe the false ego.

COMMENTARY

In Sāñkhya philosophy, the ego is the "I am" identity. It arises from a preconception of what we understand to be greatness, which is prior produced from the desire to be great, which prior arises from the sense of insecurity. When this sense of insecurity overwhelms a person, then even though they have the ideas of greatness, their ego is weak: They no longer consider themselves great, or even capable of achieving greatness. The sense of insecurity paralyzes the person, which is sometimes called anxiety and depression. The confidence in one's ability to do great things instead is called the ahaṅkāra or false ego. This ego drives a person toward hard work and a sense of accomplishment. Such a person takes pride in their actions, and says: "I have done this". Factually, all the activities were done by the body; the soul simply chose what must be done, based on the available opportunities, and the bodily capabilities. The person who realizes the truth about the soul, also realizes that all claims about "I have done this" are factually false. Those achievements are due to the body, although attributing the activity to the soul is not false because the body acts under the direction of the soul. Thus, two contradictory ideas must be understood simultaneously. First, the pride in the achievements of the body is falsely attributed to the soul. Second, those achievements would not arise without the soul. Hence, we cannot reject the soul's existence, and we cannot feel proud about the body's achievements, or depressed due to their absence.

Sūtra 3.2.16
सन्दग्धिस्तूपचारः
sandigdhastūpacāraḥ

sandigdha—doubtful; tu—but; upacāraḥ—the secondary activities.

TRANSLATION

The secondary activities (in the body) are but doubtful.

COMMENTARY

This statement was also made previously after noting that the bodily changes are secondary effects of the soul. Then, the statement meant that the bodily activity will remain indeterministic without the soul. Subsequently, the reality of the ego was also recognized, but as something different from the soul. Therefore, this particular statement about indeterminism must be taken to mean that merely the presence of the soul would not completely determine the differences between the body types or their activities. Rather, the soul must be the agency that determines the ego, and the ego then determines the body.

Sūtra 3.2.17
न तु शरीरवशिेषाद्यज्ञदत्त वष्णुिमत्रियोर्ज्ञानवषियः
na tu śarīraviśeṣādyajñadatta viṣṇumitrayorjñānaviṣayaḥ

na—not; tu—but; śarīra—body; viśeṣāt—from the specific; yajña-datta—the person called Yajñadatta; viṣṇumitrayoh—of the person called Viṣṇumitra; jñāna—knowledge; viṣayaḥ—the object.

TRANSLATION

But, from the individual bodies of Yajñadatta and Viṣṇumitra, the object (i.e., the soul that controls these individual bodies) is not known.

COMMENTARY

This sūtra further nuances the description of the soul. In previous sūtras, it has been said that the body works under the soul's control, that the soul's presence can be detected from the body's functioning, and yet bodily successes or failures should not be attributed to the soul. This sūtra extends this point by saying that the soul cannot be known from the body. That is, the bodily gender is not the soul's gender; the bodily color is not the soul's color; the age of the body is the not soul's age. Even though the soul's effects are seen on the body, the soul is not the body. Just like a car will not drive itself; it needs a driver, and so the driver's actions result in effects in the car, but the driver is not the car.

Sūtra 3.2.18

अहमतिि मुख्ययोग्याभ्यां शब्दवद्व्यतरिकाव्यभचारािद्वशिेष सद्धिेर्नागमकिः

ahamiti mukhyayogyābhyāṁ śabdavadvyatirekāvyabhicārādviśeṣa siddhernāgamikaḥ

ahamiti—I am the only; mukhya—the master; yogyābhyāṁ—by the union; śabdavat—sound-like; vyatireka—exclusive; avyabhicārāt—from the undivided; viśeṣa—individual; siddheh—achieved; na—not; āgamikaḥ—scriptural.

TRANSLATION

That I am the only master by the union with the sound-like (body), an exclusive individual is achieved from the undivided, is not scriptural doctrine.

COMMENTARY

This sūtra attacks the impersonal doctrine in which Brahman is divided into separate individual souls by the union with māyā. If this combination is removed, then oneness is attained. The impersonalists quote the Upaniśad statement "aham brahmasmi", built from three roots—aham or I-ness, brahma or Brahman, and asmi—identity or type—and neglect the last root of asmita which means identity or type. Thus, "aham brahmasmi", is taken to mean "I am Brahman" when the correct meaning is that "I-ness is of Brahman type". Right now, if you ask someone who they are, then they will say: "I am human", "I am man or woman", "I am black or white", "I am tall or short", etc. Thus, their asmita or self-identity comprises of many types—human, man, woman, black, white, tall, short, etc.

The Upanišad says that you are none of these things; your type is Brahman—that is sat-chit-ānanda. Type-based thinking is also the outcome of a semantic viewpoint in which whatever we call the body is not a substance, but meaning. Similarly, the soul is also a unique meaning, within the class of meanings that are true, right, and good, as opposed to material meanings, which are false, wrong, and bad. When this semantic view of matter is rejected, then Brahman becomes a "substance" and māyā becomes the cause of dividing this substance into objects—just like clay is divided into lumps and then given a potted form. Now, the impersonalist claims that there is only one substance—clay—and there are numerous pots; therefore, when the pots are broken, we are left with clay. This substantivalist doctrine of the soul is rejected here. In fact, it is not just refuted as a wrong idea that could be justified based on Vedic texts, but an un-Vedic idea. Unfortunately, it is the dominant view of Vedic philosophy the present and touted as the alternative to modern materialism. But the fact is that it cannot be used to understand matter scientifically. If matter is not understood scientifically, then the soul is not properly distinguished from matter. As a result, the doctrine fails on both counts of science and religion.

Sūtra 3.2.19

सुखदुख ज्ञाननिष्पत्त्यविशेषादैकात्म्यम्

sukhaduḥkha jñānaniṣpattyaviśeṣādaikātmyam

sukhaduḥkha—happiness and distress; jñāna—knowledge; niṣpatti—produces; aviśeṣāt—from the universal; eka—one; ātmyam—soul-nature.

TRANSLATION

From the universal is produced the knowledge of happiness and distress and the one soul-nature.

COMMENTARY

The impersonalists recognize only two categories—Brahman and māyā—but this sūtra introduces a third category—the Universal—from which both the soul and matter are produced. The impersonalists like to say that what we call "God" is nothing but Brahman descended into matter and covered by it, just like a soul. The difference is simply that "God" is an enlightened soul, while the "soul" is non-enlightened. Then, the difference between the soul and God is simply enlightenment; if you become enlightened, then you also become God. These claims, however, are concoctions of the impersonalist mind. As we have discussed, the soul enters the material world trying to become the master. This desire for mastery was termed "mukhya" in the last sūtra. When the soul fails to obtain mastery by acquiring material things, then it decides to become the master by renouncing matter. This renunciation of matter and a pseudo-acceptance of Vedic texts, while rejecting the primary principle of surrender to the Lord, seems like religion, but it is only the desire for mastery in disguise.

Sūtra 3.2.20

व्यवस्थातो नाना

vyavasthāto nānā

vyavasthātah—arrangement; nānā—of the many.

TRANSLATION

(Also produced from the Universal) is the arrangement of the many.

COMMENTARY

The arrangement of many things requires a hierarchical organization, in which there is a singular controller at the top, and the diversities below are controlled. There can be several levels of control in which a controller is also controlled. Such hierarchical organization is seen in the case of governments and businesses. This sūtra states that the Universal manifests the system of hierarchical organization, which means that a leader or mukhya must be at the top. The impersonalist likes to think that there is no leader or mukhya, as there are no individuals, and the individuality of the soul is an illusion created by māyā.

This problem with this doctrine is this—It moves all the complexity of our experience—the varieties of emotions, the diversities of cognitions and conations, and the numerous arrangements through relationships—into a single bucket called "māyā", and then rejects the entire bucket as an "illusion", thus simplifying the doctrine of religion. This simplicity now attracts two kinds of people—(a) those who are not intelligent and cannot understand the complexity but would like to consider themselves superior by rejecting it, and (b) those who are envious of the Lord, or scared of responsibility, retribution, and punishment for their own choices. Such so-called religious people produce neither science nor religion. They cannot produce science because they have rejected matter as an illusion, so why this illusion is governed by rational order becomes impossible to explicate. And they cannot produce religion because God has already been rejected—as yet another illusion. Thus, of the three categories that the Vedas discuss—God, soul, and matter—two are designated as illusory. Only the soul is partially real, as even the soul's individuality is illusory.

With so much variety in the illusion and so little reality, the onus of explaining how this reality produces the illusion falls on the impersonalist. But the impersonalist escapes this responsibility because (1) the people loving this doctrine are not intelligent and hence they do not ask deep questions about how the illusion came into existence, and (2) they are relieved of the pressure of responsibility, retribution, and punishment by thinking that there is no God. Impersonalism creates armchair philosophers who neither have the urgency to ask important questions nor are they concerned about the absence of answers.

Sūtra 3.2.21

शास्त्रसामर्थ्याच्च

śāstrasāmarthyācca

śāstra—the scripture; sāmarthyāt—from the prowess; ca—also.

TRANSLATION

Also produced from the prowess (of the Universal) are the scriptures.

COMMENTARY

This sūtra states that the Lord also creates the scriptures as the knowledge of the soul, matter, and their origin—He Himself. The existence of these scriptures is also a problem for the impersonalist, because if only the Brahman is real, then scriptures must also be illusory. But the impersonalist gets around this problem by saying that scriptures are created by "enlightened souls". But the question is: How did these souls get enlightened without the scriptures? Did they perform a rational-empirical process to become enlightened, and then wrote the scriptures to help other non-enlightened souls? If so, then why should anyone else believe in the scriptures, instead of the rational-empirical process? If scriptures are the creations of a rational-empirical process, then shouldn't everyone be qualified to create their own scriptures by the same process? Then again, as already stated by the impersonalist, the rational-empirical process is an illusion. So, how did the process of practicing illusion produce enlightenment? Thus, numerous problems are created with regard to knowledge when impersonalism is accepted. First, how did these scriptures arise? Second, how can true knowledge arise by an illusory process? And third, why shouldn't anyone else produce arbitrary scriptures based on the same illusory process?

CHAPTER 4

Section 1

Sūtra 4.1.1

सदकारणवन्नित्यम्

sadakāraṇavannityam

sat—that which exists; kāraṇavat—just like the cause; nityam—eternal.

TRANSLATION

That which exists is eternal, just like the cause.

COMMENTARY

After challenging many premises of impersonalism, this sūtra criticizes the main idea, namely, that the material world is temporary, and whatever is temporary must be an illusion. It argues that even ordinary things that we see—e.g., tables and chairs—are eternally existent; they are just not eternally visible to us. How are they eternal? Because they are concepts that are eternally possible. They become manifest in our vision by the combination of three kinds of possibilities—the universal, individual, and contextual. The combination is temporary, but the ingredients are not. Even the temporary things exist, and they are produced from the eternal; so, the material world is not an illusion.

And yet, it is *false*. Just like the statement "I love you" is eternally possible, is sometimes manifest, and it can be true or false. The truth of the statement depends on it being consistent with a person's thoughts, feelings, beliefs, etc. and anything that is not consistent with deeper reality is false. Thus, the statement "I love you" can be false if it is uttered without similar types of thoughts, beliefs, and feelings. The root of these inconsistencies is the soul which takes shelter in false identities, unable to accept the reality that it is a servant of the Lord. Sometimes the truth is revealed, namely, that the soul is helpless. And sometimes, the truth is hidden, namely, that the soul pretends to be great.

Temporariness is the outcome of an inconsistency between what the reality is, and what we want it to be. When the truth is revealed, and we don't want to accept it, we create an illusion hoping that it will last. But it doesn't. Why? Because the truth reveals itself again. So, if we stopped our attempts to create a false identity, and accepted the truth, then the inconsistency would end, and that would end the change. Does this mean that the world is temporary? Or does this mean that our childish attempts to suppress the truth are temporary?

The impersonalist confuses these two very different things and claims that the world is temporary and hence false. By that measure, even the scriptures would be temporary, and even rational-empirical methods would be illusory. That would entail that there is no source of knowledge. If we have to distrust everything in here, then why would we not distrust impersonalism too?

Sūtra 4.1.2

तस्य कार्यं लिङ्गम्

tasya kāryaṁ liṅgam

tasya—of that (eternal truth); kāryaṁ—effects; liṅgam—the symptoms.

TRANSLATION

The symptoms of that eternal truth are the effects (of that truth).

COMMENTARY

All experience is produced by the combination of the universal, individual, and contextual; these three, and their various subparts, are eternal. And yet, their combinations can be temporary. Thus, this sūtra states that the symptoms we experience are the effects of the eternal truth, but they are temporary.

Sūtra 4.1.3
कारणभावात् कार्याभावः
kāraṇabhāvāt kāryābhāvaḥ

kāraṇabhāvāt—from the nature of the cause; kāryābhāvaḥ—the nature of the effects.

TRANSLATION

From the nature of the cause, the nature of the effects.

COMMENTARY

The material and spiritual worlds have identical ingredients. But due to inner contradictions between the various levels of reality, what we see in this world is almost never the truth, or at least not the whole truth. The falsity or illusion arises because the superficial reality is inconsistent with the deeper reality. If we created weapons out of paper, and clothes out of steel, then both weapons and clothes would not truly be those things. That doesn't mean that paper, steel, weapons, or clothes are false. It just means that the combination of paper and weapon, and clothes and steel is incorrect. The spiritual and material worlds have the same ingredients—paper, clothes, weapons, and steel. And yet, the spiritual world is eternal, because the combinations are *appropriate.*

The cause of these two worlds has all the properties that we eventually perceive. And yet, by creating *inappropriate* combinations we create a false nature in which the apparent and deeper realities are mutually inconsistent. Therefore, the difference between matter and spirit is very simple—inappropriate and appropriate combinations. If the desire in the soul is to become something that it is truly not, then it creates inappropriate combinations out of its own wishful thinking, but that inappropriate nature of things remains temporary. If on the other hand, the desire in the soul is to be what it truly is, then that desire produces appropriate combinations, which are then eternal. Since both material and spiritual worlds have the same ingredients, therefore, they have a common cause in the Lord. But the difference in the soul's desire produces the difference. Therefore, the temporary world is produced out of the soul's desires; what we see in the material world is a reflection of what earlier existed in the soul.

Sūtra 4.1.4
अनित्य इति विशेषतःप्रतिषेधभावः
anitya iti viśeṣataḥ pratiṣedhabhāvaḥ

anitya—temporary; iti—thus; viśeṣataḥ—the individuals or specifics; pratiṣedha—forbidden; bhāvaḥ—nature or existence.

TRANSLATION

Thus, the temporariness of individuals or specifics is forbidden nature.

COMMENTARY

Many people are prepared to accept the eternal nature of the universals, but not of the individuals. For instance, in Plato's philosophy, the universals are accepted to be eternal but the symbols of these universals—e.g., the actual tables and chairs in this world—are temporary. This discrepancy arose because the Greeks treated the material world to be 'substance', which was amorphous, and it obtained a 'form' when it combined with some universal. But what is a substance? Is it not some taste, smell, touch, color, hardness, roughness, etc.? If we closely analyze substance, then it also becomes a collection of universals, and its instantiation or what we call 'matter' must also require individuals.

The impersonalist insists that there is only one substance—Brahman—and all the properties (universals) and things (individuals) are due to māyā. The impersonalist may also agree that the universals are eternal, and must reject the eternity of the individuals to account for the changing nature of the world. But then, how are these individuals created? Why are there many dogs and cats, instead of just one? If we say that māyā itself creates these individuals, then we must end up with materialism, as there is absolutely no need for Brahman. Similarly, if the individuality is created by māyā, then all the subsequent choices of a person, which arise due to their personal choices, must also be the by-product of māyā, and no individual should be held responsible for those choices. Then why are some people suffering while others are happy? Why is someone poor while others are rich? Why are some people beautiful, while others are ugly?

When we consider all the problems arising from the rejection of individuality, then we can conclude that individuality is also eternally real.

This applies not just to the individuality of the soul, but also to the material particles. And yet, this individuality is just like the universality—it may not always be manifest. Hence, the soul can 'merge' into Brahman, and appear to lose its individuality, not because there is no individuality, but because it is unmanifest. Likewise, all the material particles can merge into a single individual, not because these particles are not eternal, but because individuality is unmanifest.

Sūtra 4.1.5
अविद्या
avidyā

avidyā—ignorance or delusion.

TRANSLATION

(The temporariness of individuals) is ignorance or delusion.

COMMENTARY

The soul is a part of the Lord. The part is not merged into the whole; the whole is not an epiphenomenon of the parts; and the whole and the parts are not truly separable, although they are conceptually distinct. The materialist says that the whole is reducible to the parts, and has no separate reality. The impersonalist says that the parts are merged into the whole, and have no separate reality. Many modern non-Vedic philosophies draw a stark distinction between soul and God. But the Vedic texts reject all these varied viewpoints.

The soul and God are like cow and mammal. The cow is not merged into the mammal; the mammal doesn't reduce to cows, horses, dogs, and cats; and the cow cannot truly be separated from the mammal, although they are distinct: the cow is a mammal but the mammal is not a cow. Thus, various kinds of doctrines—diversity without unity, unity without diversity, or unity reduced to diversity—are rejected in the Vedic texts. The previous sūtra stated that the temporariness of the individual is forbidden nature, and this sūtra says that if someone doesn't accept that, then that position is delusional or ignorant. This is a direct reference to impersonalism which rejects the individuality of the soul. The use of strong words like ignorance or delusion indicates how stridently Vedic texts reject such ideas. And yet, many people faithfully adhere to them. Perhaps, if they study the Six Systems of Philosophy, then can know the truth.

Sūtra 4.1.6

महत्यनेकद्रव्यवत्त्वात् रूपाच्चोपलब्धिः

mahatyanekadravyavattvāt rūpāccopalabdhiḥ

mahat—greatness; aneka—many; dravyavattvāt—from object-like; rūpa—forms; ca—also; upalabdhiḥ—obtained or produced.

TRANSLATION

From mahattattva, many object-like forms are also obtained or produced.

COMMENTARY

As we have discussed earlier, the Sāñkhya system describes five categories of Brahman, pradhāna, prakṛti, mahattattva, and ahaṃkāra. The pradhāna is produced from the combination of Brahman and māyā or the sense of "I am not (great)". That inadequacy leads to the desire to be the pradhāna or the master. The specific type of inadequacy that the soul feels transforms into the desire for a specific type of mastery, which is called prakṛti, or the material "personality". That desire produces the principles of greatness called mahattattva—which if truly acquired would make the soul truly great. These principles then produce the ahaṃkāra or the ego, namely, the idea that "I am great". Thus, through a five-step process, the original "I am not great" becomes "I am great". This sense of greatness is false because it is produced from inadequacy. It is an outward projection of greatness from the inner feeling of its absence. Therefore, when the ego is hurt a little, then the feeling of inadequacy returns quickly to the surface. It sometimes manifests as anger and frustration, and at other times into anxiety and depression. It is the root cause of all the misery in the world.

Since the soul is covered by māyā, therefore, the "I am" of the soul becomes "I am not great" due to māyā, which becomes "I want to be great" due to pradhāna, which becomes "I want to be great in this specific way" due to prakṛti, which becomes "I must have the qualities of greatness" due to mahattattva, and then "I am great since I have great qualities" which is called ahaṃkāra.

The ego or the ahaṃkāra is a false identity, and it springs out of mahattattva. This sūtra refers to that ego, which springs from mahattattva. However, it would not spring if there was no soul, which felt inadequate and then wanted to become great, and then would eventually consider itself great.

The term 'individuality' therefore essentially indicates pride in oneself. Individualistic cultures encourage the inculcation of pride and confidence in oneself, to the point that a person disregards the individuality and pride of others. Such cultures perpetuate the illusion of greatness in each person, which is very dangerous because the moment that pride is destroyed, self-loathing sets in. The destruction of pride is inevitable and every egoistic culture eventually wallows in anxiety and depression because they have learned to cover up the fear and insecurity by a sense of illusory pride. Any display of weakness is frowned upon in such cultures, but there are no profound reasons to be truly proud of. Thus, if the superficial reasons for pride are removed, then a person becomes aimless. Their resurrection out of that miserable state is realizing their spiritual identity. But instead of teaching that spirituality, the materialists try to reinforce a false sense of pride in their nation, race, culture, materialistic goals, etc.

In the context of matter, too, the individuality or ahaṃkāra springs out of the universal principles of greatness or mahattattva. In simple terms, the individual things are manifest out of the universal concepts. These individual things then further manifest other universals like objectivity, quality, and activity, which we have discussed earlier. Therefore, it is hard to separate individuality and universality because the universals manifest from the individual, and the individuals manifest from the universals. That separation is made contextually—e.g., the individual called the ahaṃkāra manifests from the universal called mahattattva, and the universals called objectivity, quality, and activity manifest from the individual called ahaṃkāra. Sāñkhya also describes the latter process where the ahaṃkāra is said to divide into three modes called sattvic, rajasic, and tamasic. As we have discussed earlier, the activity manifests from the object, and the quality manifests from the activity. In this way, enormous variety is embedded inside each simple idea and manifest from within it.

Sūtra 4.1.7

सत्यपि द्रव्यत्वे महत्त्वे रूपसंस्काराभावाद्वायोरनुपलब्धिः

satyapi dravyatve mahattve rūpasaṁskārābhāvādvāyoranupalabdhiḥ

satyapi—even though existing; dravyatve—objectivity; mahattve—greatness; rūpa—form; saṁskāra—impressions; abhāvāt—from the absence; vāyoh—the Air element; anupalabdhiḥ—non-obtainment or non-accessibility.

TRANSLATION

Even though objectivity, greatness, and form are existing, from the absence of the Air element, they are not obtained or not perceived (i.e., those object-like forms can be spoken of and can be thought, but they cannot be touched).

COMMENTARY

As we have discussed earlier, the material nature constructs an inverted-tree like structure, which we can simply call "space". Every individual thing, property, activity—including the senses, mind, intellect, ego, and the moral sense—are simply parts of this tree-like space. All the trunks, branches, twigs, and leaves of this tree can be given a name or number. As a result, we can speak about the entire tree in ordinary language. However, because the meanings of these words vary considerably, therefore, they generate different kinds of experiences. The physical description of reality simply involves studying the tree as names or numbers. But the semantic description must treat it as meaning.

These meanings can be cognitively classified into three categories—sensations, concepts, and judgments. The sensation words have a greater emotive aspect; the concepts have a greater cognitive aspect, and the judgments have a greater relational aspect. Since everything is comprised of these three modes, therefore, every part of the tree can be described in terms of these components. A good example of this fact is the use of sensations even at the level of mental concepts. For example, we use terms like "black heart", "green with envy", "obtuse character", "rough demeanor", "shallow talk", "deep ideas", "hard life", "coming down heavy", "sweet person", "bitter truth", and so on, to describe purely mental entities that should not be associated with sensations. And yet, these terms are applicable because everything has sensual, cognitive, and judgment components. If you use the term "deep ideas" to describe something, you mean three things—(a) something is hard to reach, (b) these are ideas, and (c) they are something to be respected and valued. The idea is the cognition, the respect tied to it is a judgment, and the hard-to-reach aspect is sensual.

With this background, we can understand this sūtra as describing the individuals manifest due to ahaṃkāra as being devoid of the sensual components of touch, sight, taste, and smell. These individuals are rather like words and numbers which don't yet have cognitive, relational, and emotional components. This sūtra states that even though objectivity, greatness, and form are present, within these individuals, these are not manifest as sense perception. Objectivity is the identification of the individual as a table or chair. The greatness is the claim that this table or chair is of good or bad quality, expensive or cheap. And the form is the association of the table or chair with some shape, size, color, weight, etc. Thus, the individuals are just pure thing-in-themselves entities that cannot be classified, judged, or perceived. And yet, we can say that these are "individual things". The type of object, its sense perceivable qualities, and whether the object is great or not, will be manifest subsequently from these individuals. Until then, there is a thingness without an associated experience.

A good way to understand this stage of existence is to grasp the use of words like "this" and "that", "here" and "there", etc. These pronouns identify individual entities without saying whether they are tables or chairs, great or not, or what their shape, size, color, etc. are. These manifest subsequently.

We must remember that the individual is created *after* some greatness has been identified, and the type of greatness is the reason for its individuation. And yet, the greatness remains hidden from the sense perception of others. Therefore, these statements pertaining to the absence of greatness, objectivity, and form should be understood as pertaining to the perception of *others*. They are not statements about the factual absence of all the qualities of greatness.

Sūtra 4.1.8

अनेकद्रव्यसमवायात् रूपविशेषाच्च रूपोपलब्धिः

anekadravyasamavāyāt rūpaviśeṣācca rūpopalabdhiḥ

aneka—many; dravya—objects; samavāyāt—from the

inherent presence; rūpa—form; viśeṣa—specific; ca—also; rūpa—form; upalabdhiḥ—obtained.

TRANSLATION

From the inherent presence of many objects, a specific form is obtained.

COMMENTARY

This sūtra states that the specific form of the object, namely, its conceptual type such as table or chair, its properties like shape and size, its greatness—i.e., whether it is expensive or cheap—and its relation to other things which define whether it is placed in kitchen or bedroom, are manifest from the object. This means that the potentiality of numerous possibilities about that individual exists within the individual, and they are manifest from that individual. The numerous potentialities of being different things are called "many objects" here, and they are said to be inherently present in the individual. And yet, since one or few of these potentialities manifest, therefore, a specific form is created.

Sūtra 4.1.9

तेन रसगन्धस्पर्शेषु ज्ञानं व्याख्यातम्

tena rasagandhasparśeṣu jñānaṁ vyākhyātam

tena—by that; rasa—taste; gandha—smell; sparśeṣu—of touch; jñānaṁ—knowledge; vyākhyātam—is described or explained.

TRANSLATION

By that, the knowledge of taste, smell, and touch is described.

COMMENTARY

The last sūtra noted the manifestation of objectivities along with a form, which should, in the given context, be understood as the visible shape, color, etc. This sūtra now describes the manifestation of even more properties of that object, noting three such properties—taste, smell, and touch. The term rūpa or 'form' has many meanings. First, it can denote a conceptual object. Second, it can represent a structure, such as that of a table. Third, it can also denote the property of color, shape, size, etc. The order of manifestation is that there is a conceptual object, which then expands into a structure which we can call the 'design' of the object, as it comprises of many functional parts. This structure then further expands into the atomic units of taste, touch, smell, and sight. However, given the subtle distinction between the 'design' and shape and size, the term rūpa or form is noted only once in the previous sūtra. This doesn't mean that touch follows the shape and size; as we have discussed, the element Air is subtler than the Fire element. So, the implication is not that the components of vision such as shape and color are manifest *before* the touch is manifest. This is just the terminology where both design and shape are called rūpa.

Sūtra 4.1.10

तस्याभावादव्यभिचारः

tasyābhāvādavyabhicāraḥ

tasya—of that; ābhāvāt—from the absence; avyabhicāraḥ—the unity.

TRANSLATION

From the absence of that (form, touch, smell, taste), the unity.

COMMENTARY

The properties of taste, touch, smell, and sight create various aspects of an object. Likewise, the structural design creates many parts. But if we remove the sensed properties, then we can think of the design, or the conceptual object, as one entity. This entity also has a deeper level individuality of being "this" or "that", without having a conceptual object-type or even a structural design.

Sūtra 4.1.11

संख्याःपरिमाणानि पृथक्त्वं संयोग वभिागौ परत्वापरत्वे कर्म च पद्रव्यसमवायात् चाक्षुषाणि

saṁkhyāḥ parimāṇāni pṛthaktvaṁ saṁyoga vibhāgau paratvāparatve karma ca rūpadravyasamavāyāt cākṣuṣāṇi

saṁkhyāḥ—numbers; parimāṇāni—quantities; pṛthaktvaṁ—separateness; saṁyoga—union; vibhāgau—and division; paratvāparatve—in the superior and inferior; karma—activity; ca—also; rūpa—shape (quality); dravya—objects; samavāyāt—from the inherent presence; cākṣuṣāṇi—the visible things.

TRANSLATION

Numbers, quantities, separateness, union, and division, in the superior and inferior objects, qualities, and activities—these are from the inherent presence of the visible things.

COMMENTARY

The materialist doctrine of variety in nature is that it arises due to varied combinations of some fundamental particles. The Vaiśeṣika, and other Vedic systems, dispute this idea; variety is not due to the combination of things; it rather springs out of some primordial state of matter. Just like meaning exists in the mind as an idea, but when it is expressed into a sentence, then there are individual words that are separated from other words, and then they are also combined into a structure, similarly, variety springs out of the unity. Once this variety has sprung, then it has to be distinguished using concepts, identified using concepts and ordered as prior or posterior, superior and inferior, using concepts. This distinguishing, identifying, and sequencing then leads to numbering and counting. Thus, this sūtra states that the basic principle is not numbering and counting, upon which materialism is based. It is rather founded on how variety springs out of unity from an inherent unmanifest state.

Sūtra 4.1.12

अरूपिष्वचाक्षुषाणि

arūpiṣvacākṣuṣāṇi

arūpiṣu—in that which is without form; acākṣuṣāṇi—invisible things.

TRANSLATION

In that which is without form, there are invisible things.

COMMENTARY

The impersonalist says that Brahman is formless, and form is added externally by māyā. But this sūtra says that even if something seems formless, the form is hidden inside that thing, and it springs out of the formless just like a tree grows out of the seed. Just like the ordinary seed requires some environment—soil, water, air—to sprout, similarly, the soul also requires the presence of the Lord to manifest its form. If the Lord is forgotten, then the soul remains formless, unaware of its true nature. In this formless state, there is always a question: Who am I? What is the purpose of my existence? This question can then lead the soul either to a material or a spiritual body. If the soul contacts matter, then matter develops into a form in the soul's presence, which the soul considers its own form although that form is external and temporary. If the soul contacts the Lord, then the soul develops into a form, which is the soul's true and eternal form, and yet, it is manifest only through the Lord's contact.

In this way, the soul is like soil and water for matter, because matter unfolds the hidden form in the soul's presence. And the Lord is like the soil and water for the soul, because the soul unfurls the hidden form in the Lord's presence. The chanting of the Lord's names is a simple way to associate with the Lord, and it is compared to the soil and water for the soul-seed. In this way, the soul is considered superior to matter because matter remains unmanifest without the soul's presence. Similarly, the Lord is considered superior to the soul because the soul form remains unmanifest without the Lord's presence. The Lord, however, is always manifest, and therefore nothing else is needed to cause the manifestation of other things. In fact, the soul-seed and the matter-seed are themselves the products of the manifestation from the Lord. As parts of the Lord, they are just like Him, but since they are controlled by the Lord, therefore, they are not equal to the Lord. The Brahman and māyā are therefore two kinds of seeds in which the māyā unfurls due to Brahman and the Brahman unfurls due to the Param Brahman. He is param or supreme, because He is also a living entity, and yet, as the whole truth, He controls the soul's true unfurling.

Sūtra 4.1.13

एतेन गुणत्वे भावे च सर्वेन्द्रियं ज्ञानं व्याख्यातम्

etena guṇatve bhāve ca sarvendriyaṁ jñānaṁ vyākhyātam

etena—in this way; guṇatve—in the qualities; bhāve—in the existent; ca—also; sarvendriyaṁ—all senses; jñānaṁ—knowledge; vyākhyātam—is described.

TRANSLATION

In this way also, the knowledge in the qualities, in the existents, and of all the senses, is described.

COMMENTARY

Sense perception requires three kinds of entities—an objective reality, a sense that perceives that reality, and the quality or property which is present in the objective reality and can be present in the senses. In Sāñkhya, these three are called bhūta, indriya, and tanmātra. For example, if you see an apple, then the objective existence of the apple is called bhūta, and the senses of perception are called indriya. The shape, color, size, etc. are the tanmātra and they exist in the apple and can exist in the senses (during sense perception). Therefore, sense perception is the process of unfurling the tanmātra from within the senses. In this unfurling, the sense is like the seed, and the apple is like water and soil that causes the seed to sprout. Thus, when the process of perception is described, then it is said that the tanmātra is manifest from the indriya, such that color, shape, size, etc. are the by-products of our senses—under the influence of the water and the soil of the real apple. Different water and soil will produce a different kind of color, shape, and size, so there is a one-to-one correspondence between the thing we see and the world that triggers the perception. This correspondence between perception and reality makes us say that the apple itself has taste, touch, smell, etc. even though these are produced by our senses.

The water and soil of sense perception—i.e., the apple—are also manifestations of an individual from within the universal—the concept apple—and its properties of color, shape, and size are manifestations from within the individual. The individual apple manifests from the universal apple under the presence of a soul. Therefore, the soul is the water and soil for the seed of universal apple to sprout. If the soul did not exist, then the apple would not sprout, and then its successive properties would also not be manifest. In this way, some entities manifest due to the presence of other material entities, but eventually, a soul is necessary to manifest those entities. Similarly, the Lord is necessary to manifest the soul. The difference is only that the Lord is completely autonomous, the soul is less autonomous, and matter is the least autonomous. Hence, the Lord can control the soul, and the soul can control matter. As the soul identifies with matter, it loses the ability to control matter and is controlled by it. Thus, the purpose of knowledge is to understand how the soul is different from matter, causes the material manifestation, but is still subordinate to the Lord.

All material things are some limited potentialities—they are not infinite, and they are not fixed. The potentialities in each thing are also more likely or less likely due to their hierarchical organization. As a result, these possibilities can be associated with probabilities, and they are, in modern atomic theory. But this probabilistic description of matter is an incomplete understanding. If we understand how the potentiality is hidden inside each thing, how it is organized hierarchically, how some external conditions trigger the manifestation of these potentialities, and which condition triggers which potentiality, then we can describe matter perfectly. If something is not perceived, then the potentiality lies hidden inside, and perception is the process of triggering that potentiality.

Section 2

Sūtra 4.2.1

तत्पुनःपृथिव्यादिकार्यद्रव्यं त्रिविधिं शरीरेन्द्रयिविषियसंज्ञकम्

tatpunaḥ pṛthivyādikāryadravyaṁ trividhaṁ
śarīrendriyaviṣayasaṁjñakam

tat—that; punaḥ—again; pṛthivi—the Earth element; ādi—etc.; kārya—effect; dravyaṁ—conceptual objects; trividhaṁ—three-fold; śarīra—body; indriya—senses; viṣaya—the sense-objects; saṁjñakam—nomenclature.

TRANSLATION

Again, these effect-objects such as the Earth element, etc., are known in a three-fold nomenclature—the body, the senses, and the sense-objects.

COMMENTARY

The senses and the sense-objects have been discussed earlier, and the nature of the body is discussed in the next sūtra. As we have noted earlier, the terms five elements are sometimes restricted to describing the sense-objects. But at other times, properties such as hardness, roughness, heat, coldness, loudness, softness, color, shape, and size, etc. are also attributed to thoughts, judgments, intentions, and morals. Thus, there can be big ideas, rough judgments, circular intentions, and cold morals. This sūtra applies this principle to the senses. Our senses themselves can be hot and cold, hard and rough, etc. The presence of a certain quality in the senses makes us attracted to those qualities, and also makes it easier for us to understand those qualities when such qualities are present. Thus, those who are emotionally cold naturally understand those who have the same nature but find it hard to understand those with an emotionally warm nature. Such natures are either incomprehensible or disliked or both.

Sūtra 4.2.2

प्रत्यक्षाप्रत्यक्षाणां संयोगस्याप्रत्यक्षत्वात् पञ्चात्मकं न विद्यते

pratyakṣāpratyakṣāṇāṁ saṁyogasyāpratyakṣatvāt pañcātmakaṁ na vidyate

pratyakṣāpratyakṣāṇāṁ—of perceptible and imperceptible; saṁyogasya—of union; apratyakṣatvāt—due to that which is imperceptible; pañcātmakaṁ—the body comprised of five-fold elements; na—not; vidyate—known.

TRANSLATION

By the union of perceptible and imperceptible, the body comprising of the five-fold elements is not known due to that which is imperceptible.

COMMENTARY

The materialist says that the body is reducible to chemicals, the chemicals to atoms, and the atoms to subatomic particles, because while these particles, atoms, and chemicals can be perceived, their combination into a structure—as cells, organs, systems, and the entire body—is imperceptible. This is just like a people organization in which we can see the people, but we cannot see the hierarchical organization structure. That doesn't mean it doesn't exist; it also doesn't mean that the hierarchical structure has no empirical effects. And yet, we cannot perceive the structure by the senses because it is not taste, touch, smell, sound, and sight. And yet, it is still possible to apply sense-perceptible qualities to it. For example, we can say that the organizational structure is hard and heavy, big or small, flat or steep, bitter or sweet, etc. In this way, the five elements, even when not sense perceivable can be used to describe structures. This description involves another mode of nature than the sense perception.

Sūtra 4.2.3

गुणान्तराप्रादुर्भावाच्च न त्र्यात्मकम्

guṇāntarāprādurbhāvācca na tryātmakam

guṇāntara—differences of qualities; aprādurbhāvāt—from not being manifest; ca—also; na—not; tryātmakam—in a three-fold manner.

TRANSLATION

The differences of qualities (caused by the combination of perceptible and imperceptible) from not being manifest are not in a three-fold manner.

COMMENTARY

As we discussed before, the combination of redness with light, rose, and cross produces different kinds of meanings—a red light means stop, a red rose means love, and a red cross means life. The qualities of love, life, and danger exist within redness, and they are evoked due to the presence of contexts. The difference is that the quality is associated with the whole structure, rather than its individual parts. Therefore, while the parts are divided in three ways—e.g., knower, known, and knowing—the structure is the combination of these three parts and hence undivided. Therefore, if we say that the structure is 'hard' or 'heavy' it is not about one part being hard or heavy; it is about the whole structure being hard or heavy. Of course, a larger structure can be divided into smaller parts, and each such part can also be heavy or light, hard or soft. But the methods of dividing a structure are four-fold, seven-fold, and so on. This sūtra simply says that they are not three-fold. That doesn't mean that the structure cannot be subdivided. It just means that the division is not three-fold.

Sūtra 4.2.4

अणुसंयोगस्त्वप्रतिषिद्धः

aṇusaṁyogastvapratiṣiddhaḥ

aṇusaṁyogah—the combination of atoms; tu—but; apratiṣiddhaḥ—not forbidden.

TRANSLATION

(It is not three-fold because) the combination of atoms is not forbidden.

COMMENTARY

Even a casual look at molecular structures, protein folding patterns, organizational structures, and various ways of arranging things in a room, indicates that there is practically no limit to how many structures can be created. Each such structure evokes different properties out of each part and gives the whole new properties. And yet, there is no systematic way of classifying them. We can still associate sense perceivable properties to these structures, but since they are the properties of the structure, therefore, they cannot be created by the composition of the atoms. This problem is generally called non-linearity in modern science where removing a small part doesn't necessarily have a small effect. Linearity applies to the sense perceivable atoms. For instance, there can be an apple that lacks sweetness but looks just like another apple with sweetness. By the ability to remove one property at a time, we are sometimes led to reductionist linearity—namely, that the whole is nothing but the combination of the parts. But the structural combination defies such linearity because a car with three wheels is not a functional car. The removal of different parts has different effects on the whole, and these effects depend on the structural relationship between the parts. General methods of classification can be applied to linear systems, but they cannot be applied to non-linear systems. Hence, each combination of the parts has some unique properties which can't be reduced to the parts.

Sūtra 4.2.5

तत्र शरीरं द्वविधिं योनजिमयोनजिं च

tatra śarīraṁ dvividhaṁ yonijamayonijaṁ ca

tatra—there; śarīraṁ—the body; dvividhaṁ—two-fold; yonijam—born from a female reproducing organ; ayonijaṁ—not born from female reproducing organ; ca—also.

TRANSLATION

There are also two-fold divisions of the body—born from a female reproducing organ and not born from the female reproducing organ.

COMMENTARY

After saying that the body structures are not produced out of three-fold classification, this sūtra says that the bodies are of two types—produced from a sexual union and not produced from a sexual union. The next few sūtras will further clarify how this two-fold classification is not a rigid method.

Sūtra 4.2.6

अनियतदिग्देशपूर्वकत्वात्

aniyatadigdeśapūrvakatvāt

aniyata—not fixed; dig—direction; deśa—place; pūrvakatvāt—as if from the prior production.

TRANSLATION

(These bodies) don't have a fixed direction and place as from prior production.

COMMENTARY

This sūtra rejects the idea of strict inheritance of bodily properties stating that these bodies can also differ in direction and place—i.e., structure—and the bodily structure of the children may differ from those of the parent(s).

Sūtra 4.2.7

धर्मविशेषाच्च

dharmaviśeṣācca

dharma—nature; viśeṣāt—from a unique individual; ca—also.

TRANSLATION

There can also be unique individual natures (in the different bodies).

COMMENTARY

This is a well-known fact that children can differ from their parents in their color, height, facial features, bodily shape, and other such bodily traits.

Sūtra 4.2.8
समाख्याभावाच्च
samākhyābhāvācca

samākhya—a uniform classification; abhāvāt—from the absence; ca—also.

TRANSLATION

Also from the absence of a uniform classification (uniqueness is accepted).

COMMENTARY

Even when methods of classification are used in identifying bodies, these are broad categories. No two humans for instance have identical facial features.

Sūtra 4.2.9
संज्ञाया आदित्वात्
saṁjñāyā āditvāt

saṁjñāyā—the nomenclature; āditvāt—from the origin (i.e., parents).

TRANSLATION

The nomenclature (of body types) is from the origin (i.e., the parents).

COMMENTARY

This is a rejection of the modern evolutionary theory in which mutations in one species can produce another species. The fact is that mutations in dogs never produce cats. The mutations in bacteria never produce viruses. There can be differences between parent(s) and children, due to which a strict set of attributes cannot be assigned to the species. But those differences don't mean that they are different species. They are merely differences within the species.

Sūtra 4.2.10
सन्त्ययोनिजाः
santyayonijāḥ

santi—there exist; ayonijāḥ—those not born from sexual union.

TRANSLATION
There exist body types that are not born from sexual union.

COMMENTARY
A wide variety of asexual species are known today; this sūtra accepts them.

Sūtra 4.2.11
वेदलिङ्गाच्च
vedaliṅgācca

vedaliṅgāt—from the symptoms of knowledge; ca—also.

TRANSLATION
Body types are also distinguished based on the symptoms of knowledge.

COMMENTARY
All species of life have some capacity to understand their environment and act in their defense. The capacity to represent the environment as knowledge, therefore, exists in all species of life. However, the different species vary in their capacity to feel emotions, and the understanding of right and wrong. The human species is unique in its capacity to ask the questions of truth, the laws of nature, creativity in terms of art, music, and literature. Other species have knowledge about what to eat, what is safe or not, and how to survive in their environment. This type of knowledge is not considered great, but it is still knowledge.

CHAPTER 5

Section 1

Sūtra 5.1.1

आत्मसंयोग प्रयत्नाभ्यां हस्ते करम

ātmasaṁyoga prayatnābhyāṁ haste karma

ātmasaṁyoga—the union of the self; prayatnābhyāṁ—from the effort; haste—in the hands; karma—activity.

TRANSLATION

From the union and effort of the soul, there is an activity in the hands.

COMMENTARY

Matter exists in a state of potentiality, and it is activated by choices. It may not always be our choice; it can also be someone else's choice. But it is always activated by a choice. Therefore, the activity of the hands is attributed to the soul. Subsequent sūtras will clarify the nature of this soul-body interaction.

Sūtra 5.1.2

तथा हस्तसंयोगाच्च मुसले करम

tathā hastasaṁyogācca musale karma

tathā—in the same way; hastasaṁyogāt—from the union with the hands; ca—also; musale—in the pestle; karma—activity.

TRANSLATION

In the same way, from the union with the hands, there is also activity in the pestle.

COMMENTARY

Most of us are fairly comfortable in thinking about how hands move the pestle, but we don't understand how the soul moves the hand. This is because we have become accustomed to thinking of hands and pestle as physical things, while the soul is considered a non-physical thing. The fact is that the soul, hand, and pestle are not physical things. They are the potentials for meaning-forms. The hand is thus a potentiality for pushing, holding, movement, etc. What we call the 'hand' is a collection of infinite potentials, and one of those potentials is activated at one moment. When we see the hand at rest, that is one potential; when we see the hand moving, that is another potential; when we see the hand holding a pestle, that is yet another potential. The pestle is similarly literally infinite potentials, one of which can be selected by the hand. The soul is also a potential for infinite emotions, cognitions, and relations. The difference is simply that in the soul, the potentiality can become an actuality without an external selection. This is not the case with matter; matter always needs an external agency to select one of the many potentialities. Thus, all over Vedic philosophy, matter is called 'inert', whereas the soul is called 'active'. The relation between the hand and the pestle is however similar to the relation between the soul and the hands in the sense that the hand selects one of the many potentials out of the pestle potentiality, and the soul selects one of the many potentials out of the hand potentiality. Therefore, even though soul and matter are different, the *relationship* between the soul and the hand is just like that between the hand and the pestle—both relationships perform the job of making a selection.

Sūtra 5.1.3

अभिघातजे मुसलादौ कर्मणि व्यतिरेकादकारणं हस्तसंयोगः

abhighātaje musalādau karmaṇi vyatirekādakāraṇaṁ hastasaṁyogaḥ

abhighātaje—produced by hitting; musalādau—originating from the pestle; karmaṇi—the activities; vyatirekāt—due to the exclusion; akāraṇaṁ—not the causes; hastasaṁyogaḥ—the union of the hands.

TRANSLATION

The union of the hands is not the cause of the activities originating from the pestle and produced by hitting due to the exclusion (of hands and pestle).

COMMENTARY

When a person is shot dead by a bullet, the *cause* of the death is the bullet, but the *responsibility* for the action is assigned to the shooter. The shooter could put forward a facetious argument: I did not kill the person; it was the bullet. But this argument is rejected, and causality is traced backwards to what initiated the bullet's firing. The question is: How far backwards must we trace this causal chain? For example, should we say that the cook who fed the shooter in the morning gave him the energy to fire the bullet, and so it was the cook who must be held responsible for the shooting? After all, if he had not supplied the food, then the shooter would not have had the energy to fire. So, the cook set into motion a chain of events by feeding the shooter, which then led to the shooting. Or, should we go even further backwards, and blame the parents for giving birth to a shooter? Or even further to his grandparents or great-grandparents?

Modern physical theories cannot answer these questions, because they have no role for choices. Hence, they cannot say that the shooter made a choice for shooting. The food produced by the cook doesn't *determine* the shooting; from the actions of the cook, there are many possible alternative forward trajectories, one of which was chosen by the shooter. That choice makes the person responsible for the shooting, rather than the gun (which has no choice), or the cook (whose choices don't determine the outcome). In this way, when choice is inducted into the conversation, then we trace the causality back to the nearest prior action which made the outcome deterministic, and not further backward where the outcome was non-deterministic. Thus, if a mafia boss forces a foot soldier to shoot, the main culprit for the shooting is the boss rather than the foot soldier, since the boss's choices determined the pulling of the trigger. The foot soldier in this case plays a role similar to the gun—i.e., absence of choice.

In this way, there is a subtle distinction between *cause* and *responsibility*. The bullet is always the cause of death, but the responsibility of death may be assigned to the gun manufacturer if the gun fires without the trigger being pulled, to someone who modified the gun to fire accidentally, to the shooter if he fires with the intention to kill, or even to the mafia boss who ordered the killing. In all such cases, we trace the causality back to the nearest prior choice that made the outcome inevitable. And by that, we can clearly distinguish between the cause of an effect and the responsibility for the cause itself.

With this background, we can understand this sūtra—if the pestle hits grain, then the effect of crushing the grain is not attributed to the hands: It is attributed to the pestle. Then, the responsibility for crushing the grain is not attributed to the pestle: It is attributed to the hands. Thus, the pestle is the cause, and the hands are responsible. This sūtra says that the hands are not the cause of the effect—i.e., the crushing of the grain by the pestle. This should be read in the context of the distinction between causality and responsibility. This point will become evident by the nature of the soul's involvement in the next sūtra.

Sūtra 5.1.4

तथात्मसंयोगो हस्तकर्मणि

tathātmasaṁyogo hastakarmaṇi

tathā—in the same way; ātmasaṁyogah—the union of the self; hasta-karmaṇi—the actions of the hands.

TRANSLATION

In the same way, the union of the self (causes) the actions of the hands (without the effects being attributed to the self).

COMMENTARY

Just as the pestle is the cause of grain being crushed, but the hand is responsible for the pestle's movement, similarly, the hand is the cause of the selection of a potential from the pestle, while the soul is responsible for the selection of the potential in the hand. This difference between cause and responsibility can be pushed backward until we find that cause for which nothing else is responsible. For example, if an employee were crushing the grain using a pestle upon the instructions of an employer, then the responsibility for the action goes to the employer—partially or wholly. The chain of cause and responsibility terminates when we can legitimately say that others are not responsible for a cause. Rather, a person has made a choice due to their own personality.

Sūtra 5.1.5
अभिघातान्मुसलसंयोगाद्धस्ते कर्म
abhighātānmusalasaṁyogāddhaste karma

abhighātān—on the end of hitting; musala—pestle; saṁyogāt—from the union; haste—hands; karma—activity.

TRANSLATION

At the end of hitting, from the union of the pestle and hands, there is activity.

COMMENTARY

This sūtra makes another key point about cause and responsibility by distinguishing between two terms—kāraṇa or cause, and karma or activity. Suppose a bullet is fired, but it misses the target. In that case, the responsibility for shooting would not be assigned to the shooter—even though he did shoot. Hence, the cause lies at the beginning of the activity, and the responsibility lies at the end—if the activity was completed. If that activity was incomplete, or it failed to achieve the intended objective, then the karma is not considered complete, and hence the responsibility cannot be assigned, even though there was still a cause of the shooting. One of the cardinal principles of the Vedic theory of karma is that mere good or bad intentions don't produce good or bad karma. Similarly, actions based on good or bad intentions produce less good or bad if they are incomplete, miss the target, or were performed incorrectly. The fullest extent of good or bad karma is created when the actions are complete, and they were the intended consequences. As a result, most ritualistic practices are forbidden in the present age because, despite good intentions, the performer misses the target by performing them incorrectly. Half a chair is not half-price of a full chair. In fact, half a chair would be priced at the same value as the wood that comprises it. In the same way, actions that don't achieve the results are not considered activities, even though there is a cause and effect. The meaning of karma or activity here is that which determines some reward or punishment.

Sūtra 5.1.6
आत्मकर्म हस्तसंयोगाच्च
ātmakarma hastasaṁyogācca

ātmakarma—the actions of the soul; hasta—hands; saṁyogāt—from the union with the hands; ca—also.

TRANSLATION
Also, the actions of the soul from the union with the hands.

COMMENTARY
Just as the responsibility of the hand in crushing the grain is assigned when the grain is crushed, similarly, the soul's responsibility is assigned after the action is complete. Thus, the soul's karma is created on the action's completion.

Sūtra 5.1.7
संयोगाभावे गुरुत्वात् पतनम्
saṁyogābhāve gurutvāt patanam

saṁyoga—union; abhāve—in the absence; gurutvāt—as if from the heaviness; patanam—falling down.

TRANSLATION
In the absence of the soul's union, (activities are) just like falling down due to heaviness (i.e., karma is not created in such situations).

COMMENTARY
Nature is also moving due to the effect of time, and time activates certain possibilities in this nature automatically. When such potentialities are activated without the soul's involvement, then the actions are not due to the soul's involvement. In such cases, the soul is not held responsible for such outcomes. This sūtra compares such outcomes of objects falling down due to heaviness.

It is notable that in Vedic philosophy, automatic actions are also called 'dharma' or duty. Accordingly, 'dharma' is also sometimes considered 'nature'. For example, it is the dharma of fire to heat things. It means that there is a deity of fire that enacts a duty to convert the potentiality into an actuality. Without this deity, fire can have the property of heat, but others will not get burnt by it. Thus, the burning due to fire is not an automatic conclusion; that burn is due to a conscious intervention, which is the responsibility, duty, or the dharma of a deity called Agni. However, because Agni burns things as a matter of performing his duty, therefore, the burning is not considered good or bad action.

Sūtra 5.1.8

नोदनविशेषाभावान्नोर्ध्वं न तिर्यग्गमनम्

nodanaviśeṣābhāvānnordhvaṁ na tiryaggamanam

nodana—removing; viśeṣa—specifics; abhāvāt—from the absence; na—not; urdhvaṁ—vertical; na—not; tiryak—horizontal; gamanam—movement.

TRANSLATION

Without removing some specifics, no vertical or horizontal movement.

COMMENTARY

The tree of concepts is like a pine tree in which there are many levels of branches, twigs, and leaves. As we have discussed, the sense-perception concepts can be applied not just to objects and sensations, but also to thoughts, judgments, intentions, and morals. Hence, each level in the tree embodies a different category of concepts—objects, sensations, senses, mind, intellect, ego, and the moral sense. Likewise, each level of branches, twigs, and leaves in the tree is similar—the innermost branches are abstract, and progressively they are more detailed with the detailed structure mimicking the hierarchy of the five elements. Hence, there are hard objects, the sensation of hardness, difficult to assimilate ideas (which are called hard to grasp), tough judgments (which are hard to accept for everyone), rigid ego (which is intolerant of others), and valuing rigidity as a virtue (e.g., remaining tough and inflexible as a virtue).

Moving vertically in this tree means moving to a higher level—i.e., from objects to sensations to senses to mind to intellect to ego to the moral sense. And moving horizontally—e.g., in the case of sensations—means moving from smell to taste to sight to touch to sound. In both cases, some specifics or details must be removed. For example, the Water element has touch, sight, and taste, but no smell. Therefore, in moving horizontally from Earth to Water, the property of smell must be removed. Likewise, to grasp the idea of a table, we must remove the consideration of the differences of various tables, and just focus on the similarity in them. Thus, the removal of details can move us upward or inward.

But that doesn't mean that every removal will indeed move us inward or upward. For example, removing the tires of a car doesn't provide an understanding of what we mean by vehicles. But the converse is true—unless we remove some details, we cannot understand the abstract. A good example of this fact is that when we see an Alsatian and we say "It is a dog" we have already removed the unique properties of the Alsatians and seen the similarities with other types of dogs such as Poodles and Huskies. So, obtaining the more abstract idea requires us to remove the details, and some removals move the consciousness inward and some removals move the consciousness upwards.

Thus, the statement "by removing details we get the abstract" is incorrect because removing some details doesn't always produce the abstract. But the converse statement "without removing details we cannot get the abstract" is correct. This sūtra makes the latter statement. The indication is that we should not think about object motion; we are not talking about the vertical and horizontal movement of physical objects. We are rather talking about the upward and inward movement of consciousness. This movement requires conceptual thinking, in which without relinquishing the details, we cannot know the abstract. This understanding of the tree of concepts is the basis on which spiritual progress is commonly called the inward and upward movement of the soul.

Sūtra 5.1.9

प्रयत्नविशेषान्नोदन विशेषः

prayatnaviśeṣānnodana viśeṣaḥ

prayatna—effort; viśeṣāt—from the individual; nodana—removing; viśeṣaḥ—the specific.

TRANSLATION

From the individual or specific effort, the specifics are removed.

COMMENTARY

Once we understand the conceptual tree, and the progress of consciousness as inward and upward movement, then we recognize that to know the abstract truth, we have to relinquish the details. This requires a process in which the details are removed one by one, and each removal moves our consciousness away from some or the other detail. A yogi is taught renunciation from the world because this is the only way that he can understand the complete truth. The person who is absorbed in the minute details of everyday life cannot understand the nature of the complete truth. A progressive spiritual life is thus designed to successively cut our attachments to this world—initially the parents, then the children, then the wife, and eventually the place of living. In the Varṇāśrama system, for example, a person enters into the Sannyasa order of life where he renounces all relationships to children, wife, home, and wealth; he roams from one place to another, never staying in one place for more than three days. If we know that nothing is permanent, or doesn't last longer than three days, then we will never be attached to it. Thus, by cutting all attachments, the consciousness is elevated to understand the Absolute Truth. This sūtra refers to the gradual but progressive process of cutting out details, one at a time. Each progressive step in this process of detachment requires a separate effort. Generally, the efforts get increasingly difficult with the successive detachments.

Sūtra 5.1.10

नोदनविशेषादुदसनविशेषः

nodanaviśeṣādudasanaviśeṣaḥ

nodana—removing; viśeṣāt—from specific; udasana—rising; viśeṣaḥ—specific.

TRANSLATION

Specific rising from specific removing.

COMMENTARY

In the tree of concepts, consciousness can take innumerable paths. Some people might prefer to give up one attachment first, while others prefer something else. As a result, the Vedic system permits literally infinite paths for progress, although that doesn't mean that every path leads to upliftment—some paths also take one outward and downward instead of inward and upward. This sūtra refers to the fact that by removing a particular kind of specific or detail, a specific type of upliftment is achieved. As long as one is making some upward and/or inward movement, the process is considered spiritual. If a person is moving downward and outward, their path is considered material.

Sūtra 5.1.11

हस्तकर्मणा दारककर्म व्याख्यातम्

hastakarmaṇā dārakakarma vyākhyātam

hastakarmaṇā—the actions of hands; dārakakarma—the actions of a child; vyākhyātam—described.

TRANSLATION

The actions of hands are described as the actions of a child.

COMMENTARY

The inverted tree of meanings can also be visualized as a family tree, in which the soul becomes the 'parent' and the hand becomes a 'child'.

Sūtra 5.1.12

तथा दग्धस्य विस्फोटने

tathā dagdhasya visphoṭane

tathā—in the same way; dagdhasya—of burning; visphoṭane—in an explosion.

TRANSLATION

In the same way (the phenomenon) of burning in an explosion.

COMMENTARY

The more abstract concept applies to a larger domain of specifics. As a result, we get an anti-reductionist description of a phenomenon in which the macroscopic phenomenon is described as the 'parent' and the microscopic phenomenon is described as its 'child'. This sūtra gives an example: If things in a house have been burnt due to explosion, the explosion is the macroscopic phenomenon and can be called the 'parent' and the burning is the microscopic phenomenon and can be called the 'child'. The explosion has other 'children' apart from burning, namely, that things are scattered around instead of being organized, and what was earlier a whole thing, has been broken into pieces. So, we can recursively apply the idea of an explosion to a toy—not only has the house exploded, but the toy has also 'exploded'—it is burnt, broken into pieces, and scattered, just like the house. The recursive application of the idea seems paradoxical because it implies that the more abstract concept is not just the macroscopic description, but is also immanent in the things to which it is applied. But that paradox is the result of physical thinking, which is also reductionist.

Of course, if something in the house hasn't burnt due to an explosion, but may have been broken into pieces, which are also scattered, then we will say that the thing has exploded, although the effects of the explosion are not fully manifest. This too can happen sometimes, just like the cow body is developed based on the cow-mind, but the mind is not fully developed in the cow.

Sūtra 5.1.13
यत्नाभावे प्रसुप्तस्य चलनम्
yatnābhāve prasuptasya calanam

yatna—effort; abhāve—in the absence; prasuptasya—of sleeping; calanam—the behavior.

TRANSLATION

In the absence of effort, the behavior of sleeping.

COMMENTARY

Matter lies in a state of dormancy, from which it is activated by the choices of the soul. We have earlier called this the state of possibility which is converted to reality by the soul. This sūtra compares this state to someone sleeping.

Sūtra 5.1.14
तृणे कर्म वायुसंयोगात्
tṛṇe karma vāyusaṁyogāt

tṛṇe—in the pieces of grass; karma—activity; vāyusaṁyogāt—from the union with the Air element.

TRANSLATION

Activity in the pieces of grass arises from the union with the Air element.

COMMENTARY

The Air element has the properties of touch, and one such property is what modern science called 'pressure' or 'push'. The difference between modern science and Vaiśeṣika is that modern science will say that the "air is blowing"—which means that there is something that is pushing or applying pressure on air—whereas Vaiśeṣika will say that it is simply "union" with Air. Thus, when ordinary things are moved due to the application of pressure, the descriptions are radically different. Modern science would say that something was moving, and it transferred its energy to something else, thereby causing it to move. Vaiśeṣika would say that the so-called energy was a latent possibility and it was activated. When it combined with the object, then the object started moving. This movement is one of the inherent potentialities in the grass, but it can be activated by the presence of the Air. The difference is subtle but important. In the case of transfer of energy, the air loses its energy and transfers it to the grass. But in the case of activation of a potentiality in the grass, the Air may not lose its energy, and yet, its presence can manifest a potentiality in the grass.

Just like in the presence of an angry person, others can also become angry; or, in the presence of a happy person, others may become happy. To make others happy, we don't have to lose our happiness. Likewise, to educate others, we don't have to become ignorant. As a result, the classical principles of energy conservation must be rejected when matter is described as meaning because happiness and knowledge can be spread without making someone else unhappy and ignorant. That happiness or knowledge which is manifest in the other person was previously a potentiality in that person; it is not provided as force or pressure from outside; it is rather "activated" from a "dormant" state in the presence of a certain kind of meaning. Since it was previously present as a potentiality within, therefore, the principle of conservation is not truly violated; after all, it previously existed as a "potential energy" inside that thing. And yet, since we could not observe its existence, as it was previously unmanifest, therefore, the principle of energy conservation would seem violated.

Sūtra 5.1.15

मणिगमनं सूच्यभिसर्पणमदृष्टकारणम्

maṇigamanaṁ sūcyabhisarpaṇamadṛṣṭakāraṇam

maṇigamanaṁ—the movement of a jewel; sūci—needle; abhisarpaṇam—slow approach; adṛṣṭa—invisible; kāraṇam—cause.

TRANSLATION

The movement of a jewel, the slow approach of a needle, have invisible causes.

COMMENTARY

This sūtra further extends the example of grass moving due to air—where the air seems invisible—into movements of a needle and a jewel that don't seem to have invisible causes, and yet it calls them invisible. For example, if grass moved in a field, the materialist would say that the "wind is blowing". But Vaiśeṣika would say that the element Air combined with the grass, and thereby activated a preexisting potential of movement in the grass. The same principle is now extended to cases where it seems that the hands are pushing the needle or a jewel is shaking because of our bodily movement. These too are moving because of the combination of Air. This means that when the potentiality of movement manifests in our hands—by the combination of the soul that selects a potential—then this manifest potential selects or triggers other potentials to manifest. In this case, that selected potential is the needle's movement.

In this way, two apparently contradictory claims are reconciled. First, that everything that is manifest is manifest from "within". If you become angry, then the anger was preexisting within you as a potential, and it was simply manifest from within. Second, that external things are the cause of the property manifestation. Thus, the presence of an insult or another angry person can make you angry. The difference is simply this: If you are purified of the inner anger, then the presence of another angry person cannot make you angry. Conversely, if there is a lot of anger within you, a small insult or provocation will cause you to go into a violent rage. So, the external cause of an insult or provocation is the same, but the effects can be magnified, minimized, or be non-existent. This means that external causality is insufficient to explain the observed effects.

However, if we said that everything is produced from within without an external trigger, then we would clearly not explain why people become angry only upon a provocation even as they are otherwise quite peaceful. Therefore, external causation is necessary to explain the emergence of phenomena, but that explanation must be complemented by the internal emergence explanation.

A good example of this dichotomy is dreaming and waking experiences. During waking, there is an external trigger due to which some potentials in our senses are activated. But during dreaming, those potentials are activated without an external trigger. Since dreams are possible, therefore, we can say that everything that we perceive exists as a potential within our senses. But since those potentials can be triggered by external causes, therefore, we must say that this dormant reality is sometimes activated due to some external factors. It can well be manifest due to internal causation—e.g., when the soul reactivates a potential in our senses, and we perceive something in our dreams. Thus, both internal and external causes must be accepted for a complete explanation.

Sūtra 5.1.16

इषावयुगपत् संयोगविशेषाःकर्मान्यत्वे हेतुः

iṣāvayugapat saṁyogaviśeṣāḥ karmānyatve hetuḥ

iṣāu—controller; ayugapat—without the union; saṁyoga—union; viśeṣāḥ—the specifics; karma—activity; anyatve—in the others; hetuḥ—the cause.

TRANSLATION

Without the union of a controller, the activity is caused by the union of specifics in the others.

COMMENTARY

Dreams are caused by the existence of the soul along with a subtle body of impressions that lie latent within us. This is internally triggered causation by the presence of the soul. Similarly, the movement of our hands is caused by the selection of a potentiality in the hand. This is also internal causation. But sometimes, effects can be manifest even due to external causes, which in turn must be attributed to the presence of external controllers. Thus, for example, the wind blows due to a controller called Vayu; the fire burns us due to the presence of an external controller called Agni. These controllers are the demigods who activate the potentiality even when we are not activating it consciously.

Our body digests food even without our conscious intervention. The body fights diseases even without our conscious intervention. The materialist attributes these things to 'chemicals', but those chemicals are simply potentials. What activates the potential? There is always a controller activating these potentials, but the controller may not be us. It can be other living entities just like us, or even superior living entities who activate the potentials in nature, but remain invisible to us. This sūtra refers to other causes, that are external to us, although it attributes this causality to the 'specifics' in the other things. If we extend the same thinking about the soul activating the potentials in our body, then we can say that even the external triggers are activated by other controllers.

Sūtra 5.1.17

नोदनादादयमषिोःकर्म तत्कर्मकारताच्च संस्कारादुत्तरं तथोत्तरमुत्तरं च

nodanādādyamiṣoḥ karma tatkarmakāritācca saṁskāráduttaraṁ
tathottaramuttaraṁ

nodanāt—from the removal; ādyam—the original; iṣaḥ—the controller; karma—activity; tatkarma—that activity; kārita—the doer; ca—also; saṁskārāt—from the impressions; uttaraṁ—subsequently; tatha—in the same way; uttaramuttaraṁ—subsequent to the subsequent.

TRANSLATION

From the removal, the original controller, activity, that activity (which caused the activity), and the doer (are understood). In the same way, from the impressions, the subsequent, and the subsequent to the subsequent.

COMMENTARY

The original controller is the Supreme Lord and He causes the manifestation of potentialities to a state where they can be chosen by the soul. That is, they become mentally perceivable as possibilities, and they are then further activated by the senses. The doer is the soul, which then triggers some activity, which then triggers another activity until the intended goal is achieved.

But sometimes, the impressions of the soul automatically trigger some thoughts and desires, which are then accepted by the soul, and that acceptance activates those thoughts and desires as choices of the soul, which then trigger the succession of activities. The impressions are latent and they can be activated by the soul, or they can be automatically activated by time, which is also a form of the Supreme Lord. In this way, the Lord is the supreme and original controller because He can activate latent impressions and He activates the potentialities into a state where the soul can activate them further as his activities.

Sūtra 5.1.18

संस्काराभावे गुरुत्वात् पतनम्

saṁskārābhāve gurutvāt patanam

saṁskāra—impressions; abhāve—in the absence; gurutvāt—as if due to heaviness; patanam—falling.

TRANSLATION

In the absence of impressions, as if due to falling due to heaviness.

COMMENTARY

When the soul is purified of all latent impressions, then these impressions don't trigger thoughts and desires. Now, the soul can act out of its volition and control the body. Otherwise, the body keeps working automatically due to time activating the potentials—through a long chain of causation that also involves the demigods. These demigods can also act out of their volition, and they do act as a matter of duty, which is why this automatic activity in matter is sometimes called 'dharma' or duty. But if the demigods become unwilling, or their good karma which gives them the power over material elements is over, then they are replaced by time to a different set of souls who become the demigods.

Thus, even when the demigods are said to be controlling the material nature, they are secondary controllers working under the direction of the Supreme Lord. They are replaceable from their position of power and control, but the Lord cannot be replaced from His position. Therefore, the demigods are posts or positions occupied for a brief period of time, when the Lord is the position. There is hence no difference between the Lord and His being a controller.

Section 2

Sūtra 5.2.1

नोदनाभिघातात् संयुक्तसंयोगाच्च पृथिव्यां कर्म

nodanābhighātāt saṁyuktasaṁyogācca pṛthivyāṁ karma

nodana—removing; abhighātāt—by breaking; saṁyukta—combined; saṁyogāt—from the union; ca—also; pṛthivyāṁ—in Earth; karma—activity.

TRANSLATION

Activity in the Earth is also due to removing by breaking and combining by a union.

COMMENTARY

This sūtra speaks about the ordinary method of creating complex objects by combining simpler objects and creating simpler objects by dividing complex objects. The combination, however, produces a hierarchical structure in which one property is dominant and the other is subordinate. For example, if two smells are combined, then one is always dominant and the other is subordinate. This dominant-subordinate structure can also be changed. The dominant property is said to be in greater "proportion" in physical thinking, but it is not the quantity of the quality that makes it dominant. It is rather the dominant position of the property in the hierarchical structure. For example, if pungent and sweet smells are mixed, and the sweet smell is dominant, then from a physical perspective, one would say that the proportion of the sweet smell is higher. But from the semantic perspective, one would say that the sweet smell is in a dominant position and the pungent smell is in a subordinate position. Therefore, these combinations by union and breaking should also be viewed hierarchically.

This sūtra states that the creation of such structures or the breaking of the structures is activity or karma. The properties are universals, and they are eternal. The individual instantiation of that property is also eternal, but it can be hidden. Finally, even the structure is eternal, but it can be unmanifest. Therefore, karma is the manifestation of these individuals and structures from the unmanifest. Since by creation or destruction, one structure appears and the other disappears, therefore, it seems like the structures are temporary. But if we think in this way, then structures would not be conserved, and whatever is not conserved cannot be considered real. Whatever is not real cannot be studied scientifically. Therefore, to study these structures scientifically, we have to say that they are eternal possibilities, and yet they lie unmanifest. When one structure is manifest, then the other is unmanifest. This creates a sense of temporariness in the material world because something is appearing and disappearing, but that is not the only thing happening here; rather, each change also results in the production or destruction of something called karma or 'activity'.

For example, if you buy some food in exchange for money, then your money is gone but you have obtained food. Similarly, the seller has lost the food but gained some money. So, structural change creates a record—just like money changing hands—and if we look at karma and change together, then they are conserved. This is a different notion of conservation and reality than physical change and conservation where energy moves from one object to another, but money doesn't move in the reverse direction. Therefore, to study conservation, we have to rely exclusively on the total amount of energy. If, however, a chef has mixed ingredients to create a tasty recipe, then he has created value, which is then compensated by the money he receives by giving it to someone else.

Hence, activity can be described as the creation and destruction of value. In every value creation, some value is destroyed: e.g., by cooking the raw ingredients, those ingredients are no longer available. But if someone can compensate the chef by paying him money in return, then that money or value was created in the act of transforming one structure into another. This value is temporary because after some time the food would be inedible. Therefore, even if the value is not destroyed by some combination or separation, it is destroyed automatically, and by that destruction, we can say that karma comes to an end. So, the study of activity is about manifesting something unmanifest, which is then called value, which can then be exchanged, but it is eventually lost. When it is lost, then the manifest reality goes back into the unmanifest state again. As a result, even when change occurs, the material reality remains eternal.

Because modern science doesn't study structures, therefore, it also cannot talk about value. Since value is absent, therefore, science also cannot talk about intention to create and consume value, or that we like or dislike certain types of structures. As a result, economics is separated from physics. Science is now reduced to the study of particles and structures are said to be either created randomly, or by human effort, but the result of that effort is outside science.

These descriptions of activity should therefore be treated as not merely physical movement, but the production (or destruction) of value, such that a new kind of phenomenon—namely the circulation of value—can be studied. In this description of nature, the economic value would also be objective—it is the structural change produced by some effort, which involves the senses and the mind. The abilities in the senses and the mind can then be spoken of as previously created values, so a capable body is obtained due to past good karma. If our abilities are used to destroy value, then the past good karma—which gave us the ability—is destroyed, and the new value is not created. The result of such destructive activities is that the next body of the soul remains incapable of producing value. Thus, as people indulge in destructive activities, their minds become uncreative, their intellect becomes dumber, and their senses become incapable. Conversely, if they create value rather than destroying it, then their subsequent lives give them capable bodies, minds, and intellects, using which they can produce even more value. Thus, the science of morality is not separate from the science of matter; it seems separate when we minimize the study of matter to particles, physical laws of energy conservation, and adopt materialism.

Sūtra 5.2.2

तद्विशेषेणादृष्टकारितम्

tadviśeṣeṇādṛṣṭakāritam

tat—that (activity of union and separation); viśeṣeṇa—in the specifics; adṛṣṭa—invisible; kāritam—causation.

TRANSLATION

That activity of union and separation (rests) in the specifics as invisible causation.

COMMENTARY

If we recall the distinction between cause and responsibility, then the activity produces some value that rests in the material object, and the responsibility is assigned to the soul. The hierarchical structural relationship is invisible to the senses, but its effects can be perceived. Similarly, the karma or responsibility for the actions assigned to the soul remains invisible, but its effects are perceivable. Economics rests on the objective value in things, and the price commanded by a commodity must rest on this objective value. Modern economics ignores this objective value in things and determines prices by supply and demand. This leads to price inflation when the demand rises, and price deflation when the demand falls. These price instabilities then create other cycles of boom and bust. To create a stable economy, we must understand that value is objectively present in things, although it remains invisible. Similarly, karma remains invisible but it is like money that we choose to spend to acquire things. If we don't have the money, then we cannot buy things. Similarly, if we don't have karma, then we cannot get a good life. All these things can be understood from the simple ideas of causation and responsibility for that causation, and the idea that some activities create value, while other activities destroy the value.

Sūtra 5.2.3

अपां संयोगाभावे गुरुत्वात् पतनम्

apāṁ saṁyogābhāve gurutvāt patanam

apāṁ—Water; saṁyoga—union; abhāve—in the absence; gurutvāt—as if heaviness; patanam—falling.

TRANSLATION

In the absence of union with Water, as if falling due to heaviness.

COMMENTARY

The same statement was made earlier in two contexts—(a) the soul's union with the body, and (b) the soul's union with impressions. The union essentially activates a possibility, whereupon the responsibility of that selection is attributed to the soul. But if the soul doesn't make that selection, then time automatically selects. As a result, our choices are not the sole cause of change. Blood circulation, food digestion, immunity, etc. are working automatically without our conscious intervention. This automated working is due to the demigods working under the control of time. But this automated working is compared to things falling down automatically due to heaviness. All elements can work automatically, and hence the universe evolves without our intervention, or even despite it because time forces changes, which seems automatic because it is outside our control. However, it is under the control of the Supreme Lord. The basic principles of choices controlling matter are the same; the persons exercising these choices, however, are different. Thus, nature is not working due to some mathematical laws; it is working due to choices—ours or the Lord's.

Sūtra 5.2.4

द्रवत्वात् स्यन्दनम्

dravatvāt syandanam

dravatvāt—from fluidity; syandanam—flowing.

TRANSLATION

(An example of automatic working) is from fluidity, there is flowing.

COMMENTARY

The property of fluidity is present in the Water element but it is unmanifest when fluids are stored in a vessel. Modern science would now say that there is a force of gravitation that acts on the fluid, but the vessel that stores the fluid compensates for that pressure and prevents the fluid from flowing. The Vaiśeṣika philosophy would instead say that the properties of the vessel present the context in which the property of fluidity is unmanifest. When that context is removed, then the property of fluidity is manifest. Just like redness combined with rose, light, and cross manifests new properties in redness, similarly, the context reveals and hides the properties. Physical theories can explain some of these manifestations—e.g., the flow of fluids. But they cannot explain how we feel nervous in some places, happy and excited in other places, why some people naturally make us angry and upset, how certain environments naturally produce allergies in us, and how new meanings are created by context.

The clearest example of such contextual manifestation in modern science is the entanglement and non-locality in atomic theory where a change in one part of a system automatically changes the other parts—without a transfer of energy or force. Most physicists like to think that these are unique properties of microscopic particles, but they must disappear for macroscopic systems where all change must occur through locality or the transfer of energy. But the Vaiśeṣika system will explain even the macroscopic phenomena in terms of contextual manifestation. As a result, when one property is unmanifest, then another property is manifest; an example being the flowing of fluids outside a vessel.

Sūtra 5.2.5

नाड्या वायुसंयोगादारोहणम्

nāḍyā vāyusaṁyogādārohaṇam

nāḍyā—reed; vāyu—Air; saṁyogāt—from a union; ārohaṇam—rising up.

TRANSLATION

The rising of reed from a union with Air.

COMMENTARY

This is another example of a commonplace phenomenon of reed (a type of long grass) floating in the air, which is explained differently than how most people like to think. A naïve view is that when air "blows" then the reed flies. In this way of thinking, the blowing of the air is considered a force, which makes the reed fly. But this sūtra presents a different idea about that flying: the combination with the Air element manifests the properties of lightness and movement. As a result, there is no "force" being exerted by Air. Rather, Air is "combining" with the reed to produce a movement. Naïve interpretations of these texts take a very simplistic view to say that "the reed flies due to air", which is such an obvious claim (if we view it as wind blowing the grass), that one is led to assume that both the reader and the author must not be very intelligent. The fact is that these are not trivial or obvious statements. There is no need to repeat the obvious, or what everyone can see and is led to believe from their everyday experience. These are rather rejections of commonsensical ideas about motion and change, with the alternative explanation that is more encompassing.

These statements become necessary when we have to explain non-local phenomena in the same way as those phenomena that we have traditionally explained using local methods—i.e., that some force pushes things and causes them to move. Since non-locality cannot be explained using local methods, therefore, local explanations must be replaced by a non-local methodology.

Sūtra 5.2.6
नोदनापीडनात् संयुक्तसंयोगाच्च
nodanāpīḍanāt saṁyuktasaṁyogācca

nodana—removing; āpīḍanāt—from not being forceful; saṁyukta—mixing; saṁyogāt—from the union; ca—also.

TRANSLATION

(The effects) from removing not being forceful, (the effects) from mixing and union also (not forceful).

COMMENTARY

The term pīḍan signifies torture, pain, and exploitation. Modern science is based on this philosophy of forcing things to our benefit. Francis Bacon, for example, thought of experimentation as the "inquisition" of nature in which nature is compelled to reveal its secrets. Bacon was a legal inquisitor involved in the trials and torture of the witches, which was common during his time. He viewed scientific experimentation in the same vein—torture nature like a witch to make her reveal her secrets because that will give us control over her.

The Vedic system of knowledge is based on a different idea: Present the right context, and nature will reveal a different property. But every time you are doing that, you are creating karma, so be sure to do the right thing. We cannot enslave nature; rather, nature constantly enslaves us. The soul, however, enters the material world with the false idea of mastery and tries to dominate nature. The soul doesn't realize that every action has a consequence, and bad consequences of actions take away the power to control and master. Then, when a person becomes weak and helpless in front of nature's power, then he feels miserable. So, instead of going through a false pride and then misery, Vedic philosophy teaches us the science of matter, and how to use it responsibly.

Sūtra 5.2.7

वृक्षाभिसर्पणमित्यदृष्टकारितम्

vṛkṣābhisarpaṇamityadṛṣṭakāritam

vṛkṣa—tree; abhisarpaṇam—moving slowly; iti—thus; adṛṣṭa—the invisible; kāritam—actions.

TRANSLATION

The tree moves slowly; thus are the actions of the invisible.

COMMENTARY

Even if we have accumulated good karma, we cannot consume it all at once. And if we have accumulated bad karma, we cannot suffer all of it at once. Similarly, bad karma cannot be slowed to a point where it becomes easily bearable. The results of karma are always delivered at a certain rate—not faster or slower. However, the extent of good and bad changes. The person who suffers a lot reaps karma at the same rate as the person who enjoys a lot—the difference is simply that the karma being reaped is significantly bad or good. Thus, this sūtra says that the "tree moves slowly"—comparing the growth and decline of karma to a tree that takes many seasons to grow from seed and produce fruits. The karma we are reaping right now was a seed sown much earlier. In the meantime, we may have stopped sinful activities, transformed our nature to be good people, but that karma must still produce the fruits even after a long time. As long as there is any material desire, the karma will produce good or bad results according to that desire—i.e., it will either fulfill that desire or frustrate it. Karma is destroyed completely only when all the desires are vanquished.

Sūtra 5.2.8

अपां सङ्घातो वलियनं च तेजःसंयोगात्

apāṁ saṅghāto vilayanaṁ ca tejaḥ saṁyogāt

apāṁ—Water; saṅghātah—structure; vilayanaṁ—merged within; ca—also; tejaḥ—Fire; saṁyogāt—from the union.

TRANSLATION

Also, the structure of Water is merged within, from the union with Fire.

COMMENTARY

An earlier sūtra described how Water has the properties of viscosity. Another sūtra described how Water has the property of coolness, while Fire has the property of heat. This sūtra says that from the union with Fire, the structural properties of Water are destroyed. This means that some properties of Water—e.g., taste—are possessed even in the individual Water atoms. But other properties like viscosity are present in the Water atoms but they are contextually manifest in the presence of other atoms. We can call these the structural properties of Water, but that doesn't mean that they are only in the structure; they are also in the Water atoms, but they are revealed only in the context of other atoms. It is these structural properties—which are in the Water atoms but manifest in the presence of other Water atoms—that are hidden in combination with Fire. Modern science says that a unique type of force called the Van Der Vaal force creates weak chemical bonds, which are responsible for viscosity and surface tension in water. In Vaiśeṣika, these are the contextual properties of Water, which means that they are in Water, but they are revealed in a context. The term vilaya means "merged within", indicating that the structural properties of Water were "projected outward" in the presence of other Water atoms. There is no English equivalent to this term, but we can say that these properties were previously manifest, and when combined with Fire, they are unmanifest.

In simple terms, the property of taste is possessed by each Water atom, while properties like fluidity are the properties of a collection of Water atoms. A collection of Water atoms, when organized in a structure, can also be treated as a single object. And that object—also Water—manifests the property of fluidity or viscosity. This means that when Water atoms are combined, a new contextual property is revealed, which is a possessed property but was earlier unmanifest. When Water is heated by Fire, then the structure of Water is destroyed and the contextual property of viscosity is hidden. It manifests again when Fire is removed. The implication is that by mixing these atoms, hidden properties are revealed, so if we wanted to know all the properties in an atom, we would have to mix it—i.e., subject it to numerous contexts—one after another.

Sūtra 5.2.9
तत्र विस्फूर्जतुर्लिङ्गम्
tatra visphūrjaturliṅgam

tatra—there; visphūrjatuh—born by bursting of energy; liṅgam—symptoms.

TRANSLATION

There, the symptoms are born by the bursting of energy.

COMMENTARY

The term visphūrjatuh comprises two other terms—visphur which means bursting out, and ūrjatah which means born from the energy. There are no English equivalents for these terms, but we can say that the unmanifest properties are hidden as potential energy within, and they burst out as manifest reality. This manifestation is just like a bomb that throws out particles that were previously within it. This means that even properties like fluidity are within the Water atoms, but they are contextually manifest in the presence of other atoms.

In modern science, most of these contextually manifest properties are called epiphenomena, implying that they are the secondary outcomes of some primary properties. A good example is fluidity; the primary property (according to modern science) is water's chemical formula (H2O) and the secondary phenomenon is fluidity. That means, fluidity is not "within" water, and yet, it appears due to Van Der Vaal forces. Science, therefore, speculates that even the mind could be an epiphenomenon of the brain. That is, none of the brain parts have any meaning, but the collection of these parts becomes meaningful.

The Vaiśeṣika system instead indicates that all epiphenomenal properties are present within Water atoms, but they burst out being born of latent energy. Hence, we can say that Water atoms have fluidity, but we cannot observe it because that property is latent within the atoms. The Sāñkhya system uses the term Satkāryavāda to describe the same emergence of properties—the effect eternally exists within the cause and is sometimes manifest from within.

Sūtra 5.2.10
वैदिकं च
vaidikaṁ ca

vaidikaṁ—Vedic philosophy; ca—also.

TRANSLATION

This is also Vedic philosophy.

COMMENTARY

This sūtra clarifies that the description of the bursting out of energy is not merely Vaiśeṣika statements; rather these are also Vedic statements. As we have noted, the same idea is presented in Sāñkhya as Satkāryavāda. It is presented in Vedānta as vyakta and avyakta, or manifest and unmanifest. It is called abhāva and bhava or absence and presence in Nyāya philosophy. Thus, the terminologies often differ but the doctrines of manifestation are not different.

Sūtra 5.2.11
अपां संयोगाद्विभागाच्च स्तनयित्नोः
apāṁ saṁyogādvibhāgācca stanayitnoḥ

apāṁ—Water; saṁyogāt—from the union; vibhāgāt—from the division; ca—also; stanayitnoḥ—thunder clouds.

TRANSLATION

From the union and division of Water, also thunder clouds (are created).

COMMENTARY

This sūtra describes thunder clouds as a byproduct of the structural organization of the Water atoms. This structural organization involves the union and division of atoms. Each such structure can also be spoken of as an individual object—the root of the tree from which the rest of the structure springs forth.

Sūtra 5.2.12

पृथिवीकर्मणा तेजःकर्म वायुकर्म च व्याख्यातम्

pṛthivīkarmaṇā tejaḥ karma vāyukarma ca vyākhyātam

pṛthivī—Earth; karmaṇā—the actions of; tejaḥ—Fire; karma—the actions; vāyu—Air; karma—actions; ca—also; vyākhyātam—explained.

TRANSLATION

The actions of Earth can be explained as the actions of Fire and the actions of Air.

COMMENTARY

This sūtra states that the structural effects of the Earth atoms can also be explained as if they were the effects of the combination of Fire and Air atoms. Explicating these sūtras requires a detailed scientific theory in which the atoms of Earth, Water, Fire, and Air are studied as the interactions of meanings.

Sūtra 5.2.13

अग्नेरूर्ध्वज्वलनं वायोस्तिर्यग्गमनं अणूनां मनसश्चाद्यं कर्मादृष्टकारितम्

agnerūrdhvajvalanaṁ vāyostiryaggamanaṁ aṇūnāṁ manasaścādyaṁ karmādṛṣṭakāritam

agner—of Fire; ūrdhvajvalanaṁ—vertical burning; vāyoh—of Air; tiryak—horizontal; gamanaṁ—movement; aṇūnāṁ—of the atoms; manasah—of the mind; ca—also; ādyaṁ—the origin of; karma—activity; adṛṣṭakāritam—the invisible activity.

TRANSLATION

The origin of the vertical burning of Fire atoms, the origin of the horizontal movement of Air atoms, and the origin of the mind's activity, are also due to the invisible activity.

COMMENTARY

The upward movement of the Fire atoms and the inward movement of the Air atoms represents the creation of greater order. When the senses of sight and touch are withdrawn inward, and we lose the perception of the world (assuming that we are already not smelling and tasting), then the mind rises upward. Conversely, when the senses are engrossed with the material world, then the mind also falls. In simple terms, living in solitude and cutting oneself off from sense perception elevates the mind. Conversely, interacting with the world and indulging in sensory stimulation degrades the mind. The symptom of a degraded mind is that it is incapable of understanding deeper levels of reality.

Modern society preaches social interactions and the technologies of communication have ensured that people are always hooked into sensory stimulation from the world, destroying all solitude. The result is that people hooked into this sensory stimulation have lost their capacity to think about deeper subjects, or even grasp the nature of deeper realities—even if they are presented with intuitive examples from the everyday world. If we talk about an abstract reality without examples, then they cannot understand anything. And if we give them intuitive examples of such reality, then they equate the reality to those examples, because they cannot extract the idea from the example. This is the result of the dumbing of the mind due to excessive sense enjoyments.

Western societies are leading examples of such superficiality—everything is judged by how it "looks". People are not interested in anything deep. They just want to "look" good—i.e., wearing fancy clothes, applying fancy makeup, driving in a fancy car, and talking in a fancy way. There is absolutely no depth in the person. If we talk about the mind, then people say: It must be the brain. If we talk about intellect, then people say: It must be the neural connections in the brain. If we talk about morality, then people say: It must be nothing but the behaviors in relation to other people. And if we talk about feelings of happiness, then people say: It must be a chemical. In this way, by excessive sensory preoccupation, the mind is completely dumbed, since they lose the capacity to understand the existence of a deeper reality. Even if we try to teach them about a deeper level of reality, they always visualize it in terms of sense perception.

This sūtra explains that this inward and upward or downward and outward movement is the effect of invisible activity. The Sāñkhya system explains this invisible activity in greater detail as the modifications of the chitta, guna, karma, and time. The guna is the habits we have acquired; if we indulge in sense perception, then we also create habits of sense perception, and these habits then force the consciousness toward more sense perception. If we indulge in sense perception, then the mind loses the capacity to understand abstract ideas such as thought, judgment, intention, and morality. And due to these habits and loss of capacity, karma delivers all good and bad results in terms of sense perception. Thus, even if there is good karma, it is very hard to translate it into the acquisition of good ideas, morals, intentions, and judgments. People rather think of good karma as good clothes, a good house, a good spouse, and a good car. If time triggers chitta, karma, and guna, then a person gets engrossed in sensory activities. And if the effect of time ceases, then the person goes to sleep. This superficial existence is the gateway to entry into animal forms of life.

Sūtra 5.2.14

हस्तकर्मणा मनसःकर्म व्याख्यातम्

hastakarmaṇā manasaḥ karma vyākhyātam

hastakarmaṇā—the activities of hands; manasaḥ—of mind; karma—activity; vyākhyātam—explained.

TRANSLATION

The activities of the hands are explained by the activity of the mind.

COMMENTARY

As we have discussed, the concepts of sense perception can also be applied to the mind. For example, we describe mental understanding as "grasping of ideas"—as if the mind were like a hand that could hold things. Similarly, we speak of mental models as "visualization"—as if the mind were an eye looking at a picture. We say that people should "speak their mind"—as if the mind were the organ of speech. And we use metaphors such as "journey of the mind"—as if the mind had legs by which it was traveling on a journey. The fact is the very opposite: The activities of the senses—e.g., grasping, visualization, speaking, and walking—begin in the mind. The difference is simply that the sensory metaphors of each of the five senses of knowledge and action can be applied to the mind, but the metaphors of one sense cannot be applied to the other senses (unless we use mental metaphors—e.g., "my hand has a mind of its own").

Thus, while explaining any sensory activity, we have to invoke the activity of the mind, because the activity originates in the mind, and gradually becomes the activity of the body. When the senses are habituated to sense perception, then they drag the mind along. In some Vedic texts, this is described as a man who is dragged in different directions by his wives. The mind seems helpless in such cases, but even then, by withdrawing the mind, the senses can be controlled. Therefore, even when the senses force the mind, it is only by the mind acquiescing to that force from the senses. This acquiescing is sometimes called "willing" of the mind—the mind willingly goes along with the senses. If the mind is unwilling, then the senses cannot trigger the mind; rather, the mind will control the senses. Therefore, the actions of the hands have to be ultimately explained in terms of the mind's actions—even if that activity is acquiescing.

Sūtra 5.2.15

आत्मेन्द्रयिमनोर्ऽथसन्निकिर्षात् सुख दुखे

ātmendriyamanor'thasannikarṣāt sukha duḥkhe

ātma—soul; indriya—senses; manah—mind; artha—the object; sannikarṣāt—from proximity and attraction; sukha—happiness; duḥkhe—distress.

TRANSLATION

From the proximity and attraction of the soul, senses, and the mind to their objects, there is happiness and distress.

COMMENTARY

The senses and the mind have two kinds of natures—(1) the nature of likes and dislikes, which is called their 'guna', and (2) the nature of abilities or capacities by which certain types of activities are easily performed by the senses, and certain types of meanings are easily understood by the mind. The third kind of meaning is karma, which also resides in the senses and the mind, and it brings the senses and the mind into contact with their objects. If the objects are liked due to the guna, then happiness is created; if they are disliked, then distress is created. Happiness and distress are not directly due to the contact of the senses and the mind with their objects, but due to the likes and dislikes innate in them. Thus, a yogi who has become free of likes and dislikes doesn't enjoy or suffer due to the contact with the sense- and mental- objects. Therefore, this sūtra should be viewed as referring to the general class of people in whom happiness and distress are automatically triggered by the interaction with the objects.

Sūtra 5.2.16

तदनारम्भ आत्मस्थे मनसि शरीरस्य दुखाभाव:संयोगः

tadanārambha ātmasthe manasi śarīrasya duḥkhābhāvaḥ saṁyogaḥ

tat—that; anārambha—without a beginning; ātmasthe—situated in the self; manasi—the nature of mind; śarīrasya—of the body; duḥkhābhāvaḥ—the absence of unhappiness; saṁyogaḥ—in the communion.

TRANSLATION

In the communion, with that which is without a beginning, (the soul) has the nature of the body and the mind situated in the self, devoid of all unhappiness.

COMMENTARY

This sūtra describes the state of the communion of the soul with the Lord, Who is said to have no beginning. In this state, the soul is not devoid of thinking or perceiving capacities. However, these capacities are "situated in the self". In simple terms, the body and the mind of the soul are *parts* of the soul. Just like a tree grows from a seed, similarly, the soul's true body and mind develop from the seed of devotion to the Lord. This is not a material body that is external to the soul, and exists as its covering, under the pretentious attempt at greatness. This spiritual body is rather internal to the soul, and springs out of the soul. Just like various material qualities spring out of material energy called pradhāna, similarly, the soul's spiritual body also springs out from within the soul.

The material body delivers both happiness and distress, but the spiritual body is devoid of distress because all distresses are outcomes of bad karma, which is produced under the ignorance of the Lord's existence, or negligence of His happiness. When the soul is devoted to the Lord, all its actions are perfect—they are neither good nor bad, and hence they don't lead to repeated bodies or the soul's transmigration. Then, there is no need for a material body to deliver the results of karma. The soul now enjoys loving devotion to the Lord.

This devotion, and the resulting happiness, are the creations of the soul; they are not supplied from outside. As a result, there is no dependence on anything else to be happy. All happiness is derived from serving the Lord, and this service is spontaneous—i.e., not governed by considerations of gain or loss. The soul's mind and body are simply engaged in finding out the best way to serve the Lord. Each soul has a unique mind and body, by which they calculate the best method to serve the Lord differently. So, their uniqueness is not imaginary; there is genuine uniqueness that makes their devotion and themselves unique.

Sūtra 5.2.17

अपसर्पणमुपसर्पणमशति पीतसंयोगाःकार्यान्तर संयोगाश्चेत्यदृष्टकारतिानि

apasarpaṇamupasarpaṇamaśita pītasaṁyogāḥ kāryāntara saṁyogāścetyadṛṣṭakāritāni

apasarpaṇam—moving away slowly; upasarpaṇam—approaching slowly; aśita—having eaten; pīta—having drunk; saṁyogāḥ—by the communion; kāryāntara—the differences of effects; saṁyogāt—from the communion; ca—also; iti—in this way; adṛṣṭa—the invisible; kāritāni—the activities.

TRANSLATION

Moving away slowly, approaching slowly, eating and drinking by the communion (of the invisible), and also the difference of effects from the communion (of the invisible), in this way, there are the effects of the invisible.

COMMENTARY

As we have discussed, the invisible comprises chitta, guna, and karma, and constitutes the "unconscious body" of the soul so its existence is not even revealed to each soul even during introspection. So, it is "invisible" not just from the perspective of sense perception, but also from the perspective of inner introspection. The unconscious body is the cause of all conscious activities.

For example, the karma or destiny of the soul slowly moves the soul in a direction even if the guna or the desires of the soul are different. Thus, we might imagine that our goal in life is to become a soldier, but karma can move life in a direction away from the military and towards an academic career. These processes are very slow. Then there is a fast process, such as eating and drinking. If we have good karma, then we can choose the kind of food and drink. But if we don't, then karma gives us some food or drink that we may not enjoy.

Finally, even the determination of whether the intended effects of actions are produced or not is decided by karma and guna. We might act with all good intentions, but the results may not be proportionate to our effort. And then, sometimes we might not do anything, and still get good results. We cannot see how the "invisible" sometimes fulfills our desires without effort, and sometimes frustrates them despite our efforts. But this reality can be understood if we recognize that matter is meaning, that actions have consequences, and these consequences then become the basis of the acquisition of further meaning.

Sūtra 5.2.18

तदभावे संयोगाभावो ऽप्रादुर्भावश्च मोक्षः

adabhāve saṁyogābhāvo 'prādurbhāvaśca mokṣaḥ

tadabhāve—in the absence of that; saṁyoga—union; abhāvah—absence; aprādurbhāva—not born; ca—also; mokṣaḥ—liberation from this world.

TRANSLATION

In the absence of that (invisible reality), the union (with the world) and the (feeling of) absence (i.e., desire) are not born; that is liberation.

COMMENTARY

This sūtra gives more insights into the nature of the "invisible reality" by citing two examples—one that causes the union with the world and is called karma, and the other that leads to the feeling of absence or inadequacy called guna. Just like a dog with a collar sometimes feels secure because he has a collar, and then sometimes feels constrained by the collar, similarly, the soul due to the covering called guna sometimes feels secure and sometimes insecure. The feeling of security is that some of his desires are being fulfilled and he feels secure in that life; this is called avaraṇātmika. The feeling of insecurity is that he is not the other things, and some of his desires are not being fulfilled and this is called prakśepātmika. The latter is the force that "throws" the soul out of the comfort zone and makes him struggle in this world. The prakśepātmika is also called abhāva or the feeling that something is missing. When the soul starts struggling to fulfill his desires, then karma delivers some fulfillment and some frustration by creating circumstances of interaction with the world.

When the invisible reality is destroyed, then the feeling of frustration is destroyed, the struggle for fulfillment is gone, and the forcible union with the world to find the fulfillment (which is perceived as absence) is overcome. This state devoid of frustration, and the desire to overcome it, is called liberation.

Sūtra 5.2.19

द्रव्यगुणकर्मनिष्पत्तिवैधर्म्यादभावस्तमः

dravyaguṇakarmaniṣpattivaidharmyādabhāvastamaḥ

dravya—object; guṇa—quality; karma—activity; niṣpatti—falling out; vaidharmyāt—from the opposing nature; abhāvah—the absence; tamaḥ—darkness.

TRANSLATION

The object, quality, and activity falling out from the opposing nature of absence is darkness.

COMMENTARY

The last sūtra referred to absence as an invisible cause, and this sūtra explains why it is invisible: It has an opposing nature to object, quality, and activity because it is the *absence* of an object, quality, and activity. This absence exists in us as desire, and it begins with the feeling of inadequacy or incompleteness. Thus, even when the soul is not desiring anything, the material nature creates fear, insecurity, inadequacy, and incompleteness in the soul. The material nature tells the soul: You don't have enough money, you are not powerful, you are ugly, you are not famous, you don't know so many things, you are stuck in one place and haven't seen all the places, and therefore, your life is mediocre. If the soul was detached from material nature, then it will ignore this message from the material nature. But the soul identifies with that message and starts believing it to be the truth. Now, a feeling of absence, emptiness, frustration, and desolation is created and the soul starts struggling to overcome it.

The nature of frustration is the very opposite of the nature of fulfillment. They are like ball and socket: The socket is the frustration and the ball is the means to fill that socket and overcome the frustration. Each type of frustration is a unique type of socket, and the means to overcome the frustration is a unique type of ball. This socket of frustration is called māyā, or "that which is not". It is also called abhāva because it is the absence of the ball. The uniqueness here is simply that we normally think that the ball is something external to the socket and must be supplied from the outside to fill the socket. But in Nyāya and Vaiśeṣika, this ball is produced by the socket—from within the socket.

As we have discussed, the absence is like a question or a problem, and the answer to that question or the solution to the problem emerges from within the question or the problem. Similarly, the Sāñkhya system describes that pradhāna emerges from māyā. Just as māyā is the problem, similarly, pradhāna is the idea that "I can solve the problem because I am a master at solving problems".

From this sense of mastery, the soul applies itself to the problem, and the solution—which is called prakṛti—is created. This is the ball that fits the socket. Then, we employ some universal principles of morality, which are called mahattattva, to judge if the solution is right—i.e., whether it is appropriate for us to use such a solution. For example, if the solution is illegal, then even if the solution might work, it is dropped. Then we employ the ego to judge if this solution will be good for me. If the solution is legal and righteous, but it is not good for me, then the solution is rejected by the soul. But if the solution is judged to be good, then the intellect is employed to determine if the solution will practically work in the real world. If the solution will not work, then it is rejected even if we determine that it is righteous and good for me. Once we determine that the solution will work, then the details are ironed out by the mind. Then the solution progresses into the implementation by the senses, and finally, it becomes a material product that we perceive through the senses.

But the sense of mastery created by solving problems is illusory because each solution creates a new problem. That problem then creates a new inadequacy, which creates a new solution. In this way, the soul is caught in the vicious cycle of creating endless problems and solutions, and he alternates between the despondency of seeing problems and the thrill of seeing solutions.

Thus, māyā is called tamas or darkness in this sūtra, because the problems and the solutions are real, but they are not *our* problems, and the solutions have nothing to do with *us*. We have just accepted some random problem as our problem, and we suffer from the problem and then enjoy the solution. Just like people entertain themselves by solving puzzles, where the puzzle is voluntarily accepted as a real problem, and its solution creates some thrill, similarly, the soul spends its time solving puzzles that are not the puzzles of the soul.

Sūtra 5.2.20

तेजसो द्रव्यान्तरेणावरणाच्च

tejaso dravyāntareṇāvaraṇācca

tejasah—of light; dravyāntareṇa—by the difference in objects; āvaraṇāt—from the covering; ca—also.

TRANSLATION

Also, light is known by the difference in objects from the covering.

COMMENTARY

This last sūtra stated that the objects, qualities, and activities being produced from the opposing nature of absence is "darkness". And this sūtra says that being able to know the true nature of objects, as they exist different from the "covering" of appearances is "light". The cardinal example in epistemology is the distinction between a rope and a snake; they look alike, but one is harmless and the other is not. So, being able to know the true nature of things is the basis on which we can determine whether it is harmful or harmless. The "light" tells us about the nature of things, and "darkness" makes us hanker for them.

Sūtra 5.2.21

दिक्कालावाकाशं च क्रियावद्वैधर्म्यान्निष्क्रियाणि

dikkālāvākāśaṁ ca kriyāvadvaidharmyānniṣkriyāṇi

dik—direction; kālāu—of time; ākāśaṁ—space; ca—also; kriyāvat—as if activity; vaidharmyāt—from the opposing nature; niṣkriyāṇi—devoid of activity.

TRANSLATION

The apparent activities of direction, space, and time, are also from the opposing nature which is devoid of activity.

COMMENTARY

When space is understood as an inverted tree, then it has two kinds of activities—(a) the branches, twigs, and leaves grow out, and thereby new phenomena are manifest, or (b) the branches, twigs, and leaves fall back in, and thereby the phenomena become unmanifest. However, when something has become manifest, it hasn't been "created". And when it is unmanifest, it hasn't been "destroyed". The appearance and disappearance are merely apparent phenomena that give the false impression of creation and destruction. This apparent change in an eternal reality is called kriyāvat in this sūtra, and this activity arises from the opposing nature of absence which was detailed in the last sūtra. This sūtra further states that the absence—i.e., the question or problem—is "inactive" while the answer or the solution is just "seemingly active".

Sūtra 5.2.22

एतेन कर्माणि गुणाश्च व्याख्याताः

etena karmāṇi guṇāśca vyākhyātāḥ

etena—by these; karmāṇi—the actions; guṇāśca—also the qualities; vyākhyātāḥ—are explained.

TRANSLATION

By these actions, the qualities are also explained.

COMMENTARY

As earlier discussed, the objects give birth to the activities which then give birth to qualities. The object is in the mode of sattva-guna, activity is in the mode of rajo-guna, and the qualities are in the mode of tamo-guna.

As these successive realities manifest one after another, the initial understanding of an object is that it exists, but is totally invisible; the next understanding of the object is that exists and it is invisible, but its effects are visible; finally, the third understanding of the object is that it exists, its effects are visible, and even the object's qualities are visible. So, in the third stage, we can measure the object by its qualities. In the second stage, we can measure the effects, but not the object. And in the first stage, we cannot measure neither the effects nor the qualities. And yet, because this object can manifest qualities and activities, therefore, it exists.

Sūtra 5.2.23

नष्क्रियाणां समवायःकर्मभ्यो नषिद्धिः

niṣkriyāṇāṁ samavāyaḥ karmabhyo niṣiddhaḥ

niṣkriyāṇāṁ—of the inactivities; samavāyaḥ—combination; karmabhyo—to the karma or activity; niṣiddhaḥ—forbidden.

TRANSLATION

The combination of the inactivities to karma or activity is forbidden.

COMMENTARY

An earlier sūtra stated that the absence is inactive, while the presence is active. Inactivity means that unless a soul is present, a problem is not really a problem, and therefore, the problem will not be solved without a soul. A problem manifests into a solution only when a soul is present. However, if a solution has manifested, then it will automatically produce a problem; this production of the problem from the solution doesn't require the soul. We can restate this thesis a little differently: To create order and information, a soul must intervene; but the disorder is created automatically even without conscious intervention.

Thus, when something is present, the absence also exists, but it remains inactive. When the soul interacts with this absence, then it becomes active: It becomes a problem, desire, or intention for the soul. Then, the soul's presence leads to the creation of a solution, which automatically comes with a problem. Thus, for instance, even when people are trying to solve a problem, they may not be trying to create new problems; and yet, problems are automatically created. When a problem is created, the soul can tolerate the problem, and not try to solve it. Or, it can consider that a serious problem and attempt a solution.

By tolerating the problem, rather than trying to solve it, we avoid producing new solutions and thereby new problems. We just bear the consequences of the present problem. This is the recommended way of life for the yogi, who learns to tolerate the problems because he knows that karma acts in multifarious ways and the problems can change form, but they cannot be avoided.

This sūtra states that if there is an inactive problem, then it cannot become an active solution just because there is so much activity. In physical sciences, if a ball is at rest, then another moving ball can hit it, and that will cause the inactive ball to start moving. This simplistic idea of the active combining with the inactive to make it active is rejected here. A ball will not automatically hit another ball unless we consider the inactivity of the ball a problem, and we revector the energy of another ball to solve this problem. Thus, if someone is playing billiards, then they can push the ball using another ball because the inactive ball at a fixed position is a problem that the billiards player is trying to solve. If this static ball wasn't a problem, then the inactive ball will remain inactive. Conversely, if a ball has been hit, it will become active, and then again inactive after attaining a new state, and that inactive state automatically constitutes a problem—but it will be inactive unless we start considering it as a problem.

This doctrine of presence and absence helps us see how consciousness is essential to ordinary activities, like the motion of billiard balls. If only presence is acknowledged, then science becomes deterministic; in this deterministic science, there are no problems and no solutions; things just happen one after another and we might designate them as problems or solutions, but that doesn't change the course of the activity. But Vaiśeṣika and Nyāya describe this process quite differently as presence and absence, activity and inactivity, order and disorder, solution and problem, answer and question. There is an automatic component of change, and there is a conscious intervention needed for change.

Sūtra 5.2.24

कारणं त्वसमवायिनो गुणाः

kāraṇaṁ tvasamavāyino guṇāḥ

kāraṇaṁ—to the cause; tu—but; asamavāyinah—non-combinative; guṇāḥ—the qualities.

TRANSLATION

The qualities are but non-combinative to the cause (the absence of qualities).

COMMENTARY

The statements made about objects and activities previously, namely, that the activity doesn't combine with inactivity, and the absence doesn't combine with the presence, are here extended to the qualities. Something cold doesn't automatically cause the flow of heat; hunger doesn't automatically cause the flow of food into the stomach. We have to consider these absences as a problem, and that requires a conscious intervention. This problem is best illustrated in atomic theory where energy exists in a system, but it is not automatically emitted; the emission is indeterministic. If it is emitted, it is not emitted to everything; there is a selective emission and absorption, which is also indeterministic. The solution to this indeterminism is that there are invisible causes of guna, karma, and chitta, which act under the influence of time. Each of these three causes requires a conscious entity; if we don't incorporate these invisible causes, and the conscious entity in science, then the explanation will be incomplete.

Sūtra 5.2.25

गुणैर्दिक् व्याख्याता

guṇairdik vyākhyātā

guṇair—the qualities; dik—directions of space; vyākhyātā—explained.

TRANSLATION

The qualities are explained as directions of space.

COMMENTARY

The space of meanings is like a tree in which the trunks, branches, twigs, etc. are three things—(a) they are objects, (b) they are spaces within which there are more objects, and (c) they are directions in the higher space. For example, the property of color is a space in which there are objects or shades such as yellow, red, and green. Then, the property of color is an object in the space of vision. And the property of color is also a direction in the space of vision.

Modern science recognizes some dimensions such as mass, charge, energy, momentum, etc. and two sides of an equation must have the same dimensionality. However, modern science also tries to reduce all these properties to a four-dimensional space-time. For example, energy is the property of homogeneity of time; the property of momentum is the homogeneity of space; the property of mass is the curvature of the dimensions, etc. The Vaiśeṣika and the other Vedic systems don't attempt this reduction; they describe space as a tree with infinite branches in which each branch is a space, an object, and a dimension. These three descriptions are based on three distinct perspectives on the same thing.

From the perspective of a trunk, a branch is an object and a dimension. And from the perspective of the twig, the branch is a space. The dual interpretation of something as an object and a dimension exists even in atomic theory where each quantum particle is treated as a mathematically orthogonal function. That orthogonality of the functions means that the object is also a dimension. But since the hierarchical construction is missing, therefore, these quantum objects do not themselves become 'spaces' that 'contain' other objects and dimensions. Such a hierarchical construction requires us to treat these objects, dimensions, and spaces semantically—e.g., they are like concept of color, which is an object inside the vision space, it is a dimensionality of vision, and it is a space that contains other concepts like yellow, green, blue, etc. Each of these descriptions is non-commutative, which means that we cannot apply them simultaneously. They are the 'modes' of nature; we have to use these modes alternately.

Sūtra 5.2.26

कारणेन कालः

kāraṇena kālaḥ

kāraṇena—by the causation; kālaḥ—time.

TRANSLATION

By the causation (of objects, qualities, activities) time (is explained).

COMMENTARY

One of the fundamental differences in modern science and Vedic description of nature is that causality is tied to matter in science, but it is tied to time in the Vedic description. The tree of objects, qualities, and activities is eternal, but it is not eternally manifest. The manifestation and unmanifestation are caused by time. Time, however, determines what will happen, matter determines how it will happen, and the soul determines who will partake in that event. For example, time determines how many people will fall sick; matter determines how that sickness will spread from one person to another; and the soul's guna, karma, and chitta determine whether that specific person will fall sick. Therefore, time is not the only cause, although it is the primary cause—what will happen is determined first, the mechanism of its occurrence is determined next, and the participants in that event are determined last. As individuals, we can choose to not participate in bad worldly events, and we can become catalysts for good events. But we cannot change the collective outcomes themselves.

CHAPTER 6

Section 1

Sūtra 6.1.1

बुद्धिपूर्वा वाक्यकृतिर्वेदे

buddhipūrvā vākyakṛtirvede

buddhi—intelligence; pūrvā—prior to; vākyakṛtih—the statements were created; vede—in the Vedas.

TRANSLATION

The statements in the Vedas were created prior to intelligence.

COMMENTARY

The intellect is the instrument of judging the truth. To judge any truth, we must have some axioms, based on which truth can be judged. A logical or rational system can only employ logic or rationality to derive conclusions if the axioms are already present. These axioms, however, remain choices in modern rationality and they are chosen to solve a specific problem. If the problem changes, then the axioms can change—suited to solve that problem. This sūtra states that the statements of the Vedas were created before the judgment of truth was created, which means that a set of axioms were presented suited to solve the problem of life—namely, liberation from material existence. If these axioms are accepted, then the ultimate goal of life can be achieved easily.

Sūtra 6.1.2

ब्राह्मणे संज्ञाकर्म सिद्धिलिङ्गम्

brāhmaṇe saṃjñākarma siddhiliṅgam

brāhmaṇe—in the Brahmana portion of the Vedas; saṃjñākarma—the nouns and verbs; siddhiliṅgam—are the symbols of perfection.

TRANSLATION

In the Brahmana portion of the Vedas, the nouns and verbs are the symbols of perfection (i.e., they are perfect truths, which can be used to judge truth).

COMMENTARY

The truth of the Vedas can be verified rationally and empirically, provided we understand that rational and empirical verification requires many levels of understanding. For example, a statement like "I love you" can be verified superficially as the exchange of gifts, but the mere exchange of gifts doesn't certify the truth. To validate the truth of "I love you", we have to also look at deeper realities—the thoughts in the mind, the beliefs in the intellect, the intentions in the ego, and the values in the moral sense. This is because the axioms by which we judge the truth are our choices. Those axioms are chosen by the problem, and the problem is itself chosen by the values. The values are then chosen by the soul. And the soul gets the meaning of its existence in relation to God. Unless the deepest level of self-evident meanings is grasped, and the truth is established in relation to those self-evident meanings, the truth cannot be established. The most fundamental basis for judging the truth is the meaning of existence or life. If this meaning is perfectly understood, then everything else can be judged in relation to it—whatever is consistent with that meaning of existence is true, and everything else is false. This sūtra states that the Brahmana portion of the Vedas presents this summarized understanding of the truth.

Sūtra 6.1.3

बुद्धपूिर्वो ददातिः

buddhipūrvo dadātiḥ

buddhi—intellect; pūrvah—prior to; dadātiḥ—(the Vedas) give.

TRANSLATION

The (Vedas give the knowledge) that is prior to the intellect.

COMMENTARY

If Vedic knowledge is accepted as the basis of judging the truth, then everything can be perfectly achieved. This includes material well-being and spiritual attainment. This system of knowledge is perfect: We can analyze this perfection rationally by studying the Vedas, and we can verify it empirically by implementing the teachings. Modern systems of knowledge are created speculatively—each department of knowledge studies a small portion of our experience, postulates beliefs suited for that small portion, and disregards everything else. As a result, there are many contradictions between different departments of knowledge, and between many theories in each department. Each of these contradictory theories is also incomplete and imperfect because it doesn't explain all the observations or experiences. Instead, false theories either lead to confirmation bias or disregard for facts that don't fit the theory.

Perfect knowledge is free from these problems; it is not just suited for the problems and facts that we are aware of presently, but also to facts and problems that we haven't yet encountered. If this system of knowledge is adopted, then we don't have to change our theories and understanding of reality every day since the same truth will be confirmed through every new encounter.

Sūtra 6.1.4

तथा प्रतग्रिरहः

tathā pratigrahaḥ

tathā—in the same way; pratigrahaḥ—the acceptance.

TRANSLATION

In the same way, the acceptance (of Vedic knowledge is prior to intellect).

COMMENTARY

Modern science suffers from numerous problems of inconsistency and incompleteness, but people have put their *faith* in the scientific method—they believe that someday in the future science will solve all their problems. Similarly, a student goes to a teacher under the faith that the teacher will answer all their questions. This kind of faith is necessary to approach any teacher or system of knowledge. Unless we are prepared to invest the time and energy in understanding a system of knowledge or listening respectfully to a teacher, nothing can ever be gained. The same is true for Vedic knowledge. Of course, we have to approach a learned teacher who can present the Vedic knowledge perfectly. But that doesn't mean that we will know everything before we accept the teacher. So, faith in the teacher precedes the understanding. Now, we might ask: What leads to this faith? And the answer is that we must look at qualities deeper than the intellect—namely, intentions and values. If a person values profits and glory and is prepared to sacrifice the truth for it, then such a person can never be the source of truth. Therefore, faith is not established whimsically. It is established on the basis of the personal character of the teacher. If the teachers are drunkards and womanizers, manipulators and liars, then their teachings will also be compromised. People putting their faith in such teachers will also be cheated. Therefore, in the Vedic system, the teachers—called Brahmanas—are always above reproach due to their perfect character. They embody moral values which make them trustworthy. Faith in these teachers leads to the truth.

Sūtra 6.1.5

आत्मान्तरगुणानामात्मान्तरे ऽकारणत्वात्

ātmāntaraguṇānāmātmāntare 'kāraṇatvāt

ātmāntaraguṇa—the differences in the qualities of the soul; anāmātmāntare—in that which is not the difference between the souls; akāraṇatvāt—as if from the uncaused.

TRANSLATION

The differences in the qualities of the soul, in that which is not the difference between the souls, is as if from the uncaused.

COMMENTARY

All souls have three properties, which are called sat, chit, and ānanda. However, there are immense varieties within this basic nature of the soul. The variety in sat leads to diverse relationships; the variety in chit leads to various types of bodies which are in turn the cognitive and conative abilities, and the variety in ānanda leads to different kinds of desires which then lead to different kinds of pleasure. The impersonalist says that the differences between the souls is caused by māyā, which is external to the soul. But this sūtra says that the differences in the soul are uncaused; they are the innate properties of the soul. However, this innate personality of the soul cannot be recognized unless we recognize the difference of the soul from that of the external covering of māyā. This means three things: (1) we must know that the relationships of this world are not the true relationships, (2) the body of cognition and conation is not the real body, and (3) the pleasure of the senses and the mind is not the real pleasure. The Brahman realization is the understanding that the soul is different from the material covering. But it is not the end; specifically, separating the soul from matter is not the same as recognizing the true spiritual nature of the soul, and its innate or uncaused (i.e., not external) relationships, pleasures, cognitions, and conations. This realization of the true nature of the soul's qualities requires progress beyond the Brahman realization into devotion to the Lord because the relationships, pleasures, cognitions, and conations are in relation to the Lord. If the self is recognized as different from matter, but the Lord is not recognized, then Brahman simply means the end of all relationships, cognitions, conations, and pleasures. This is better than material life, but not the perfection of life.

The term ātmāntaraguṇa can also be understood as the soul's internal qualities, rather than the differences between the souls. Similarly, anāmātmāntare can also be understood as differences that are not the true nature of the self. The former would now refer to the soul, and the latter to the body, its relationships, and pleasures. This sūtra can now be translated to mean: "The true qualities of the soul in the material body of false differences are uncaused by the body". The sūtra's purport will be unchanged even with this alternate translation.

Sūtra 6.1.6

तद्दुष्टभोजने न विद्यते

taddusṭabhojane na vidyate

tat—that; duṣṭabhojane—in wicked eating; na—not; vidyate—known.

TRANSLATION

Wicked eating is not known in that (soul's true nature).

COMMENTARY

The term "wicked eating" refers to selfish enjoyment. The selfish person wants to accumulate wealth and power and competes with others in this accumulation. If the wealth and power are accumulated, then they are used to exploit the others, and this exploitation is called "enjoyment". It is a sadistic kind of pleasure in which the fact that one has something that the others do not have is considered the measure of success and superiority. This sūtra says that this wicked nature doesn't exist in the soul. The soul by nature is altruistic and loving: It wants to make others happy and happily serves the other souls. The soul sometimes competes with other souls in giving rather than taking. Therefore, even if competition exists, it is due to loving nature, not wickedness.

Sūtra 6.1.7

दुष्टं हिंसायाम्

duṣṭaṃ hiṃsāyām

duṣṭaṃ—the wicked; hiṃsāyām—indulging in violence.

TRANSLATION

The wicked are engaged in violence.

COMMENTARY

Modern society is based on the evil ideas of competition, self-aggrandizement, and the accumulation of wealth. This wealth is accumulated by killing trees and animals, recklessly exploiting natural resources such as minerals, water, and land, and the poor, weak, and helpless people who toil day and night for the benefit of those who have wickedly accumulated power and wealth.

Some religions endorse this violence as their God-given birthright to enjoy the wealth and resources, simply by their virtue of accepting membership into an institution. They are unable to realize that other living entities are also the children of God. They exploit everyone and everything believing that God gave them such rights. Such wickedness is not religion, because it is not the nature of the soul, or even of God. It is a mental concoction to rationalize otherwise reprehensible behavior by giving it the pretense of religious practice. Irreligious people who have no desire for spiritual upliftment, but want uninhibited enjoyment without moral accountability, take to such pseudo religions.

Sūtra 6.1.8

तस्य समभिव्याहारतो दोषः

tasya samabhivyāhārato doṣaḥ

tasya—of those; samabhivyāhāratah—associating and interacting; doṣaḥ—faults.

TRANSLATION

The association and interactions of those (wicked) are faulty.

COMMENTARY

The selfish and wicked people often come across as friends, trying to do good to the world, but their friendship is the masquerade for cheating. They are not interested in the good of anyone, but only interested in accumulating more power and wealth so that they can exploit and control others even more.

Sūtra 6.1.9

तददुष्टे न विद्यते

tadaduṣṭe na vidyate

tad—those; aduṣṭe—innocence; na—not; vidyate—known.

TRANSLATION

Innocence is not known to exist in the (wicked).

COMMENTARY

Those who advance the philosophy of accumulation, competition, and reckless enjoyment should be rejected in all possible ways—their ideas should be rejected, their schemes for so-called advancement must be rejected, and all their apparently charitable and philanthropic activities must be rejected. This is because there is no innocence in them; everything has an ulterior motive, and that motive is not the well-being of others; it is always their self-advancement.

Sūtra 6.1.10
पुनर्विशिष्टे प्रवृत्तिः
punarviśiṣṭe pravṛttiḥ

punarviśiṣṭe—repeatedly going into details; pravṛttiḥ—tendency.

TRANSLATION
The wicked have the tendency to repeatedly go into details.

COMMENTARY
Reality is constructed from the simple and abstract to the complex and detailed. Those who know the truth can state it very simply and easily in an intuitive manner. But those who are wicked, question these simple and intuitive truths and try to create "clarity" by producing enormous complexity. By hair-splitting simple and intuitive ideas, they confuse everyone and everything. They make things so complex that nobody can truly understand what is going on. Then they exploit the loopholes in this complexity to gain control. All wicked people have a tendency to create complexity and chaos by obfuscating the simple truth, and ensure that others are lost in the ensuing confusion. The complexity gets so scary that most people give up even trying to understand it. They simply relinquish all control to the so-called "experts" who designed and produced that complexity in the first place. Even if someone tries to demystify that complexity, the wicked throw more jargon and terminology to create confusion so that the common person cannot decide for themselves. Then, these "experts" come forward with "solutions" designed to advance their power.

Sūtra 6.1.11
समे हीने वा प्रवृत्तिः
same hīne vā pravṛttiḥ

same—in the equality; hīne—in the inferior; vā—alternatively; pravṛttiḥ—tendency.

TRANSLATION

Alternatively, the tendency for claiming equality with the inferior.

COMMENTARY

In the inverted tree, the details are inferior and the abstract is superior. The last sūtra stated that the wicked have the tendency for going into complexity, disregarding the simplicity, and this sūtra states that they have a tendency for equating everything with the most inferior type of reality. This inferior reality is the perceptions of the five senses. The wicked claim that there is nothing other than this reality; for example, even sensations, thoughts, judgments, intentions, morals, and the soul are by-products of this material reality. Similarly, there is no karma, no soul, and no God. Whatever we call the mind is just chemicals. Thus, every superior reality has to be reduced to something inferior. By degrading everything, which is called 'reductionism', the wicked intellectual feels great and he calls this degradation or reduction of higher reality 'progress'.

Sūtra 6.1.12

एतेन हीनसमवशिष्टि धार्मिकेभ्यःपरस्वादानं व्याख्यातम्

etena hīnasamaviśiṣṭa dhārmikebhyaḥ parasvādānaṃ vyākhyātam

etena—by this; hīnasamaviśiṣṭa—equality to the inferior and the detailed; dhārmikebhyaḥ—the religious systems; parasva—another's property; ādānaṃ—eating or consuming; vyākhyātam—explained.

TRANSLATION

By this (tendency to claim) equality to the inferior and the detailed, the religious systems of consuming another's property are explained (by the wicked).

COMMENTARY

This sūtra succinctly explains the modern doctrine of capitalism as arising from a materialistic foundation in which homo sapiens (or one who is capable of discerning) is reduced to homo economicus (or one who is a consumer). Since there is nothing beyond the body, and the body is just a bag of chemicals, therefore, there cannot be anything more profound than the satisfaction of the body. The highest goal of this life is ensuring that the body survives for the longest time, and the accumulation of property is one of the means to that survival. Society is structured as an exploitative pyramid in which wealth created by the work of the poorest sections flows upwards to the richest. With increasing wealth and power, the richest gain greater control over the poor and weak. The accumulation of wealth and power is called the 'dharma' or religious duty of each person, and the immoral ways for exploiting the weak are legalized.

Sūtra 6.1.13

तथा वरिुद्धानां त्यागः

tathā viruddhānāṃ tyāgaḥ

tathā—in the same way; viruddhānāṃ—the oppositions; tyāgaḥ—to sacrifice or renunciation.

TRANSLATION

In the same way, the oppositions to sacrifice and renunciation (are explained by the wicked).

COMMENTARY

The wicked elevate the principles of selfishness, competition, survival, gaining power, and stealing from others to the level of a scientific theory. The moral virtues of sacrifice, renunciation, charity, altruism, are thus opposed as the remnants of religion which is now claimed to have no scientific basis.

Sūtra 6.1.14

हीने परे त्यागः

hīne pare tyāgaḥ

hīne—in the inferior; pare—in the others; tyāgaḥ—sacrifice.

TRANSLATION

(The inferior) in the others is sacrifice in the (pursuit of) the inferior.

COMMENTARY

This sūtra explains the doctrine of Social Darwinism in which the fittest survive, and since fitness to survive is a virtue, therefore, through the destruction of the unfit, the society is collectively elevated to those who are fitter. Thus, stealing from others is not considered unvirtuous. It is rather considered the means to the progress of society in which the weak and unintelligent are gradually destroyed, and the offspring of the powerful and intelligent inherit the power and wealth of their parents, thereby propagating their genes. When this process is repeated over several generations, the Social Darwinist claims, humanity as a whole is vastly improved because only the genes of the competent and successful are propagated while the genes of the incompetent are not.

Sūtra 6.1.15

समे आत्मत्यागःपरत्यागो वा

same ātmatyāgaḥ paratyāgo vā

same—in the equality; ātmatyāgaḥ—the sacrifice of the self; paratyāgah—the sacrifice of the others; vā—or.

TRANSLATION

In the equality (of our existence to the lowermost detailed reality), it is either the sacrifice of the self or the sacrifice of others.

COMMENTARY

The materialists follow the philosophy of "kill or be killed". If my neck is on the line, then it is better than I take yours before you get a chance to take mine. In this way, society is degraded to a dog-eat-dog world. Morality doesn't really matter, because both are dogs anyway. However, since the more powerful dog will kill the weaker dog, therefore, after a few iterations, only the powerful dogs will survive, and they will then compete with other such dogs.

Sūtra 6.1.16

विशिष्टे आत्मत्याग इति

viśiṣṭe ātmatyāga iti

viśiṣṭe—in the details; ātmatyāga—the self-sacrifice; iti—thus.

TRANSLATION

Thus, the sacrifice of the self in the pursuit of the details.

COMMENTARY

Materialists also invent the ideologies of nationalism to encourage some people to die for the protection and well-being of others. But that nation is not truly a superior ideology; it is the same (or even worse) ideology of selfish survival, exploiting the weak, and sacrificing the poor for the richer. But this false ideology of wealth and power is sold to the people of a nation as a morally superior and worthy goal, incentivizing them to make sacrifices. But the creators of that ideology, or the people who benefit from it, are not concerned about those who sacrifice their lives. It is necessary evil propaganda used to extend their wealth and power, and if some lives have to be sacrificed for it, so be it.

Section 2

Sūtra 6.2.1

दृष्टादृष्ट प्रयोजनानां दृष्टाभावे प्रयोजनमभ्युदयाय

dṛṣṭādṛṣṭa prayojanānāṃ dṛṣṭābhāve prayojanamabhyudayāya

dṛṣṭādṛṣṭa—visible and invisible; prayojanānāṃ—purposes; dṛṣṭābhāve—in the absence of visibility; prayojanam—purpose; abhyudayāya—as the elevating principle.

TRANSLATION

In the absence of the visibility of purposes in the visible and invisible, the purpose is the elevating principle.

COMMENTARY

After describing the ideology of materialists and wicked who reject the existence of a purpose—ostensibly because it is not visible—this sūtra states that the purpose of everything is that it leads to moral and virtuous elevation and progress. Therefore, we might see some evil in society but that evil will lead to something more virtuous and moral. That evil exists for the purification of the society, or of the individual, by which they are purified of their past sinful actions. Similarly, the purpose in ordinary things—such as tables and chairs—is that they should be used for a moral and virtuous purpose. Thus, if we see some evil, then we should understand that it is not purposeless; its purpose is the purification of past sins. And if we see something that seems just a material object, then it still has a purpose—and that purpose is the principle of elevation.

Sūtra 6.2.2

अभिषेचनोपवास ब्रह्मचर्यगुरुकुलवासवानप्रस्थ यज्ञदान प्रोक्षणदिङ् नक्षत्रमन्त्रकालनियमाश्चादृष्टाय

abhiṣecanopavāsa brahmacaryagurukulavāsavānaprastha yajñadāna prokṣaṇadiṅnakṣatramantrakālaniyamāścādṛṣṭāya

abhiṣecana—bathing for purifying; upavāsa—fasting; brahmacarya—celibacy; gurukulavāsa—residing in the teacher's school; vanaprastha—going to the forest; yajñadāna—sacrifice and charity; prokṣaṇa—consecration; diṅnakṣatra—the daily performances; mantra—chanting; kāla—time; niyamāt—from the regulations; ca—also; adṛṣṭāya—for the invisible.

TRANSLATION

Bathing for purifying, fasting, celibacy, residing in the teacher's school, going to the forest, sacrifice, charity, consecration, the daily performances, chanting of mantras, based on time and regulations is also for (seeing) the invisible.

COMMENTARY

The last sūtra stated that everything has an elevating purpose, but this purpose is often invisible. This sūtra prescribes many kinds of activities that lead to the vision of that invisible purpose. In other words, if our life is degraded, then we cannot see a higher purpose in reality. Rather, we will see everything on the same level as our degraded existence. Therefore, those people who cannot see the elevated purpose in everything should be considered degraded. The purpose is not objectively absent, although its vision is missing. If we want to see that elevated purpose, then we have to elevate ourselves to a virtuous and moral life. This is a general principle pervading across Vedic philosophy that everyone cannot see everything. Rather, our vision is conditioned by the capacity of the chitta, which is like the goggles through which we perceive. If the goggles are covered with dirt, then the reality cannot be perceived. Therefore, philosophy alone is not enough to realize the nature of the truth. It is only a glimpse into the nature of the truth, and after learning about that nature, and realizing our inability to see it, we must endeavor to purify the chitta. Once the goggles of the chitta are purified, then we will also see the reality clearly. In this case, by our purification, we will see an elevated purpose in everything.

Sūtra 6.2.3
चातुराश्रम्यमुपधा अनुपधाश्च
cāturāśramyamupadhā anupadhāśca

cāturāśramyam—the four āśraṃa; upadhā—the false designations; anupadhāt—from the true designations; ca—also.

TRANSLATION

The four āśraṃa are also from the true and false designations.

COMMENTARY

The soul is covered by the guna, karma, and chitta, and some parts of this covering are elevating, while others are degrading. The four classes of society are meant to use the elevating aspects of guna, karma, and chitta for further elevation, and to correct the degrading aspects of guna, karma, and chitta. Thus, by the elevating abilities in the chitta, the desires of guna, and the good karma, one can perform many elevating activities that lead to further elevation. And by the inabilities in the chitta, the bad desires, and the bad karma, one would suffer, and thereby give up those bad desires, acquire the abilities, and purify oneself of the bad karma. The result completely depends on the combination of which types of karma, guna, and chitta are combined. If we combine bad guna with good karma, then our evil desires lead to degradation due to good karma, but those actions then produce bad karma which leads to greater suffering. Conversely, if we use our good karma only for the good guna, and bad karma only for the bad guna, then we are gradually elevated and purified of all inauspiciousness. Thus, the combination of good and bad has an elevating purpose.

Sūtra 6.2.4
भावदोष उपधादोषो ऽनुपधा
bhāvadoṣa upadhādoṣo 'nupadhā

bhāvadoṣa—the faults of desires; upadhādoṣah—the faults of faults designations; anupadhā—the faults of the true designations.

TRANSLATION

The faults of desires are the faults of true and false designations.

COMMENTARY

Since everything has an elevating purpose, therefore, factually nothing is faulty. It just seems faulty to us due to our desires. Thus, for instance, if we have desires for material luxuries, then poverty seems like a problem. But if we have the goal for spiritual elevation, then poverty seems like a blessing that detaches us from the material world and prevents the creation of habits of enjoyment which then bind us to the repeated cycle of birth and death. Likewise, if we have desires for material enjoyment, then wealth becomes a bondage to the world as it entices us toward greater sense pleasures. But if we have the desire for spiritual upliftment, then the same wealth becomes the source of upliftment as it is used for propagating the knowledge of the soul and God. Thus, neither poverty nor wealth are good or bad designations. It depends on our perspective or desire. If the desire is elevated, then material designations lead to elevation. If the desire is degraded, then material designations lead to degradation.

Sūtra 6.2.5

यदष्टिरूपरसगन्धस्पर्शं प्रोक्षितमभ्युक्षितं च तच्छुचि

yadiṣṭarūparasagandhasparśaṃ prokṣitamabhyukṣitaṃ ca tacchuci

yat—that which; iṣṭa—the Lord or sacred rite; rūpa—form; rasa—taste; gandha—smell; sparśaṃ—touch; prokṣitam—offering; abhyukṣitaṃ—offering with glorifying mantras; ca—also; tat—that; shuci—pure.

TRANSLATION

The form, taste, smell, and touch that is offered to the Lord (or sacred rite) with or without glorifying mantras, is also pure.

COMMENTARY

The terms prokṣitam and abhyukṣitaṃ are technical names used to denote rites of offering without and with the chanting of mantras, respectively. The term iṣṭa has several meanings, such as desirable, revered, etc. In the context of the offering (with and without the mantras) noted in this sūtra, this term references the Lord who receives the offering. When demigods are worshiped, the term iṣṭa-devata is generally used. Without the suffix, iṣṭa means the Lord.

The last sūtra spoke about the purification of desires by which the ordinary good or bad circumstances become the source of spiritual elevation. And this sūtra says that whatever is offered to the Lord with glorifying mantras becomes pure. The implication is that everything is meant to serve the Lord and their purpose—which was earlier said to be hidden or invisible—is that they are used in such service. The elevation in spiritual life is also using our sensual and mental energies to serve the Lord. By that service, the senses and the mind are offered to the Lord, for the purpose of His glorification, just like the offering of taste, smell, touch, and form. Since everything can be used to glorify the Lord, therefore, everything can be used for spiritual upliftment and that is the auspiciousness in everything. Nothing is inauspicious if used in the Lord's service.

Sūtra 6.2.6

अशुचीति शुचिप्रतिषेधः

aśucīti śucipratiṣedhaḥ

aśuci—the impure; iti—thus; śuci—the pure; pratiṣedhaḥ—forbidding.

TRANSLATION

In this way, the impure is the forbidding (or the opposite) of the pure.

COMMENTARY

Our bodies, senses, and minds, or even the things that they interact with, are impure when not used in the Lord's service. They seem good when the senses, mind, and body are fulfilled, and they seem bad otherwise. But the fact is that they are always pure as they can lead us to purity. And when not used in the Lord's service, they are always impure. This idea can be easily understood if we think of a gun: If it is used for the protection of the innocent, then it is good; if it is used to hurt the innocent, then it is bad. Since it can be used to protect the innocent, its real purpose is that of protection. But when it is used to hurt the innocent, then it has been contaminated by our materialistic desires. Thus, our desires—if pure—perceive the purpose of everything correctly, and that purpose is spiritual elevation. The impure desires instead contaminate everything. Thus, the reality is pure, but it is contaminated by our own desires. Under that contamination, it degrades us, even though its purpose is elevation.

Sūtra 6.2.7
अर्थान्तरं च
arthāntaraṃ ca

arthāntaraṃ—the differences of purpose; ca—also.

TRANSLATION
The differences of purpose are also (due to forbidding the true purpose).

COMMENTARY
When the service of the Lord is disregarded as the pure purpose, then many impure purposes are created. These include serving the body, serving the society, serving the nation, etc. In each such service, something else is not served; in fact, those serving their body tend to render a disservice to other bodies; those serving one society tend to hurt other societies; those serving one nation fight with others serving other nations. And all these kinds of service do not lead to spiritual upliftment because the body, society, or nation are temporary designations of the soul. When the soul is neglected in preference for the other designations, then the true purpose of life, and of other things, is disregarded.

Sūtra 6.2.8
अयतस्य शुचिभोजनादभ्युदयो न विद्यते नियमाभावाद् विद्यते वाऽर्थान्तरत्वाद् यमस्य
ayatasya śucibhojanādabhyudayo na vidyate niyamābhāvād vidyate vār'thāntaratvād yamasya

ayatasya—not endeavoring (for the true purpose); śuci—pure; bhojanāt—from the consumption of food; abhyudayah—elevation; na—not; vidyate—known; niyama—regulation; abhāvāt—from the absence of; vidyate—known; vā—or; arthāntaratvāt—as if an alternative purpose; yamasya—than restraint.

TRANSLATION

Not endeavoring for the true purpose by the consumption of pure food, elevation is not known due to the absence of regulation; alternatively, what is known is an imaginary purpose than the restraint (of consumption).

COMMENTARY

The previous sūtras have spoken of the nature of pure and impure as the Lord's service and this sūtra explicitly states that if the pure purpose is not adopted, then the elevating nature of reality is not known. Rather, the person is absorbed in unrestrained consumption, under some imaginary purpose.

Sūtra 6.2.9

असति चाभावात्

asati cābhāvāt

asati—falsity; ca—also; abhāvāt—from the absence.

TRANSLATION

From the absence (of true purpose), there is also falsity.

COMMENTARY

If we read scriptures but don't know their true purpose, then we will also misunderstand what they are saying. Therefore, the sincere students of scriptures are advised to study under an enlightened master, because that master can inform the students about the true purpose of scriptures, and the understanding of purpose then leads to the correct grasping of the scriptural statements. The purpose of something is an objective reality, but it is invisible to sense perception. And yet, it is the basis on which the meanings must be understood. Similarly, if the purpose of life is not understood, then we think that the body, senses, and the mind are meant for enjoyment, rather than upliftment. We fail to see the preciousness of human life and how the possession of a superior intellect can lead us to a better result. We just use it for mundane activities. Just like someone might use a diamond as a paperweight, similarly, not knowing the true purpose leads to the wastage of life in mundane activities.

Sūtra 6.2.10
सुखाद्रागः
sukhādrāgaḥ

sukhāt—from happiness; rāgaḥ—attachments.

TRANSLATION

Attachments arise from happiness.

COMMENTARY

The material body is not physical stuff because it comprises deeper levels of reality that we cannot sensually perceive. One such reality is attachment to things. A physical object cannot develop an attachment to anything. But our bodies get habituated to different kinds of foods, clothes, places of living, relationships, and people—because they have been the source of happiness in the past. Then, mere separation from these things becomes a source of unhappiness, and habits of repeated interaction with these things are formed. Thus, happiness initially leads to attachment, and eventually to suffering, because someday those things that have given us happiness will be taken away from us. Similarly, the suffering caused by things leads to detachment from those things, but that detachment eventually leads to happiness as the person is free of attachments. Thus, whatever seems suffering, in the beginning, can be a source of happiness, and whatever seems happiness, in the beginning, can be a source of suffering.

Sūtra 6.2.11
तन्मयत्वाच्च
tanmayatvācca

tanmayatvāt—from absorption of the mind into the body; ca—also.

TRANSLATION

(Attachments arise) also from the absorption of the mind into the body.

COMMENTARY

Attachments would not arise simply from interaction with the world if our consciousness is not absorbed in the body. The person who realizes that they are different from the body, treats the material pleasures and pains as temporary. They are neither attached to the sources of pleasures nor scared of the sources of pain. Therefore, the term 'also' here means that for pleasure to give rise to attachment, the person must also be identifying himself with the body.

Sūtra 6.2.12

अदृष्टाच्च

adṛṣṭācca

adṛṣṭāt—from the invisible; ca—also.

TRANSLATION

(Attachments arise) also from the invisible.

COMMENTARY

As we have earlier discussed, the invisible reality exists as the sense of absence, inadequacy, and incompleteness in a person. Each person feels inadequate in some respect, and the moment they find something that overcomes that sense of incompleteness, they become attached to it. Thus, deep bonds of attachment and attraction are instantly formed between some people because they complement and overcome their respective senses of inadequacy. This sūtra says that this is one of the causes of the attachment—apart from the previous two reasons: (a) happiness and (b) the mind's absorption into the body.

Sūtra 6.2.13

जातविशीषाच्च

jātiviśeṣācca

jātiviśeṣāt—from the specific classes or species; ca—also.

TRANSLATION

(Attachments arise) also from the specific classes or species of life.

COMMENTARY

The chitta carries impressions from past lives, and it gives us special insight into different aspects of the world that we live in. For example, if the soul has previously been into a dog's body, and those impressions are still active in the chitta, then he or she has a special insight into the dog. That makes them especially attracted to dogs. Likewise, some people are especially attracted to trees, because their chitta gives them a deeper insight into tree life. We tend to like things that we can understand, and we tend to dislike things that we cannot understand. Therefore, our capacity to understand things, based on our previous acquaintances with those things, also plays an important role in the formation of attachments. The things that we especially capable of are also often the things that we are able to use to produce good results, and that desire for happiness then makes us attached to those things. For instance, those who are especially gifted at music become attached to music because they are good at it. Thus, sometimes we may be very capable of certain kinds of things although not attached to them. And sometimes we may be attached to things although not very capable of doing them. This sūtra speaks of the situation in which our gifts and abilities create the successes, which lead to happiness and then to attachment. All these are by-products of the impressions left in the chitta.

Sūtra 6.2.14

इच्छाद्वेषपूर्विका धर्माधर्म प्रवृत्तिः

icchādveṣapūrvikā dharmādharma pravṛttiḥ

icchādveṣa—desire and aversion; pūrvikā—from the past; dharma—nature or duty; adharma—unnatural and non-duty; pravṛttiḥ—the tendencies.

TRANSLATION

The tendencies of nature or duty, unnatural and non-duty, desire and aversion are from the past.

COMMENTARY

The term 'dharma' has three meanings—(a) the desires of enjoyment intentions; this meaning of 'dharma' indicates that they are driven towards certain types of pleasures and goals, (b) the potentialities of knowledge and action, which can become real; this meaning of 'dharma' means 'nature', and (c) their duty or responsibility, due to which they are supposed to do certain things. The term icchādveṣa indicates the first type of dharma, and the terms dharma and adharma indicate the second and third types of dharma. We can also call them desire, ability, and responsibility, and they are hence also called guna, chitta, and karma. The gunas are habits of enjoyment and likes produced due to past actions that produced happiness; if something led to happiness in the past, we are inclined to repeat those same things in order to gain happiness. The chitta is the abilities or potentialities of knowledge and action, which then limit what we can do and know; these abilities are produced due to previous engagement in certain types of actions. As the saying goes: Practice makes perfect, repeated engagement in certain types of activities makes us skilled in those things. Karma is the cause of our circumstances, the role in society, and these roles entail a duty, which is also called dharma. By performing this dharma correctly, we become free of karma, but these roles are themselves produced due to past actions. In this way, the entire unconscious body of the soul is created due to past activities. It might be habits, skills, or consequences of actions. Sometimes they are distinguished as guna, chitta, and karma, and sometimes they are collectively designated as 'dharma'. This sūtra designates them collectively.

Sūtra 6.2.15

तत्संयोगो वभिागः

tatsaṃyogo vibhāgaḥ

tat—that; saṃyogah—by union; vibhāgaḥ—the divisions.

TRANSLATION

By union with that (three-fold dharma) the divisions (are created).

COMMENTARY

All the variety of this material world is a by-product of the variety in the unconscious body. The different species of life are the by-products of guna and chitta—each species of life has unique habits and capabilities. And these species of life are placed in different environments and eco-systems due to their karma. Thus, all variety can be succinctly construed in three ways—abilities, desires, and circumstances. This variety is also the consequence of the soul identifying with the unconscious body. This unconscious body is automatically triggered by time, and it produces a subtle modification, which is called vikāra or vṛitti in Yoga philosophy. When the soul identifies with this vikāra or vṛitti, it gives the "approval" for its existence simply by identifying with it. The subtle reality now manifests into some grosser reality, and the soul again identifies with that change and thereby gives its "approval". Then, an even grosser reality is produced. In this way, the soul is constrained by some desires, abilities, and circumstances, which then produce modifications, but the soul's identification with those changes creates further changes, and the variety of the world is produced.

Sūtra 6.2.16

आत्मकर्मसु मोक्षो व्याख्यातः

ātmakarmasu mokṣo vyākhyātaḥ

ātmakarmasu—by the actions of the soul; mokṣah—liberation; vyākhyātaḥ—explained.

TRANSLATION

By the actions of the soul, liberation is explained.

COMMENTARY

The 'action of the soul' in the materially conditioned state is just a choice—accept or reject. If the soul identifies with something, then it gives approval for its existence, and that is 'accept'. If the soul does not identify with something, then it doesn't give approval for its existence, and that is 'reject'. Thus, choice naturally emerges from the "I am" of the soul. If a desire arises due to guna, and the soul identifies with it, then "I am" becomes "I am desiring". The consciousness of the soul is now said to be 'present'. If the soul rejects that desire, then "I am" does not become "I am desiring" and the consciousness of the soul is 'absent'. By identification with material reality, the soul is caught in the material nature and undergoes the cycle of birth and death. But if the soul learns how to distinguish itself from the material reality, then it can also reject the automatically produced modification as *its* nature. Then, there is a material need or desire, but that is not "my desire" or "my need". This leads to liberation.

Chapter 7

Section 1

Sūtra 7.1.1

उक्ता गुणाः

uktā guṇāḥ

uktā—have been stated; guṇāḥ—the qualities.

TRANSLATION

The qualities have been stated.

COMMENTARY

The following sūtras revisit and detail the nature of the aforementioned qualities. As we can recall, four qualities—smell, taste, form, and touch—were noted earlier, corresponding to four elements—Earth, Water, Fire, and Air.

Sūtra 7.1.2

पृथिव्यादि रूपरसगन्धस्पर्शा द्रव्यानित्यत्वादनित्याश्च

pṛthivyādi rūparasagandhasparśā dravyānityatvādanityāśca

pṛthivyādi—Earth etc.; rūpa—form; rasa—taste; gandha—smell; sparśā—touch; dravya—objects; anityatvāt—as if from temporary; anitya—temporary; ca—also.

TRANSLATION

The elements of Earth etc., the qualities such as form, taste, smell, and touch, and objects are as if from temporary and they are temporary.

COMMENTARY

The material nature is eternal, but it is not eternally manifest. Even the qualities such as taste, touch, smell, and sight are not eternally manifest, although they exist eternally in an unmanifest form. Therefore, the term "as if from temporary" is used to refer to this apparent temporariness. When this manifest form becomes unmanifest, then it appears to be temporary. Thus, the manifest and unmanifest states of reality are used to claim both eternity and temporariness. The next sūtra explains that the material nature is always eternal.

Sūtra 7.1.3

एतेन नित्येषु नित्यत्वमुक्तम्

etena nityeṣu nityatvamuktam

etena—by this; nityeṣu—in the eternal; nityatvam—eternity; uktam—stated.

TRANSLATION

By this, eternity is stated in the eternal.

COMMENTARY

The material energy is eternal, but its manifestations are temporary. Since the manifestation emerges out of the eternal, and then returns to the unmanifest state, therefore, it is sometimes said to be eternal and sometimes temporary.

Sūtra 7.1.4

अप्सु तेजसि वायौ च नित्या द्रव्यनित्यत्वात्

apsu tejasi vāyau ca nityā dravyanityatvāt

apsu—in Water; tejasi—in Fire; vāyau—in Air; ca—also; nityā—eternal; dravyanityatvāt—objectivity from eternity.

TRANSLATION

In Water, Fire, Air also eternal objectivity (is present) from eternity.

COMMENTARY

As we have discussed earlier, the individuals can manifest from the universals, and the universals can manifest from the individuals. All this potentiality exists eternally but a very small portion of that potentiality is manifest occasionally. This occasional manifestation is due to time and the soul. Therefore, the atoms of Earth, Water, Fire, Air, etc. are considered eternal, although they may often be unmanifest. Likewise, the combinations of these atoms—e.g., our bodies—are considered eternal although they do become unmanifest.

Sūtra 7.1.5

अनित्येष्वनित्या द्रव्यनित्यत्वात्

anityeṣvanityā dravyānityatvāt

anityeṣu—in the temporary; anityā—the temporary; dravya—objectivity; nityatvāt—from the eternity.

TRANSLATION

In the temporary, the temporary objectivity is from eternity.

COMMENTARY

The objects that we see around us seem temporary, but they are eternal. Due to the effect of time and the soul, they appear to be temporary. Therefore, this world is also said to be a place of birth and death, even though everything that is manifest is eternally present even when it appears to be unmanifest.

Sūtra 7.1.6

कारणगुणपूर्वकाःपृथिव्यां पाकजाः

kāraṇaguṇapūrvakāḥ pṛthivyāṃ pākajāḥ

kāraṇa—the cause; guṇa—qualities; pūrvakāḥ—previous; pṛthivyāṃ—in Earth; pākajāḥ—the unborn in the food.

TRANSLATION

The cause of qualities is the previously existing qualities unborn in the food.

COMMENTARY

The previous sūtra spoke about the eternity of the objects, and this sūtra speaks about the eternity of the qualities. They are said to be 'unborn' here.

Sūtra 7.1.7

एकद्रव्यत्वात्

ekadravyatvāt

eka—one; dravyatvāt—as if from an object.

TRANSLATION

(The qualities and objects) are as if from a single object.

COMMENTARY

The reality that manifests is not just eternal; it is also unified. That unification arises because there is a single source of the manifestation in the Lord. He is the complete truth, and the manifest things are the partial expressions of the manifest truth. Just like the sentences in a book express different meanings, but the book originates from an idea, similarly, the whole truth expands into diversity but that diversity is not independent realities. They are rather related to each other by virtue of being part of the book. Nevertheless, the idea that originates the book, and the book itself, are distinct. Therefore, if the book is destroyed, then the idea is not destroyed; but if the idea did not exist, then the book also cannot be manifest. Therefore, the manifested reality is said to be at once different and non-different from the source: The difference is that the meaning existed when the book did not exist, and the non-difference is that when the book exists, then it embodies the same meaning that existed prior.

Sūtra 7.1.8

अणोर्महतश्चोपलब्ध्यनुपलब्धी नित्ये व्याख्याते

aṇormahataścopalabdhyanupalabdhī nitye vyākhyāte

aṇoh—of the atom; mahatah—greatness; ca—also;

upalabdhi—perceived; anupalabdhī—not perceived; nitye—in the eternal; vyākhyāte—explained.

TRANSLATION

It is explained that the greatness of the atom is also perceived and not perceived in the eternal.

COMMENTARY

Everything in this world has some great qualities, and by those great qualities it is identified. But everything is also missing some great qualities by which it is distinguished from other things. However, the Lord possesses all the great qualities in full; these qualities are partially present in the things that have expanded from Him. All these great qualities, however, are not simultaneously visible; they are rather visible in different contextual relationships to the Lord. Each contextual relationship reveals some greatness and hides other greatness. Therefore, this sūtra states that these qualities are perceived and not perceived in the Lord, because the perception depends on the contextual relationship.

Sūtra 7.1.9

कारण बहुत्वाच्च

kāraṇa bahutvācca

kāraṇa—the cause; bahutvāt—from the plurality; ca—also.

TRANSLATION

From the plurality of causes also (many atoms are produced).

COMMENTARY

The impersonalist says that the one source of everything cannot produce many things; this production must be caused by māyā. But the Lord is single, and yet, He has all the qualities in a combined form. These qualities are the various aspects of the Lord, which are revealed in different contexts. When these qualities are separated, then numerous diverse things are produced.

Sūtra 7.1.10
अतो वपिरतिमणु
ato viparitamaṇu

atah—therefore; viparitam—the opposite; aṇu—atom.

TRANSLATION

Therefore, the opposite atom.

COMMENTARY

Since the Lord has all the qualities, therefore, He also has opposite qualities. He is kind and cruel, beautiful and ugly, bitter and sweet, the smallest and the biggest. The atoms are the symbols of these qualities. Since the qualities are mutually opposed, therefore, the meaning in the symbol is also mutually opposed.

Sūtra 7.1.11
अणु महदतिि तिस्मनि् वशिषभावात् वशिोषाभावाच्च
aṇu mahaditi tasmin viśeṣabhāvāt viśeṣābhāvācca

aṇu—atom; mahat—greatness; iti—thus; tasmin—in that; viśeṣa—specific; bhāvāt—from presence; viśeṣa—specific; abhāvāt—from absence; ca—also.

TRANSLATION

The greatness in the atom is thus from the presence of specific qualities and the absence of specific qualities.

COMMENTARY

The separation of qualities means that the sweetness atom is different from the bitterness atom. The heat atom is different from the cold atom. And so on. When one quality is present in the atom, the opposite quality is missing.

Sūtra 7.1.12
एककालत्वात्
ekakālatvāt

ekakālatvāt—from the simultaneity (of the opposites).

TRANSLATION
(The atoms are) from the simultaneity (of the opposites).

COMMENTARY
The impersonalist says that the Absolute Truth is devoid of all qualities; it is neither hot nor cold, neither bitter nor sweet. But this sūtra says that the Absolute Truth simultaneously possesses all qualities; it is both hot and cold, both bitter and sweet. The material world, however, separates these qualities, such that the bitterness atom is separate from the sweetness atom. The impersonalist conceives qualities based on this separation—he says that if all qualities are opposed to the other qualities, then how can we obtain unity? The unity would become logically contradictory if it comprises the opposites. This sūtra however states that the Absolute Truth is all the qualities simultaneously. The resolution of the contradiction is that these qualities are not manifest simultaneously. As has already been stated previously, the qualities are perceived and not perceived. The perception and non-perception depend on the context. Even though the qualities exist simultaneously, the context reveals their presence.

Sūtra 7.1.13
दृष्टान्ताच्च
dṛṣṭāntācca

dṛṣṭāntāt—from the standard; ca—also.

TRANSLATION
(The atoms are) also from the standard (of the qualities).

COMMENTARY
When standards are conceived physically, then any object can become a standard. For example, both kilogram and pound can be the standard of

weight. However, when standards are conceived semantically, then the pure and perfect entity is always the standard. This sūtra states that atoms are produced from this perfect standard. As we have discussed earlier, the universal can expand into many individuals, which are the instances of the universal. The individual atoms are the symbolic instances of the source, and the source is the standard from which they have expanded. The difference is simply that in the standard, all the qualities are present simultaneously, but in expansions, many of these qualities are missing. Due to these missing qualities, we can say that each individual entity is a *partial expression* of the standard, and only the standard is the whole truth. We can also say that the expansions are parts of the whole truth since they partially manifest or express the standard's qualities.

Sūtra 7.1.14

अणुत्वमहत्त्वयोरणुत्वमहत्त्वाभावःकर्मगुणैर्व्याख्यातः

aṇutvamahattvayoraṇutvamahattvābhāvaḥ karmaguṇairvyākhyātaḥ

aṇutva—atomicity; mahattvayoh—and greatness; aṇutva—atomicity; mahattva—greatness; abhāvaḥ—the absence; karma—activity; guṇair—of qualities; vyākhyātaḥ—the explanation.

TRANSLATION

The explanation of qualities and activities is the absence of atomicity and greatness in the atomicity and greatness.

COMMENTARY

The ordinary qualities that we perceive by the senses can be logically divided into atomic qualities, but the world of things that we perceive is always a combination of qualities. Thus, even though we can logically separate the properties of shape and color, we cannot find anything that is just shape without color, or just color without shape. Since the qualities are always combined, therefore, the world of qualities is the absence of atomicity. Similarly, since the qualities are present in everything as a mixture of many qualities, therefore, the pure nature of each quality is not fully manifest in those mixtures. To understand this, we have to recognize that each quality hides some aspect of the other qualities. This is easily seen when opposite qualities like bitter and sweet or hot and cold are combined—the result is neither purely bitter nor sweet, neither purely hot nor cold. It is harder to see this in the case of a combination of qualities such as shape and color. But we can understand it by realizing that all the qualities are orthogonal 'dimensions' of a space of meanings and that orthogonality is defined by all the member qualities collectively. Therefore, if a new quality is added to an ensemble, then the other qualities must be modified to maintain orthogonality. This modification of the qualities means that none of the qualities are perfectly represented in a collection. The presence of other qualities in the ensemble makes each quality imperfect, and that imperfection is called the absence of 'greatness' in this sūtra. Quite simply, each quality is partially hidden in a mixture of qualities, as the other qualities obfuscate it.

Thus, the ordinary qualities and activities are not atomic because the qualities are always mixed. And the ordinary qualities and activities are not greatness because the pure nature of each quality is modified by other qualities. Even when we contextually observe one quality, what we get is not pure quality. We rather get the quality that has been modified by the presence of other qualities. This modification of qualities is called 'entanglement' in atomic theory. The members of an entangled ensemble are mutually orthogonal dimensions. Therefore, the addition or removal of a quality modifies each member.

We can also explain this idea by how 'knowledge' is present in subjects like mathematics, physics, chemistry, etc., and yet, we cannot say that knowledge is mathematics, or knowledge is physics, or knowledge is chemistry. We can, however, make the reverse claim—mathematics is knowledge. Since "mathematics is knowledge", therefore, knowledge is present in mathematics. And yet, the pure form of knowledge is modified by the presence of other attributes. Therefore, knowledge is not mathematics, but mathematics is knowledge.

Sūtra 7.1.15

कर्मभिः कर्माणि गुणैश्च गुणा व्याख्याताः

karmabhiḥ karmāṇi guṇaiśca guṇā vyākhyātāḥ

karmabhiḥ—by activity; karmāṇi—the actions; guṇaiśca—also by qualities; guṇā—the qualities; vyākhyātāḥ—explained.

TRANSLATION

By activity, the activities, also by qualities the qualities, are explained.

COMMENTARY

Complex qualities and activities can be created by combining simpler qualities and activities. Again, the presence of additional qualities or activities in a mixture must modify all the qualities. Hence, the mixtures of qualities or activities cannot be the original pure and perfect ideas or forms prior to mixing.

Sūtra 7.1.16

अणुत्वमहत्त्वाभ्यां कर्मगुणाश्च व्याख्याताः

aṇutvamahattvābhyāṃ karmaguṇāśca vyākhyātāḥ

aṇutva—atomicity; mahattvābhyāṃ—and greatness; karma—activity; guṇa—qualities; ca—also; vyākhyātāḥ—are explained.

TRANSLATION

Activities and qualities are also explained as atomicity and greatness.

COMMENTARY

The sūtra prior to the last one said that the qualities and activities are defined by the absence of atomicity and greatness, and this sūtra states the opposite: The qualities and activities can be explained by the atomicity and greatness. These seemingly contradictory statements are reconciled if we recognize that the original pure and perfect qualities are present in each thing, but they are modified by the presence of the other qualities. Due to this modification, we cannot say that the qualities are present in their original pure form. And yet we also cannot deny the presence of the qualities in a modified form. The similarity between the pure and the modified forms of qualities leads us to the conclusion that to explain the modified form we must use the original and pure form. As a result, the original and pure qualities are present and can be used to explain the ordinary qualities, and yet, in another sense, they are not present purely. The absence of pure forms was noted earlier, and this sūtra states that we can understand the world in terms of atomicity and greatness. This is because even if the qualities are not present in their pure form, they are still present impurely. This imperfect presence is still the quality's presence, although imperfect.

Sūtra 7.1.17

एतेन दीर्घत्व ह्रस्वत्वे व्याख्याते

etena dīrghatva hrasvatve vyākhyāte

etena—by this; dīrghatva—bigness; hrasvatve—in the smallness; vyākhyāte—explained.

TRANSLATION

By this, the bigness in the smallness is explained.

COMMENTARY

The bigness is pure quality, and the smallness is the modification of that quality, by which some of the bigness is obfuscated. As we have discussed earlier, each thing has some qualities of greatness, but since these qualities are not manifest in a pure form, therefore, greatness is always partial. And yet, we also cannot say that the thing has absolutely no greatness. Therefore, the correct conclusion is that the original greatness is present, but it is covered by layers of obfuscations produced by other qualities. These layers of obfuscations hide the purity of the quality. The combination of the pure quality and its obfuscations appears as impure quality, even though the pure quality is always present.

We can think of an unmarried man who is a good friend to another person—he always comes to help his friend whenever the need arises. But if this man gets married, then the additional relationship with his wife makes him a less ideal friend—sometimes he doesn't come to help the friend in need. When this man has children, then he becomes even less of an ideal friend—because now there are more instances in which he doesn't come to the help of the friend. In this way, by mixing qualities, the nature of each quality is obfuscated. That obfuscation does not mean the absence of the original quality—a married man with children can still be a friend, although the friendship is no longer ideal.

Sūtra 7.1.18
अनित्ये ऽनित्यम्
anitye 'nityam

anitye—in the temporary; anityam—the temporariness.

TRANSLATION

(In this way) the temporariness in the temporary (is explained).

COMMENTARY

If some qualities are added to an ensemble, other qualities are modified. Similarly, if the qualities are removed, again, there is a modification to the remaining qualities. The question is: Does the addition of qualities bring the qualities closer to their pure form? Or does the removal of qualities bring them closer to the pure form? Since no quality can exist by itself, therefore, the pure form of the quality in isolation cannot be defined by removing all the other qualities. The pure form has to be defined by adding all possible qualities. Thus, the pure and perfect form of each quality is seen when *all* the possible qualities are present. As qualities are removed, each quality becomes slightly imperfect.

Therefore, while temporariness can be defined by the addition and removal of qualities, the addition of more qualities makes the ensemble more perfect. Conversely, the removal of qualities makes each quality less perfect. Change through the addition and removal of qualities therefore can be directed toward greater or lesser perfection. And that change constitutes temporariness.

Sūtra 7.1.19
नित्ये नित्यम्
nitye nityam

nitye—in the eternal; nityam—eternity.

TRANSLATION

(In this way) the eternity in the eternal (is explained).

COMMENTARY

Eternity is the scenario in which all the possible qualities are already present. This 'eternity' has earlier been called the source of everything, so in this context, it means the Lord from Whom everything manifests. The Lord possesses all the qualities. And in this state, each quality has its pure and perfect form. Even if some quality is added, there is no change to these forms because they are already in their pure form. And since no quality can be removed by the addition of qualities, therefore, the Lord's form of qualities is never diminished. In the material world, everything has a limited number of qualities. By this limitation of qualities, each of the qualities also has an imperfect form. But the Lord is all the qualities simultaneously, and that also makes each quality pure.

Sūtra 7.1.20

नित्यं परिमण्डलम्

nityaṃ parimaṇḍalam

nityaṃ—the eternal; parimaṇḍalam—circular or spherical.

TRANSLATION

The eternal is circular or spherical.

COMMENTARY

The circularity here should be understood in contrast to hierarchy. Conceptual hierarchies modify the root concept by the addition of other concepts. For example, a 'black table' is the modification of 'table' by the addition of 'black'. A 'long black table' is the modification of 'table' by the addition of 'long' and 'black'. When 'table' is modified by these additions, then the pure form of 'table' is obfuscated by 'long' and 'black', because if we took the 'long black table' as the pure 'table', then a 'short white table' would no longer be a 'table'. Therefore, we must say that 'table' is present in a 'long black table' but it has been partially obfuscated. This obfuscation of 'table' is achieved by a hierarchy—the property 'table' is the root, the property 'black' is the trunk, and the property 'black' is the branch. During perception, we focus on one of these qualities at a time—so we sometimes see a 'table', then 'black', and then 'long'. The mind then constructs a picture that combines these properties. In some minds, blackness can be the prominent property, such that they might say that the 'black table' is a subclass of black things. In other minds, tableness can be the prominent property, such that a 'black table' is the subclass of the class 'table'.

This hierarchical construction must be discarded if all the properties are equally prominent, and replaced by perfect symmetry. The statement about the eternal truth being spherical or symmetrical is not about a particular shape, because that shape is just one of the numerous properties. This is rather a statement about the symmetry in the collection of properties, which is analogously described as a sphere or circle. It means that none of the properties is more or less prominent. The Nyāya system explains this differently by stating that all the qualities are present inside each quality. Therefore, even if we see only one quality, it doesn't mean that the other qualities are absent. Each part or aspect of the Lord is therefore complete because it comprises all the possible qualities. Thus, the Lord can use His eyes for seeing, but that is not the only function of the eyes. By His eyes, the Lord can also eat, hold, walk, or impregnate. Thus, each part of the Lord is the Lord fully. The mutual exclusion of qualities that exists in the material world doesn't exist in the Lord. Since each quality is the completeness of all qualities, therefore, all the qualities are equivalent. This equivalence means that no quality is superior or inferior. Unlike our bodies where the head is superior to the hands, this is not the case with the Lord. When the property of superiority and inferiority of qualities is discarded, then there are many qualities, but they are not organized hierarchically. The presence of all these qualities without a hierarchy is referred to here as 'circularity'.

Sūtra 7.1.21
अविद्या च विद्यालिङ्गम्

avidyā ca vidyāliṅgam

avidyā—ignorance; ca—also; vidyā—knowledge; liṅgam—symptom.

TRANSLATION
Ignorance is also a symptom of knowledge.

COMMENTARY
The knowledge of the perfect truth exists in all of us, but it is covered by many layers of negations called māyā. When the truth is negated, then

ignorance is produced. But negation requires an assertion; without the assertion, the negation has no independent existence. Therefore, if someone says that "unicorns do not exist", then they are assuming the existence of a meaning called 'unicorn'. If the meaning 'unicorn' was impossible, then the statement "unicorns do not exist" would also be impossible. When reality is defined as meaning, then it comprises everything conceivable. If we can think of something, then it exists as a possibility. It may not be available to our sense perception, but it can become sense perceivable using the same process by which the other possibilities are converted into reality. The invisibility of unicorns can therefore be described as a layer of negation on top of the possibility. If that layer of invisibility is removed, then, the unicorns will become visible. That layer of invisibility thus covers our vision and creates *our ignorance*. That ignorance would not exist if the possibility did not exist, because there would be no need to cover the vision of something that is impossible. Impossibility would simply mean inconceivability and inconceivable things cannot be spoken of. Therefore, all negations indicate the existence of the assertion, and the negation is a layer of ignorance that covers our vision of the thing we cannot see.

Sūtra 7.1.22

वभिवान्महानाकाश:तथा चात्मा

vibhavānmahānākāśaḥ tathā cātmā

vibhavāt—from that which is the nature of wealth; mahāna—great; ākāśaḥ—space; tathā—in the same way; ca—also; ātmā—the soul.

TRANSLATION

The great space is from that which is the nature of wealth; in the same way, the soul also (is an expansion).

COMMENTARY

The impersonalists use the terms mahākāśh and ghatākāśh to denote the Brahman (the great space) and the individual consciousness (the potted space). The claim is that if the pots of individual consciousness are broken, then the soul merges into Brahman. These pots are also said to be constituted by māyā in impersonalism. But this sūtra states that the mahākāśh or Brahman is expanded from the Supreme Lord who is the very nature of wealth. The term vibhava actually denotes six qualities—knowledge, beauty, wealth, power, fame, and renunciation. They are collectively called the 'opulences' of the Lord, so the term vibhava which means 'wealth' is also sometimes used to denote the Lord. These opulences expand into a mahākāśh or a "great space" which is like an inverted tree in which the root is the Lord. The soul is then described to be just like a bird that hops from one branch of the tree to another. The soul is also said to be an expansion of the Lord in this sūtra. These expansions are just like the concept 'mammal' expanding into other concepts such as 'cow', 'horse', 'dog', 'cat', etc. In one sense, the expanded reality is a part of the whole, and in another sense, the whole doesn't reduce to the expanded parts. Therefore, the material space and the soul are partial expressions of the full wealth in the Lord, and the Lord is distinct from these expansions. Thus, in a single sūtra, many contentions of impersonalism are simultaneously refuted: (1) mahākāśh is not the ultimate reality, (2) mahākāśh is expanded from the Supreme Lord, (3) the Supreme Lord is not devoid of qualities, (4) He is called vibhavat or one whose nature is wealth, and (5) the soul is also expanded from the Supreme Lord.

Sūtra 7.1.23

तदभावादणु मनः

tadabhāvādaṇu manaḥ

tat—that; ahāvāt—from the absence; aṇu—atom; manaḥ—mind.

TRANSLATION

From the absence of that (the Lord), the atoms of mind (or thought).

COMMENTARY

The materialistic mind is defined by ideas disconnected from the Lord. The spiritual mind is defined as the ideas that are connected to the Lord. The ideas of the materialistic mind believe that matter exists of its own accord. Most materialists also think that the soul is merely an epiphenomenon of matter. But even if someone thinks that the soul is different from matter, but doesn't see the connection between matter and the Lord, his ideas are also considered materialistic. Similarly, if someone thinks that there is no connection between the soul and God, their spiritualism is also quite like materialism, because they think that both matter and soul have no relation to God. When the connection between matter and God, and soul and God, is perceived, then the same reality transforms into spiritualism. The materialistic ideas are illusory, because God is present as an immanent truth inside an idea, if we trace the origin of that idea. But materialism tries not to trace that origin; it postulates some ideas as *axioms* supposing that they are self-evident truths, rather than created truths. The difference between various kinds of materialism is how deep their axioms are.

The impersonalists also suppose that consciousness is an axiom, and to avoid the conclusion that each individual consciousness is a separate axiom, they try to reduce the individuals to a singular Brahman. After all, a system with infinite axioms would not be considered a perfect system. All these systems are materialistic because they axiomatize what is not an axiom. The true axiom is the Supreme Lord; He is all the qualities, He is a conscious person, and He has desires. When He expands, the souls also get the Lord's qualities, consciousness, and desires in part. By His expansion, matter also gets the Lord's qualities, the capacity to connect and relate, and intentionality. Therefore, matter is also a conscious person, just like the soul. The difference between matter and soul is that the soul can act of its own accord, while matter always acts on the direction of the Lord. Just like a faithful servant doesn't do anything unless the master asks for it, similarly, matter acts on the direction of the Lord. Due to this faithfulness to the master, matter is sometimes called 'inert' although it is not. It seems to be inert because it only acts on the direction of the master.

The soul on the other hand can act even against the master's will, but that action is considered the misuse of free will. There is also a third spiritual energy beyond matter and soul, which spontaneously acts in the service of the Lord. Unlike the material energy, where the Lord has to ask it to do something, the spiritual energy acts spontaneously to fulfill the Lord's wishes. All these three energies are expansions of the Lord, but we can visualize them as three kinds of servants: (1) the material energy is a faithful servant that waits on the instructions and executes them faithfully, (2) the spiritual energy is a faithful servant that does what the Lord wants without waiting for the Lord to ask for it, and (3) the soul, which can become an errant misbehaved servant who acts impetuously not realizing or totally disregarding the consequences of his actions.

Since these three forms of the Lord's energies are expanded from the

Lord, therefore, the Lord has all these three natures. First, He has the nature to do what is required and no more. Second, He has the nature to act spontaneously for the good, even if not asked for. Third, He has the nature to act impetuously, disregarding the outcomes of actions. The soul takes its impetuous nature from the Lord and thinks that he can be *independently* impetuous. That independence, or absence of the Lord, is the fault in the soul according to this sūtra. If the soul is liberated, it can act impetuously, but that impetuous nature is in relation to the Lord. That impetuous action that totally disregards one's own well-being and only considers the Lord's happiness is the limit of perfection.

Sūtra 7.1.24

गुणैर्दिग्व्याख्याता

guṇairdigvyākhyātā

guṇair—the qualities; dik—directions; vyākhyātā—explained.

TRANSLATION

The qualities are explained as directions.

COMMENTARY

This sūtra occurred earlier too, and it is repeated here, after noting that the material mind is the absence of the Lord. The different directions in space are different kinds of absence of the Lord. Since the Lord is the sum total of all qualities, the different types of absences of the Lord create material qualities which are missing in the other qualities. Thus, a 'separated' space of mutually exclusive qualities is produced by removing the whole truth from the parts.

This absence of the Lord is not real; the Lord is factually immanent in everything as the Paramātma. However, the soul's vision is covered in a way that it doesn't perceive this separation. For example, when cows, horses, dogs, and cats are expanded from a mammal, then we might refuse to see how they are similar in nature, and therefore, must have expanded from a common source. Instead, we might say that cows, horses, dogs, and cats are independent realities and treat them as axioms. This axiomatization of details, disregarding the abstract (which is also the deeper reality), doesn't mean that it is real. It is just real in our mental vision of reality. The reality is that the qualities are separated as directions, but the whole truth is immanent in each quality, and by that immanence, it is connected to the whole truth. But if we cannot perceive that immanence, we think that these directions are physically separated entities.

An earlier sūtra stated that ignorance is also the symptom of knowledge. In this case, the knowledge is that the whole truth is immanent in everything, and ignorance is that parts are separated from each other. This ignorance, which was earlier stated to be the mind devoid of the understanding of the Lord, is the covering of the soul that blocks the vision of deeper realities because the soul doesn't want to see the deeper reality. If that deeper reality was perceived, the mentality of independence would have to be discarded. To support its desire for independence, the soul buries itself into ignorance by wearing the goggles that filter the truth—especially the truth of the Lord's existence.

Sūtra 7.1.25

कारणेन कालः

kāraṇena kālaḥ

kāraṇena—the cause of this; kālaḥ—time.

TRANSLATION

The cause of this (separation of qualities) is time.

COMMENTARY

This sūtra also occurred previously, but in the present context, it means that when a material mind devoid of the understanding of the Lord is produced, then time causes the appearance and disappearance of things. Thereby, everything that we have previously axiomatized as reality sometimes appears and sometimes disappears. This appearance and disappearance of our axioms tell us that they are not truly real, and thus we go searching again for the real axioms. Temporariness is thus associated with ignorance. If we have false ideas, then nature will force a change by which we are compelled to change our ideas. If this change did not exist, then we would continue to hold our false ideas as truth. But we are compelled to change our ideas because time destroys our beliefs by changing reality. Thus, material nature is not purposeless; it has a purpose to bring us to the proper understanding of the truth, and the destruction of false beliefs is the way to achieve it. The soul doesn't want to give up its desire for independence, and it is compelled to keep facing destruction.

Section 2

Sūtra 7.2.1

रुपरसगन्धस्पर्शव्यतिरेकादर्थान्तरमेकत्वम्

ruparasagandhasparśavyatirekādarthāntaramekatvam

rupa—form; rasa—taste; gandha—smell; sparśa—touch; vyatirekāt—from the mutual exclusion; arthāntaram—a difference of meaning; ekatvam—unity.

TRANSLATION

From the mutual exclusion, form, taste, smell, and touch have a difference in meaning from the unity.

COMMENTARY

This sūtra refers to the conceptual distinction between the source of the qualities (which is called the unity here) and the qualities themselves. This distinction entails that the source has an effect on the sense perceivable qualities, but the source itself cannot be obtained through sense perception. This, as we have discussed earlier, is typical of all the causes that are deeper than the sense perceivable qualities. For example, mental states such as happiness and distress have effects on the body, but these effects cannot be explained simply by sense perception because triggers for such chemicals would remain unexplained.

Sūtra 7.2.2

तथा पृथक्त्वम्

tathā pṛthaktvam

tathā—in the same way; pṛthaktvam—the separateness.

TRANSLATION

In the same way, separateness (is different from unity).

COMMENTARY

This sūtra refers to the individual instances of the qualities noted above.

Sūtra 7.2.3

एकत्वैकपृथक्त्वयोरेकत्वैकपृथक्त्वाभावो ऽणुत्वमहत्त्वाभ्यां व्याख्यातः

ekatvaikapṛthaktvayorekatvaikapṛthaktvābhāvo 'ṇutvamahattvābhyāṃ vyākhyātaḥ

ekatva—oneness; eka—one; pṛthaktvayoh—in the separateness; ekatva—oneness; eka—one; pṛthaktva—separateness; abhāvah—absence; aṇutva—atomicity mahattvābhyāṃ—from greatness; vyākhyātaḥ—is explained.

TRANSLATION

The absence of oneness, one, and separateness in the oneness, one, and separateness is explained by atomicity arising from greatness.

COMMENTARY

The sūtra describes a paradox and its solution. The paradox is that there is simultaneous diversity and oneness. The existence of diversity is the absence of oneness, and the existence of oneness is the absence of diversity. The diversity exists because the whole truth is divided into parts. And the oneness exists because the whole truth is immanent in the parts. Since both unity and diversity exist, therefore, separateness and oneness are absent. Similarly, the "one" is transcendent to the parts, therefore, the "one" is absent from the diversity.

The "one" from which the diversity expands comprises all the diversity, and yet, the diversity is not separated in the "one". Therefore, there is no separateness (as there is oneness), and there is no oneness (because there is diversity). Similarly, the "one" is absent from the "one" because It has the desire for self-knowledge; that desire can exist only when the "one" doesn't know itself. This desire for self-knowledge is called abhāva due to which the self misses itself and desires to unite with itself; that union creates self-knowledge.

Thus, paradoxically, there is one (the source of everything), there is diversity (or separateness), and there is unity in diversity (the oneness). And yet, in another sense, the one is missing from the diversity and itself, the diversity is missing in the one, and unity—even though present—is apparently missing because it is not perceived in the material condition. This leads to the paradox of one, oneness, and separateness, namely that they are at once present and absent. The resolution of the paradox is that oneness counters separateness, the separateness counters oneness, and yet both are reconciled in the one. This one expands into many due to the one missing from itself; therefore, another paradox of presence and absence is created, but the paradox is resolved if we understand this "one" as a personality with the desire for self-knowledge.

Once we understand the paradox and its resolution, then we can understand the role of atomicity and greatness. The greatness is the transcendent whole truth, and the atomicity is the immanent representation of this whole truth within all partial truths. Just like a mammal is present within a cow, and in one sense mammal is transcendent, and in another sense immanent, in the same way, the Absolute Truth is transcendent as greatness and immanent as atomicity. Thus, He is both the greatest and the smallest. His immanence in everything is the unity in everything; His transcendence being divided into parts is the diversity, and His transcendental personality is the one. Thus, the Lord is inside everything, outside everything, and everything. These three realizations about the Absolute Truth are called Paramātma, Bhagavan, and Brahman, respectively. Brahman is everything; Paramātma is the immanent truth inside everything, and Bhagavan is the transcendent truth outside everything.

If we only acknowledge diversity, then there would be no unity, and there would be no origin. If we say that there is one source for everything, but that source is transcendent, then there would be no way to *know* that source from the things. Such a postulate would become indistinguishable from arbitrary hypotheses. Hence, in addition to diversity, and a single source of diversity, we must acknowledge a unity that is immanent inside the diversity. This immanent truth creates unity in diversity and is the means to know the transcendent one: We can look deep inside anything, and know the source of everything.

Sūtra 7.2.4

नःिसंखयत्वात् करमगुणानां सरवैकत्वं न वदियते

niḥ saṃkhyatvāt karmaguṇānāṃ sarvaikatvaṃ na vidyate

niḥ—without; saṃkhyatvāt—from number-like; karma—activity; guṇānāṃ—qualities; sarva—all; ekatvaṃ—unity; na—not vidyate—known.

TRANSLATION

Without being manifested from number-like, the unity of all activities and qualities cannot be known.

COMMENTARY

This sūtra states the Sāñkhya position in which all qualities and activities are essentially numbers, but these numbers are meanings. Their interaction is based on the logic of meaning interaction, and their successive manifestation is the manifestation of one number from within another. Based on the nature of numbers, their manifestation and interaction can be studied scientifically. Logic and numbers are therefore applicable to the study of qualities and activities because the qualities and activities are themselves numbers. But these are not quantitative numbers; each number rather symbolizes a type of meaning.

Sūtra 7.2.5

भ्रान्तं तत्

bhrāntaṃ tat

bhrāntaṃ—confusing; tat—that.

TRANSLATION

That (unity due to manifestation from number-like) is confusing.

COMMENTARY

In modern science, we think of the world as matter and force, not as numbers. Matter is understood in terms of its properties like mass and charge, energy, and momentum. Forces are similarly conceived as gravity, electromagnetism, etc. How can all these things be just numbers? Despite the successes of modern science and its reliance on numbers and equations, we still don't understand why mathematics can be so successful in describing the nature of reality. This confusion is the result of thinking of numbers as quantities, rather than types of meaning. Conversely, those who don't feel confused about this success use that success to proclaim materialism when factually all that science does is numbers and equations. This sūtra answers the twin confusions about why science works, as well as why materialism is false despite its success.

The answer to the question about why science works is that nature is numbers, and the equations of science treat reality as numbers. The successes of science owe to the fact that it has gotten one idea correct—namely, that nature should be described using mathematics. By capturing some properties of the number aggregates, science has become successful. However, the aggregation of numbers doesn't necessarily produce a number that would be obtained by the addition of constituent numbers. Numbers also have complex contextual properties due to the inverted-tree-like structure in which they are produced.

A number, for instance, can be treated in three ways—an object, a quality, and an activity. A number like 10 can sometimes refer to a particular individual—e.g., employee number 10. Then, it can refer to the quality of tenness. And it can refer to an activity (e.g., if numbers are used as instructions in computers). Whether a number is an object, quality, or activity cannot be determined independently of context. But since each number is some quality, activity, or object, therefore, the result of number aggregation cannot simply be obtained by the addition of numbers. Such addition amounts to adding qualities to activities to objects—which cannot be added since they are entities of different types.

Just as apples and oranges can be added to obtain the total number of fruits, but not the total number of apples or oranges, similarly, sometimes number addition works if it pertains to a more abstract concept. And sometimes it doesn't work if we think that the addition pertains to the total number of oranges or apples. As a result, modern science is a mixture of some successes and many failures. The successes are not due to materialism; they are attributable to the fact that reality is numbers. And the failures are due to the fact that numbers are not quantities but types. Each number has a unique type, which includes the type of being an object, quality, or activity. The qualities, activities, and objects are subdivided into many subtypes. And the combination of these types requires an alternative system of type combining. That system will simultaneously undermine materialism, and produce a science that is far more powerful than current science because it accounts for the typed nature of reality.

Sūtra 7.2.6

एकत्वाभावाद्भक्तिस्तु न विद्यते

ekatvābhāvādbhaktistu na vidyate

ekatva—unity; abhāvāt—from the absence; bhakti—attachment; tu—but; na—not; vidyate—known.

TRANSLATION

But from the absence of unity (between objects, qualities, and activities), the attachments (between them) cannot be known.

COMMENTARY

The last sūtra stated that the unity between objects, qualities, and activities is very confusing, and this sūtra counters—but, if we don't consider this unity then we cannot explain how these things are combined. This is the doctrine of similar things combine with similar things, and dissimilar things cannot interact. Therefore, if activities are disparate from qualities, then they cannot be produced from qualities, nor can they modify objects. Hence, even though the unity between objects, qualities, and activities is confusing, it must be accepted because the alternative makes it impossible to understand the nature of reality.

Sūtra 7.2.7

कार्यकारणयोरेकत्वैकपृथक्त्वाभावादेकत्वैकपृथक्त्वं न विद्यते

kāryakāraṇayorekatvaikapṛthaktvābhāvādekatvaikapṛthaktvaṃ na vidyate

kārya—effect; kāraṇayoh—and the cause; ekatva—unity; eka—one; pṛthaktva—separateness; abhāvāt—from the absence; ekatva—unity; eka—one; pṛthaktvaṃ—separateness; na—not; vidyate—known.

TRANSLATION

The oneness, unity, and separateness of cause and effect are not known from the absence of oneness, unity, and separateness.

COMMENTARY

This sūtra revisits the paradox we have discussed earlier. To recall, the paradox is that (a) there is one cause for everything, (b) there are many things produced from that cause, and (c) all these varied things have unity. The last two create the paradox of *unity in diversity*, and the first two create the paradox of *diversity in the unity*. If diversity did not exist in the unity, then many things could not be created from that unity. Similarly, if unity did not exist in the diversity, then the many produced things could not interact with each other.

The previous sūtras have elaborated on the nature of the unity—namely, that they are all numbers, and hence they can combine and interact. But this unity is qualitative—we are talking about the property of numerosity and then treating all the individual numbers as the subclasses of that numerosity. If we remove either of the above three—oneness, unity, and separateness—then we cannot explain (a) the single source for everything, (b) many manifested things, and (c) the basis for interaction between these things. Thus, a pure singularity of cause doesn't work as it leads to only one effect, rather than many effects. A pure plurality of causes and effects doesn't work because we cannot explain why these things are able to interact with each other without a similarity, which requires a single source of causation. Hence, by removing any one of these three principles of unity, oneness, and separateness, we lose the basis for all three.

Sūtra 7.2.8

एतदनित्ययोर्व्याख्यातम्

etadanityayorvyākhyātam

etat—in this way; anityayoh—temporariness; vyākhyātam—explained.

TRANSLATION

In this way, temporariness is explained.

COMMENTARY

The effects are many and separate from the causes. But they have also emerged from the cause. Since they were originally present within the cause, therefore, they are not truly separate. And yet, because they have separated, therefore, they are not truly identical to the cause. This is the doctrine of non-difference, non-duality, and non-exclusion. The temporariness of the material world is that the effects are sometimes manifest and sometimes unmanifest. But if they are manifest, they are both separated and non-separated from the cause. Then, when they are unmanifest, they are still non-separated from the cause. The manifestation of the effect also creates an immanent representation of the cause in the effect, by which we can know the cause from the effect. If that immanent representation did not exist, then we would not be able to determine the cause—just by observing the effect. Therefore, the immanent representation of the Lord, which is also called the Paramātma, is temporarily manifest when the effects are manifest from the cause. When the effects merge back into the cause, then this temporary manifestation also disappears. Thus, the Paramātma form of the Lord is not eternally present; this form exists only so long as the material world exists. The transcendent form, however, always exists.

Sūtra 7.2.9

अन्यतरकर्मज उभयकर्मजःसंयोगजश्च संयोगः

anyatarakarmaja ubhayakarmajaḥ saṃyogajaśca saṃyogaḥ

anyatara—other; karmaja—born from an action; ubhaya—both; karmajaḥ—born from an action; saṃyogaja—born from a conjunction; ca—also; saṃyogaḥ—conjunction.

TRANSLATION

A conjunction is that which is born from the action of the other, born from the action of both, or born from conjunction (of the two).

COMMENTARY

This sūtra explains three kinds of causation as follows:

One thing acts on another thing to produce a third thing. In this case, the two original things are not modified, but a third thing is produced. Since a third thing is produced from the second thing, the second thing is divided into parts by this production. For example, the utterance of harsh speech can make a person angry. In this case, the harsh speech is the first thing, the person who later becomes angry is the second thing, and the resulting anger is the third thing. Assuming that the listener isn't changed by the harsh speech, and the speaker is unruffled by the outcome, the result of harsh speech is a unidirectional action of producing anger.

Two things act mutually on each other to produce a third thing. In this case, both things are modified by mutual action, and the original causes become unmanifest, while new causes are manifest. For example, when harsh words are exchanged by two parties leading to an irrevocable breakdown of their mutual relationship.

Two things combine to produce a third thing. In this case, the two things are modified by their mutual interaction but the new state has greater similarity than their states previously. For example, when harsh words are exchanged between two parties but they realize their respective mistakes and come to a common understanding. In this state, the meanings in them have been combined.

Sūtra 7.2.10

एतेन वभिागो व्याख्यातः

etena vibhāgo vyākhyātaḥ

etena—in this way; vibhāgah—divisions; vyākhyātaḥ—explained.

TRANSLATION

In this way, the divisions are explained.

COMMENTARY

This sūtra is notable in how it describes divisions as the outcome of conjunctions. As we have discussed earlier, each thing is the potentiality for many things, and these potentialities manifest when things are combined. The manifestation of a potentiality is the subdivision of that thing because it now comes to exhibit a property that wasn't previously visible. When a division occurs due to the action of one thing on another, a new property—e.g., anger in a person—is visible, when he might have been calm otherwise. Now, we can say that this person can both be angry and calm. Similarly, when division occurs due to the mutual effect of two things on each other, and they are both modified by that interaction, then a new property manifests while the older property becomes unmanifest. For instance, if two calm people argue with each other, and they both exhibit anger, then the property of their relationship, which might have been based on mutual respect earlier, could be destroyed. In one sense, they are the same people, and in another sense, they are not mutually related anymore. This again produces a subdivision in the person, such that they can exhibit the property of relatedness or not. Finally, if they mutually exchange kind words, the relationship may be restored, as they develop a mutual understanding and come closer than before due to that understanding, and again, in one sense they are the same people and, in another sense, they are now different, and we could say that they had the potentiality for this improved understanding earlier but it was missing due to different ideas or misunderstandings about each other. Then, we can say that they had the potential for both understanding and misunderstanding but one of them is manifest after another. In this way, as things combine with each other, they manifest new properties of qualities and that manifestation is the subdivision of that thing into subparts, which is why this sūtra states that by the process of combination, subdivisions are created.

Sūtra 7.2.11

संयोगवभिागयोःसंयोगवभिागाभावःअणुत्वमहत्त्वाभ्यां व्याख्यातः

saṃyogavibhāgayoḥ saṃyogavibhāgābhāvaḥ
aṇutvamahattvābhyāṃ vyākhyātaḥ

saṃyoga—conjunction; vibhāgayoḥ—and division; saṃyoga—conjunction; vibhāga—division; abhāvaḥ—the absence; aṇutva—atomicity; mahattvābhyāṃ—from the greatness; vyākhyātaḥ—is explained.

TRANSLATION

Conjunction and division are explained from the absence of atomicity and greatness in the conjunction and division.

COMMENTARY

Why do two things combine? Modern science says that they combine due to some 'force' between them. That force is due to a natural property (such as mass) that exists in the things exerting force on each other, and this force is always exerted on all the things that possess this property. But atomic theory has shown that this force is not always exerted, and not to everything in the universe. It is rather exerted toward selective things at selective times. The idea of 'force' now fails because is it not applicable to everything, everywhere, and everywhen. This sūtra offers a reprieve to this problem: The forces are not exerted to everything, everywhere, and everywhen; they are exerted only when the 'absence' of a property—which would be manifest by their interaction—appears. The potentiality for that property always exists, but the absence of that property doesn't always exist. Its appearance causes their mutual interaction.

For example, we have the capacity to eat food, but that doesn't mean that we are constantly eating everything, everywhere, and everywhen. Rather, sometimes, an absence of food—i.e., hunger—appears in us, and that causes the interaction with the food. The hunger may also be great or small, and accordingly, we might eat different amounts of things, which then limits the interaction with the food to certain places, times, and things. If we are greatly hungry, then we might eat a full meal, and if we have a little hunger, then we will eat a snack. The interaction is essentially determined by the appearance of hunger.

Thus, there are two doctrines of interaction. In the first doctrine adopted by modern science, change is caused by a presence of a property that exerts a force on the presence of other properties. In the second doctrine described by Vaiśeṣika, change is caused by the absence of a property which causes a conjunction that then produces a new property (as already described above).

The difference between these doctrines is that the force exerted by physical properties acts on everything, everywhere, and everywhen, while the absence appears sometimes, to somethings, at some places. Hunger can be controlled by our will, so even though it appears automatically, its effects—i.e., the interactions with food resulting from its appearance—are not deterministic. When the doctrine of causality is changed from the presence of properties to their absence, then Yoga practices teach us how to control the urges of such as hunger. The ability to control these urges indicates that matter can be controlled by our will, although if our urges are not controlled, then a person acts like an automaton.

This sūtra also notes two kinds of absences—of atomicity and greatness. These are respectively the hunger for falling lower or rising higher. The hunger for atomicity is the urge to unite with details to create a small modification. And the hunger for greatness is the urge to unite with the abstract to create a big change. Most people presently equate all urges to the hunger for small material things. For example, two friends like to constantly chit-chat and "stay in touch" exchanging pointless tidbits. Or people develop the habit to nibble constantly. In this way, they keep descending from greatness to atomicity. In contrast, there is the opposite urge to renounce these entanglements and rise to greatness. Due to these two kinds of urges, a person either rises inward and upward or downward and outward. But the cause of this change is the existence of an urge.

Even spiritual life depends on an inner urge. If this urge is missing, then to some extent a person can rely on a guru to force them, thereby substituting their urge with the urge in the teacher to uplift them. But this urge in the teacher is, ultimately, not a substitute. One must have a strong inner urge to uplift themselves. Spiritual progress therefore cannot arise due to an external force.

Sūtra 7.2.12

कर्मभिःकिर्माणि गुणैर्गुणा अणुत्व महत्त्वाभ्यामिति

karmabhiḥ karmāṇi guṇairguṇā aṇutva mahattvābhyāmiti

karmabhiḥ—by actions; karmāṇi—actions; guṇair—by qualities; guṇā—qualities; aṇutva—atomicity; mahattvābhyām—and greatness; iti—thus.

TRANSLATION

Thus, by actions, the activities are great or atomic, and by qualities, the qualities are great or atomic.

COMMENTARY

The abstract qualities are great, and the detailed qualities are atomic. Similarly, the abstract activities are great and the detailed activities are atomic. When some activity comprises abstractness, then it is considered great. Conversely, when some activity comprises details, then it is considered atomic. Thus, for instance, thinking is a greater activity than talking or eating. Then, judging the truth, right, and good, is an even greater activity than thinking. Enjoying the association with moral values is a greater pleasure than enjoying food. And the moral values are a greater quality than the food's taste.

Sūtra 7.2.13

युतसिद्ध्यभावात् कार्यकारणयोःसंयोगविभागौ न विद्येते

yutasiddhyabhāvāt kāryakāraṇayoḥ saṃyogavibhāgau na vidyete

yutasiddhi—having attained perfection; abhāvāt—from the absence; kārya—effect; kāraṇayoḥ—and cause; saṃyoga—conjunction; vibhāgau—and division; na—not; vidyete—are known.

TRANSLATION

Having attained perfection, the conjunction and division arising as the effects of the absence of the cause are not known.

COMMENTARY

This sūtra states that the causality that is driven by the appearance of absence ceases when one attains perfection. In simple terms, when the spiritual urges arise in the soul, the material urges end. Now, the soul controls the body, rather than the body controlling the soul. The spiritual urges are based on devotion to the Lord, and the perfect soul works for the Lord's pleasure.

Sūtra 7.2.14

गुणत्वात

guṇatvāt

guṇatvāt—from the habits previously formed.

TRANSLATION

(The causality of absence arises) from the habits previously formed.

COMMENTARY

Everyone doesn't get the same urges. Rather, based on the previous habits of enjoyment—which are called guna—the urges are created by time. These habits exist in the subtle body, and when the soul identifies with the urge, he believes that it is his urge, when it is factually a product of the material guna. When the soul is perfected, he stops identifying with the body. As a result, even if the urge for hunger and sleep is produced, the soul entertains these urges to maintain the body. But the soul is not distressed by these urges. Just like an operator can feed oil into a machine, or repair it if is malfunctioning, similarly, the perfected soul maintains the body like an instrument, to be used in the Lord's service. There is no attachment to the instrument, because if one instrument is destroyed, then another one would be available for the soul's use. In this way, perfection means complete detachment from bodily urges.

Sūtra 7.2.15

गुणो ऽपि विभाव्यते

guṇo 'pi vibhāvyate

guṇah—the qualities; api—even; vibhāvyate—in the establishment.

TRANSLATION

Even in the establishment (of perfection), the qualities (exist).

COMMENTARY

The material energy is like an instrument, which possesses many qualities. The soul, however, is not devoid of qualities. The soul's qualities rather spring from within a primordial state of the soul, just like the material qualities spring from within the primordial state of the material energy. When the soul is covered by material energy, the qualities of its body, senses, and mind are not the soul's true qualities. They are rather the impressions of habits formed previously, which automatically generate urges. This is why the soul's qualities are rejected as true qualities. This sūtra however says that the qualities exist even after the soul's perfection. This claim can be understood in two ways. First, the material body exists, but it is the instrument used by the soul (not the instrument that controls the soul). Second, the soul is able to control the instrument only because it has its own qualities, which then lead to urges and desires. If the soul did not have its own urges, then upon detachment from the body, it would become completely inactive, and ultimately leave the body. But even the liberated soul continues to live in the body and uses it as an instrument. This state is sometimes called jīvan-mukta or "liberated even while living in a material body". This control is possible because the capacity to choose is not destroyed. And this capacity for choosing can be used only when there is desire and urge. Without any desire, there are no choices, because there is no preference for one outcome over another. Therefore, the liberated soul acts because he has spiritual urges—produced out of the soul, rather than the body.

Sūtra 7.2.16
नष्क्रियत्वात्
niṣkriyatvāt

niṣkriyatvāt—from as if inactive state.

TRANSLATION
(The soul's activities) are as if from the inactive state.

COMMENTARY
As we have discussed earlier, all material activities are conducted under the influence of fear, insecurity, anxiety, and incompleteness. The soul feels inadequate and tries to overcome that inadequacy, and that attempt to become great and conquer the inadequacy produces material activities. This inadequacy appears as the 'absence' of something, and hence it is called māyā—or "that which is not". This māyā is also said to be comprised of three qualities of sattva, rajas, and tamas, and hence the cause of this activity resulting from inadequacy is also called guna. The sattva-guna represents the cognition that the soul lacks the knowledge and understanding of reality. The rajo-guna represents the realization the soul is incapable of many things. And tamo-guna represents the realization that the soul doesn't have access to many kinds of things. Thus, under the inadequacy of tamo-guna, the soul tries to acquire things. Under the inadequacy of rajo-guna, it tries to develop new skills. And under the inadequacy of sattva-guna, it tries to understand the nature of reality, including its own nature. The sattva-guna inadequacy is considered better than the inadequacies produced by rajo-guna and tamo-guna, but they are still inadequacies. The liberation of the soul is the liberation from māyā and hence inadequacy. Once this anxiety, fear, and insecurity are destroyed, the soul becomes inactive, because the activity was previously driven by the sense of incompleteness.

However, on further progress from the freedom from material anxieties, a new kind of urge and desire develops in the soul, in which it acts voluntarily out of love of the Lord, rather than the fear of the material condition. The fear compels a person to act, but love is voluntary. When actions are performed under fear, then a result is always expected. But when actions are performed under love, then the activity of love is itself sufficient. This type of activity is considered 'inactive' in contrast to the material 'activity' driven by fear.

Sūtra 7.2.17

असति नास्तीति च प्रयोगात्

asati nāstīti ca prayogāt

asati—the false and temporary; na—not; astī—existent; iti—thus; ca—also; prayogāt—from the application or use.

TRANSLATION

From the application or use (of the body), thus it is also concluded that the false and temporary does not exist (only the eternal exists).

COMMENTARY

In Vedic philosophy, there is a distinction between 'reality' and 'existence'. False sentences like "the sky is purple" can exist, but they are not true; therefore, even though they exist, they are not accorded 'reality'. As we have discussed earlier, even ignorance is the mark of truth, because ignorance is created by hiding parts of the truth. This hiding is also produced by māyā or 'absence'. Just like if you hide one of the legs from a chair, then you see a three-legged chair which seems like a novelty, but this vision is produced from two things—(a) there is a real chair, and (b) one of the legs from the chair has been hidden. This three-legged chair, however, has no *reality* although it *exists* in our vision. We can also call this distinction between reality and appearance, where the appearances are produced due to hiding of reality, or filtering of some truths.

The liberated soul realizes that the notion of me and mine—e.g., this is my body, or the body is me—is an illusion. By this illusion, we might profess some rights and duties, demands and supplies, but they are not real. However, a subtle distinction is required here: The distinction is that the body is not unreal, although my *identification* with the body is unreal. This is because if the body was truly me, then I would not have to give up the body. You cannot be kicked out of a house that you own; you can be kicked out of the rental property. In the same way, the body is real as a rental property, and hence the idea that "this body is me" is false. Based on this distinction, two visions of unreality are created. The impersonalist says that rental property itself doesn't exist, and we simply hallucinate its existence. But the personalist says that the rental property exists, and we live in that property, but the identification with the property is false. Thus, something that ceases to be me, was never me to begin with.

In this sense, the temporariness of the body is taken to mean that the body is not me. It has temporarily been assigned to me, so we can temporarily call it 'mine', but not 'me'. Thus, this sūtra says that using the body, we come to conclude that the body is not me. The impersonalist would not say "by using the body we conclude that it is false"; after all, if you are successfully able to use the body, then the natural conclusion is that it is real. But if you are using the body as an instrument, then you come to the conclusion that it is not *me*. Hence, false and temporary is the idea that "I am the body", and it is said to not exist.

This sūtra comes after those that discuss the liberation from material urges. This means that unless these urges are destroyed, there is always a remnant of bodily identification. Only when the soul starts acting spontaneously and independent of bodily urges does a complete detachment from the body arise.

Sūtra 7.2.18

शब्दार्थावसम्बन्धौ

śabdārthāvasambandhau

śabda—word; arthāu—to meaning; asambandhau—no relation.

TRANSLATION

The word to meaning has no relation.

COMMENTARY

It is practically impossible to determine the meaning of individual words because the same word can be interpreted in different ways. For example, the term 'artha' itself sometimes denotes 'meaning', sometimes an 'object', sometimes a 'purpose', etc. Likewise, the term 'śabda' sometimes denotes scripture, sometimes verbal testimony, sometimes sound, and sometimes word. The context delineates the meaning of the words. But that doesn't mean that the word-meaning relation is arbitrary. This sūtra specifically notes the "word to meaning" relation as being arbitrary. The "meaning to word" relation is, however, not arbitrary. If we know what we want to say, then we can translate that deterministically into words. But if we know the words, then we cannot deterministically translate the sound of words into meaning. The meaning originally exists as an intention or purpose. This purpose or intention then expands into a structure—which we generally called the grammatical structure. This structure is then populated by words, which can be unique to a language. If the words have been expressed in a sentence, then the words are deterministic, the grammar is slightly less deterministic, and the intention is least deterministic. The process of understanding requires us to overcome indeterminism.

The overcoming of indeterminism requires us to know many things: (a) the dictionary meanings, (b) the grammar, and (c) the mind of the speaker or author who spoke or wrote those words. Each of these three can be contextually nuanced. For example, the dictionary meanings can change, the grammar can evolve, and the speaker may have different intentions in speaking different words. This is the reason why an independent study of the Vedic texts is prohibited; the student is always advised to go to an enlightened teacher who has himself learned from another teacher—to understand the speaker's *intention*. The prospective student is also advised to humbly ask questions, clarify their understanding, and serve the teacher so that the true intention is revealed. The dictionary words can be memorized; the grammar can also be learned by practice. But the intention of the speaker can never be obtained in this way.

Sūtra 7.2.19

संयोगिनो दण्डात् समवायिनो विशेषाच्च

saṃyogino daṇḍāt samavāyino viśeṣācca

saṃyoginah—the conjunction; daṇḍāt—due to the stick or staff; samavāyinah—inherence; viśeṣāt—from the specifics or details; ca—also.

TRANSLATION

(The word to meaning can be known) also from the inherence of the specifics or details that are in conjunction due to the stick or staff.

COMMENTARY

This sūtra uses the inverted tree model to explain the relation between word and meaning. The meaning is the intention, the grammatical structure is the expansion of this intention into an inverted tree structure that looks like the branches of the tree, and the words are the leaves or fruits attached to these branches. The fruit has some properties due to which we can broadly eliminate some possible meanings. But just as apples can look like nectarines, similarly, the perfect meanings of words cannot be known by just observing the words. We have to rather look beyond the fruit—into the whole tree, the nature of its trunks and branches, and the nature of the leaves, to determine if the tree is nectarine or apple. Once we determine that the tree is an apple, then the fruits on that tree will also be apples. In the same way, when the larger context has been understood, then the words can be interpreted. In short, meanings are determined by understanding the speaker, his intentions, his culture, and context, before we interpret the words. We can call this the top-down understanding of meaning because it begins in the person, then understands their intentions, then understands the context, then grasps the grammar, and finally looks at the words. Most people try to read the words and don't try to know the author. Without knowing the speaker or author, they try to grasp the meanings. But this sūtra states that we can understand the meaning by understanding the bigger context—i.e., the branches, that ultimately lead us to the tree's root.

The term 'inherence' indicates the existence of the parts (the specific details) in the whole. To understand these parts, we have to understand the whole first. This whole constitutes the understanding of the person and his intentions. It is not the physical aggregation of the parts; it is a different and deeper kind of reality. If the speaker is not properly understood, then the text is also prone to many misinterpretations. Hence, it is imperative to follow the guru-disciple succession in which the tradition is taught because it clarifies the intention. Once that intention is clear to the reader, then the text also becomes clear.

Sūtra 7.2.20
सामयिकः शब्दादर्थप्रत्ययः
sāmayikaḥ śabdādarthapratyayaḥ

sāmayikaḥ—the time, place, context, and tradition; śabdāt—from the words; artha—the meaning; pratyayaḥ—parts or components.

TRANSLATION

From the time, place, context, and tradition of the words, the meanings are parts or components (of the words).

COMMENTARY

A word can be visualized as the superposition of many possible meanings, and the context, time, place, and tradition select one particular meaning. Just like a block of wood can be alternately seen as a table, chair, or firewood, similarly, each word is a superposition of all possible interpretations. A specific interpretation springs out of the word, just like the tableness or chairness springs out of a block of wood under the proper contextual circumstances. Therefore, it is incorrect to say that the words don't have a meaning; they have all possible meanings. It is also incorrect to say that the meaning is supplied by the mind because the meaning is objectively present in the word as its cause. However, we cannot perceive the cause by our senses; we have to treat the perceived object as a superposition of meanings, and then select one of the possible meanings. This general principle of context producing a new quality is not unique to the word interpretations. We have discussed earlier how ordinary things produce new meanings in different contexts. That principle applies here too.

Sūtra 7.2.21
एकदिक्काभ्यामेककालाभ्यां सन्निकृष्टविप्रकृष्टाभ्यां परमपरञ्च
ekadikkābhyāmekakālābhyāṃ sannikṛṣṭaviprakṛṣṭābhyāṃ paramaparañca

eka—one; dikkābhyām—from many directions; eka—one; kālābhyāṃ—from many times; sannikṛṣṭa—by proximity and attraction; viprakṛṣṭābhyāṃ—from many distant possibilities; paramaparā—the tradition; ca—also.

TRANSLATION

Also, one from many directions, one from many times, (is selected) by proximity and attraction to a tradition from the many distant possibilities.

COMMENTARY

When the word is seen as the superposition of many meanings, then each meaning represents a different direction (as we have discussed, these meanings are orthogonal dimensions). Each direction is also selected at a specific time because these directions are not simultaneously manifest. This sūtra states that the selection of the meaning of the words is determined by the paramparā or tradition. Thus, the same word can be used in different contexts, places, and times to mean something different. The enlightened teacher imparts the correct meaning to the students, by explaining the intended meaning. The Vedānta system notes another method for determining the intended meaning, which is that all the texts must be reconciled to obtain a mutually consistent meaning. Inconsistencies in understanding the Vedic texts mean that the interpretation is incorrect. The correct interpretation is that which reconciles all statements.

The term paramparā can also be translated as "superior to the superior", which means that the meanings inferred from a text can be organized in a hierarchy. The superior meaning is that which reconciles all the texts, and the inferior meaning is that which creates contradictions in the meanings. As we increase our understanding, we see greater harmony, simplicity, and unity in the texts—assuming, of course, that the texts are not themselves contradictory. This creates a problem for the interpreters—when their interpretations are incorrect, and these result in a seeming contradiction, they suppose that the texts themselves are contradictory. The paramparā helps us resolve this conundrum—it shows how the texts are coherent and yet multi-faceted, by presenting their meaning according to the guru-disciple succession of received knowledge.

Sūtra 7.2.22

कारणपरत्वात् कारणापरत्वाच्च

kāraṇaparatvāt kāraṇāparatvācca

kāraṇa—the cause; paratvāt—from the superior; kāraṇa—cause; aparatvāt—from the inferior; ca—also.

TRANSLATION

The cause (of meaning) can be superior, and the cause can be inferior.

COMMENTARY

The Nyāya system of philosophy explains how the same reality is perceived in different ways by different people: They see what they are because the capacities for perception and understanding are the goggles through which we see. In Sāñkhya, these goggles are called the chitta, and they are different capacities for perception, action, and understanding. These goggles are superior or inferior. Therefore, it is not enough to merely go to a teacher to understand the meaning; one must also practice a path of purification to perceive these meanings themselves. If this purification is not performed, then the same reality is interpreted according to our inferior goggles, and it remains imperfect. We then see many faults in the scriptures, and our interpretation of the speaker is conditioned by our own ideas and the cultural and social presuppositions.

Sūtra 7.2.23

परत्वापरत्वयोःपरत्वापरत्वाभावो ऽणुत्वमहत्त्वाभ्यां व्याख्यातः

paratvāparatvayoḥ paratvāparatvābhāvo 'ṇutvamahattvābhyāṃ vyākhyātaḥ

paratva—superiority; aparatvayoḥ—in the inferiority; paratva—superiority; aparatva—inferiority; abhāvah—absence; aṇutva—atomicity; mahattvābhyāṃ—from the greatness; vyākhyātaḥ—explained.

TRANSLATION

(The perception) of superiority and inferiority in superiority and inferiority is explained on the basis of the absence of atomicity and greatness.

COMMENTARY

The doctrine of abhāva or absence is revisited here and used to explain the process of interpretation. This abhāva, as we have discussed, appears as hunger and desire in us. If we are hungry for superior meaning, then we find the superior meaning even in things that are inferior. Conversely, if we are hungry for inferior meaning, then we find the inferior meaning even in the things that are superior. All reality, as was noted earlier, has an elevating purpose. Therefore, factually there is no inferior reality; it just appears to be inferior to those who don't understand the elevating purpose. For example, the trials and tribulations of life have an inferior interpretation—namely, that life is meaningless suffering. But the same difficulties have a superior interpretation—namely, that by the troubles in life, the soul is purified of its material contaminations. Thus, some people voluntarily perform austerities to purify themselves, while others run away from difficulties, or fail to utilize them for their own upliftment.

We discussed earlier how everything is produced due to an absence, urge, or desire. This sūtra uses that idea to explain the interpretation of words: Based on our desire, urge, or hunger, we see different things in the same reality. If our urges are inferior, then we find inferior meanings in everything. And if our urges are superior, then we find the superior meanings in everything. The conclusion is that all possible interpretations of texts are not equivalent. Rather, we have to understand the superior or inferior nature of the author and the reader. If the author is superior and the reader is inferior, then the reader will not find the truth: He will just keep thinking that the author is also inferior like him. Conversely, if the reader is superior and the author is inferior, then the superior reader will always find something to appreciate even in the inferior work.

Sūtra 7.2.24

कर्मभिःकर्माणि

karmabhiḥ karmāṇi

karmabhiḥ—by actions; karmāṇi—the actions.

TRANSLATION

By the (previous) actions, the (subsequent) actions.

COMMENTARY

This sūtra was stated earlier, where the meaning was that complex actions are created from the combination of simpler actions. But in the present context, where we are discussing the superior and inferior interpretations, this sūtra means that unless one has performed superior activities, he or she cannot understand that other people can also perform superior activities. For example, many modern interpreters of Vedic texts think that their statements are the conjectures of a "human mind" speculating on the nature of reality because they cannot imagine that someone might have the perfect insight into the nature of reality. Since their lives are mediocre and cynical, they impute that cynicism and mediocrity on others. It is has become standard practice today to say that the Vedic texts could not have been written by one person—Veda Vyas. Why? Because the mediocre historians studying these texts have probably written one or two books in their lives, and they cannot imagine how someone can write hundreds of books. So, they extrapolate their mediocrity to others and claim that if a vast body of texts exists, then it must be the work of many authors.

The Vedic system discourages such people from reading the Vedic texts and sometimes forbids them. The nuisance interpreters then take offense at this rejection and claim that the Vedic system was creating an artificial superiority for the Brahmanas. Again, this is what the inferior mind is capable of—seeing a problem in good advice. But we must note that this advice is based on sound judgment. For example, those who haven't performed great deeds in their life are advised to engage in karma-yoga—i.e., first, perform great things without a desire for any results. If you can do that, then you will also understand how the authors of great philosophies were performing a great deed for the other people without desiring results. Their motives were pure, and their knowledge was pure. But the person who hasn't performed great deeds unselfishly cannot understand the greatness in others. Thus, by previous actions, new actions.

Sūtra 7.2.25

गुणैर्गुणाः

guṇairguṇāḥ

guṇair—by qualities; guṇāḥ—qualities.

TRANSLATION

By the (previous) qualities, (new) qualities.

COMMENTARY

This sūtra was also presented earlier where the meaning was that complex qualities are created by the combination of simple qualities. In the present context, where the discussion is about superior and inferior interpretations, the meaning is that if a person has developed inferior qualities, then they cannot perceive superior qualities. For example, a selfish person cannot conceive of good intentions in other people; he thinks that every good deed must involve a conspiracy to cheat. Indeed, a good person is seen as a cunning selfish person who hides his true intentions from others much better than other selfish people. Thus, those who cannot understand the Vedic texts think that these texts are factually meaningless. That they are produced by a group of people who did not have a coherent ideology. That they wrote these texts because they were motivated by the desire for name and power. Or, that they deliberately made these texts complicated so that they remain inaccessible to the outsiders.

Sūtra 7.2.26

इहेदमितियितःकार्यकारणयोःस समवायः

ihedamiti yataḥ kāryakāraṇayoḥ sa samavāyaḥ

iha—here; idam—-this; iti—thus; yataḥ—just as; kāryakāraṇayoḥ—effect and cause; sa—that; samavāyaḥ—the inherence.

TRANSLATION

Just as the effect and cause are here and this, that inherence (of meaning in the texts) is thus (the same as here and this).

COMMENTARY

This sūtra summarizes the 'here' and 'this' mentality of ordinary people. They cannot understand things that they haven't seen 'here'—i.e., in their personal lives, being lived on the Earth planet. And they cannot accept the existence of things that are not 'this'—i.e., the ordinary things that they can see. Due to their mundane vision, everything has to be reduced to 'here' and 'this'—i.e., it must be available in front of their eyes, and just like mundane things. They cannot understand how there are things that are not 'here' and 'this'—i.e., they are not available in our sense perception, and they are not like what we see. This, as has been explained, is due to their acquired qualities and previous activities. If they change their qualities and activities, they too can understand. But they must first believe that there is something beyond 'here' and 'this'.

Sūtra 7.2.27
दरव्यत्वगुणत्व प्रतषिधःभावेन व्याख्याता
dravyatvaguṇatva pratiṣedhaḥ bhāvena vyākhyātā

dravyatva—objectivity; guṇatva—qualityness; pratiṣedhaḥ—by removing; bhāvena—the meaning in it; vyākhyātā—is explained.

TRANSLATION
By removing (material) objectivity and qualities, the meaning in it is explained.

COMMENTARY
The true nature of reality is hidden from everyone's vision unless their material qualities are removed. We have to also stop thinking in terms of objects, and think in terms of meanings. When the goggles of vision are purified, not just Vedic texts, but everything else is understood in its true nature. Therefore, the Vedic system doesn't prescribe complex experimental arrangements to understand reality. It prescribes the purification of consciousness. When the soul is purified of its material encumbrances, then it sees everything clearly.

Sūtra 7.2.28
तत्त्वम्भावेन
tattvambhāvena

tattvam—the true nature; bhāvena—the meaning in it.

TRANSLATION
The true nature (of everything) is the meaning in it.

COMMENTARY
Meanings have several levels. At the grossest level, these meanings are

seen as sense percepts (such as red, round, and sweet). Deeper than that meaning is the properties (such as color, shape, and taste). Deeper than that is the object concept (such as an apple). Deeper than that is the belief that apples are red, round, and sweet, which is used to judge the truth of sense perception and mental intuition. Deeper than that is the belief that apples are good for health. And deeper than that is the idea that health is a value or virtue. Even deeper than that is the desire for health. And even deeper than that is the soul who chooses. In this way, the true nature of everything is understood if we grasp all the tiers of meanings, but it must include the understanding of the person or soul. If the soul is neglected, then gradually all the levels of meaning are neglected. Ultimately, even the reality of sense perceivable qualities is rejected, and a material world devoid of meaning, contextuality, and purpose is produced. Modern science is that redacted understanding of meaning as something physical. But it is not the true nature of reality. It is a collection of false ideas that opportunistically use the multiple levels of meaning when it suits a materialistic agenda and rejects it when it doesn't. This material science is also a meaning, created by some souls with a purpose—the purpose to enjoy without responsibility. But it cannot be successful because it is ignorant about the true nature of reality.

CHAPTER 8

Section 1

Sūtra 8.1.1

द्रव्येषु ज्ञानं व्याख्यातम्

dravyeṣu jñānaṃ vyākhyātam

dravyeṣu—in the object; jñānaṃ—knowledge; vyākhyātam—is explained.

TRANSLATION

Knowledge is explained to exist in the objects.

COMMENTARY

In modern science, objects have no 'inside' and there is nothing 'inside' the object. But, as this sūtra explains, conceptual objects carry meanings. We can classify these meanings into three categories. First, there is the meaning of what the object itself is; for example, the object represents an entity such as 'table' or 'chair'. Second, there is the meaning of an object's relation to other objects; for instance, there is an objective property of whom the table belongs to, such that "my table" is not merely a property in my mind; it is objectively in the table. Third, there is the meaning about the purpose of the object; for instance, the table is supposed to be used for studying, rather than being burnt as firewood. Thus, jñāna is meaning or artha, and this artha has many interpretations—(1) it is a type of object, (2) the object is owned by me, and (3) it has a purpose.

These three types of meanings become apparent when we think of sentences. A sentence has some cognitive meaning. It has a speaker, and the sentence is related to the speaker. And it was uttered by the speaker for a purpose. To determine the sentence's meaning, we have to know who spoke it, and why they spoke it, besides what was said. The three types of meaning in the sentence are therefore who, why, and what. If we only look at a sentence but don't know who spoke it, and why they spoke it, then the meaning is incompletely known. Similarly, all objects—even tables and chairs—have three kinds of meaning. An ordinary product for example has the name of the manufacturer imprinted on it, and sometimes the name of the owner is imprinted on the product as well. This establishes the relationship to other objects. Similarly, the product has an intended use, which is prescribed in the "terms and conditions of use" when the product is bought. Since we cannot perceive the purpose and relationship, and only see what it is, therefore, the manufacturer, owner, terms and conditions, etc. are printed on paper and accompany the products we purchase. But removing that piece of paper from the product doesn't void those facts. This is because those facts are a part of the product, although they are invisible.

Sūtra 8.1.2

तत्रात्मा मनश्चाप्रत्यक्षे

tatrātmā manaścāpratyakṣe

tatra—there; ātmā—the soul; manas—mind; ca—also; apratyakṣe—in the non-perceivable form.

TRANSLATION

There, the soul and the mind are also present in a non-perceivable form.

COMMENTARY

The 'soul' here denotes the owner or the creator of the product. For instance, the works of Shakespeare are attributed to Shakespeare even after his death. When a property is purchased, the ownership doesn't change with time, even if the body becomes old. The 'mind' here denotes the purpose for which the thing is meant to be used; it represents the intention for which the product was meant for. A good example of this intended use is that even if one buys a property but uses it for unlawful purposes, that property can be confiscated by the government. Within lawful uses, the property belongs to the person who paid for it. Thus, in addition to what a thing can do, there is additional information about who is supposed to use it, and for purposes can they use it. This sūtra states that the purpose and relation exist in objects in an imperceivable form. Therefore, information about ownership, the name of the manufacturer, the serial number of the product, and the terms and conditions are sometimes imprinted on the objects themselves, and sometimes given as a document.

Sūtra 8.1.3
ज्ञाननिर्देशे ज्ञाननिष्पत्तिविधिरुक्तः
jñānanirdeśe jñānaniṣpattividhiruktaḥ

jñāna—knowledge; nirdeśe—in the command or order; jñāna—knowledge; niṣpatti—concluded; vidhir—the process or method; uktaḥ—stated.

TRANSLATION

This knowledge is stated as the knowledge in the command or order, and the knowledge which is concluded by the process or method.

COMMENTARY

A command or order is issued by someone to someone; the command is therefore related to the sender and the receiver. Similarly, the command has a purpose that must translate into a particular set of activities which are called process or method. Ludwig Wittgenstein spoke extensively about these two kinds of meanings. He cites the example of a mechanic who gives commands to his assistant and the assistant executes those commands. For instance, if the mechanic says "hammer" then the assistant gets him the hammer. If the mechanic says "wrench" then the assistant gets him a wrench. Wittgenstein argued that the words "hammer" and "wrench" have contextual meanings, which can be understood if we know the effects they produce. He called these "speech acts". A speech act makes the three kinds of meanings we discussed above apparent in one sense and obfuscates their distinction in another sense. What is said, why it is said, and whom it is said by to whom, are three distinct kinds of meanings. Different words could be used by other mechanics and assistants for the same purpose, so the purpose and the words are different. Likewise, the same persons can use the same words for a different purpose, so, the person and the purpose are different. By separating these three kinds of meanings, and then seeing how they are combined uniquely in each context, we get a theory of meaning that comprises three aspects—cognition, relation, and intention. Each of these three can be individually varied while keeping the other two unchanged. But more importantly, these three aspects are inherent in the words themselves. Thus, who is saying, and why they are saying it, is as important as what they are saying. However, only the 'what' is seen in the sentence; 'who' and 'why' are not. Hence, the 'who' is attributed to the soul, and 'why' to the mind. But these are also stated to be immanent in the objects themselves.

Sūtra 8.1.4

गुणकर्मसु सन्निकृष्टेषु ज्ञाननिष्पत्तेःद्रव्यं कारणम्

guṇakarmasu sannikṛṣṭeṣu jñānaniṣpatteḥ dravyaṃ kāraṇam

guṇakarmasu—in the qualities and activities; sannikṛṣṭeṣu—in the proximity and attraction; jñāna—knowledge; niṣpatteḥ—logically produced; dravyaṃ—object; kāraṇam—the cause.

TRANSLATION

The object is the cause of the knowledge being logically produced in the qualities and activities in the proximity and attraction (to other objects).

COMMENTARY

The previous sūtras spoke about how the knowledge of purpose and relation is created in the objects, and this sūtra states that once it has been created in the object, the object becomes the cause of the propagation of this knowledge into the qualities and activities. As we have earlier discussed, the qualities and activities are immanent in the objects, and manifest from these objects. This sūtra further states that the knowledge of the objects, along with the other immanent knowledge in them about the relations to other objects and the purpose of that object, is immanent in the qualities and activities of the objects. This immanence of knowledge creates an 'awareness' in qualities and activities about the purpose for which they are acting, and the things toward which they are acting. In modern science, objects act on other objects due to a force, devoid of any 'awareness' of why they are acting, and on whom they are acting. The physical properties are not 'aware' of which objects they pertain to, and the purpose of that object. But these sūtras indicate that ordinary objects, qualities, and activities have an 'awareness' of the meaning, purpose, and relation to other things. This awareness is not 'consciousness', but it is close to it; it is called jñāna or knowledge which can also be considered an informational representation.

Essentially, every object (along with its qualities and activities) carries a 'picture' of the external reality, and it acts in relation to other objects through three things—(a) what it is, (b) what its purpose is, and (c) the picture of the world. While we cannot say that material objects are 'conscious' we can still say that they 'know' about the world through a representation of the world. The distinction between matter and consciousness is now subtle—consciousness specifically means free will, or the ability to create a new purpose, choose which things to relate to or focus upon, and select which abilities to utilize when. Matter on the other hand is devoid of this free will, although there is a fixed purpose, a fixed set of abilities, and a fixed set of relations to the external reality. Barring the property of free will or the power of choice, matter possesses the same three capacities for cognition, relation, and intention just as the soul.

Sūtra 8.1.5

सामान्यविशेषेषु सामान्यविशेषाभावात् तदेव ज्ञानम्

sāmānyaviśeṣeṣu sāmānyaviśeṣābhāvāt tadeva jñānam

sāmānyaviśeṣeṣu—in the general and the specific; sāmānya—the general; viśeṣa—the specific; abhāvāt—from the absence; tadeva—of that; jñānam—knowledge.

TRANSLATION

The knowledge of that (object, quality, and activity) is produced from the absence of the general and specific in the general and specific.

COMMENTARY

After stating that the knowledge of the external world exists in the objects, this sūtra caveats the previous statement by the doctrine of absence. Namely, that the knowledge of the external world exists only when there is the hunger or urge for the external world created as their absence. We can illustrate this idea by the example of the hunger for food in our bodies. When the body is not hungry, then the thoughts about food don't arise, and we remain unaware of food stuffs, even if they are around us. We become aware of their existence if hunger arises because then a representation of the external world is created in us. According to this sūtra, this is not a unique situation about our bodies. It is rather true of all material objects. The knowledge representation of the external world is created when there is an urge to interact, and this urge arises when the absence of general and specific is created within the general and specific.

As we have discussed, in the abstract, there is a natural absence for the specific, and in the specific, there is a natural absence of the abstract. But this absence need not become an urge or hunger, and in such a situation, matter will not evolve to a new state. It evolves when the absence becomes an urge. The bodily urges such as hunger, sleep, and sex are therefore not unique to our bodies. They are rather properties of matter which exist in all material objects. Therefore, instead of thinking that matter is just physical properties, and then imagining that the bodily urges are created by the interaction of these properties, Vaiśeṣika changes the paradigm—now, matter has novel properties of knowledge (cognition, relation, and intention) and the 'feeling' of absence. Thereby, the biology of living bodies needs no special consideration if the physics of matter is suitably modified to accommodate knowledge and absence.

Sūtra 8.1.6

सामान्यविशेषापेक्षं द्रव्यगुणकर्मसु

sāmānyaviśeṣāpekṣaṃ dravyaguṇakarmasu

sāmānya—the general; viśeṣa—the specific; apekṣaṃ—relative to; dravya—object; guṇa—quality; karmasu—and activity.

TRANSLATION

The general and specific (spoken of in the last sūtra, in regards to the absence leading to knowledge) are relative to the object, quality, and activity.

COMMENTARY

This sūtra clarifies the previous one by saying that the terms 'general' and 'specific' are just denotations of abstract and detailed, and they can be applied to any object, any quality, and any activity. This means that the knowledge of the external world exists at all levels of abstraction and detailing, although it appears only when the urge or absence of that abstraction and detailing appears. For example, if the absence of food arises in the mind, then it can percolate downward into the senses, and the nose will then feel the absence for food's smell, the tongue will feel the absence of food's taste, the eyes will feel the absence of food's sight. Likewise, if the smell of food enters the nose, then it can propagate upwards and trigger the absence of food in the mind, which can then propagate downward and trigger the urge to taste in the tongue. In this way, the urges can propagate upward and downward and create more urges. Similarly, if the urge ceases in one sense, then it can propagate upward and downward and cease the urge in the other senses. That cessation will then result in the cessation of the activity, and suddenly the whole body is satiated. As is commonly known, even a hungry person can lose their appetite simply by hearing unpleasant words, seeing unpleasant things, or smelling unpleasant odors.

Sūtra 8.1.7

द्रव्ये द्रव्यगुणकर्मापेक्षम्

dravye dravyaguṇakarmāpekṣam

dravye—in the object; dravya—object; guṇa—quality; karma—activity; apekṣam—relative to.

TRANSLATION

(The general and specific) in the object are relative to the object, quality, and activity.

COMMENTARY

Some people have the urge to understand the entire universe; other people are interested only in their nation and society, and yet others are only desirous to know about their immediate family and work environment. This difference between the people arises due to their own nature; each such personality can be thought of as a different kind of object, which develops different kinds or urges, and then they acquire different kinds of knowledge. Therefore, there are no universal prescriptions about all objects developing all kinds of urges to know everything, have all the purposes, or have all kinds of knowledge. This sūtra hence states that the urges for the general and specific are dependent on the object, quality, and activity. This means that different kinds of urges will develop in different individuals of different qualities, activities, and natures.

Sūtra 8.1.8

गुणकर्मसु गुणकर्माभावात् गुणकर्मापेक्षं न विद्यते

guṇakarmasu guṇakarmābhāvāt guṇakarmāpekṣaṃ na vidyate

guṇakarmasu—in qualities and activities; guṇa—quality; karma—activity; abhāvāt—from the absence; guṇa—quality; karma—activity; apekṣaṃ—relative to; na—not; vidyate—known.

TRANSLATION

From the absence of quality and activity in quality and activity, relativity to the quality and activity is not known.

COMMENTARY

We cannot admire the leadership qualities of criminals, and then say that we dislike their criminal activities. We cannot admire the intellect of the atheists, and then dislike their atheistic propaganda. We cannot appreciate the destructive qualities of bombs, and then criticize their use for destruction. Qualities and activities are separate modes in nature, but they are not separable. Rather, each quality comes along with certain activities compatible with it.

Hence, if we admire the leadership qualities of criminals, then we will either appreciate and justify their criminal activities, or we will reject both their qualities and activities. If we admire the intellect of the atheists, then we will either appreciate and support their atheistic propaganda, or we will reject both their propaganda and intellect. If we like the destructive potential in bombs, then we will either support their use for bombing, or reject the destructive potential of bombs along with their use for destruction. In this way, isolated attraction for merely the qualities or activities cannot exist. Wherever one type of attraction is present, the other type of attraction must also be present.

Sūtra 8.1.9

समवायिनिःश्वैत्याच्छ्वैत्य बुद्धेश्च श्वेते बुद्धिस्ते एते कार्यकारणभूते

samavāyinaḥ śvaityācchvaitya buddheśca
śvete buddhiste ete kāryakāraṇabhūte

samavāyinaḥ—inherence; śvaityāt—from purity; śvaitya—purity; buddheh—intellect; ca—also; śvete—in purity; buddhi—knowledge; te—these; ete—those; kārya—effect; kāraṇa—cause; bhūta—in existents.

TRANSLATION

From the inherence of purity, purity (is produced), and the intellect in purity (produces) pure knowledge of these effects and those causes in existents.

COMMENTARY

In the last sūtra, we noted how qualities and activities cannot be separated. This sūtra phrases the same idea differently by speaking of causes and effects. The qualities are the causes, and the activities are their effects. If the quality of purity exists in us, then our actions are also pure. Conversely, if the qualities of impurity exist in us, then our actions are also impure. Furthermore, when the pure quality exists in us, then we can truly understand the nature of cause and effect—both in the pure and the impure things. Conversely, if the quality of purity doesn't exist in us, then we cannot understand the true nature of the causes and effects. Therefore, knowledge of causes and effects doesn't require instruments and experiments; it requires the seeker to become a pure person. When that purity is acquired, then everything is automatically understood.

Sūtra 8.1.10

द्रव्येष्वनितरेतरकारणाः

dravyeṣvanitaretarakāraṇāḥ

dravyeṣu—in the objects; anitaretara—not other; kāraṇāḥ—causes.

TRANSLATION

In the objects, the causes are not others (i.e., not different).

COMMENTARY

The last sūtra cited the human example of knowledge, and stated that purity of the intellect produces the purity of knowledge. This sūtra says that this principle can also be applied to the objects. Thus, objects with the quality of sattva-guna, will produce actions that are in sattva-guna; the objects with the quality of rajo-guna will produce effects that are in rajo-guna; and the objects with the quality of tamo-guna will produce effects that are in tamo-guna.

Sūtra 8.1.11

कारणायौगपद्यात् कारणक्रमाच्च घटपटादिबुद्धीनां क्रमो न हेतुफलभावात्

kāraṇāyaugapadyāt kāraṇakramācca ghaṭapaṭādibuddhīnāṃ kramo na hetuphalabhāvāt

kāraṇa—cause; ayaugapadyāt—from the non-simultaneity; kāraṇa—cause; kramāt—from the sequence; ca—also; ghaṭa—pot; paṭa—cloth; ādi—etc.; buddhīnāṃ—the way of thinking; kramah—sequence; na—not; hetu—cause; phala—result; bhāvāt—from the existence.

TRANSLATION

From the existence of the result, the cause is not (deduced). From the non-simultaneity of causes, from the sequence of causes, (the cause is not deduced). Also, from the pot and cloth, etc. type of thinking (the cause is not deduced).

COMMENTARY

This sūtra criticizes many mundane methods of deriving causes. First, it notes that simply by observing the effect, we cannot deduce the cause. Why? Because the same effect can be produced by other causes. The effects underdetermine the causes, although the causes fully determine the effects. Therefore, we must proceed from causes to effects, rather than from effects to causes. Second, the mere non-simultaneity and succession of causes cannot be used as the explanation of effects. Why? Because the effects are not always produced due to other manifest things (the non-simultaneity and succession of causes assumes that the cause must be manifest). Effects may also be produced due to what was previously unmanifest, but becomes manifest due to a context, time, place, or interaction. Third, it ridicules the mundane thinking about objects calling them ghaṭapaṭa way of thinking—i.e., thinking that the world is comprised of pots and clothes. In modern language, we use the terms billiard balls and water waves; these two are deemed inappropriate for deducing the causes.

Then what is the correct method of understanding the cause? The answer was given in the last sūtra: We have to purify our intellect. If the intellect is purified, then sometimes the causes can be deduced from effects; sometimes, the non-simultaneity and succession of events will mean that they are the cause of an effect; and sometimes, the pot and cloth thinking will also work. But at other times, we will also look at the unmanifest as a potential cause for an effect; we will also consider things that might be manifest but outside our current vision as the potential causes. More importantly, we will always try to understand the nature of reality before we try to explain its effects. The successes in predicting the behavior do not determine the truth. Rather, the purity of the intellect by which the role of the senses, mind, knowledge, and purpose are understood in causation will play a crucial role in cause-effect prediction.

Thus, the methods of science and religion are identical. Religion is not based merely on faith; when the senses, mind, intellect, and consciousness are purified, then the soul and God are directly perceived. Likewise, science is not based on material experimentation; when the senses, mind, intellect, and consciousness are purified, then the true nature of material causation is known. Hence, whether we are interested in science or religion, the method is the same, and if that the method is followed, then the results of both are obtained.

Section 2

Sūtra 8.2.1

अयमेष त्वया कृतं भोजयैनं इति बुद्ध्यपेक्षम्

ayameṣa tvayā kṛtaṃ bhojayainaṃ iti buddhyapekṣam

ayam—this; eṣa—running; tvayā—by you; kṛtaṃ—done; bhojaya—food; enaṃ—for him; iti—thus; buddhi—intellect; apekṣam—one-sided.

TRANSLATION

"This is running", "this was done by you", "this is food for him", thus is the one-sided intellect.

COMMENTARY

The last sūtra noted several ways in which causality cannot be understood, and this sūtra clarifies the reason—all these methods of deciding the causation are 'one-sided'—i.e., they look at what is manifest and ignore the unmanifest. The next sūtra clarifies the one-sided nature of the mundane intellect. The term apekṣa means focusing on, having regard for, etc. In the contexts where two things are being discussed, it generally means that one thing is defined in relation to the other. Therefore, we can translate apekṣa as "relative to". But the meanings of focusing on, or having regard for, etc., also have a connotation of not focusing on, or not having regard for, etc. In that sense, the term apekṣa also means partial or one-sided. This latter meaning is relevant in this case.

Sūtra 8.2.2

दृष्टेषु भावाददृष्टेष्वभावात्

dṛṣṭeṣu bhāvādadṛṣṭeṣvabhāvāt

dṛṣṭeṣu—in the vision; bhāvāt—from the presence; adṛṣṭeṣu—in the non-vision; abhāvāt—from the absence.

TRANSLATION

(The effects) from the presence are in the vision; (the effects) from the absence are not in the vision.

COMMENTARY

The above statements such as "this is running", "this was done by you", "this is food for him" are all based on what we can perceive by our senses. The causality based on presence of properties has been rejected previously many times. The foregoing sūtras have explained how causality is based on absence, because matter is simply potentiality. To activate that potentiality, there has to be something that selects one potential over another. That selection of potentiality is stated to be the appearance of absence, which exists like an urge. This absence is invisible until it produces an effect. But when it produces an effect, it is one of many possible effects that could have been produced. Therefore, if we use the presence method to determine an effect, then the results will always be indeterministic—the effect was one of many possible effects. Why did this particular effect come about instead of the other possible effects? To overcome this indeterminism, we have to include the causal effects of absence too.

Sūtra 8.2.3

अर्थ इति द्रव्यगुणकर्मसु

artha iti dravyaguṇakarmasu

artha—meaning or purpose; iti—thus; dravya—object; guṇa—quality; karmasu—and activity.

TRANSLATION

This is the meaning or purpose of object, quality, and activity (i.e., that it explains not just what is visible, but also what is not visible).

COMMENTARY

Unlike the manifest properties that are ordinarily used for understanding the effects, the Vaiśeṣika system employs the notion of objects, qualities, and activities which can also be unmanifest. An object, for instance, exists, without any manifest qualities and activities. The subsequent effects are then explained by the manifestation of qualities and activities from the preexisting object.

Sūtra 8.2.4

द्रव्येषु पञ्चात्मकत्वं प्रतिषिद्धम्

dravyeṣu pañcātmakatvaṃ pratiṣiddham

dravyeṣu—in the objects; pañcātmakatvaṃ—caused by the five-fold nature of the self; pratiṣiddham—each proven by careful study.

TRANSLATION

The five-fold nature in the object is caused by the five-fold nature of the self—each one proved by careful study.

COMMENTARY

The properties of smell, taste, sight, touch, and sound exist in matter, because these properties exist in the soul. The soul has spiritual senses which are capable of smell, taste, sight, touch, and sound, and it has a spiritual body that has smell, taste, sight, touch, and sound. The properties in matter are therefore not an accident. They are present in matter as the reflections of the soul's properties. Thus, even the study of matter gives us a preliminary understanding of the nature of the soul. Also, the material energy is a soul and is considered divine. She just acts subordinate to the Lord, obeying His will, and the Lord controls the material energy in the form of Eternal Time. Since the material energy fulfills many of the soul's wishes due to his good karma, therefore, the soul starts believing that the material energy is "dead" or "inert" and the soul is fully in control of this energy when the fact is that She is far more powerful than the soul, but acts "dead" in order to fulfill the Lord's wishes to let the soul enjoy his karma. This realization, however, is overturned when bad karma arises. Then, the soul realizes that he is not in control because despite his best efforts he doesn't get the desired results, and is forced to suffer despite not wishing it.

Sūtra 8.2.5

भूयस्त्वात् गन्धवत्त्वाच्च पृथिवी गन्धज्ञाने प्रकृतिः

bhūyastvāt gandhavattvācca pṛthivī gandhajñāne prakṛtiḥ

bhūyastvāt—from the greater; gandhavattvāt—from just like smell; ca—also; pṛthivī—Earth; gandha—smell; jñāne—in knowledge; prakṛtiḥ—nature.

TRANSLATION

From the greater (i.e., the soul) and from its property of just like smell, the knowledge of smell, and the nature of smell, exists in the Earth.

COMMENTARY

The last sūtra explained that the five-fold properties in matter exist due to the soul, and this sūtra further clarifies this for the property of smell. The property of smell in the soul is called gandavat or "just like smell", to distinguish it from the smell found in Earth. Similarly, the property of smell in matter is divided into two parts—(a) the knowledge of smell, and (b) the nature of smell—thereby indicating that material energy creates both the property of smell and the senses by which we smell. In this way, every property in the soul is reflected in matter, and by that reflection, the soul knows itself in various ways. Just like someone can put on various kinds of makeup to have their photo taken, similarly, the various kinds of bodies are the soul's covering that distort the true nature of the soul, but the soul considers that distorted picture its real nature.

Sūtra 8.2.6

तथापस्तेजो वायुश्च रसरूपस्पर्शाविशेषात्

tathāpastejo vāyuśca rasarūpasparśāviśeṣāt

tathā—in the same way; apas—Water; tejah—Fire; vāyu—Air; ca—also; rasa—taste; rūpa—form; sparśa—touch; aviśeṣāt—from the universals.

TRANSLATION

In the same way, from the universals of taste, form, and touch (in the soul), the elements of Water, Fire, and Air (are produced).

COMMENTARY

In the last two sūtras, a general statement about all properties being manifest from the soul, and a specific statement about the smell being manifest were made. This sūtra extends that understanding to taste, form, and touch. It also uses the term aviśeṣa or universals regarding these properties indicating two things—(a) these properties are universal across all souls, and (b) they are universals in matter. However, they appear in matter *from* the universal in the soul. Therefore, matter acquires a form due to the presence of the soul. At the end of the material creation, when the souls are withdrawn from the universe, the material energy loses its form. Just like the shape of the glove is modeled after the shape of the hand, and the glove looks just like the hand when the hand is within the glove, similarly, the material energy becomes formless when the soul leaves the material energy. This formless state of the material energy is called its primordial state. This view of soul and matter is the exact opposite of impersonalism in which the soul is formless and it acquires a form due to matter. The Vaiśeṣika position is that matter is formless and the soul gives it form.

CHAPTER 9

Section 1

Sūtra 9.1.1

क्रियागुणव्यपदेशाभावात् प्रागसत्

kriyāguṇavyapadeśābhāvāt prāgasat

kriyā—activity; guṇa—qualities; vyapadeśa—logically concluded; abhāvāt—from the absence; prāk—before; asat—temporary.

TRANSLATION

Activities and qualities are logically concluded from the absence, which is before (the activities and qualities) and temporary.

COMMENTARY

The manifestation of qualities and activities from the absence has been noted earlier; this sūtra adds that this absence is temporary. We can understand this temporariness as the question that comes before the answer is produced, but once the question has been answered, the question ceases to exist.

Sūtra 9.1.2

सदसत्

sadasat

sadasat—eternal and temporary.

TRANSLATION

(The qualities and activities) are eternal and temporary.

COMMENTARY

The potentiality is eternal, but its manifestation is temporary. Thus, as potentials, qualities and activities are eternal, but have a temporary manifestation.

Sūtra 9.1.3

असतःक्रियागुणव्यपदेशाभावादर्थान्तरम्

asataḥ kriyāguṇavyapadeśābhāvādarthāntaram

asataḥ—temporary; kriyā—activity; guṇa—quality; vyapadeśa—logically concluded; abhāvāt—from the absence; arthāntaram—a difference of meaning.

TRANSLATION

The temporary activity and quality are logically concluded from the absence, which is the difference of meaning.

COMMENTARY

The differences of meaning in the qualities and activities are attributed here to the difference in the absence that precedes their manifestation. If qualities and activities are the answers, then their cause is the difference in the questions.

Sūtra 9.1.4

सच्चासत्

saccāsat

sat—eternal; ca—also; asat—temporary.

TRANSLATION

(The absence is) also eternal and temporary.

COMMENTARY

An earlier sūtra stated that the qualities and activities are eternal and temporary, but the absence is manifest temporarily—like a question that ceases to exist when the answer is obtained. But this position is revised here and the question is also said to be eternal—i.e., it is occasionally manifest and unmanifest. When the question disappears upon the appearance of the answer, the question hasn't truly ceased to exist; it has just become causally inefficacious.

Sūtra 9.1.5

यच्चान्यदसदतस्तदसत्

yaccānyadasadatastadasat

yat—that which; ca—also; anyat—different; asat—temporary; atah—therefore; tat—that; asat—temporary.

TRANSLATION

Also, that which is different from the temporary is therefore that temporary (i.e., although the effect is different from the cause, is effectively the same).

COMMENTARY

After the previous sūtras which noted that both qualities and activities, and their cause—the absence—are temporary and eternal, this sūtra dissolves the strict distinction between the manifested reality and the cause of their manifestation by saying that since the appearance of the answer dissolves the question and vice versa, therefore, in some sense, they are to be considered the same.

Sūtra 9.1.6

असदिति भूतप्रत्यक्षाभावात् भूतस्मृतेर्विरोधिप्रत्यक्षवत्

asaditi bhūtapratyakṣābhāvāt bhūtasmṛtervirodhipratyakṣavat

asat—temporary; iti—thus; bhūta—entities; pratyakṣa—direct perception; abhāvāt—from the absence; bhūta—entities; smṛteh—remembered or recollected; virodhi—opposite; pratyakṣavat—as if direct perception.

TRANSLATION

Due to the absence of the direct perception of entities that are thus stated to be temporary, the opposite entities are remembered as if direct perception.

COMMENTARY

In modern science, sometimes the electron movement is visualized as the movement of an electron 'hole' in the reverse direction. Similarly, if something was kept at a certain place for a long time, its movement leads to the perception of a 'hole' in the place where that thing was kept previously. Likewise, if a person in our home dies, we might perceive the home to be 'empty'. In all these ways, we perceive the absence as if it were a direct perception of the thing. Thus, this sūtra states that entities that cannot be perceived by direct perception can still be perceived using our memory or recollection just like direct perception.

Sūtra 9.1.7

तथाभावे भावप्रत्यक्षाच्च

tathābhāve bhāvapratyakṣācca

tatha—in the same way; abhāve—in the absence; bhava—the presence; pratyakṣāt—from the direct perception; ca—also.

TRANSLATION

In the same way, in the absence, the presence is also seen from direct perception (of the absence).

COMMENTARY

The absence of objects, qualities, and activities can leave behind a 'hole' which is absence in one sense, but their form is just the opposite of the form of presence. Thus, from the absence we can perceive the nature of the presence. The presence is directly perceived, and because of the opposite nature of the form of absence, this presence of absence is perceived as a potential presence. A common example is an ability of some people to stand in a desert and visualize a big city. Or to stand on some empty land and visualize the appearance of a big building. Or to see a new future built upon the ruins of the present. What they are seeing is absence, but in that absence, they can see a presence.

Sūtra 9.1.8
एतेनाघटो ऽगौरधर्मश्च व्याख्याताः
etenāghaṭo 'gauradharmaśca vyākhyātāḥ

etena—by this; aghaṭah—the non-pot; agau—non-cow; adharma—non-duty; ca—also; vyākhyātāḥ—are explained.

TRANSLATION

By this (perception of the absence of a presence), terms like non-pot, non-cow, non-duty are also explained.

COMMENTARY

When we see a cow, and we say "this not a horse", we are perceiving the absence of a horse in the cow. This is generally taken to be a mere euphemism by most people, but this sūtra states that the presence of the non-horse in the cow is real—i.e., there is something within the cow that exists as the non-horse. The negations of concepts are therefore not merely logical in nature. Instead, there is an ontological presence of the absence. If this ontological absence was unreal, then the claim that a cow is not a horse would merely be a linguistic construct, a manner of speaking about the world, but not a fact about reality. To assert that a cow is not a horse, we must invoke the presence of not-horse in the cow. However, as we have discussed earlier, these absences are not always manifest. Therefore, it is not always necessary for us to invoke the not-horse presence in the cow. This presence must rather be invoked contextually.

An example of such a distinction arises when we see a cow grazing in a field. In this situation, we say that the "cow is not the field" and the "field is not the cow". If instead, the cow was standing against the backdrop of a wall or a mountain, then we would invoke additional types of presences—not-wall and not-mountain. Thus, the cow against the backdrop of a field is not identical to the cow against the backdrop of a wall or a mountain. Something additional exists in the cow in different situations, so this presence is context-sensitive. The implication is that when things are mutually compared, contrasted, or contextualized, then that relationship adds something to the objects themselves. In a comparison of cars alone, we don't invoke the not-a-truck contrast. This contrast is invoked when the cars are grouped together with the trucks. Hence, the act of grouping things together—or what we call 'sets' in modern mathematics—is not a mere aggregation of independent objects. Rather, if we group things, then we make a change to each of those things, such that they obtain the property of not being the other things—specific to that particular group.

This logical distinguishability of things in groups is seen in modern atomic theory where adding particles into an ensemble changes all the particles because each particle must be not-the-other-particle. Due to this property of being not-the-other-particle in each particle, the particles are said to be mathematically orthogonal. Similarly, the particles are said to be mutually 'entangled' because of the presence of the property of not-the-other-particle in each particle. Thus, these ideas about the presence of an absence are not a euphemism. They have accurate scientific counterparts which require us to eschew classical materialism. When we think of the world in terms of concepts, rather than physical things, then a group of concepts acquires a presence of the absence of the other concepts, and that presence is context-sensitive. Hence, if the group is changed, then a different type of presence of absence would be found in each thing.

Sūtra 9.1.9

अभूतं नास्तीत्यनर्थान्तरम्

abhūtaṃ nāstītyanarthāntaram

abhūtaṃ—non-existence; nāsti—doesn't exist; iti—claiming in this way; anarthāntaram—is a meaningless distinction.

TRANSLATION

The claim that "non-existence doesn't exist" is a meaningless distinction.

COMMENTARY

This sūtra restates the doctrine of absence as abhūtaṃ; bhūta means something that exists, and abhūta means something that doesn't exist. It goes on to state that "non-existence doesn't exist" is a meaningless distinction, implying that if we have to claim that "a cow is not a horse" then we must say that within cow there *exists* something called not-horse. Only then can the claim be considered true ontologically, rather than just logically. The potentiality for these abhūta always exists, but this potentiality only manifests in different contexts. Thus, for instance, "man is not a woman" appears inside a man only in contextual relation to women. If there are no women, then the men remain unaware of this distinction to women. Their behavior in the company of women is modified, relative to their behavior in the company of other men. Bodily consciousness—especially of gender—therefore increases in the presence of the opposite sex and this consciousness disappears in the absence of the opposite sex. The explanation of this consciousness is that each man is modified by the manifestation of a new property called not-woman in the presence of a woman.

Sūtra 9.1.10

नास्ति घटो गेहे इति सतो घटस्य गेहसंसर्गप्रतिषेधः

nāsti ghaṭo gehe iti sato ghaṭasya gehasaṃsargapratiṣedhaḥ

nāsti—doesn't exist; ghaṭah—a pot; gehe—in the room; iti—this type of statement; satah—is true; ghaṭasya—of the pot; geha—room; saṃsarga—association; pratiṣedhaḥ—is negated or prevented.

TRANSLATION

The statement that "a pot doesn't exist in the room" is true when the association of the pot and the room has been negated or prevented.

COMMENTARY

This sūtra advances a simple argument against the proponents of presence as the only source for knowledge. If the pot is not present in a room, how can we claim its absence, unless we are able to perceive the absence? If presence is the only source of knowledge, then we can only make *positive* claims about the things that are present in the room. We cannot make *negative* claims about presence, because such absences are not perceived (according to the person who claims that knowledge is only via presence). Therefore, claims such as "the pot doesn't exist in the room" would not be true because they cannot be verified. But the claim also cannot be called false because the evidence is unavailable. The Nyāya Sūtra explains this idea beautifully by stating that "the absence of evidence is not the evidence of absence". Therefore, if we cannot gather the evidence for the pot's existence, then we cannot conclude that the pot is indeed absent. The conclusion will be that we can neither confirm nor deny the claim that "the pot doesn't exist in the room" and this claim becomes indeterminate—i.e., neither true nor false. The only way that we can confirm or deny this claim is if we say that there is a presence in the room that is the pot's absence.

Sūtra 9.1.11

आत्मन्यात्ममनसोःसंयोगादात्मप्रत्यक्षम्

ātmanyātmamanasoḥ saṃyogādātmapratyakṣam

ātmani—in the soul; ātma—the soul; manasoḥ—of the mind; saṃyogāt—from the combination; ātma—the soul; pratyakṣam—is directly perceived.

TRANSLATION

From the combination of the soul and the mind, the soul is directly perceived in the soul.

COMMENTARY

In the earlier portions of this text, the soul and the mind were identified as objects. Then, it was said that the objects carry a representational knowledge of the other objects. Later, it was also said that this knowledge arises due to an absence, and that absence could be of the superior or the inferior. By recalling all these statements, we can understand this sūtra. The representation of one object inside another is like a picture within an object. For the sake of illustration, we can think of the soul and the mind as two mirrors; the mind-mirror reflects the soul within it, and the soul-mirror reflects the mind within it. Through this recursive reflection, the soul obtains a picture of the mind-mirror within itself, which then has the soul as a represented object within it. By this process of seeing the reflection of the soul in the mind-mirror, the soul obtains a direct perception of itself, quite like we perceive our body by looking into an ordinary mirror. The paradox here is that the seer is also the seen; how can something see itself? And the answer to that paradox is that the seer sees a reflection of itself in the mind-mirror, and thus obtains a direct perception.

The implication is that self-consciousness requires a mind. If the mind is removed, then self-consciousness cannot be obtained. Therefore, the impersonalist doesn't truly have self-knowledge, because there is no mind. Of course, there is a sense of being or existence, quite like we know that we exist even when we don't see ourselves in the mirror. However, that doesn't mean we know our shape, size, color, features, etc. We know about these things when we look at ourselves in the mirror. In the same way, the impersonal realization of the self is the knowledge that "I exist (eternally)" even when there is no mind. As a result, we can say that we are different from the mind, and the body. But the true features of the soul—its qualities and activities, which must exist in each object—cannot be known. The mind facilitates that type of knowledge. Hence, the state of the soul with a spiritual body is superior because, through that body, the soul can perceive its qualities and activities, beyond its existence. The impersonal realization of the soul simply facilitates a sense of being.

Of course, to see the self-reflection in the mind, we must have the urge to know the self. If this urge doesn't exist, then the knowledge of the self will not appear. As we have discussed earlier, the knowledge of the other objects appears only after the appearance of an 'absence'. If our mind is absorbed in the perception of the external world, then it has no urge to know the self. At this time, the mirror of the mind will reflect tables and chairs, rather than the self. So, to see the self, we must withdraw the mind from the external world, and create an urge to see the self. Then, the same mirror can reflect the self. Hence, the materialists cannot see the self, because their minds are absorbed in the perception of tables and chairs. They have no urge to see the self, and they claim that the self doesn't exist; it is merely the construction of material elements. Since their urges are driven toward these elements, they cannot see the self.

Sūtra 9.1.12

तथा द्रव्यान्तरेषु प्रत्यक्षम्

tathā dravyāntareṣu pratyakṣam

tathā—in the same way; dravya—object; antareṣu—in the other or different; pratyakṣam—direct perception.

TRANSLATION

In the same way, in the case of other or different objects, there is direct perception (of those objects).

COMMENTARY

As we have discussed earlier, there are many kinds of objects. The object called the intellect judges the truth of the meanings present in the mind. Therefore, if the soul is reflected in the mind, then the intellect can judge whether this is the true nature of the soul, and the soul can then perceive that judgment of the truth. Similarly, the object called the ego judges the goodness of the meaning present in the mind. Therefore, if the soul is reflected in the mind, then the ego can judge if the soul is a good person, and the soul can then perceive that judgment of the goodness in the ego. Likewise, the object called the moral sense judges the rightness of the meaning present in the mind. If the soul is reflected in the mind, then the moral sense can judge if the soul is a righteous person, and the soul can then perceive that judgment of righteousness in the moral sense. Likewise, through the senses of smell, taste, sight, touch, and sound, the soul can perceive its form, color, size, the sound of its voice, and so on.

When all these perceptions are obtained, then the material body remains no longer material; it is rather transformed into a spiritual body, because every sense now reflects the nature of the self, and through the body, we obtain nothing other than self-knowledge. The body no longer remains a problem, because it has become the source for various types of self-realization of the soul.

Sūtra 9.1.13

असमाहितान्तःकरणा उपसंहृतसमाधयस्तेषाञ्च

asamāhitāntaḥ karaṇā upasaṃhṛtasamādhayasteṣāñca

asamāhita—that which is not merged; antaḥkaraṇā—the internal instrument; upasaṃhṛta—progressing toward merger; samādhayah—samādhi; teṣām—they; ca—also.

TRANSLATION

For those whose internal instrument is not merged (in self-awareness) but are slowly progressing toward merger into a samādhi, they also (can see).

COMMENTARY

Self-awareness is not merely a destination; it is also a journey. Those people who are introspective, constantly evaluate the self—e.g., Am I a good person? Have I been righteous in my actions? Is this my true nature, or am I acting falsely out of external compulsions and provocations? They may not see a reflection of the self in the senses, but they can see their reflection in the "inner instrument" which comprises of four parts—mind, intellect, ego, and the moral sense. Thus, if someone says that the self doesn't exist, or there is no soul, we should infer that the person's "inner instrument" is either dysfunctional or remains unutilized for introspective purposes. This is, by and large, the case for most people who are so absorbed in worldly affairs that they are unable to see the reflection of the self in the inner instrument. They can, however, learn to perceive the self if they stay in seclusion, and stop worldly interactions. The problem is that most people cannot tolerate solitude. The moment they are isolated, their inner instrument is disturbed and it seeks external gratification. This disturbance is a clear indicator that their minds are turned outwardly.

Sūtra 9.1.14

तत्समवायात्कर्मगुणेषु

tatsamavāyātkarmaguṇeṣu

tat—that; samavāyāt—from the inherence; karma—activity; guṇeṣu—in the qualities.

TRANSLATION

That (perception of the self) is from the inherence in qualities and activities.

COMMENTARY

The last sūtra stated that even a person progressing toward samādhi can see the self, and this sūtra clarifies that this vision of the self is contaminated by material qualities and activities. The material qualities are guna or desires, due to which a person thinks that their material likes and dislikes are truly their spiritual nature. Similarly, all that a person has been able to do, or is doing, due to their karma is believed to be the soul's actions. The picture of the soul covered by guna and karma is not the true picture. The true picture is that which is eternal, springs automatically out of the self, and works despite the odds presented by guna and karma. Of course, even a partially true picture is better than none at all, and therefore, the vision of the self in the internal instrument was encouraged in the last sūtra, but this sūtra clarifies that it is not the pure self.

Sūtra 9.1.15
आत्मसमवायादात्मगुणेषु
ātmasamavāyādātmaguṇeṣu

ātma—the soul; samavāyāt—from the inherence; ātma—the soul; guṇeṣu—in the qualities.

TRANSLATION

The soul (is truly perceived) from the inherence in the soul's qualities.

COMMENTARY

This sūtra makes it evident that the soul has its own qualities, that are different from the material qualities. There is knowledge in the soul, due to which the conviction in the spiritual matter never dies. There is beauty in the soul by which it attracts respect and affection from everyone. There are similarly qualities of power, heroism, and richness in the soul. Due to the soul's power, it is never overcome by fear, insecurity, and anxiety, even when the material situation seems dangerous. Due to its heroism, the soul is capable of leadership even in difficult situations. And due to the richness, the soul always remains aristocratic and noble and stays above mundane partisan interests. Finally, there is renunciation in the soul by which it is not enamored by respect or disturbed by criticism. Each of these qualities is compromised due to the material influence, and when this compromised picture is seen, then it is not judged to be true, right, and good. After all, who wants to see themselves as ignorant, ugly, weak, lazy, poor, and disturbed people? The result of a compromised picture is that the soul's attention is immediately drawn away from it, into other things where the inexorable guilt from seeing a compromised self is not stoked.

The conclusion is that if we want to be absorbed in the self, then the self must also be great. If the self doesn't have the great qualities, then seeing that self makes the person unhappy and guilty, and that quickly alters the focus away from the self into other things. Thus, unless the qualities of greatness are acquired, the attention on the self is always temporary. The permanence of self-consciousness is attained only when the greatness becomes permanent.

All these great qualities of the soul are innate to the soul, and therefore don't have to be acquired. One must, however, remove the material contamination that diminishes these qualities. Thus, every person has innate greatness, but that greatness is not always visible. Therefore, every yoga practice recommends the purification of consciousness as the process by which one can always remain self-conscious. Most yoga practitioners don't understand this basic principle; they simply advise people to "meditate" without realizing that this meditation cannot be sustained unless the self is purified of contamination. Thus, the realized practitioners of yoga don't emphasize "meditation". They rather emphasize self-purification because they know that once the material contamination is completely destroyed, self-absorption is automatically attained. The processes of purification are many and varied, and they include the acquisition of knowledge, the performance of duties, and devotion to the Lord. Once these are perfected, then the absorption in the self becomes an automatic fact.

Section 2

Sūtra 9.2.1

अस्येदं कार्यं कारणं संयोगि विरोधि समवायि चेति लैङ्गिकम्

asyedaṃ kāryaṃ kāraṇaṃ saṃyogi virodhi samavāyi ceti laiṅgikam

asya—of this; idaṃ—this; kāryaṃ—effects; kāraṇaṃ—causes; saṃyogi—cooperative; virodhi—opposing; samavāyi—inherent; ca—also; iti—thus; laiṅgikam—the symptoms.

TRANSLATION

The symptoms (of the true perception of self) are thus: the effects of this, the cause this, and (the cognition of) cooperative, opposing, and inherent.

COMMENTARY

As we have discussed earlier, spiritual attainment automatically brings perfect material knowledge, and thus purification of intellect was earlier noted as the method for obtaining true knowledge. This sūtra further draws a distinction between the cooperative, opposing, and inherent factors, with regard to the self. Renunciation of luxuries, for instance, is a cooperative factor in spiritual progress, but since the soul is distinct from the body, therefore, living a life of poverty is not an inherently spiritual quality. Likewise, fasting, austerities, and penances are cooperative factors in spiritual progress, but torturing the body is not an inherently spiritual quality. This distinction between spiritual and material is often mistaken by ignorant people to mean that if the soul is distinct from the body, then sense pleasure and material accumulation must be equivalent to their opposites. This is not true. Austerity and renunciation are 'cooperative' factors in spiritual progress, and sense indulgence and material accumulations are 'opposing' factors. Both cooperative and opposing factors are distinct from the 'inherent' qualities. True knowledge results not just in an understanding of material nature, but also in the understanding of the distinction between matter and soul, and which qualities in matter are favorable to spiritual progress (even though they are material), and which qualities are unfavorable. Hence, the truly enlightened person accepts some material things that are favorable for spiritual progress and rejects other unfavorable things. Blanket acceptance or blanket rejection of all material things is not the symptom of spiritual advancement.

Sūtra 9.2.2

अस्येदं कार्य कारणसम्बन्धश्चावयवाद्भवति

asyedaṃ kārya kāraṇasambandhaścāvayavādbhavati

asya—of this; idaṃ—this; kārya—effect; kāraṇa—cause; sambandha—relationship; ca—also; avayavāt—from the parts; bhavati—appears.

TRANSLATION

The relationship between this cause and the effect of this (cause) also appears from the parts.

COMMENTARY

In modern science, one object has an effect on another object, and that's the limit of causality. But in Vaiśeṣika, Sāñkhya, and other systems, there is another kind of causality in which the whole acts on the parts and the parts act on the whole. It is not merely the action of a part to part, or whole to whole. Those types of actions, as we have seen, result in the creation of an absence (an urge) and presence (knowledge). But even for that presence and absence to appear, there must be potentiality in an object to manifest those possibilities. That potentiality is a part, and the object is the whole. When it manifests a possibility, the whole has acted on the part to manifest it. Likewise, when a part manifests, it can change the nature of the whole. Thus, the doctrine of causality is modified to include the relationship between whole and part as the causes and effects. This type of causation is different from the part-to-part and whole-to-whole causation, and hence the sūtra uses the term 'also appears', thereby indicating that the other types of causations are not denied, but this one is included.

Sūtra 9.2.3

एतेन शाब्दं व्याख्यातम्

etena śābdaṃ vyākhyātam

etena—by this; śābdaṃ—literature; vyākhyātam—is explained.

TRANSLATION

By this (whole to part causal relationship), literature is explained.

COMMENTARY

A literary text is organized hierarchically and this hierarchy is visible from the table of contents, which divides the text into chapters, sections, paragraphs, and sentences. The text begins with a core idea, which is then expanded into many parts over the course of the text. This is causality from whole to part.

Sūtra 9.2.4

हेतुरपदेशो लङ्गिं प्रमाणं करणमित्यनर्थान्तरम्

heturapadeśo liṅgaṃ pramāṇaṃ karaṇamityanarthāntaram

hetuh—reason; apadeśah—reference; liṅgaṃ—symptom; pramāṇaṃ—proof; karaṇam—cause; iti—thus; anarthāntaram—meaningless distinctions.

TRANSLATION

Reason, reference, symptom, proof, cause, etc. are meaningless distinctions.

COMMENTARY

The same object is spoken of in many ways. It is sometimes called a cause when related to an effect. This cause is not irrational; since it is purposeful and rational, therefore, it is also called the reason for something happening. Then, sometimes, it is the thing behind the experiences, so it is the reference of the experiences. And sometimes that reference is the cause of an appearance or experience, therefore, that appearance is considered the symptom of the reality. If the appearance is true, then it also indicates the nature of the object. Thus, many names are used to describe reality, but they do not have separate meanings.

Sūtra 9.2.5
अस्येदमिति बुद्ध्यपेक्षितत्वात्
asyedamiti buddhyapekṣitatvāt

asya—of this; idam—this; iti—thus; buddhi—intellect; apekṣitatvāt—from the relativity.

TRANSLATION

Words such as 'this' and 'of this' are from the relativity of the intellect.

COMMENTARY

The term 'this' can be employed to refer to any object, quality, or activity. The term 'of this' is however reserved for qualities and activities *of* an object. The problem is that we can also refer to "the object *of* the quality" thereby using 'of' to refer to the object, rather than merely to the quality. Likewise, we can use the term 'of' as "the effect of a cause" and "the cause of an effect". In the former case, we are tracing the effect from a cause, and in the latter case, we are tracing the cause from an effect. These are merely relative positions of preference.

Sūtra 9.2.6
आत्मनःसंयोगविशेषात् संस्काराच्च स्मृतिः
ātmanaḥ saṃyogaviśeṣāt saṃskārācca smṛtiḥ

ātmanaḥ—the soul; saṃyoga—union; viśeṣāt—from the specifics; saṃskārāt—from the habits; ca—also; smṛtiḥ—memory or recollection.

TRANSLATION

The union of the soul (with the other objects) is from the specifics (i.e., the objects), from the habits, and also from the memory or recollection.

COMMENTARY

This sūtra notes three kinds of causes of the soul's interaction with the material world. First, there are habits of enjoyment that the soul has previously formed that draw the soul toward the material world. This is the primary cause of the soul's engagement with the world, and it constitutes a 'desire'. Second, there are latent memories which if recalled subsequently drive the production of desire. These memories are also called the chitta, which harbors the impressions from the past life. Third, there are objects which then drive the memory, or create an impression, which then leads to a desire, which then results in an interaction. This interaction with the world can be forced and is called karma. Thus, there are three key causes, and they are called guna, chitta, and karma. Of these, the guna is the most important; if the desires of enjoyment are destroyed, then even if past memories are recollected, the engagement with the world doesn't happen. Likewise, if the desires are destroyed, then even if a person comes into contact with the world of enjoyment, the engagement is not triggered. Thus, the purification of desires is the most fundamental goal of spiritual attainment. Once these desires are purified, the chitta is also purified, and eventually, the karma is either finished (after it has been endured) or destroyed (if the guna and the chitta are already pure and karma serves no purpose).

Sūtra 9.2.7

तथा स्वप्नः

tathā svapnaḥ

tathā—in the same way; svapnaḥ—dreams.

TRANSLATION

In the same way, interactions of the soul with material objects in the dream are also caused by three types of causes (as noted in the previous sūtra).

COMMENTARY

Dreams are experientially indistinguishable from waking experience. The difference is just that during waking, the experience is produced as a result of an interaction with the external world, and during dreaming, the experience is manifested out of the mind and the senses themselves. The mind and senses are therefore not merely consumers of material information. They are also the producers of material information. The Vedic doctrine of causality is that originally the mind manifests the senses, the senses manifest the properties (tanmātra) and the properties then manifest the objects. Thus, the external world is produced from an internal reality. This process of the creation of the external from the internal is seen during dreaming, and therefore, the dreaming experience is considered superior to the waking experience. This sūtra notes that the cause of the dreaming experience is also the chitta, guna, and karma. The Sāñkhya system elaborates this idea through a description of three kinds of 'bodies' which are called subtle, gendered, and gross. The subtle body comprises guna, chitta, and karma; the gendered body comprises the moral sense, ego, intellect, mind, senses, and their properties; and the gross body comprises the five elements that encode the properties. Material energy thus develops progressively from a subtle cause into a gross world. The dreaming experience replicates this process of subtle to gross manifestation, while the waking experience changes the process from gross to subtle. However, during waking, the subtle to gross processes also occur, and therefore, the waking experience is more complex.

Sūtra 9.2.8

स्वप्नान्तिकम्

svapnāntikam

svapna—dreaming; āntikam—the closest (to the causal process).

TRANSLATION

Dreaming is closest (to the causal process).

COMMENTARY

The Yoga system describes four states of consciousness—waking, dreaming, deep sleep, and transcendent. The transcendent state constitutes the observer's self-awareness or the sense of 'being', and other than the choices it exercises in permitting or denying the manifestation from the subtle state, it plays no other causal role. The deep sleep state constitutes the unconscious in which the chitta, guna, and karma are mostly inactive. Therefore, these two states do not afford a good understanding of the causal process. The process is best understood through the dreaming experience where the subtle body manifests into experiences of the moral sense, ego, intellect, mind, and senses. The dreaming experience, however, doesn't lead to the formation of new desires, karma, or abilities, contrary to the waking experience. Therefore, it is a pure one-way manifestation from the subtle reality to experience. The waking experience on the other hand also leads to the formation of new habits, karma, and abilities.

Sūtra 9.2.9
धर्माच्च
dharmācca

dharmāt—from the duties; ca—also.

TRANSLATION
From the duties also (the experience is explained).

COMMENTARY
The production of karma depends on the dharma. If duties are neglected, then bad karma is produced. If duties are performed with the desire for a result, then good karma is produced. This good and bad karma then leads to different kinds of encounters with the world, and then to the soul's experience. Since the current discussion is about the production of experience, therefore, dharma—in the sense of moral strictures, guidelines, rules, and principles also play an important role. For example, even if we have bad past habits, inabilities to perform our duty, and bad karma that prevents us from doing our duty effectively, the acceptance of dharma and trying to fulfill our duties to the best of our ability and opportunity—with no desire for rewards in return—leads to liberation.

Sūtra 9.2.10
इन्द्रयिदोषात्संस्कारदोषाच्चाविद्या
indriyadoṣātsaṃskāradoṣāccāvidyā

indriya—senses; doṣāt—from the faults; saṃskāra—habits; doṣāt—from the faults; ca—also; avidyā—ignorance.

TRANSLATION
Ignorance is created from the faults of the senses and faulty habits.

COMMENTARY

This sūtra discusses two kinds of ignorance—one that arises because our senses are incapable of perception, and the other because we have adopted the habit of thinking and the desire to see reality in a certain way. The first type of ignorance—arising from the faults in the senses—is easy to understand; we must remember that the term 'senses' doesn't just include the five senses for taste, smell, touch, sound, and sight. They also include the mind, intellect, ego, and the moral sense. Most of us, for instance, are unable to see other people's thoughts; many of us are often cheated by other people's deceit; we think that they are honest moral people, but they turn out to be untruthful. These faults are products of our incapacities of perception, but they are not due to a deliberate desire or bias in perception. The second type of ignorance is that which arises due to a chosen bias, habit, or desire. The materialist, for instance, is not just incapable of seeing a deeper reality but *chooses* not to accept its existence even if the materialist explanation falls short, or is not the simplest explanation. While all of us have the experience of the five senses, but materialism cannot explain how these qualities arise, the materialist refuses to accept the reality of anything other than physical properties. When the indeterminism of physical theories indicates a clear role for choice, the materialist tries to invent complicated schemes to avoid that conclusion. This choice, bias, habit, or desire is self-created and is the second—although more onerous—cause of ignorance.

Sūtra 9.2.11

तद्दुष्टज्ञानम्

taddusṭajñānam

tat—that; duṣṭa—wicked; jñānam—knowledge.

TRANSLATION

That (which is produced by ignorance) is wicked knowledge.

COMMENTARY

In the name of scientific discovery and progress, which is a euphemism for accumulating more wealth, materialists have destroyed innumerable human lives, many species of plants and animals, polluted the water, air, forests, and mountains, and brought untold suffering on all forms of life. The materialists refuse to put into balance the little progress they have achieved against the massive cumulative destruction they have brought. They think that all that was destroyed was worth the little economic prosperity for some time. This is the nature of wickedness. It causes more harm than good and refuses to accept responsibility. Nature easily counteracts this wickedness—the law of karma subjects every wicked person to the same wickedness as they have wrought on others. The wicked person learns the truth of his nature by facing the music.

Sūtra 9.2.12
अदुष्टं विद्या
aduṣṭaṃ vidyā

aduṣṭaṃ—non-wicked; vidyā—true knowledge.

TRANSLATION
True knowledge is non-wicked.

COMMENTARY
True knowledge is that which recognizes the many tiers of reality, the laws of choice and consequence, the cycle of birth and death, and the pleasure or pain that comes as a result of one's past actions. This knowledge is not just rational and empirical, but also moral and spiritually uplifting. It leads to the realization of the soul's distinction from the body, why the soul suffers in the material world due to ignorance, and the process by which the ignorance is destroyed and the state of true happiness is attained. That state of spiritual perfection is devoid of envy, greed, and egotism, and their consequences. It is a state in which the soul is devoted to the Lord, and hence respectful toward His entire creation. A spiritually elevated person lifts everyone and harms no one. He is completely devoid of wickedness because he has true knowledge. Thus, knowledge is not epitomized by material prosperity. It is rather epitomized by personal character. The wicked personality is also the ignorant personality.

Sūtra 9.2.13
आर्षं सिद्धदर्शनं च धर्मेभ्यः
ārṣaṃ siddhadarśanaṃ ca dharmebhyaḥ

ārṣaṃ—sacred; siddha—perfect; darśanaṃ—vision; ca—also; dharmebhyaḥ—dutiful.

TRANSLATION

The sacred person has both perfect vision and dutifulness.

COMMENTARY

Modern intelligentsia has separated the questions of truth from that of right and good. But this is not the Vedic system. That which doesn't lead to the right and good is also not considered true. There is hence not merely a faith in the knowability of reality, but also in the morality and goodness of reality. The knower of the truth is therefore also a sacred person. And the wicked person is the ignorant person. The questions of truth, right, and good may be separate, but the answer to the questions is one and the same. Anything that fails one of these three tests is considered to have failed to answer all three questions.

CHAPTER 10

Section 1

Sūtra 10.1.1

इष्टानिष्टकारणविशेषाद्विरोधाच्च मिथः सुखदुखयोर्थान्तरभावः

iṣṭāniṣṭakāraṇaviśeṣādvirodhācca mithaḥ sukhaduḥkhayorthāntarabhāvaḥ

iṣṭa—desirable; aniṣṭa—the undesirable; kāraṇa—cause; viśeṣāt—from the specific; virodhāt—from the opposing; ca—also; mithaḥ—with each other or mutually; sukha—happiness; duḥkhayoh—and distress; arthāntara—the difference in meaning; bhāvaḥ—the existence or nature.

TRANSLATION

The desirable and the undesirable, from some specific and its opposite are also mutually (opposed) as happiness and distress. Their difference in meaning (between pleasure/desirable, or pain/undesirable) is their (opposite) nature.

COMMENTARY

This sūtra gives insight into the existence of opposites in nature, as they are said to produce opposite effects—pleasure and pain. The qualitative opposition in the pleasure and pain means that their causes must also be opposite. This is quite different from modern science where matter has quantitative property, and qualities like 'hot' and 'cold' are subjective feelings, rather than objective reality. Similarly, hard and soft, etc. are not objective realities, but subjective perceptions in modern science. Vaiśeṣika treats this problem differently as the existence of opposite qualities in nature. Thus, nature must be construed in terms of opposites like hot and cold, hard and soft. If the quantitative description of nature in modern science is replaced by a qualitative reality, then nature's properties must be described in terms opposites, instead of linearly.

These opposites are still numbers and we can think of each quality as a dimension, and the opposites as the extremes of positive and negative numbers. However, by this opposition, the dimension also becomes bounded: It doesn't infinitely extend to infinity on either extreme. In Sāñkhya, these opposites are identified as tamo-guna and rajo-guna, which then emanate as separated aspects of sattva-guna, which is *neither* of these two gunas. This 'neither' state of sattva-guna can be understood as the origin or the 'zero' of the dimension. But it is not a quantitative zero. Rather, the zero on each dimension has a different meaning—it is the state devoid of the extremes of that particular property.

For example, the quality of tamo-guna creates laziness and the quality of rajo-guna creates hyperactivity. The quality of sattva-guna is the balance between the two—the state of performing one's duties without expecting the results. Under tamo-guna, a person generally neglects their duties, because it involves hard work. And under rajo-guna, one excitedly engages in hard work, hoping that he will obtain great results by it. The 'neither hard work nor laziness' state is when one doesn't neglect the duties (because the work is difficult) nor does he engage in hyperactivity (since the results can be pleasurable). Just doing what needs to be done, as a matter of duty, is the middle ground between the two extremes. This is the 'origin' or the 'zero' of the dimension from which two extreme opposites of laziness and hyperactivity are produced. As a result, sometimes, the world is described as three qualities—duty, hyperactivity, and laziness. And sometimes, only the opposites of hyperactivity and laziness are described. The former leads to three qualities, and the latter to mutual opposites. They are not different claims, but different types of quality emphases.

Sūtra 10.1.2

संशयनिर्णयान्तराभावश्च ज्ञानान्तरत्वे हेतुः

saṃśayanirṇayāntarābhāvaśca jñānāntaratve hetuḥ

saṃśaya—doubt; nirṇaya—ascertainment; antara—difference; abhāva—absence; ca—also; jñānāntaratve—present inside knowledge as different (opposites); hetuḥ—the reason or cause.

TRANSLATION

The difference between doubt and ascertainment is the absence (of each other); they are present inside knowledge as different (opposite) causes.

COMMENTARY

This sūtra moves from the doctrine of two to the doctrine of three. The two categories of doubt and ascertainment are the opposite, but they are present inside knowledge—which is the third entity—as different kinds of causes.

The Buddhist doctrine of reality says that the reality is comprised of opposites, which are mutually defined, and the opposites are co-produced. The combination of these opposites, however, is nothingness, because when opposites are combined, then the combinations must dissolve each of the opposites. This sūtra counters that idea: The combination of opposites doesn't cancel these opposites when they are combined. The combination instead produces a third category which is qualitatively different from the previous two categories.

This third category is called 'knowledge' here, when the other two categories are called 'doubt' and 'ascertainment'. The point is that all answers are considered answers only in relation to a question. Without the question, there is no meaning to an answer. Similarly, doubt is like the question, and the ascertainment is like the answer. They exist as mutually defined opposites—i.e., the doubt lacks the answer, and the answer lacks the doubt. But this leads to a new problem: How did the doubt arise? Did the doubt arise before the answer? If doubt arises when nothing exists, how can it come into existence? The existence of doubt must at least require the existence of a doubter, in whom the doubt can arise. Similarly, a question cannot arise without some premise. Even if the question is as generic as "What is the nature of reality?" it is assumed that there is a reality and it must have a nature. This sūtra answers the question: There is a reality and it has a nature, but the reality doesn't know its own nature. Therefore, within the reality a doubt arises: What is my nature? And then within that reality the doubt is answered: The nature of reality is discovered by reality. That discovery of the reality prompted by a doubt is not outside the reality. Rather, both doubt and the answer to the doubt must exist within the reality itself.

Therefore, the reality is 'knowledge', the doubt about the nature of reality is the first opposite, and the answer to that doubt is the second opposite.

In simple terms, reality becomes self-aware, and it must be understood in terms of three categories—a premise, a question, and an answer. The existence of the premise leads to a question, and the existence of the question leads to an answer. But all these things are happening within reality. Therefore, the doubt about reality is a part of reality, just as the answer to the doubt is a part of reality. This tripartite understanding of reality is sometimes called sat-chit-ānanda. The chit is the existence, in that existence a doubt, question, or desire arises: Who am I? This question of reality about its nature is ānanda. And then the answer to the question is provided, which is called sat. That answer or sat is merely the awareness of chit. If the answer to the question about reality was different from reality, then the answer would not be 'truth'. Therefore, there are two states—(a) truth exists, and (b) the truth is known due to awareness.

Therefore, we can also say that chit is knowledge, sat is the awareness of knowledge, and ānanda is the question that leads to that awareness. This process of an existence becoming aware of itself is the basic process by which that singular existence expands into diversity. Essentially, there is a reality, which produces an answer after a question, but that answer then becomes a new premise, and then produces a new question, which then leads to a new answer.

The recursive application of this process of premise, question, and answer produces the diversity because there are three types of questions and answers. These three types of questions and answers pertain to truth, right, and good. So, the question "What is the nature of reality?" is the question about truth. But it is not the only question. Inside that question are two other hidden questions, namely, "Is knowing reality a virtue?" and "Is the knowledge of reality good?" The question of virtue arises even before the question of knowledge. If knowing reality was not a virtue, then the question would not automatically arise. But even if the question arises, and the reality is known, but the knowledge is not good, then, the questioning will stop. We can apply this idea to scientific inquiry. Science is initially justified because knowing the nature of reality is itself a virtue, and those who ask such a question are doing something virtuous. Science doesn't become immoral or illegal because questioning is itself a virtue. Then, by the practice of science, we obtain the nature of reality, which is the truth. Finally, we apply that knowledge to produce some technology that does some good. Even if technology wasn't being produced by knowledge, knowing the nature of the truth would still be a virtue. Indeed, this is why philosophy was practiced in ancient times—its goal was not to produce technology but to answer basic questions about existence because asking these questions was a virtuous act. Subsequently, pragmatism arose and the issue of virtuosness was discarded, and replaced by the funding for knowledge precisely because it produces some technology. But factually, the question of virtuosness doesn't go away with the appearance of technology. It now reappears in the technological context: Is it virtuous to produce a technology? For example, if technology gave us food, but killed a number of living entities, should we do science?

The answer to this question is "no" because if we do something unvirtuous, then we will also face a lie, that is not good. Why? Because inside the right is good and truth, and inside the unvirtuous is false and bad. If we choose the unvirtuous, then we cannot avoid the consequences of false and bad. That false and bad would automatically emerge from the unvirtuous eventually.

Thus, the quest for right and good is hidden inside the quest for truth. Likewise, the quest for truth and good is hidden inside the quest for right. And the quest for right and truth is hidden inside the quest for good. In simple terms, we will not seek knowledge if such a search was not right and good. We will not seek good if knowledge were impossible and it was not right. And we will not seek right if knowledge were impossible and it was not good. Thus, two questions are hidden inside each question. Similarly, two answers are hidden inside each answer. And two premises are hidden inside each premise.

In summary, we can say that there are three fundamental principles. But since two of them are inside one, therefore, there is only one principle. And since the combination of three principles produces enormous variety, therefore, there are many principles. In this way, reality can be said to be one, two, three, or many. These are not contradictory if their foundation is understood.

Sūtra 10.1.3

तयोर्निष्पत्तिः प्रत्यक्षलैङ्गिकाभ्याम्

tayorniṣpattiḥ pratyakṣalaiṅgikābhyām

tayoh—from that (doubt and ascertainment); niṣpattiḥ—falls out; pratyakṣa—directly perception; laiṅgikābhyām—and rational inference.

TRANSLATION

From that (doubt and ascertainment) falls out direct perception and rational inference.

COMMENTARY

The answer to a question constitutes the direct perception because the answer is the awareness of reality. Likewise, the question and answer arise from the premise, because the succession of these three principles is rationality. In this way, epistemology—or the process of knowing—becomes the ontology of reality comprising three principles that produce the reality's self-awareness. The awareness of reality is epistemology, and the process is produced by an ontology of three principles. The process of ontology is also rationality. Therefore, direct perception, rational inference, and ontology are interwoven.

Sūtra 10.1.4

अभूदित्यपि

abhūdityapi

abhūt—the future (or not the past); iti—thus; api—even.

TRANSLATION

This will also be the case in the future (i.e., this doctrine will never be false).

COMMENTARY

This sūtra expands on the above thesis and attributes the passing of time to a rational process of the succession of premises, questions, and answers. This time is dialectical rather than linear because it is not merely a succession of moments. It is rather a rational process that alternates between premise, question, and answer. The premise can be that I have a body, the question can be that the body is hungry, and the answer can be food. When the food is consumed—by combining the question and the answer—then the combination is a new premise, namely, an energized body. This new premise then leads to a new question: What should I do? Which then leads to a new answer about some activity. When that question and answer are combined, a new activity is produced, which becomes a new premise, and the process repeats endlessly.

The generation of the question from the premise, or the generation of answers from the question is not deterministic. Therefore, even though there are considerations of truth, right, and good, we can ignore some or all these considerations. Thus, after eating food, we may ask the question "What should I do now?" and the answer could be "sleep" instead of "work". If the answer is "work" there can be many subsequent types of questions and answers.

Sūtra 10.1.5
सति च कार्यादर्शनात्
sati ca kāryādarśanāt

sati—exists; ca—also; kārya—effect; adarśanāt—from the non-perception.

TRANSLATION

This principle exists also for effects caused by the non-perception (of truth).

COMMENTARY

The variability in the questions and answers means that reason involves choices: Everyone doesn't see the same problem in a premise, and everyone isn't led to the same answer for a given question. These questions and answers are produced from a history of previous questions and answers. The history of previous questions is called guna, and the history of previous answers is called chitta. If the questions are bad, and the answers are wrong, then a third entity—called karma—is also produced, which then leads us to false answers which are also bad responses to the questions. Thus, along with choice, there is also responsibility. Choices of questions and answers are not completely free. Why? Because two principles are always embedded inside the third. Therefore, if we make a wrong choice, then it will produce false answers and bad answers. If we instead make the right choice, then it will produce true answers and good answers. The true answers will be stable, and the good answers will be pleasing. The wrong answers will be unstable and the bad answers will be displeasing. Thus, by various kinds of wrong choices, we can obtain unstable good answers, stable bad answers, and unstable bad answers, all of which are undesirable. Conversely, the right choices will always produce stable good answers. In the limiting case, righteous action leads to stability (i.e., eternity) and goodness (i.e., happiness). This righteous eternal good is the purpose of human life. But if we don't understand that purpose, then there is still a law of nature that produces various kinds of alternatives, whether or not we understand the lawfulness.

Sūtra 10.1.6

एकार्थसमवायि कारणान्तरेषु दृष्टत्वात्

ekārthasamavāyi kāraṇāntareṣu dṛṣṭatvāt

ekārtha—a singular purpose; samavāyi—inherent; kāraṇāntareṣu—in the different kinds of causes; dṛṣṭatvāt—from the perception of reality.

TRANSLATION

From the perception of reality, we can understand that a singular purpose is inherent in all the different kinds of causes (which is knowing the truth).

COMMENTARY

The basic mechanism underlying reality is knowing the nature of reality. That reality is also right and good. But, the process of the creation of awareness involves a choice, due to which we can also choose the wrong and the bad. That wrong and bad will also be false, due to the inherence of wrong and bad inside false. This makes the mechanism of self-knowledge also *self-correcting*. That is, there is freedom in reality to know the reality differently. But if reality is known as falsity, then the result is also wrong and bad, which forces a correction. This corrective mechanism is not separate from the process of self-knowledge. Thus, external mechanisms are not required to say whether the knowledge is true or false. The standard for truth is that it must produce happiness. If that happiness is not being produced, then we must alter the understanding of the truth.

In this way, this sūtra states, that we can understand that there is only one principle underlying reality—the principle of knowing the truth. But since there is a choice in knowing the truth, therefore, the choices can be wrong, and the consequences will be bad. That alternative route however forces a correction, and eventually brings us to that truth which is also righteous and pleasing. When that goal of knowing the right, good, truth is accomplished, the alternative route to making wrong, bad, and false choices end. The self-correcting nature of the process of reality reconciles reason, choices, and causal explanations.

Sūtra 10.1.7

एकदेशे इत्येकस्मिन् शरिःपृष्ठमुदरं मर्माणि तद्विशेषस्तद्विशेषेभ्यः

ekadeśe ityekasmin śiraḥ pṛṣṭhamudaraṃ marmāṇi tadviśeṣastadviśeṣebhyaḥ

ekadeśe—in one place; iti—thus; ekasmin—in that one; śiraḥ—the head; pṛṣṭham—the behind; udaraṃ—the stomach; marmāṇi—vital points in the body; tat—that; viśeṣa—specific; tat—that; viśeṣebhyaḥ—due to the specific.

TRANSLATION

Thus, in one place, in that one is the head, the behind, the stomach, and the vital points; those specifics are those (specifics) due to the specific.

COMMENTARY

This sūtra visualizes all of reality as a single body in which the different parts are just like the head, behind, stomach, and vital points. They are all different attempts of reality to become self-aware. But they are also different due to their free will or choices. Each soul is therefore a part of reality, just like a different part of a body, and it knows itself in a different way. The different positions of the soul in this reality are a by-product of its different choices.

The reality is also hierarchical in the sense that the head is more important than the stomach or the behind. But just as the material body expands from the soul, similarly, the Lord is the soul and the bodily expansion is His creation. He has expanded into the reality in which everything is trying to be self-aware. That self-awareness leads to matter—which is the choice for renouncing the use of free will itself. That self-awareness leads to the soul—which is a choice for being whose nature can be determined by the Lord's will or the soul's will. And that self-awareness also leads to a spiritual reality—which is a choice in which the free will and the Lord's will are identical. Thus, we say that matter has no free will, the soul has free will which can be used or misused, and the spiritual energy is where there is free will although it is never misused. Based on this distinction, it is said that there is some spirit that is eternally liberated—i.e., it has never fallen. Then there is the spirit that was fallen and can be liberated. And then there is matter which is eternally 'fallen' in that it never uses free will. But in another sense, it is never 'fallen' because it has never misused free will.

The difference between matter and spirit is thus very subtle—it is the difference between not having a choice, and having a choice but always choosing correctly. Some people find a choice a big burden: We have to always choose correctly! Wouldn't it be better, the skeptic of free will asks, to not have a choice, because then we never have the burden of making the correct choices? The answer is that the state of choosing not to have a choice is matter; the state of choosing to have a choice that can be used or misused is the soul; and the state of choosing to have a choice that is always correctly used is spirit.

We can call these latter types of choice "meta-choices". These have already been made and they constitute an innate nature. Even those who complain about choices being a burden are not truly prepared to relinquish their choices. They just want to avoid the burdensome consequences of choices. Therefore, the soul must now learn to use the choices correctly. Since the soul can make the correct choice, therefore, it is said to be spiritual, although if it makes wrong choices, then it enters matter where it often seems that there is no choice. This seeming lack of choice is the result of wrong choices. If choices are corrected, the choice (in the sense or available alternatives) returns again. The seeming absence of choice is never truly an absence; it is merely the presence of the correct choice, and the absence of every other alternative type of choice. The conclusion is that even when choice seems to disappear, the choice for the correct alternative never disappears. That choice for the correct alternative is spirit. Therefore, the spiritual or correct choices are always available to everyone.

In summary, everything is consciousness, and everything is trying to know itself. However, the way in which they know themselves is different. Matter is defined by whatever God wills it to be. Soul is defined by the choice of what one wants, which may or may not be compatible with the Lord's wants. And spirit is defined to be what one wants but not different from what the Lord wants. This not-different from what the Lord wants is not identical to what the Lord wants. Spiritual attainment is therefore not devoid of choice; there is always a choice in what one wants to be—although it is also what the Lord wants. For example, if you join an organization, the organization doesn't force you to join a particular department; you have a choice to join a department of your choosing. But whichever department you join, you serve the organization. In that way, the members of an organization are all compatible with the organization's leader, and yet they have also exercised their free will to work in a specific department. But there are also specific individuals whom the leader trusts so much that he asks them to work in a specific department, and they accept it happily. The ask-driven move is not the same as the self-driven move. Hence, there is a very subtle difference between the soul and the spirit.

Our meta-choices can be changed, and if the soul desires, it can become matter or spirit. But it needs a very fundamental meta-change. All the prescriptions of Vedic scriptures are to correct the soul's choices, but encouraging it to make a choice—i.e., maintain its independence. The perfect self-realized souls however also teach that being fully surrendered to the Lord's will is the state of spiritual perfection. It is superior even to the soul's liberation in which the soul chooses a particular role in the organization. It is that state in which the soul takes on whatever role the Lord wants it to accept. This reality looks almost identical to the material world, with one difference—in the spiritual case, the will is surrendered, and in the material case, the will is relinquished. Since this nuance is very hard to understand, therefore, the simpler thesis of "soul is free will while matter is not free will" is emphasized as the stepping stone to the more advanced thesis of "a surrendered free will is better than free will".

Regardless of whether free will is relinquished or surrendered, the fact is that everything moves by the will of the Lord—in both material and spiritual worlds. They are just different kinds of movements based on different kinds of free will. In this way, everything is consciousness, but some consciousness is matter, some consciousness is the soul, and some consciousness is spirit.

This distinction is brought to the fore in the descriptions of Vedic cosmology, where the soul's will to be against the Lord's will is called the material world, the soul's will to be independent of the Lord's will is called Brahman, the soul's will to be compatible with the Lord's will is called Vaikuṇtha, and the soul's will surrendered to the Lord's will is called

Goloka. Other than the material world, Brahman, Vaikuṇtha, and Goloka are all considered "spiritual" in contrast to matter, because the soul's will is not against the Lord's will. But this is a preliminary understanding. The more advanced understanding is that within the "spiritual" realm, there are distinctions of free will being independent of the Lord's will, compatible with the Lord's will, and surrendered to the Lord's will. If all these distinctions, along with the distinction to matter are understood, then the complete nature of the reality and how it springs from self-awareness is known. Then, matter is also seen as consciousness, although it is the free will to relinquish free will, rather than be independent, compatible, or surrendered.

In one sense, since everything is free will, therefore, everything is Brahman. But if the free will is relinquished, that portion of Brahman becomes matter. If that free will is compatible with the Param Brahman, then it is Vaikuṇtha. And if that free will is surrendered to the Param Brahman, then it is Goloka. Finally, the Brahman is an emanation of Param Brahman, such that all the four realms described above are said to have emanated from a single source—the Lord. This sūtra compares these four realms to the head, the back, the stomach, and the vital points. The vital points are Brahman; the back is the material world; the stomach is Vaikuṇtha; and the head is Goloka. They are all considered to be the body of the Lord, but explicating this four-part understanding of the body requires profound considerations of how consciousness is of four types.

Section 2

Sūtra 10.2.1

कारणमिति द्रव्ये कार्यसमवायात्

kāraṇamiti dravye kāryasamavāyāt

kāraṇam—cause; iti—thus; dravye—in objects; kārya—effect; samavāyāt—from the inherence.

TRANSLATION

From the inherence of the effect in objects that are thus the cause.

COMMENTARY

This sūtra echoes the Satkāryavāda doctrine of the inherence of the effects in the causes. We have discussed this doctrine earlier, and it is repeated here.

Sūtra 10.2.2

संयोगाद्वा

saṃyogādvā

saṃyogāt—from the union; vā—alternatively.

TRANSLATION

Alternatively, (the effect is produced) from the union.

COMMENTARY

Even when the effect is triggered by an external agency, the external agency is only responsible for the trigger, rather than the effect itself. Similarly, when the effect occurs, it is due to the 'knowledge' of the trigger being inherent, the trigger itself being present in the cause due to the emergence of some absence. Thus, when an external agency causes an effect, the following steps occur: (a) the effect was previously latent in the cause, (b) an absence of an external cause is created, (b) a representation of the external cause is created within the cause that will spring the effect, and (c) this representation triggers the effect. One outcome of this doctrine of causation is that the cause and the effect are always *local*—since the actual trigger is the local representation rather than the remote cause. The local representation is however created in advance of the effect's manifestation. This seeming non-locality, which is always local—creates many problems for the models of causation that are local (such as in atomic theory). But these problems are not created in Vaiśeṣika due to the innate locality.

Sūtra 10.2.3

कारणे समवायात् कर्माणि

kāraṇe samavāyāt karmāṇi

kāraṇe—in the cause; samavāyāt—from the inherence; karmāṇi—actions.

TRANSLATION

(Effects are created) from the inherence of actions in the cause.

COMMENTARY

This sūtra speaks about what is happening in the external cause—namely, that there are potentialities of action, which then create the representation of the external cause in the cause which subsequently produces the effect. We can compare this potentiality to the transfer of meaning from a teacher to a student. The idea exists in the teacher, but the teacher also has some 'energy' that is expended in expressing that idea. That expenditure of energy doesn't rob the teacher of the ideas, but it does require him to exert. Due to that exertion, the quality or idea becomes a knowledge within the student. Thus, the quality is transferred from the teacher to the student, due to the teacher's efforts.

Sūtra 10.2.4

तथा रूपे कारणैकार्थसमवायाच्च

tathā rūpe kāraṇaikārthasamavāyācca

tathā—in the same way; rūpe—in many forms; kāraṇa—the cause; eka—one; artha—meaning; samavāyāt—from the inherence; ca—also.

TRANSLATION

In the same way, from the inherence of one meaning, the cause (i.e., the activity spoken of in the previous sūtra) also acts in many forms.

COMMENTARY

As we have discussed earlier, the qualities and activities are one-to-one. A knife can be used to cut or pierce—which are different kinds of actions. Likewise, the actions of cutting and piercing can be performed by many things that are not knives. Thus, qualities underdetermine the actions, and the actions underdetermine the qualities. This means that the teacher can present the same idea through different actions, and the same action can be used to express different ideas. Therefore, the effect resulting from a cause cannot be predicted deterministically if the cause expresses in a different activity. However, the effect produced by the activity can easily be explained using the same idea. This points to another kind of indeterminism—an effect can be explained by many causes, and a single cause can explain many different effects. Thus, due to the many-to-many relation between quality and activity, a many-to-many relationship between causes and effects is created. This sūtra notes that all these diverse effects of a given cause are the different 'forms' of the same cause.

Sūtra 10.2.5

कारणसमवायात् संयोगः पटस्य

kāraṇasamavāyāt saṃyogaḥ paṭasya

kāraṇa—cause; samavāyāt—from the inherence; saṃyogaḥ—the union; paṭasya—of the cloth.

TRANSLATION

The union of the cloth is from the inherence of the cause (in the threads).

COMMENTARY

This sūtra identifies a difference between the ordinary notions of causality and the Vaiśeṣika notion of the same causality. In the ordinary notion, a cloth is assembled out of threads, but the threads themselves are unchanged by that assembly: The thread outside and inside the cloth are the same thread. But in Vaiśeṣika, the thread in the cloth is different from the thread outside the cloth. The cloth assembly seems due to something that is *between the threads*, but it is deeper than that—the change is within each thread, rather than between the threads. Thus, for instance, when a man becomes a father, the fatherhood is not in *between* the father and the son. Rather, there is something inside the father, and inside the son, that identifies them as father and son. Even the relationships between things—which produce a structure—are therefore inside those things rather than in between them. Similarly, if we rearrange the furniture in a room, each such arrangement modifies each of the furniture pieces as something within them is changed, quite like the weaving of threads into a cloth changes the threads. This change in the furniture or the threads is triggered by the creation of an internal representation in the furniture pieces and the many threads.

This idea has tremendous implications for modern science. The classical picture of a molecule, for instance, is that it is comprised of atoms, and the atoms outside and inside the molecule are the same. But according to this doctrine, each of the atoms is modified when they are assembled into a molecule. Thus, there is factually no such thing as Oxygen or Nitrogen atoms from which the molecule is composed. Rather, the atoms outside the molecule are not the same as the atoms inside the molecule. As a result, the properties of molecules cannot be simply reduced to the properties of the atoms—because unique properties are created in each atom in each molecule, such that we cannot speak about universal properties of behaviors of atoms comprising molecules. Instead, we have to look at the whole molecular structure to understand each of the atoms, and then we can understand how these atoms will behave.

Thus, the chemistry of molecules doesn't simply reduce to the physics of atoms, because in each molecule the atoms have different properties and the chemical behaviors of the atoms can vary from one molecule to another. Unlike the capacity to produce general laws in physics, the capacity for such laws is practically non-existent in chemistry, because the properties are unique to each molecule, and any such law would be a highly inaccurate generalization. This problem magnifies significantly as the molecules grow in size because a minor change in one atom can produce drastic differences in molecular behavior. Again, biology doesn't reduce to chemistry because additional properties are created at each new level of organization of the chemistry into biology. Due to the failures of reduction at each level of organization, we have to totally reject reductionism and acknowledge that an object in a collection is different from the object outside the collection. A collection changes each individual thing.

Sūtra 10.2.6

कारणाकारणसमवायाच्च

kāraṇākāraṇasamavāyācca

kāraṇa—cause; akāraṇa—uncaused and spontaneous; samavāyāt—from the inherence; ca—also.

TRANSLATION

(The union of the cloth is) also from the inherence of the uncaused and spontaneous in the cause.

COMMENTARY

The term akāraṇa can be translated in three ways—causeless, uncaused, and spontaneous. By causeless, we mean something that is causally inert, and it doesn't produce an effect; it just exists within the thing without creating an effect. Since such a thing produces no effect, therefore, its existence can never be known. Its existence is as good as non-existence. This meaning of akāraṇa is practically useless, and amounts to unverifiable metaphysical assumptions.

By uncaused, we mean something that is always present in something and it was not put there due to an external cause. But this thing can have its own effects, and therefore, its existence can be detected through observation.

By spontaneous, we mean that there is no prior trigger for an action. This meaning of akāraṇa has been used twice before. First, it was used to describe the Absolute Truth, by stating that things in the Absolute Truth are uncaused—i.e., they occur spontaneously. Second, it was used in the context of the soul, by stating that the activities of the soul are uncaused—i.e., they are spontaneous. Again, their presence is not a metaphysical presupposition because they do produce effects, and by those effects, their presence can be detected. But because that action cannot be traced back to another cause, so it is spontaneous.

For this sūtra, we can take the meanings 'uncaused' and 'spontaneous', and these can be taken to refer to the immanent form of the Lord, or the immanence of the soul, or the immanence of both. That distinction between the soul and the Lord is not made in this sūtra; only the immanence of uncaused is noted. Since both of these are uncaused and act spontaneously, they can be included.

The conclusion will be that the Lord is always present in everything, it is His presence that causes the cloth to exist. Similarly, sometimes, the soul's existence along with the Lord's existence causes the material body to exist.

The question is: Why is the Lord's presence *within* the cloth necessary for the cloth to exist? And the answer has been discussed earlier—the cloth represents a unity of some threads, and the existence of this unity is a variation on the basic idea of unity in diversity, which constitutes the immanent form called Paramātma. If this unity doesn't exist, then even if the myriad atoms from the original source are created, they would just be disparate individual things. While we can surmise that the unity of fibers in a cloth forms a cloth due to a structure, the question is: Why should structures remain stable? Why doesn't a cloth comprised of individual atoms fall apart into those atoms? Why does the world comprised of bodies, societies, and organizations remain stable?

That stability of the structure is attributed to the Paramātma as the 'maintainer' of the material world (rather than its creator or destroyer). The creators and destroyers of structures are external to the structure, but the maintainer is innate to the structure. The structure exists due to Paramātma's presence.

This presence has an observable effect—stability. But the cause is not observable. Modern science tries to explain the stability of complex structures in various ways, but none of these ways are truly explanatory. For instance, some people postulate that things are stable when they are at the lowest energy. But to say that something is at the lowest energy, we have to draw a boundary between that system and the rest of the world. What creates that boundary? There is no answer to this question in modern science. Then again, is the claim that the lowest energy structures are stable the real explanation? Why would wars and explosions occur as instabilities if the prior state was already stable? Should we say that war and explosion is the state of greatest stability in nature?

The answer in this sūtra is that there is something inside everything which is itself uncaused, and spontaneously causes one effect—i.e., stability. Things remain stable as long as that cause is present. And things are destroyed to create other things when that cause is absent. The cloth, therefore, doesn't break apart into threads, and the threads don't break apart into fibers because there is something that holds them together. That something is uncaused and a spontaneous cause. We cannot explain stability if we do not accept that type of cause.

Sūtra 10.2.7

संयुक्तसमवायादग्नेर्वैशेषिकम्

saṃyuktasamavāyādagnervaiśeṣikam

saṃyukta—united; samavāyāt—from the inherence; agneh—fire; vaiśeṣikam—the philosophy of Vaiśeṣika.

TRANSLATION

From the inherence of the philosophy of Vaiśeṣika, one is united with fire (i.e., the knowledge dissipates all kinds of darkness).

COMMENTARY

This sūtra praises the Vaiśeṣika system of philosophy as the torchlight of knowledge that dissipates the darkness of ignorance about material nature.

Sūtra 10.2.8

दृष्टानां दृष्टप्रयोजनानां दृष्टाभावे प्रयोगो ऽभ्युदयाय

dṛṣṭānāṃ dṛṣṭaprayojanānāṃ dṛṣṭābhāve prayogo 'bhyudayāya

dṛṣṭānāṃ—those with the visions; dṛṣṭa—see; prayojanānāṃ—the purposes; dṛṣṭābhāve—in absence of vision; prayogah—by practical application or experimentation; abhyudayāya—arising.

TRANSLATION

Those with the visions see the purposes (of Vaiśeṣika philosophy); in the absence of vision, (that Vaiśeṣika) arises from the practical application.

COMMENTARY

This sūtra states that the Vaiśeṣika system is not just theoretical philosophy. It has been stated by those who have the vision. But if someone lacks in that vision, then that philosophy can also be understood by practical application. In short, the philosophy is amenable to practical and experimental confirmation.

Sūtra 10.2.9

तद्वचनादाम्नायस्य प्रमाण्यमिति

tadvacanādāmnāyasya pramāṇyamiti

tat—that; vacanāt—from the statements; āmnāyasya—the Vedas; pramāṇyam—provide the evidence; iti—thus.

TRANSLATION

From the statements of that (visionaries), the Vedas thus provide the evidence.

COMMENTARY

This sūtra states that Vaiśeṣika is based on the Vedic statements, as they are understood by the visionaries. But as the last sūtra stated, these statements can also be confirmed by practical experimentation and application of the ideas.

INDEX

Made in the USA
Middletown, DE
29 October 2024

63530500R00234